NUMBER TWO HUNDRED AND NINETEEN

# The Old Farmer's Almanac

CALCULATED ON A NEW AND IMPROVED PLAN FOR THE YEAR OF OUR LORD

## 2011

BEING 3RD AFTER LEAP YEAR AND (UNTIL JULY 4) 235TH YEAR OF AMERICAN INDEPENDENCE

Fitted for Boston and the New England states, with special corrections and calculations to answer for all the United States.

---

*Containing, besides the large number of Astronomical Calculations and the Farmer's Calendar for every month in the year, a variety of*

NEW, USEFUL, & ENTERTAINING MATTER.

---

*Established in 1792 by Robert B. Thomas (1766–1846)*

*The years teach much which the days never know.*

–Ralph Waldo Emerson, American writer (1803–82)

Cover T.M. registered in U.S. Patent Office

Copyright © 2010 by Yankee Publishing Incorporated
ISSN 0078-4516

Library of Congress Card No. 56-29681

*Original wood engraving by Randy Miller*

THE OLD FARMER'S ALMANAC • DUBLIN, NH 03444 • 603-563-8111 • ALMANAC.COM

## More affordable than ever. CALL NOW!

# Easy is smart with Jitterbug.

At Jitterbug, you'll enjoy live U.S. Based Customer Service 24-hours a day, 7 days a week. We offer easy-to-use services like MyWorld, that delivers your local weather forecast, exciting daily trivia, horoscopes and more, right to your Jitterbug. Together, with worldwide leader Samsung, we have created a phone with larger buttons and bigger numbers, so it's easy to use. All of this is powered by one of the most reliable networks in the country. Call our toll-free number below and order your Jitterbug today.

- No contracts or prepaid hassles
- Plans start at $14$^{99}$ a month
- Stay safe, connected and informed with services like LiveNurse, SimpleText and MyWorld
- Powerful speaker delivers clear sound
- Large keypad makes dialing easy
- Friendly, 30-Day Return Policy[1]

**866-481-3293**
CALL?
SAMSUNG

*100% U.S. Based Customer Service*

### 2 FREE GIFTS!
Free Car Charger and Leather Case
with phone activation by 11/1/10
A $43$^{99}$ value!

---

### Start now and save up to $300 a year.

| | | | |
|---|---|---|---|
| Monthly Anytime Minutes | 50 | 100 | 200 |
| Monthly Rate | $14$^{99}$ | $19$^{99}$ | $29$^{99}$ |
| Monthly Minute Carry Over | 60 Days | 60 Days | 60 Days |
| Night/Weekend Minutes | — | — | 500 |
| Operator Assistance | 24/7 | 24/7 | 24/7 |
| Long Distance Calls | FREE | FREE | FREE |
| MyCalendar | FREE | FREE | FREE |
| MyWorld | $4 | $4 | $4 New |
| Nationwide Coverage | YES | YES | YES |

Competitive share plans available. Call a Jitterbug expert to learn more.

### To order or learn more, call
# 1-866-481-3293
or visit us online at jitterbug.com/offer

SAMSUNG
Created together with worldwide leader Samsung.

**jitterbug**®

All rate plans and services require the purchase of a Jitterbug phone and a one-time set up fee of $35.00. Coverage and service is not available everywhere. Other charges and restrictions may apply. Screen images simulated. There are no additional fees to call Jitterbug's 24-hour U.S. Based Customer Service. However, for calls to an Operator in which a service is completed, minutes will be deducted from your monthly balance equal to the length of the call and any call connected by the Operator, plus an additional 5 minutes. Rate plans do not include government taxes or assessment surcharges. [1] We will refund the full price of the Jitterbug phone if it is returned within 30 days of purchase in like-new condition. We will also refund your first monthly service charge if you have less than 30 minutes of usage. If you have more than 30 minutes of usage, a per minute charge of 35 cents will apply for each minute over 30 minutes. The activation fee and shipping charges are not refundable. Savings are based on marketing materials from nationally available cellular companies as of 2010 (not including family share plans). Prices and fees are subject to change. Jitterbug is a registered trademark of GreatCall, Inc. Samsung is a registered trademark of Samsung Electronics America, Inc. and its related entities. Copyright ©2010 GreatCall, Inc.

# Get the **Tempur-Pedic®** advantage at an unmatched value...

The
**AdvantageBed**
*by Tempur-Pedic™*

The AdvantageBed makes it possible to enjoy all the benefits of **better sleep** and **better health** at an unmatched value! Unlike traditional spring mattresses that push against you causing painful pressure points, Tempur-Pedic beds are made of our proprietary TEMPUR® material.

TEMPUR material absorbs pressure, cradling your body with customized support and providing deep, rejuvenating sleep giving you **renewed daytime energy**.

Tempur-Pedic delivers all the life-improving benefits of body conforming support. Invest in more than simply a new mattress, make an investment in your health with guaranteed better sleep night after night! Rest assured...**Every Tempur-Pedic bed is backed by our 20 year Limited Warranty!**

You spend 1/3 of your life sleeping, you deserve the highest level of comfort available...**you deserve a Tempur-Pedic!**

**Which would you rather sleep on?**

*Traditional Steel Spring Mattress*

*Pressure-Absorbing TEMPUR® Material*

## Value a Tempur-Pedic...

*"Because of the stress that people feel you're not getting enough sleep. If you're not resting and feeling good you're going to have a harder time during your day. The person that values sleep, they'll value a Tempur-Pedic."*

Luci & Barry *Tempur-Pedic owners since January 2005*

**Call today for your FREE Information Kit with FREE DVD / FREE Sample / FREE Tryout Certificate**

# 888-702-8557

**or visit us online at TempurPedic.com to find a retail location near you!**

✚**TEMPUR**-PEDIC™

# Contents

## The Old Farmer's Almanac • 2011

*(continued on page 6)*

*There's more of everything at Almanac.com.*

# Contents

*(continued from page 4)*

# Local Solutions
# for Local Problems

VPG

This Almanac would not exist without our contributing writers, whose curiosity, wisdom, literary styles, and distinctive voices inform each edition. This year, we recognize two in particular.

Andrew E. Rothovius, who died on October 28, 2009, at age 86, contributed ten articles from 1983 to 1999 and assisted on numerous others. Andrew was a prodigious researcher (before computers), reader, and history buff, with a fascination for, and facility with, Almanac esoterica. He clarified, once and for all, "What on Earth Is Epact?," "New Eras: When They Began and When They Didn't," and "What to Do During a Long Sermon." (You can read these articles on Almanac.com/Rothovius.) In appreciation, we reprise, in the Calendar pages of this issue, "What a Difference a Quarter Day Makes!"

We also salute and thank Castle Freeman Jr., who concludes 29 years as author of the Farmer's Calendar essays and, in recent years, has been the voice of these in podcasts on Almanac .com. Castle's seasonal advice, insights on rural life, and observations on the natural world stand as lessons for generations of readers in our archives and others: Castle's composition for June 2009 was selected for the anthology *Best American Nonrequired Reading* (Houghton Mifflin Harcourt, 2009).

We are fortunate to have hundreds of thousands of other writers and contributors, too—friends on Facebook, Twitter, Almanac.com, and Almanac4kids .com as well as many, many more who send comments and questions through the postal service. We welcome all posts, e-mails, and letters and acknowledge as many as we can.

Beginning with the 1801 edition of this Almanac (number 9 of, now, 219), our founder, Robert B. Thomas, used this column to respond to correspondence. For example, in 1814, he wrote: "J. S. merits our thanks for his evidently kind intentions, but his poetry, we think, would do [neither] himself nor us much credit if published."

Hopefully in a more generous tone, we take up the pen here to respond to some recent dispatches:

■ C. A., a farmer in Delaware, tracked our forecasts against daily conditions in his area for the entire year. He sent both records and noted, "It turned out to be very helpful for crop insurance claims." *We are at your service. Our mission, as set forth by Robert B. Thomas, is to be "useful, with a pleasant degree of humor." We hope that the claims adjuster was likewise amused.*

■ Rev. M. H. of Maryland notes that this Almanac "has been my sidekick over the years . . . as important as a phone book." *Thank you. We pray that this edition moves us ahead of that tome in your hierarchy.*

■ F.A.B. of Massachusetts quotes from a genealogy book about an ancestor born in 1779 who was "an astronomer,

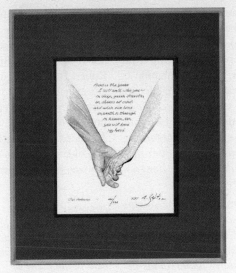

# A Most Unusual Gift of Love

THE POEM READS:

*"Across the years I will walk with you—
in deep, green forests; on shores of sand:
and when our time on earth is through,
in heaven, too, you will have my hand."*

Dear Reader,

The drawing you see above is called *The Promise*. It is completely composed of dots of ink. After writing the poem, I worked with a quill pen and placed thousands of these dots, one at a time, to create this gift in honor of my youngest brother and his wife.

Now, I have decided to offer *The Promise* to those who share and value its sentiment. Each litho is numbered and signed by hand and precisely captures the detail of the drawing. As a wedding, anniversary or Christmas gift or simply as a standard for your own home, I believe you will find it most appropriate.

Measuring 14" by 16", it is available either fully framed in a subtle copper tone with hand-cut mats of pewter and rust at $110, or in the mats alone at $95. Please add $14.50 for insured shipping and packaging. Your satisfaction is completely guaranteed.

My best wishes are with you.

**The Art of Robert Sexton, 491 Greenwich St. (at Grant), San Francisco, CA 94133**

MASTERCARD and VISA orders welcome. Please send card name, card number, address and expiration date, or phone (415) 989-1630 between noon-8 P.M. EST. Checks are also accepted. *Please allow 3 weeks for delivery.*

*The Promise* is featured with many other recent works in my book, *Journeys of the Human Heart.*
It, too, is available from the address above at $12.95 per copy postpaid. Please visit my Web site at

**www.robertsexton.com**

botanist, and chemist of note and was author and publisher for 39 years of *The New England Farmer's Almanac.*" She adds, "I would appreciate hearing from you as to whether [this] information is correct, and if so, any additional details of interest, dates, etc." *Regional almanacs proliferated at that time. Congratulations on 39 good years. Regarding the gentleman, unfortunately, our arboreal expertise, while extensive, does not extend to family trees.*

■ To P. O. in Manitoba: *Thank you for the payment for your recent order. As directed, we used the remaining funds on coffee and donuts for the shipper. The "very large staff" understands the limits of your budget.*

Perhaps our favorite missive during the past year came from a young reader of *The Old Farmer's Almanac for Kids,* who sent us "Greetings in New Hamster!" *Back at you,* and thanks to all of our younger readers who contact us about this (old) Almanac, too. For, as Robert B. Thomas wrote in 1814, "We are ever desirous to encourage the efforts of youthful genius, so far as our limits will admit."

Indeed, thank you to everyone, young and old, who keeps our mailboxes and inboxes full—and us on our toes.

J. S., June 2010

*However, it is by our works and not our words that we would be judged. These, we hope, will sustain us in the humble though proud station we have so long held in the name of*

*Your obedient servant,*

2011    THE OLD FARMER'S ALMANAC    11

# This Year at a

## EARTH IS FIRST

We're building smarter, thinking greener, and recycling more.

### HOW WE MEASURE UP

**24,000:** number of items claimed and reused every day on the "cybercurbside" site www.freecycle.org (one of several similar)

**700:** total daily weight in tons of the items above

### Unwanted Buildings Are Getting New Life

* **Giant "McMansions"** are being converted into suburban greenhouses or torn apart to build two houses with the materials.

* **Sprawling suburban communities** are being retrofitted to be more walkable.

* **Unused barns** in Montpelier, Vermont, are being made into classrooms.

**WORD OF THE YEAR . . .**

## Greenwashing:

exaggerating an item's environmental friendliness, while ignoring its not-so-beneficial aspects

Compiled by
Stacey
Kusterbeck

# Glance

## Waste Has New Worth

- Contents of **IN-HOME COMPOSTING TOILETS** are being treated with sawdust on site, removed for processing, and returned to the residences as fertilizer.

- City workers are tagging the **GARBAGE CANS** of home owners who don't recycle to shame them into compliance.

- California farmers are making **RENEWABLE ENERGY** from walnut shells and onion scraps.

- Concession stands are providing **COMPOST BINS** for customers' food scraps.

## IDEAS THAT MAKE CENTS

- **converting miscanthus,** a perennial grass, into pellets to burn in heaters

- **scallop-edge blades** (think humpback whale flippers) to improve the efficiency of windmills

- **roof shingles** as solar panels

- **games** that require recording the family's environmental "crimes" (not turning off the TV or using the clothes dryer on sunny days)

## SMALL ITEMS, BIG IMPACT

→ **Cameras worn like necklace pendants** snap pictures every 30 seconds.

→ Pocket-size **projectors put 50-inch movies** on any wall "screen."

→ **Devices calculate the energy** that household appliances use and how much each costs.

 continued ➡

# IN THE GARDEN

We're growing more of our own food and loving the land.

## HOW WE MEASURE UP

**19:** percent increase in new hobby farms and urban edible gardens as of 2009

**45:** percent increase in households that canned homegrown or organic produce in 2009

## IDEAS THAT MAKE CENTS

- **using mounded snow** to test landscape ideas, such as changing bed lines or adding bushes or trees
  *–Julie Moir Messervy, landscape designer*

- **planting economical edibles** (e.g., potatoes that taste good boiled, baked, mashed, or roasted)

- **retrofitting greenhouses** with low-cost roof vents for natural ventilation

- **butterfly and bird habitats on roofs**

- **planting shrubs** to attract pollinators and birds

- **using anti-insect netting** instead of pesticides

## Eye-catching Edibles

- ◆ **'Black Cherry'** tomato
- ◆ **'Tye Dye'** tomato (below)
- ◆ **'Skyphos'** butterhead lettuce
- ◆ **'Purple Pak'** carrot
- ◆ **'Piñata Mix'** hot pepper
- ◆ **'Petit Posy Mix'** hybrid, with brussels sprout stalks and rosettes of kale

*–Sonia Uyterhoeven, gardener for public education, The New York Botanical Garden*

–W. Atlee Burpee & Co.

## Plants Are Doing Double Duty

➔ 'Tomaccio' is a tomato that can be eaten fresh or left to dry on the stem.

➔ 'Aristotle' and 'Boxwood' basil are edible miniature topiaries.

*–Jimmy Turner, senior director of gardens, Dallas Arboretum and Botanical Garden*

## People Are Talking About . . .

- ◆ fighting the invasive vine **KUDZU** in Canada
- ◆ neighbors **SHARING YARD SPACE,** tools, and time for vegetable beds
- ◆ **REDUCING MOWING AND FERTILIZER** with 'Captiva', a slow-growing grass

continued ➡

POWERFUL PENETRATING
## *PAIN RELIEF*
You don't have to live with
joint pain anymore »

DOCTOR TESTED
CLINICALLY PROVEN

Proven innovative pain neutralizing lotion that soothes while providing temporary relief of joint pain.

Penetran+Plus patented advanced formulation provides deep penetrating pain relief, without creating a hot or cold sensation, with a pleasant lemon scent.

Penetran+Plus is a scientific victory that provides today's most effective non-prescription topical pain relief and differs from all other topical analgesic products available.

**To find a store near you or order online visit www.penetran.com (Coupon Code: Almanac) or call 800-282-5511**

Powerful Penetrating Pain Relief Lotion

| Effectiveness | Penetran +Plus |
|---|---|
| Fast Relief | ✓ YES |
| Hours Long-Lasting Relief | ✓ YES |
| Reduces Inflammation | ✓ YES |
| Clinically Proven | ✓ YES |
| Active Quaternary Ammonium | ✓ YES |
| Pleasantly Lemon Scented | ✓ YES |

# DR® LEAF and LAWN VACUUM

## LEAVES NOTHING IN ITS PATH. EXCEPT THE COMPETITION.

Put an end to fall cleanup hassle with a DR® LEAF and LAWN VACUUM. No other is built stronger or lasts longer.

**UNSTOPPABLE POWER** Collect and shred acres of leaves, pine cones, pine needles, grass clippings, nuts.

**HUGE CAPACITY** Exclusive shredding action reduces debris 10:1, for more vacuuming and less unloading.

**BUILT TO LAST** Beefy steel frame, large hoses, hard shell collector, commercial engine options.

PROFESSIONAL POWER • FOR HOMEOWNERS
DR

**Call for a FREE DVD & Catalog!**
TOLL FREE **1-800-731-0493**
**www.DRleafvac.com**

6 MONTH HANDS-ON TRIAL
69380X © 2010

# AROUND THE HOUSE

We're making things over, making things better, and often just making do.

## HOW WE MEASURE "UP"

◆ People are building tree houses to use as offices or guest rooms, instead of extending the house.

## We're Furnishing With Fewer Frills

"Over-the-top décor is still not fashionable."
*—Vern Yip, home design expert*

The trend is toward . . .

◆ upholstered goods with nailhead trim

◆ pillows with stitching and beading

◆ intricate carving on wood headboards, dining table legs, and dressers

◆ curves in sofa backs, chair backs, bathroom vanities, and accent tables

◆ drapery hung with a gentle swag

## Decorators Are Designing With . . .

◆ warm GRAYS (think charcoal, slate rock, or elephants) for walls and upholstery

◆ matte, or flat, BLACK metal for plumbing fixtures

◆ deep GREENS and PURPLES (think peacock feathers) for accent pillows, accessories, and bedding

◆ deep RED for dramatic accents

## IDEAS THAT MAKE CENTS

◆ furniture that's built to last (tables made from the reclaimed wood of old factory floors or barns built with old-growth trees)

◆ warehouses that stock impossible-to-find, generations-old (or even new) china and silverware replacement pieces

◆ mail-order knife-sharpening

## People Are Talking About . . .

◆ HANDHELD CAMERAS that "see" through walls to detect hidden wires and pipes

◆ HOUSING "BRICKS" made from dried mushrooms (they trap more heat than fiberglass insulation)

◆ CONCRETE containing titanium dioxide, which absorbs air pollution from car exhaust

continued ➡

# OUR CHANGING CULTURE

We're online, on our feet, on our game, on the move, and occasionally on edge.

## HOW WE MEASURE UP

**11.8:** hours per day in the average American's daily "information diet":

| |
|---|
| 5 hours watching television |
| 2 hours, 2 minutes listening to radio |
| 2 hours on a computer |
| 1 hour of video games |
| 36 minutes reading |
| 40 minutes on the telephone |
| 30 minutes listening to music |

## WE'RE ON THE MOVE

* **TAKING ELEVATED WALKWAYS** over city streets
* **IN THE CAR,** not the air (too costly)
* **ON BUSES** with movies and Internet access
* **GOING TENT AND RV CAMPING**

## HABITS WE'RE FORMING

➜ **Telecommuting:** This is a natural for the emerging workforce's young people, who are constantly connected (e.g., e-mailing, texting, blogging).

➜ **Home schooling:** "Online schools will make it easier and cheaper."

*–Cara Newman, editor, YoungMoney.com*

### New Terms of Endearment

**RURALPOLITANS** are families and singles relocating to the countryside.

◆

**RETROSEXUALS** are people who connect with long-lost crushes from their past.

## We Love to Compete

* **on pogo sticks,** with athletes setting high-jump records
* **in lobster-boat races** in coastal New England towns
* **in hospital kitchens,** where chefs vie to make the tastiest low-calorie meals

## People Are Talking About . . .

* **CAVE-LIKE BEDS** with TVs, sound systems, and wine coolers inside
* larger, heavier, **"HULA" HOOPS** and groups that use them
* **"CALCULATOR HOBBYISTS"** who convert the devices into miniature computers

continued ➡

2011     THE OLD FARMER'S ALMANAC     19

**This Year at a Glance**

# ON THE FASHION FRONT

We're dressing for success, whatever we perceive that to be. "It's not so matchy-matchy anymore. Everything works."

*–Marie Driscoll, retail apparel analyst,*
*Standard & Poor's*

## HOW WE MEASURE UP

**11:** percent of expected increase in hair clipper sales due to budget-conscious folks cutting their own hair

**11:** percent of expected increase in salon business repairing home cuts

## IDEAS THAT MAKE CENTS

### "TRASHION" DESIGNS

fancy outfits made from junk (e.g., rusty nails and old cassette tape)

## People are talking about . . .

- **MOVING AWAY FROM** a single skirt length or pants silhouette being "in style" and toward individual preference
- **CLOTHING LABELS THAT LET BUYERS FIND ONLINE** the designers, farmers, and factories involved in producing a garment

## The Latest in Ladieswear

"Suiting for women is going to make a big comeback." *–Cynthia Nellis, fashion expert*

### The colors

- plaid, in everything from casual camp shirts to office-ready suits
- olive and army green: "They go with everything, from purple to mustard" *–Cynthia Nellis*

### The styles

- military looks: jackets and double-breasted coats with brass buttons
- matching jackets and skirts
- fur trims: real and faux, on coats and sweaters

### After-hours attire

- T-shirts with expensive handbags, fancy jewelry with jeans and cowboy boots, and colorful accessories with neutral clothing

## Clothes That Make the Man

"Men have 'sobered up' and realized that how they look influences others."

*–Andy Gilchrist, author of*
*The Encyclopedia of Men's Clothes*

### The colors

- "stormy" charcoal and burnt brown
- reds, pinks, and yellows

continued ➡

The Davis Hill Weather Stick®

802-533-2400

davishillco@hotmail.com

P.O. Box 44, Greensboro, VT 05841

Wholesale Inquiries Welcome

$5 Each plus S&H
Min. order 2

at home in nature™

From seaside getaways to mountain retreats, the Pacific Yurt goes where you want to be.

Call today for a brochure:
1.800.944.0240
www.yurts.com

pacific yurts Inc.®

WORLD'S LEADING MANUFACTURER

*1927 Lincoln*

*1929 Surrender of Fort Sackville*

*Scarce 1942 Stamp*

# 3 Classic Mint U.S. Stamps FREE

Get 3 classic U.S. stamps in mint condition FREE! These stamps are at least 50 years old!

Send today for your three classic U.S. stamps (stamps may vary) and you'll also receive special collector's information and other interesting stamps on approval. Limit one collection. Your satisfaction is guaranteed.

**3 Classic Mint U.S. Stamps FREE**
☑ **Yes!** Send me 3 Classic Mint Postage Stamps. Limit one collection.
**Send coupon to:**
**Mystic Stamp Company, Dept. GK806**
**9700 Mill St., Camden, NY 13316-9111**

Name_____

Address _____

City/State/Zip _____

**The styles**
* polished and professional
* pleated pants

**The accessories**
* skinny ties and single-button vests
* dressy hats—dark fedoras and straw Panama hats
* Italian loafers
* lightweight scarves and pocket squares

**After-hours attire**
* dark, tailored, "power jeans" or pants resembling riding breeches
* V-neck tops and rib-hugging Ts showing chest hair
* denim with sequins and beading

# ON THE FARM

Country values, habits, and interests are sprouting everywhere.

## What's Growing

→ **cotton as food, not fiber:** Genetically engineered seeds are protein-rich.

→ **red, white, and blue potatoes:** Colored skins and/or flesh provide antioxidants.

→ **new vegetable varieties** developed by small-scale farmers to "take back the seeds" from multinational companies

**HOW WE MEASURE UP**

**600+:** number of Midwestern growers who used satellite data to assess crops and spot infestations, flooding, and storm damage in 2010

### IDEAS THAT MAKE CENTS

* **more city and suburban dwellers raising ducks, turkeys, goats, and rabbits** for food and keeping bees for honey

* **milkmen delivering to doorsteps** just-bottled milk in glass bottles

* **algae as an air-cleaner and biofuel,** grown on pods attached to urban buildings

## People are talking about . . .

* **THE DOWNSIZING OF DETROIT:** razing vacant and dilapidated homes and turning the resulting lots into productive fields and farmland

* **INCREASING RURAL PROSPERITY** through local churches, locally owned manufacturing, small colleges, and innovative farmers

continued ⇒

# Are you bothered by constant *RINGING* in your ears?

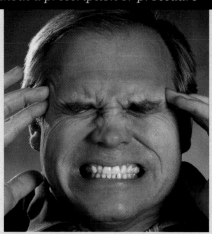

# PETS

We love our animals more than ever!

## HOW WE MEASURE UP

**1 in 3:** number of smokers who say that a pet's health would motivate them to quit

**33:** percent of bird owners who name their pet in their will

**100:** dollars saved on cat litter per year if a cat is trained to use the family toilet

**1,000:** pounds of dog poop collected each month in Ithaca, New York, in a pioneering effort to make compost for nonedible plants

## Another Reason Why Dog Is Man's Best Friend

People who walked a dog increased their speed by **28 percent** over a 12-week period, compared with a **4 percent** uptick for people who walked with people.

*–University of Missouri*

## People are talking about . . .

- **CALMING NERVOUS PETS** with animal pheromones (chemical compounds that de-stress) in sprays or collars

- **DNA TESTING** to establish a dog's precise lineage

- the average cost to **CLONE A DOG—** $144,000

continued ➡

---

# A PICTURE OF HEALTH

We're getting physical and feeling the spirit, but happiness is elusive.

## Research Results

• The **cells of sedentary people appear "older,"** while those of middle-age athletes are "younger" than those of their less-active peers, proving that exercise has an anti-aging effect at the molecular level.

• **Smokers are at additional risk** from their own "secondhand" smoke.

• **People who are outgoing, active, and less neurotic** are most likely to **live beyond age 100.**

### HOW WE MEASURE UP

**9 out of 10:** number of people who pray

**10:** difference in pounds, on average, between a man who lives in a walkable neighborhood and one who doesn't

**2,000:** number of extra steps taken each day by pedometer users

continued ➡

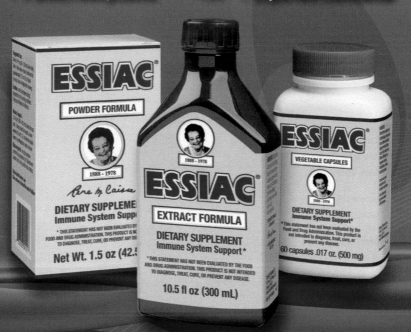

## States of Well-Being

Where people enjoy "the good life" (high job satisfaction, emotional and physical health, and more):

* **HIGHEST-RANKING (BEST FIRST)**
Hawaii, Utah, Montana
* **LOWEST-RANKING (WORST FIRST)**
Arkansas, Kentucky, West Virginia

*–Gallup-Healthways Well-Being Index*

## FRIENDLY PROVINCES

**CANADA IS . . .**

* where people in a 20-nation study would most like to live, work, or study
* home to the nationality most people would choose for a close friend

*–Anholt–GfK Roper Nation Brands Index*

## People are talking about . . .

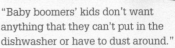

* **LABS THAT GROW HUMAN ORGANS** (muscles, blood vessels, and bladders)
* **RUNNING BAREFOOT** (which exerts less stress on the knee, hip, and ankle)

# MONEY MATTERS

We're saving, scrimping, splurging, speculating, selling, and "Scrooge-ing."

### HOW WE MEASURE UP

**1:** dollar amount budgeted per mile for food and lodging by many hikers on the Appalachian Trail

**30:** percent of people with a healthy savings habit

**82:** percent of adults surveyed who intentionally support neighborhood stores

## People are talking about . . .

* **SAFES** built into bed mattresses
* **BYPASSING BIG BOX STORES** to buy local
* **"SCROOGE-CONOMICS"** to justify not buying holiday gifts

## COLLECTIBLES:
### The Next "Big Things"

* coins
* vintage pinball machines
* space memorabilia, especially from *Apollo 11*

## Best to Bid On

→ Arts and Crafts furniture
→ Rookwood pottery
→ photographs of the Civil War and American West

*–Wes Cowan, Cincinnati, Ohio–based appraiser*

## Once Treasure, Now Trash

* Hummel figurines
* vintage beer cans
* fine china, crystal stemware, and pressed glass:

"Baby boomers' kids don't want anything that they can't put in the dishwasher or have to dust around."

*–Ken Farmer, Radford, Virginia–based appraiser*

continued ➡

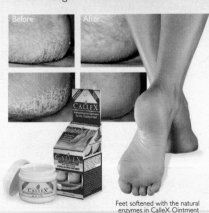

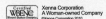

# IN THE FOOD MOOD

Life is a banquet, and we're tasting everything!

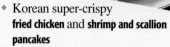

## NEW MENU OPTIONS

* **sardines** and **arctic char** (overfishing is reducing other fish stocks)
* **grits** on the side
* **"rice of the Prairies,"** an oat grain grown by Manitoba farmers
* **offal** (pig trotters and beef cheek)

## People are talking about . . .

* **BAKERIES** putting fresh-baked pies in customer's own dishes so that they can pass them off as homemade
* **ROVING FOOD TRUCKS** that announce their locations electronically
* **SHORTER INGREDIENT LABELS ON PACKAGED FOODS:** to seem "more like foods found in a home kitchen, instead of a chemistry lab"
  *–Elaine Tecklenburg, analyst at Packaged Facts*
* growing **ARTIFICIAL MEAT** in a petri dish
* **A RACE CAR** with a carrot-fiber steering wheel, potato-starch side mirrors, and cashew-cell brake pads

## Flavors We Crave

* Korean super-crispy **fried chicken** and **shrimp and scallion pancakes**
* licorice-like, sweet black **garlic**
* **homemade fermented foods** (yogurt, kimchi, and sourdough bread)
* **relaxers:** kava root, melatonin, rose hip, and valerian beverages

## IDEAS THAT MAKE CENTS

* **vending machines that reward stationary bike riders** with snacks after pedaling
* **eating (well!)** at hospital cafeterias

## Food Fads

* **pancakes with bacon-flavor butter filling**
* **waffle cones filled with chili, potatoes, or macaroni**
* **breakfast cereals in ice cream**
* **coconut water**

## THOUGHT FOR THE DAY

"People are slowing down, increasing social contacts, and feeling less pressure to buy, buy, buy. Finding 'the satisfaction of enough' is a lasting road to less stress and greater happiness."

*–Carol Holst, founder of the nonprofit group Simple Living America*

**Stacey Kusterbeck,** a frequent contributor to *The Old Farmer's Almanac,* writes about popular culture from New York State.

**BECOME A FAN** of *The Old Farmer's Almanac* on **Facebook** and **Twitter** and tell us how you're finding less stress and greater happiness this year.

# FIND THE PERFECT GIFT FOR YOUR HUNTERS.

**FREE LES KOUBA GIFT BOX WITH EACH PURCHASE!**

## GREAT HUNTING GIFTS.com

WWW.GREATHUNTINGGIFTS.COM
PHONE 888-695-1292

# FREE: THE ESSIAC HANDBOOK

Learn about the Famous Ojibway Herbal Healing Remedy

*Write for a Free Copy:*
P.O. Box 1182
Crestone, CO 81131

*Or Call Toll-Free:*
1-888-568-3036

# "Eat Your COLORS!"

−Rita Maas Studio, Inc./StockFood

Here's what Mom really meant when she told you to eat your vegetables.

BY MARGARET BOYLES

Scientific studies have confirmed that people who eat more fruit and vegetables, particularly the more deeply colored varieties, have less heart disease, cancer, diabetes, osteoporosis, and age-related neurological decline.

The secret is in the colors.

Increasingly, many health researchers have turned their attention to plant pigments—light-harvesting molecules that selectively absorb certain bandwidths of visible light and reflect others. The reflected wavelengths are the colors that we see in flowers, foliage, fruit, and vegetables. It's the pigments that deliver a variety of health-protecting benefits to the plants that make them.

"Plants are the master chemists," says Mary Ann Lila, who directs the Plants for Human Health Institute at North Carolina State University. "Because plants can't move around, they have to manufacture what they need not merely to grow, but to defend, protect, and heal themselves. It makes sense to study whether compounds that plants produce in response to stress would help a human under similar circumstances."

The first plant pigment—chlorophyll—appeared on Earth some 2.5 billion years ago. It initiates the photosynthetic reactions that produce most of the food and oxygen that sustain most animal life on Earth.

*(continued)*

35

Get the most variety of colorful fruit and vegetables you can, the most cheaply. You can't overdose on vegetables.

*–Dr. James A. Duke, retired USDA ethnobotanist and world-renowned authority on medicinal plants*

Some pigments aid photosynthesis. Others serve higher plants by attracting pollinators to their flowers and seed-dispersing animals to their fruit. Pigments protect plants from solar radiation, oxidative damage to cells, environmental stress, and attacks by microbes, insects, and animal predators. Pigments also heal damaged plant tissue, help to regulate growth, and act in many other ways still undiscovered.

Innumerable challenges face researchers looking to quantify the human health benefits of plant pigments and other compounds that plants produce. For example:

- **What provokes a plant to make more or less of a certain pigment?**

- **How do storage, processing, and cooking methods affect pigments?**

- **What is the fate of certain pigments in the human body?**

- **Are benefits to humans from plant compounds affected by genetics and/or diet?**

Beverly Clevidence, a research nutritionist with the U.S. Agricultural Research Service's Food Components and Health Laboratory since 1984, foresees the day "when individuals will receive 'phyto-nutrition' prescriptions tailored to their specific needs. Perhaps someday we will be saying, 'You're more likely to die of this type of cancer than heart disease, and you lack this particular enzyme, so you should eat more of this or that fruit or vegetable.'"

"For now," she continues, "we should apply what we know. Eat more fruit and vegetables—yes, brightly and deeply colored—but don't forget garlic, onions, and apples."

## If Fruit and Vegetables Are So Good for Us . . .

**Q:** Why don't scientists extract plant pigments identified as beneficial and put them into pills?

**A:** "Some companies have already done this, and there's a lot of research heading in this direction," says James Joseph, a neuroscientist and senior researcher at the Tufts University Human Nutrition Research Center on Aging. "But when you start taking these things apart, the compounds don't act like they do in the whole food. Extracts can even produce the opposite effect, especially in high doses."

# PLANT PIGMENTS AND YOU

**PIGMENT CLASS: Chlorophylls**

**Indicative color:** green

**Plants rich in these:** deep-green leafy greens

**In plants, these pigments** harvest light and initiate photosynthesis.

**In people, these pigments** help to deactivate carcinogens.

**Surprise!** Chlorophylls may deactivate colon and liver cancer carcinogens.

**PIGMENT CLASS: Carotenoids**

**Indicative colors:** yellow, orange to red

**Plants rich in these:** apricots, cantaloupes, carrots, leafy greens (chlorophyll masks the colors), pumpkins, sweet potatoes, tomatoes, winter squashes

**In plants, these pigments** aid in photosynthesis, protect from solar radiation, act as antioxidants, and attract pollinators and seed dispersers.

**In people, these pigments** protect the immune system, skin, and epithelial cells and may prevent heart disease, cancer, and macular degeneration.

**Surprise!** Eating carotenoids with a little fat can help the body to absorb them.

**PIGMENT CLASS: Anthocyanins**

**Indicative colors:** blue, purple-burgundy

**Plants rich in these:** black turtle beans; purple cabbage, eggplant, potatoes; red onions; red and purple grapes and berries

**In plants, these pigments** attract pollinators and seed dispersers, improve tolerance to stress, repel predators, resist disease, and prevent oxidative damage to cells.

**In people, these pigments** may prevent or reverse age-related cognitive decline and/or neuro-degenerative disease, improve vision; help to prevent cancer, heart disease, insulin resistance, and obesity; promote wound healing.

**Surprise!** Anthocyanins are water-soluble and never occur with betalains.

**PIGMENT CLASS: Betalains**

**Indicative colors:** red-violet, yellow-orange

**Plants rich in these:** beets, Swiss chard, prickly pear cactus fruit, spinach

**In plants, these pigments** protect against excess photoradiation.

**In people, these pigments** may protect against cancer, heart disease, liver damage, and ulcers.

**Surprise!** Betalains are water-soluble and never occur with anthocyanins.

**Margaret Boyles** lives and gardens in central New Hampshire and has eaten something colorful from her own ground nearly every day for more than 40 years.

**Turn the page to see what vegetables to grow for pigments**

# GROW A RAINBOW

**Try these vegetables at home for a harvest of healthy pigments!**

BY ROBIN SWEETSER

–All-America Selections

–W. Atlee Burpee & Co.

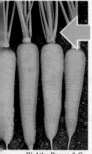

–W. Atlee Burpee & Co.

■ 'Chiogga' **beet** is an Italian heirloom. Named for a town in Italy, it is also known as the bull's-eye beet because of its red and white interior rings. Harvest at 1 inch for tender baby beets or let them fully mature. A high sugar content makes them sweet and mild. Slice them to show off the colorful rings (these don't bleed). For the highest nutritional benefit, eat the tops, too.

■ 'New Red Fire' **lettuce** tolerates heat and cold, making it a tasty, bolt-resistant choice in any garden. The ruffled leaves can be harvested as a cut-and-come-again crop or picked as an immense loose-leaf head.

■ 'Carmen' **sweet pepper** earned an All-America Selections (AAS) award in 2006. An Italian, horn-type, hybrid pepper, it grows to 6 inches long and matures from glossy green to brilliant red. 'Carmen' is sweet whether raw or cooked and high in beta-carotene.

■ 'Rose' **tomato,** an Amish heirloom, is a taste test winner. Its nearly seedless fruit weigh up to 10 ounces each and balance sweetness and acidity. The productive plants also have good disease resistance.

■ 'Touchon' **carrot** is a quick-maturing, almost coreless, French heirloom that is slender, tender, and sweet throughout its 6 to 8 inches and is excellent for making carrot juice.

■ Raw or cooked, 'Cheddar' **cauliflower** has 25 times the beta-carotene of its white cousin and fantastic flavor and texture. It keeps its color when cooked. Plant late for a fall crop; it forms large heads (up to 10 inches across) but does not do well in hot weather.

–Johnny's Selected Seeds

–Johnny's Selected Seeds

–Johnny's Selected Seeds

## The Kaleidoscope Effect

Many seed companies offer packets of mixed seeds. Look for "rainbow" mixes of beans, carrots, cauliflower, chard, peppers, and radishes.

*(continued)*

'Charentais' **melon,** a fragrant French heirloom, has exceptionally sweet and delicious orange flesh—making it perfect for desserts. Ripe fruit weigh in at 2 to 3 pounds each.

The 'Sungold' cherry **tomato** is exceptionally sweet. Its prolific plants bear early and bright 1-inch fruit. It produces in warm and cold conditions.

–W. Atlee Burpee & Co.

'Sunshine', a scarlet-orange, kabocha-type, hybrid **winter squash,** won an AAS award in 2004. Bright orange throughout, its thick, creamy, stringless flesh has a sweet, nutty flavor. Mature fruit store well.

–W. Atlee Burpee & Co.

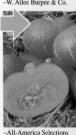

A 'Roc d'Or' **bush bean** plant bears abundant yields of slender, 6-inch-long, stringless pods that have a subtle, buttery flavor and firm, meaty texture. Better still, it is disease-resistant and tolerates cool, wet conditions. This plant grows well in a container.

–All-America Selections

Unlike some of its finicky cousins, 'Touchstone Gold' **beet** has a high germination rate and is easy to grow. Its 4-inch round roots have smooth shoulders, retain their color when cooked, and don't bleed. The best part? Its sweetness.

–Johnny's Selected Seeds

'Yellow Doll' hybrid **watermelon** is super-sweet, crisp, and very juicy. Its semicompact vines can be grown on a trellis. The almost-seedless fruit weigh 5 to 7 pounds each—convenient for the fridge.

–Johnny's Selected Seeds

'Gold Rush' **zucchini** has a rich, buttery flavor. An AAS winner in 1980, its space-saving, vigorous plants are highly productive.

–Veseys Seeds

'Maxibel' is a slender **French filet bean** of the type known as *haricots verts.* Crisp and full of flavor, it grows abundantly on 2-foot-tall plants. Its 7-inch-long pods are stringless.

–Johnny's Selected Seeds

'Apple Green' **eggplant** was developed at the University of New Hampshire by renowned plant breeder Elwyn Meader. It is mild and never seedy or bitter; its tender skin needs no peeling. The plants bear 5-inch oval fruit—even in cool, wet conditions.

–Tomato Growers Supply Company

–Johnny's Selected Seeds

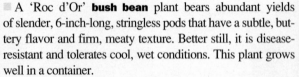
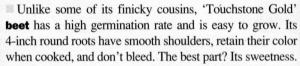

(continued)

'Early Jalapeño' **hot pepper** is used green in spicy dishes. Juicy and thick-walled, this 3-inch-long, medium-hot pepper gains heat as it matures on the plant, ripening to red. (Smoke them over mesquite to make chipotles.) Unlike most hot peppers, this has adapted widely and will set fruit in cool conditions.

–W. Atlee Burpee & Co.

'Space' **spinach** produces smooth, spoon-shape, upright leaves that are sweet and succulent raw or cooked. This is a vigorous, three-season, heat-tolerant plant.

–Johnny's Selected Seeds

'Romanesco' **zucchini** has a nutty, rich flavor. Its striped skin is deeply ribbed; slices look scalloped. Pick it young, with the flower, and steam lightly for a tender treat. Use the male blossoms for stuffing or frying.

The fast-growing 'Royal Burgundy' **bush bean** plant bears straight, smooth, 6-inch-long, stringless pods that turn green when cooked. If picked often, beans will keep coming until the first frost.

–Johnny's Selected Seeds

–Johnny's Selected Seeds

'Purple Haze' hybrid **carrot,** a 2006 AAS winner, has orange flesh and a purple exterior that fades when cooked. The 8- to 12-inch-long carrot has a sweet flavor, with a hint of spice. It's a good cool-season crop.

'Graffiti' hybrid **cauliflower** achieves its big, brilliant head without needing its outer leaves tied up. It is excellent raw or cooked (and keeps its purple color). Plant in spring and fall for two crops.

–Johnny's Selected Seeds

'All Blue' **potatoes** have deep color throughout. The tuber's soft, moist texture is best when steamed and then mashed or used in potato salad. In cool conditions, this late-season variety produces big yields of medium potatoes that keep well.

–All-America Selections

'Cherokee Purple' **tomato** is a smoky-sweet, disease-resistant heirloom from Tennessee. The mahogany skin of the 6- to 12-ounce fruit deepens as summer heats up but, when cut, its flesh glows red. Pick when its shoulders are green. □□

---

**Robin Sweetser,** a regular contributor to *The Old Farmer's Almanac All-Seasons Garden Guide,* loves cooking with colorful vegetables picked fresh from her garden in Hillsborough, New Hampshire.

–W. Atlee Burpee & Co.

–Johnny's Selected Seeds

# In His Hands

I have named this rare photograph *In His Hands*. It is a once-in-a-lifetime spiritual image captured on film. This inspirational photograph won the Gertrude Bridge Award at The Art League of New Britain's annual art show.  Information on the award and the history of how the event was recorded on film is included with each order.

11" x 14" Lithograph $35 • 8" x 10" Glossy on Archival Photo Paper $49

Price includes shipping and handling.

Orders by letter only with check enclosed to:

**Walter Gasuk • 430 Monroe Street • New Britain, CT 06052**

Email: wgasuk@comcast.net

The photo was copyrighted July 3, 1997 • Registration no. VAu 403 573

There is a receptor site in almost every cell in the human body for HGH, so its regenerative and healing effects are very comprehensive.

Growth Hormone, first synthesized in 1985 under the Reagan Orphan drug act, to treat dwarfism, was quickly recognized to stop aging in its tracks and reverse it to a remarkable degree. Since then, only the lucky and the rich have had access to it at the cost of $10,000 US per year.

The next big breakthrough was to come in 1997 when a group of doctors and scientists, developed an all-natural source product which would cause your own natural HGH to be released again and do all the remarkable things it did for you in your 20's. Now available to every adult for about the price of a coffee and donut a day.

GHR now available in America, just in time for the aging Baby Boomers and everyone else from age 30 to 90 who doesn't want to age rapidly but would rather stay young, beautiful and healthy all of the time.

The new HGH releasers are winning converts from the synthetic HGH users as well, since GHR is just as effective, is oral instead of self-injectable and is very affordable.

GHR is a natural releaser, has no known side effects, unlike the synthetic version and has no known drug interactions. Progressive doctors admit that this is the direction medicine is seeking to go, to get the body to heal itself instead of employing drugs. GHR is truly a revolutionary paradigm shift in medicine and, like any modern leap frog advance, many others will be left in the dust holding their limited, or useless drugs and remedies.

It is now thought that HGH is so comprehensive in its healing and regenerative powers that it is today, where the computer industry was twenty years ago, that it will displace so many prescription and non-prescription drugs and health remedies that it is staggering to think of.

The president of BIE Health Products stated in a recent interview, I've been waiting for these products since the 70's. We knew they would come, if only we could stay healthy and live long enough to see them! If you want to stay on top of your game, physically and mentally as you age, this product is a boon, especially for the highly skilled professionals who have made large investments in their education, and experience. Also with the failure of Congress to honor our seniors with pharmaceutical coverage policy, it's more important than ever to take pro-active steps to safeguard your health. Continued use of GHR will make a radical difference in your health, HGH is particularly helpful to the elderly who, given a choice, would rather stay independent in their own home, strong, healthy and alert enough to manage their own affairs, exercise and stay involved in their communities. Frank, age 85, walks two miles a day, plays golf, belongs to a dance club for seniors, had a girl friend again and doesn't need Viagara, passed his drivers test and is hardly ever home when we call - GHR delivers.

HGH is known to relieve symptoms of Asthma, Angina, Chronic Fatigue, Constipation, Lower back pain and Sciatica, Cataracts and Macular Degeneration, Menopause, Fibromyalgia, Regular and Diabetic Neuropathy, Hepatitis, helps Kidney Dialysis and Heart and Stroke recovery.

**For more information or to order call**
**877-849-4777**
**www.biehealth.us**

These statements have not been evaluated by the FDA. ©copyright 2000

# Plantimals on

# Parade

## *Turn your garden into a zoo.*

–Patty Hankins

Plants and animals have been keeping company since the beginning of time, so it's not surprising how many flora and fauna look-alikes have traded names. Capture and tame some of these "wildlife" specimens to transform your vegetative domain into a delightful animal kingdom.

## TOAD LILY
*Tricyrtis hirta*

This popular perennial looks little like a toad, apart from its vaguely amphibian splotches of purple, pink, or magenta, so to get the connection, take the advice of Allan Armitage, professor of horticulture at the University of Georgia: In late summer or fall, when the blossoms sparkle with a waxen sheen, turn one over to touch the three small "warts" (tiny swellings) on its back.

This Asian species requires at least partial shade and moist soil. It grows up to 2½ feet tall in slowly forming, 2- to 3-foot clumps. Some of its arching stems scramble, some lean, others stand erect. Its narrow, bamboo-like leaves are often variegated from golden to green. Hardy from Zones 4 to 9, this plant is fiercer than it appears: All parts are poisonous if ingested. *(continued)*

*by Cynthia Van Hazinga*

–animal illustrations, Renée Quintal Daily

47

# LAMBS' EARS

*Stachys byzantina*

—Our Enchanted Garden/Cheryl Binstock

**C**hildren and adults love lambs' ears for their soft-as-suede, silvery foliage. The species also has pinkish purple or white flower spikes (12 to 18 inches tall) early in the season. Some gardeners find the slightly fragrant flowers charming; others cut them off to encourage leaf growth. (Some slow-growing cultivars do not bloom.)

Let this lamb ramble over the ground or use it as soft edging, but beware: It can be invasive. Besides spreading by roots, lambs' ears self-seed profusely in Zones 4 to 8. Give them well-drained soil and remove rotted, mildewed leaves. Divide plants every 2 to 4 years, as they tend to grow from the center out.

# CANARY VINE

*Tropaeolum peregrinum*

—Christopher Whitehouse

**A**lso known as canary creeper and canary bird vine, this member of the nasturtium family will climb up to 10 feet with a fine filigree of dainty foliage and bright yellow flowers that surely provided its common name.

Grow it in view: in a window box or on a trellis or chain-link fence (if the fence does not get too hot). For an unusual effect, train it to climb an evergreen shrub or hedge; the flowers will shimmer like stars in the night sky.

Canary vine thrives in sun to partial shade and has average water needs; don't overwater. It's a tender perennial in Zones 9 to 11, a tender annual elsewhere. Its flowers are edible and taste pleasantly peppery.

*(continued)*

# SOLATUBE.
Innovation in Daylighting.

# The smarter way to brighten dark rooms.

Improve the quality of your home and your life with Solatube Daylighting Systems. Our innovative technology brings the beauty of natural light indoors in just about two hours. **You deserve the best.**

**Start planning at www.ilovedaylight.com
or call (888) SOLATUBE.**

# GOATSBEARD

*Aruncus dioicus* or *A. aethusifolius*

–Julie Krzeminski

F ast-growing goatsbeard is dramatic under maples or other tree canopies (more so near a pool or stream), waving feathery panicles of small, ivory flowers in early summer. The panicles give it its common name; they resemble the snow-white beard of a goat.

Grow it where you can see it from the south, as it tends to lean toward the sun, in moist, well-drained (even boggy) soil. It will soar 6 feet or more where it is hardy (Zones 3 to 7).

Dwarf goatsbeard *(Aruncus aethusifolius)* grows only 8 inches tall (Zones 4 to 8). This "kid" is ideal along a border or path or around flat stones.

# RED SPIDER LILY

*Lycoris radiata*

–Ken Blackwell

**O**ne of the most dramatic signs of fall in Zones 8 to 10 is clumps of red spider lily that sizzle into bloom, waving clusters of four to six flowers with long, spidery anthers. (Another spider lily, *Hymenocallis* x *festalis,* is a sparkling white.)

Native to Japan, red spider lilies give no hint of their presence until autumn rains fall. Then the brilliant, leafless flowers appear overnight. A week or so after the flowers have faded, straplike basal leaves sprout, only to deteriorate and disappear until the following autumn. Be aware that all parts are poisonous if ingested, a characteristic that helps to discourage most major pests. In their preferred habitat of full sun, spider lilies are perennial. In winter climes, red spider lilies are the stuff of dreams.

*(continued)*

# RATTLESNAKE-MASTER

*Eryngium yuccifolium*

–Jim Frazier Photography

**T**his native species is also called button eryngo and button snakeroot. It grows 2 to 6 feet tall from a short, thick rootstock and will add texture and color to almost any perennial border. Greenish-white flower heads—reminiscent of globe thistle *(Echinops ritro)* but not as showy—appear at the tip of the stem. Whitish bracts give them a rough, prickly look and feel.

Rattlesnake-master thrives in difficult soils in arid climates, although it's hardy in Zones 4 to 8 in dry glades and prairies and on sandy roadsides from Florida to Minnesota and microclimates beyond.

Why "rattlesnake"? In the 18th and 19th centuries, some Native Americans believed that if they chewed the root, blew on their hands, and then handled rattlesnakes, they would not get bitten. The root was also used in bitter teas as an antidote for various maladies, including snakebite, and to expel worms and induce vomiting.

# TURTLEHEAD

*Chelone* spp.

**N**o snapping from this faux-reptile but a characteristic tendency to draw its upper lip over its lower as if to retreat. This lusty, 2- to 6-foot-tall member of the snapdragon family gets its name from its striking, double-lip flowers in white *(C. glabra),* dark pink *(C. obliqua),* or pink-purple *(C. lyonii)* that grow in a spike or close cluster.

It's an easy perennial (to Zone 3), as long as it has moist soil. Blooming from late August to frost, the foliage is lush all summer.

–Will Stuart

*(continued)*

# Psoriasis? Dermatitis? Dandruff? Dry, Itchy Skin?

## Now you can relieve the itching and restore your skin to its clear healthy state!

**Introducing Soravil™, the scientifically advanced skin therapy system whose active ingredients are clinically proven to provide immediate relief from Psoriasis, Dermatitis, Dandruff, and other bothersome skin disorders.**

**If you suffer from an irritating skin disorder, you must try Soravil™!** Unlike anything you may have tried in the past, Soravil™ is guaranteed to provide immediate relief from the redness and irritation associated with chronic skin disorders. Our clinically tested formulas soothe, moisturize and heal dry, damaged skin...leaving it feeling smooth, supple, and healthy again! Even better, the power of Soravil™ is available in the form of Shampoo and Body Wash, so you can treat your condition as part of your daily routine. There is also easy to apply (and invisible) Body Gel and Skin Spray to take care of those stubborn flare ups. Soravil™ makes it easy for you to relieve yourself from that bothersome skin disorder.

**What are you waiting for?** If you want to relieve yourself from the suffering and rejuvenate your dry, itchy skin, it's time you tried Soravil™! This highly effective formula is guaranteed to work for you. So don't suffer any longer, call today for your risk-free trial, 1-800-711-0719, Offer # 909.

## Success Stories:

*"Right away it cleared my arms up.
I think your product is wonderful.
Thanks so much!"*
-Judy K.

*"I am amazed at the improvement that
Soravil has made to my scalp! To say
I'm delighted would be putting it lightly."*
-David L.

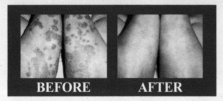

BEFORE          AFTER

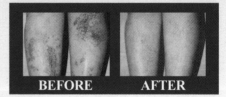

BEFORE          AFTER

## Call now and get your risk-free trial!
## 1-800-711-0719

Mention Offer # 909 and ask how you can get a **FREE SUPPLY** of our Soravil Skin Hydration Formula.

**Active Ingredient FDA Approved • Results Guaranteed
Steroid-Free Formula • Provides Immediate Relief
Works On All Skin Types • Easy Application-No Mess**

# OSTRICH FERN

*Matteuccia struthiopteris*

–Peter L. Herring

S ince the ostrich is native to Africa, it seems likely that the fern's avian nickname coincided with the fashion of imported ostrich feathers adorning women's bonnets, fans, and boas, which began around 1860, peaked in 1875, and then picked up again around the turn of the 20th century. The plume-shape, 3- to 9-foot-tall fronds are feathery!

Grow this hardy (Zones 3 to 8) native in moist, neutral, rich soil in light to full shade and stand back—it spreads rapidly through runners and clumps, adding an architectural quality to a shade garden even in winter.

In early spring, its tightly coiled fronds are a gourmet delicacy. They mature from bottom to top and, coiled up, resemble the tip of a violin (hence the plant's other name, "fiddlehead"). The curled-up fronds can cause illness when eaten raw, but foragers and cooks savor them sautéed or steamed.

*(continued)*

# ZEBRA GRASS

*Miscanthus sinensis* 'Zebrinus'

–Mike Franklin

**N**o African animal has a more distinctive coat than the zebra's, which this graceful, clumping, ornamental grass with broad, yellow-banded leaves calls to mind immediately. Growing to 6 feet tall in Zones 5 to 9, with its feathery, beige flower clusters, zebra grass, like its namesake, is a standout.

Garden designers use it as a background plant, screen, or hedge; in borders; or massed at the water's edge. It requires full sun but thrives in a wide range of soils and stands up to wind and snow. It is impervious to deer, rabbits, heat, humidity, and pollution. Be aware that it spreads rapidly and has invasive potential. Cut it back before new growth begins in the spring, when it stampedes.

# GOOSENECK LOOSESTRIFE

*Lysimachia clethroides*

**T**his aptly named plant is as aggressive as a gaggle of geese; a clump in bloom resembles a gang of webfoots on the march, stretching their long white necks to honk at an intruder.

–Sheryl Kay Oder

Gooseneck loosestrife, hardy from Zones 4 to 9, produces stout stems up to 3 feet tall. These end in nodding whorls of small, saucer-shape, white flowers in dense, tapered spikes 4 to 8 inches long, which bloom from July to September. This vigorous (some say invasive) grower has attractive leaves that turn to a rich gold in autumn.

Like its namesake, it likes to have its feet wet. Grow gooseneck loosestrife in rich and moist—but well-drained—soil.  □□

---

**Cynthia Van Hazinga,** a frequent contributor to *Old Farmer's Almanac* publications, divides her time between New York City and her garden in New Hampshire.

One of *America's* top chefs
shares special recipes and
inside tips.

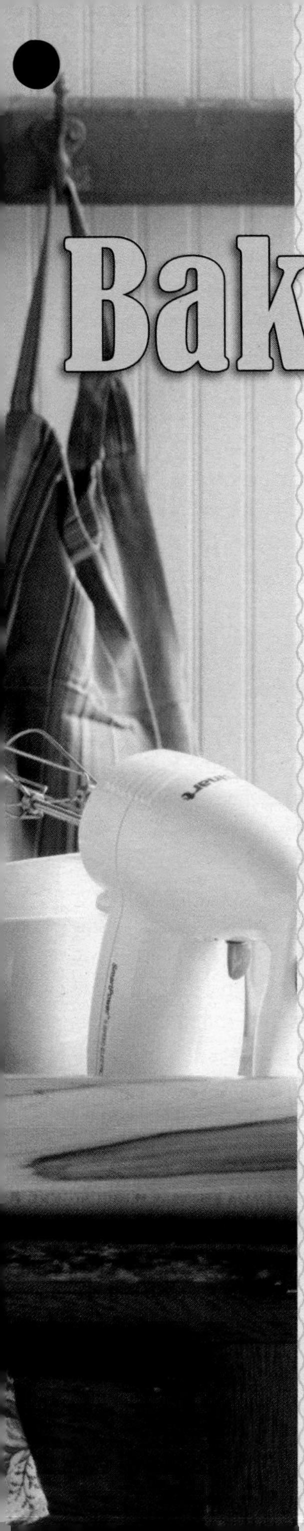

# Baker's Best

*by Ken Haedrich*

I love to bake from scratch: the tactile pleasure of handling raw ingredients, the sense of accomplishment in shaping cookies and buns, the tantalizing aroma of yeast bread in the oven—it's sheer joy. If you love to bake, you get what I mean and can't get enough opportunities to do it.

I indulge my passion throughout the year by celebrating as many special occasions as I can. Valentine's Day? Our chocoholic loved ones get Ultimate To-Die-For Chocolate Cookies. Fourth of July potluck picnic? Sign me up for Skillet Peach Pie; it's a crowd-pleaser. First PTA meeting of the year? Cranberry Beet Cake always gets an A. On birthdays, savory Monkey Bread adds to the fun.

These recipes from my baking archives—a few of my favorites—have been updated and are suitable for any event. Whether baking is new to you or a longtime love, I know that you'll enjoy them.

(RECIPES BEGIN ON NEXT PAGE)

–Alexandra Grablewski/StockFood Munich

# The Ultimate To-Die-For Chocolate Cookie

*Imagine the best brownie you've ever eaten, shaped like a cookie. These should feel soft and squishy when you take them out of the oven. They'll firm up as they cool.*

¾ cup (1½ sticks) unsalted butter

9 ounces unsweetened chocolate, coarsely chopped

3 cups sugar

6 large eggs, at room temperature

1 tablespoon vanilla extract

1½ cups walnut halves or pieces, finely chopped

3 cups all-purpose flour

2½ teaspoons baking powder

¾ teaspoon salt

1½ cups confectioners' sugar, for coating

**TIP:** *Refrigerating the cookies before wrapping makes them firmer and much easier to handle. They can be frozen in an airtight container for up to a month.*

In the top of a double boiler, melt the butter and chocolate over, not in, steaming (not simmering) water. Remove and allow the mixture to partially cool, then stir until smooth. Set aside. In a large bowl, beat the sugar and eggs for 4 minutes, or until light and airy. Add and blend in the vanilla and chocolate. Stir the walnuts into the chocolate mixture. Sift the flour, baking powder, and salt into another bowl. Stir the dry ingredients into the chocolate mixture half at a time, until the dough is evenly mixed; it will be quite soft. Cover and refrigerate for at least 4 hours, or overnight.

Set your oven rack in the middle of the oven. Preheat the oven to 325°F. Line two large cookie sheets with parchment paper. Sift the confectioners' sugar into a shallow bowl. Shape the dough into 1½-inch-diameter balls. Roll the balls in the confectioners' sugar, coating heavily. Place the balls on the sheets, leaving about 2½ inches between them. Bake the cookies one sheet at a time, for 13 minutes. When done, the cookies will have puffed but they'll seem underdone—moist in the center and puffy to the touch. That's good; remove from the oven at once. Transfer the sheet to a rack and cool the cookies for 5 minutes. Using a spatula, transfer them to the rack and finish cooling. Refrigerate 30 minutes on the rack to firm, then wrap individually in plastic wrap. **Makes about 40 large cookies.**

## Cook's Secret:

### Parchment

**Parchment is a cookie baker's best friend. This specially treated paper has a nonstick coating on both sides. Line your pans with it and you'll never have to scrub them again. Remember: You can reuse the same sheet several times, until it becomes too brittle.**

*(continued)*

# Skillet Peach Pie

*This is not your typical peach pie. It's baked in a skillet. The pastry is made with whole wheat flour, and there's only one crust, which you don't have to roll. The peaches are not peeled (the peel helps to hold the flesh together). Finally, the crust is grated like a block of cheese over the fruit. Different, yes, and oh-so-delicious.*

**PASTRY:**
¾ cup all-purpose flour
¾ cup whole wheat pastry flour*
2 teaspoons sugar
scant ½ teaspoon salt
¼ teaspoon baking powder
½ cup (1 stick) cold unsalted
  butter, cut into ¼-inch pieces
¼ cup plus 1 tablespoon cold
  water

**FILLING:**
¼ cup (½ stick) unsalted
  butter
½ cup packed light-brown sugar
6 medium peaches, halved
  lengthwise and pitted
½ cup coarsely chopped pecans
3 teaspoons sugar, divided

*For pastry:* Combine the flours, sugar, salt, and baking powder in the bowl of a food processor. Pulse to mix. Scatter the butter over the dry ingredients and pulse seven or eight times to cut in the butter. Remove the lid and sprinkle the water over the flour. Pulse again, until the pastry starts to form clumps. Do not overprocess. (The pastry may also be mixed by hand, using a pastry blender.) Turn the pastry out onto a large sheet of wax paper and pack the dough, shaping it to resemble a thick block of cheese. Wrap it in wax paper and place in the freezer for at least 1 hour, or until quite firm.

*For filling:* In a 9- or 10-inch, ovenproof (preferably cast-iron) skillet, melt the butter over medium heat. Add the brown sugar and stir, letting the mixture bubble for 15 seconds or so. Remove from the heat.

Place as many peach halves as possible flat side down in the skillet. Coarsely chop any extra peach halves and reserve them. Sprinkle the nuts in between the peaches, then sprinkle any chopped peaches over the nuts.

Set your oven rack in the middle of the oven. When the pastry is firm, preheat the oven to 375°F. Using the large holes on a box grater, grate the pastry evenly over the peaches. Sprinkle with about 2 teaspoons of sugar, then tamp down *very lightly* with your fingers. Sprinkle with the remaining sugar. Bake for 40 minutes, or until the top is golden and the pie is bubbly. Cool on a rack for at least 20 minutes before serving. **Makes 8 servings.**

*Whole wheat pastry flour, a whole grain flour made from a "soft" strain of low-protein wheat, is great for quick breads, piecrusts, and cookies.

*(continued)*

**Keep your brain sharp ... with your spice rack!!**

**Blast your belly fat ... with breakfast!**

# "VINEGAR Can Do What??"

## Just put it on your grocery list and control blood sugar, ease arthritis pain, AND make a flaky pie crust!

(By Frank K. Wood)

If you want to discover inexpensive alternatives to hundreds of costly products, you need *The Kitchen Table Book: 1,427 Kitchen Cures and Pantry Potions for Just About Every Health and Household Problem*, an informative new book just released to the public by FC&A Medical Publishing® in Peachtree City, Georgia.

Your refrigerator alone could be holding more healers than the drug companies' billion-dollar labs! You won't believe what you can do with baking soda, bananas, and so much more!

The authors provide many health tips with full explanations.

► **6** ways to dodge cancer, heart disease, diabetes, and more! Anyone can do it.

► Lower high blood pressure, relieve anxiety, and bring on restful sleep — all with one kitchen herb!

► The one fruit that lowers blood pressure and cholesterol, protects against diabetes and cancer, and can even cut your risk of dementia by over 75% — it's cheap, too!

► Common spice is a life-saver: It inhibits cancer growth, prevents blood clots, even lowers cholesterol.

► Kill disease-causing bacteria and viruses, get rid of mildew, and wipe out laundry stains. All with one inexpensive household product.

► Reduce inflammation and joint damage! A compound found in this soothing beverage could be the key!

► Give your arteries a good scrub naturally with a food from your pantry! Keep your brain sharp with a seasoning! Plus dozens more kitchen cures!

► Cut through grease and germs. Stop bacteria and mold. Even remove clothing stains and beat bathtub film! This pantry classic is all you need!

► Protect yourself from just about all forms of dementia and mental decline, simply by eating as little as 1 serving a week of this amazing food!

► Popular supplements you should never take! In foods, they heal the body. But when taken in pill form, they attack the body and cause early deaths.

► 75% of folks who lost 30 pounds or more, and kept it off, did this one thing every morning — and it's not exercise.

Learn all these amazing secrets and more. To order a copy, just return this coupon with your name and address and a check for **$9.99** plus **$3.00** shipping and handling to: **FC&A, Dept. QK-3313**, 103 Clover Green, Peachtree City, GA 30269. We will send you a copy of *The Kitchen Table Book: 1,427 Kitchen Cures and Pantry Potions for Just About Every Health and Household Problem*.

You get a no-time-limit guarantee of satisfaction or your money back.

**You must cut out and return this coupon with your order. Copies will not be accepted!**

**IMPORTANT — FREE GIFT OFFER EXPIRES IN 30 DAYS**

All orders mailed within 30 days will receive a free gift, *The Little Book of Kitchen Cures for Everyday Ailments*, **guaranteed.** **Order right away!** ©FC&A 2010

# Cranberry Beet Cake With Orange Walnut Glaze

*This cake made with beets is much more than just novel. It's scrumptious, and with its light-pink (not beet-red) hue, it's especially festive between Thanksgiving and Christmas. You can also use cooked and peeled fresh beets.*

**CAKE:**
- 1¼ cups dried sweetened cranberries
- 2½ cups all-purpose flour
- 1½ teaspoons baking powder
- 1 teaspoon baking soda
- ¾ teaspoon salt
- 1 teaspoon cinnamon
- ½ teaspoon nutmeg
- 2¼ cups sugar, divided
- 1 jar or can (16 ounces) beets (pickled or regular), drained
- 4 large eggs, at room temperature
- ¾ cup (1½ sticks) unsalted butter, very soft
- ¼ cup vegetable oil
- 2 teaspoons grated orange zest
- 2 teaspoons grated lemon zest
- 2 teaspoons vanilla extract
- ½ cup buttermilk

**GLAZE:**
- 2½ cups confectioners' sugar
- zest of 1 orange, finely grated
- ¼ cup orange juice
- 1 tablespoon lemon juice
- 1½ tablespoons unsalted butter, melted
- ¼ teaspoon vanilla extract
- 1 cup finely chopped walnuts

*For cake:* Set your oven rack in the middle of the oven. Preheat the oven to 350°F. Put the cranberries into a small bowl and add hot water to cover. Set aside.

Butter and lightly flour a fluted 10-inch Bundt pan. Sift the flour, baking powder, baking soda, salt, cinnamon, and nutmeg into a bowl. Set aside.

Put 1 cup of sugar and the drained beets into a food processor. Purée for about 30 seconds, scraping down the sides of the bowl once. Reserve.

Combine the remaining 1¼ cups of sugar and the eggs, butter, and vegetable oil in a large bowl and beat for 2 to 3 minutes, or until light and airy. Add the beet purée and beat to blend. Add the orange and lemon zests and vanilla and beat briefly, until uniform. Add half of the dry mixture, the buttermilk, and the remaining dry ingredients, beating between each on low speed, until smooth. Drain the cranberries, discarding the liquid, and fold them into the batter. Turn the batter into the Bundt pan, spreading it evenly and smoothing with a spoon. Bake for 50 minutes, or until the cake pulls away from the sides of the pan and an inserted toothpick comes out clean. Transfer the pan to a cooling rack. Cool for 15 minutes, then invert the cake onto the cooling rack. Cool briefly, but glaze the cake while it is slightly warm.

*For glaze:* Sift the confectioners' sugar into a large bowl. Add the orange zest, orange juice, and lemon juice and whisk until smooth. Whisk in the melted butter and vanilla. The glaze should have enough body to coat the cake without running everywhere; adjust as necessary.

Spoon half of the glaze over the cake. Scatter the walnuts on it, then cover the cake with the remaining glaze. **Makes 16 servings.**

*(continued)*

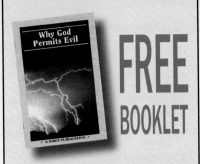

# Parmesan and Onion Monkey Bread

*Monkey bread is pull-apart bread, and most versions are sweet. This one, with herbs, cheese, and onions, is savory and makes a great stand-in for dinner rolls. Let people pull off pieces at will. (A fork helps.) It's fun!*

**1⅓ cups milk**
**9 tablespoons unsalted butter, divided: 4 cut into ¼-inch pieces**
**2 tablespoons sugar**
**1 packet (¼ ounce) active dry yeast (not instant or rapid-rise)**
**1 large egg, at room temperature, lightly beaten**
**4½ to 5 cups all-purpose flour, divided**
**2 teaspoons salt**
**2 teaspoons dried basil**
**light olive or vegetable oil, for bowl**
**1 cup finely chopped onion**
**1 cup freshly grated Parmesan cheese, divided**

Heat the milk in a saucepan until hot (almost but not simmering). Pour into a large bowl and add the four cut-up butter pieces and sugar. Stir until the butter is nearly melted. Set aside. While the milk cools, pour ¼ cup of lukewarm (105° to 115°F) water into a small bowl and sprinkle the yeast over the water. Stir briefly, then set aside for 5 to 10 minutes. When the milk mixture is slightly warmer than body temperature, stir in the yeast and beaten egg. Add 3 cups of flour and the salt and basil and beat well with a wooden spoon for 100 strokes. Cover the dough with plastic wrap and set aside for 10 minutes.

Uncover the bowl and stir in the remaining flour, about ⅓ cup at a time, until the dough pulls away from the sides of the bowl. Turn the dough out onto a lightly floured surface and knead for 8 to 10 minutes, or until the dough is elastic and supple. Use the remaining flour to keep the dough from sticking while you are kneading. Oil a large bowl. Put the dough into the bowl, turning to coat the entire surface. Cover the bowl with plastic wrap and set it aside in a warm, draft-free spot until doubled in bulk, about 1 hour. While the dough rises, melt the remaining 5 tablespoons of butter in a skillet. Add the onions and sauté over low heat for 6 minutes, stirring often. Do not let the butter or onions brown. Set aside. Butter the bottom and sides of a 9-inch springform pan.

When the dough has doubled, punch it down and turn it out onto a lightly floured surface. Knead for 1 minute. Using a dough scraper or knife, cut off pieces of dough and shape into golf ball–size rounds. Roll the dough balls in the skillet to coat with butter and bits of onion, then

## Food

place in the buttered springform pan, just touching each other.

When the bottom of the pan is covered, spoon most of the remaining onions over the dough. Sprinkle with two-thirds of the cheese. Form any remaining dough into balls, roll in the skillet, and place on top of the first layer, starting near the center and working out. Sprinkle with the remaining onions and cheese. Cover with a piece of oiled plastic wrap and set aside in a warm, draft-free spot until nearly doubled in bulk, about 45 minutes.

Place one oven rack in a lower position; remove the remaining racks. Preheat the oven to 375°F. Remove the plastic wrap and bake the bread for 40 to 45 minutes. If it starts to get dark, loosely drape a piece of aluminum foil over it for the final minutes of baking. Transfer the pan to a cooling rack. Run a butter knife down the sides to loosen, then remove the bread from the pan. Cool for 15 to 20 minutes before serving. **Makes one round loaf, about 9 servings.** □□

**Ken Haedrich,** an occasional contributor to *The Old Farmer's Almanac,* is the Julia Child Cookbook Award–winning author of a dozen cookbooks, including *Pie* (Harvard Common Press), voted Amazon.com's best cookbook of 2004.

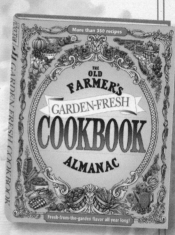

# The Old Farmer's Almanac

### Order Form

**Ordered by:**

Your Name _____

Address _____

City _____

State/Prov._____ Zip/Postal code _____

| Item # | Description | Price | Qty. | Total |
|--------|-------------|-------|------|-------|
| 05GFRESH | Garden-Fresh Cookbook (available Feb. 2011) | $19.95 | | |
| 05BZINE | Everyday Recipes (brand-new!) | $9.99 | | |
| 011GRDKT | Gardening Collection (save 31%) | $19.95 | | |
| 011WTHKT | Weather Collection (save 33%) | $19.95 | | |
| 011BASKET | Basket Collection (save 35%) | $29.95 | | |
| 011CKGKT | Cooking Collection (save 25%) | $29.95 | | |
| 03OF11CEG | 2011 Engagement Calendar | $14.99 | | |
| 03OF11CEV | 2011 Everyday Calendar | $11.99 | | |

**Method of Payment:**

☐ **Check enclosed**
payable to: The Old Farmer's Almanac

☐ **Credit card:** (checkbox below)

  ☐ Visa   ☐ MasterCard

  ☐ American Express

  ☐ Discover/NOVUS

| | | |
|---|---|---|
| 1. Order subtotal | | |
| 2. Add applicable State Sales Tax | | |
| 3. Shipping & Handling* | | $4.95 |
| 4. **TOTAL AMOUNT DUE** (in U.S. dollars) | | |

Card #: _____ Exp. Date _____

Signature: _____
*(required for credit card orders)*

THE OLD
FARMER'S
SINCE
1792
ALMANAC
BY ROBERT B. THOMAS

## Three Easy Ways to Order

 **MAIL FORM TO:**

The Old Farmer's Almanac
PO Box 4002828
Des Moines, IA 50340-2828

 **VISIT ONLINE:**

Almanac.com/Store

**CALL TOLL-FREE:**

1-800-ALMANAC
(1-800-256-2622)

*\*$4.95 shipping and handling applies to orders shipped in the U.S. only.
For orders shipped to Canada, please add $5.00 (for a total of $9.95 S&H).*

OFA2011CAT

 Cookbooks • Calendars • Gift Collections • and more!

From The Old Farmer's Almanac

## 2011 Engagement Calendar

It's easy to stay organized with this charmingly illustrated, hardbound desk calendar. The week-at-a-glance format provides ample space for appointments and notes, and each day offers a bit of useful advice, quirky history, and folklore. There are also pages to record addresses, birthdays, and anniversaries, as well as 2012 and 2013 advance planners.

140 pages • 7" x 10" • hardcover

**$14.99** • Item 03OF11CEG

## 2011 Everyday Calendar

**Do you know:**

- **How many insects live on Earth?**
- **How fast a raindrop falls?**
- **Why flowers fall off tomatoes?**

These answers and many more fun facts can be found in this cleverly illustrated, page-per-day calendar filled with household, gardening, and environmental tips and hints; proverbs; and puzzles that are sure to surprise and delight you.

This calendar and plastic base can be recycled. Gift box • 5¼" x 5½"

**$11.99** • Item 03OF11CEV

Call: 1-800-ALMANAC (1-800-256-2622)

# THE

# FACTS

## BEHIND THE

# FOLKLORE

### Scientists now—finally— admit that many weather proverbs are TRUE!

Weather proverbs—the delightful, often rhyming, couplets and colorful statements that typically link a natural event with a meteorological condition— originated centuries ago when people watched the skies, oceans, plants, and animals for clues of what to expect weatherwise. Here's why we, too, can rely on these age-old adages.

• • •

–Richard Kaylin/Getty Images

**PROVERB:**

*Fish bite more before a storm.*

**WHY** Topper Shutt, chief meteorologist for WUSA-TV in Washington, D.C., claims that the experienced fishermen he knows swear by this adage. As a low-pressure system moves across an area, air rises and cools, water vapor present in the system condenses, and rain or snow usually follows. The lower barometric pressure releases gas bubbles that cling to decaying matter at the bottom of streams and rivers. The bubbles rise to the surface, carrying the decaying matter with them. Small fish follow the particles to feed on *them.* Big fish follow the little fish to feed on *them,* and, in the end, the fishermen are the winners.

**PROVERB:**

*If there is thunder in winter, it will snow 7 days later.*

**WHY**

According to Shutt, this is true about 70 percent of the time, especially from the East Coast to the Plains. Thunder in winter is an anomaly often caused by a big dip and a big rise in the jet stream (a powerful wind current that acts like railroad tracks, guiding high and low pressure systems from west to east across North America and separating cold air in the north from warm air in the south). As cold air moves south, it replaces warm air and lifts it up, often causing thunderstorms. The cold air behind the front settles in. Depending on the strength of the front, it may hang around for many days. When the next weather system arrives several—if not exactly 7—days later, temperatures may still be cold enough to cause the moisture in the system to fall as snow.

**BY MARTIE MAJOROS**

CONTINUED

## PROVERB:

*Silver maple leaves turn over before a storm.*

**WHY**

John Fuller, chief meteorologist with KPLR-TV in St. Louis, Missouri, explains that before the arrival of a cold front, surface winds usually blow from southeast to southwest. As the front approaches, the wind shifts direction, becoming north to northwest. The unsettled winds that occur with the front flip the leaves to reveal their undersides. Silver maple leaves, more than many other leaves, turn over easily in the wind because they are broader and catch the wind more easily than smaller leaves, and their long stem allows them to twist easily in the wind.

## PROVERB:

*When dew is on the grass, rain will never come to pass.*

**WHY** Morning dew is a sign that the previous night's skies were clear, with no wind and decreasing temperatures. Clear, dry, windless conditions usually continue through the daytime. David Phillips, senior climatologist with Environment Canada, claims that this proverb is about 75 percent accurate.

## PROVERB:

*Wind in the east, good for neither man nor beast.*

**WHY** During summer and winter in mid-latitude regions, the prevailing wind blows from the west. When the wind comes from the east, a low-pressure system accompanied by precipitation usually follows. The belief behind this proverb dates from ancient Romans who would not conduct official business when the wind blew from the east. They thought that it made people more irritable and unsettled.

## PROVERB:

*Cream and milk, when they turn sour in the night, often indicate that thunderstorms are about.*

**WHY**

Before homes had refrigerators, cream and milk were often left out overnight. In winter in cold climes, this was seldom a problem. However, during summer's hot, humid nights, unrefrigerated dairy products often soured. The same hot, humid weather that spawns thunderstorms can cause bacteria in unrefrigerated milk to increase, causing it to sour and curdle. The coincidence was taken as a sign.

**PROVERB:**

*A ring around
the Moon means
rain will come
real soon.*

**WHY** A ring, or halo, around the Moon is caused when the light of
the Moon refracts through ice crystals present in high-level clouds. Although
these clouds do not produce precipitation, they often occur in advance of an
approaching low-pressure system, which often brings precipitation in the
form of rain or snow.

**PROVERB:**

*A year of snow, crops will grow.*

**WHY** A several-inch layer of snow contains more
air than ice. Trapped between the interlocking
snowflakes, the air serves to insulate the plants
beneath it. When the snow melts, the water helps to
keep the ground moist.

## GO FIGURE

Weather clues are all around us. There are no real surprises, says Environment Canada's Phillips. Before a tornado, for example, the sky may turn
green and the approaching wind might sound like a train at a distance.
Here are a few clues to making your own predictions:

■ **PAY ATTENTION TO WINDS AND CLOUDS.**
These are the big predictors of changes in barometric
pressure and resulting weather. For instance, the
adage "No weather is ill, if the wind be still" indicates
a high-pressure system, a broad area of descending
air characterized by calm winds and little cloud
formation.

■ **LISTEN.** Gordon Restoule (see page 78) lives
with waterfalls to the south and train tracks to the north.
When he hears the falls, he knows that it's going to be
warm because the sound is carried on a south wind.
When he hears the trains, he expects cold because
that sound is carried on a north wind.

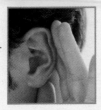

## Weather

■ **OBSERVE SHEEP, CATS, AND COWS.** Their bodies are affected by changes in air pressure. When rain is on the way, old sheep turn their backs to the wind, cats sneeze, and cows lie down.

■ **WATCH BIRDS IN FLIGHT.** Air pressure affects many birds. For example, swallows have sensitive ears; when the barometric pressure drops, they fly as close to the ground as possible, where air density is greatest. Generally, low-flying birds are signs of rain; high flyers indicate fair weather.

**Martie Majoros** lives in Burlington, Vermont, where she tries to demystify meteorology by watching weather systems as they move across Lake Champlain.

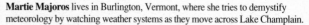

BEWARE OF

# FICKLE FORECASTS

**GORDON RESTOULE** has lived on the Dokis First Nation Reservation on the French River near Sudbury, Ontario, for 73 years. His father and grandfather taught him how to watch the animals and the skies and use his observations to predict the weather. For most of his life, his interpretations have been nearly 90 percent accurate.

Now Restoule claims that climate change is interfering with nature and the traditional habits of some animals. As a result, some proverbs have become unreliable. For example, years ago, if Restoule heard owls in a swamp at night, he was reasonably confident that rain was coming ("A screeching owl indicates cold or storm"). Now, he hears them so frequently that he claims that they don't signify anything.

Also, at one time deer would head for cover among low-branched trees such as hemlocks and pines during a cold spell or in advance of a storm. Now, Restoule says, deer gather under hardwood trees with higher canopies, such as oak, which do not provide as much protection. He attributes this change to warmer winters.

**SIMILARLY,** David Phillips of Environment Canada warns of far-forward-looking weather proverbs based on animal and plant activity. They are seldom reliable indicators of future conditions. For instance, predictions based on squirrels gathering nuts ("When squirrels lay in a large supply of nuts, expect a cold winter") or onion skins' quality ("Onion's skin very thin, mild winter coming in; onion's skin thick and tough, coming winter cold and rough") are usually indicators of the previous season's weather.

The same can be said of a heavy crop of acorns. Often, oaks form more acorns if they have experienced stress due to a drought in the previous spring or summer. □□

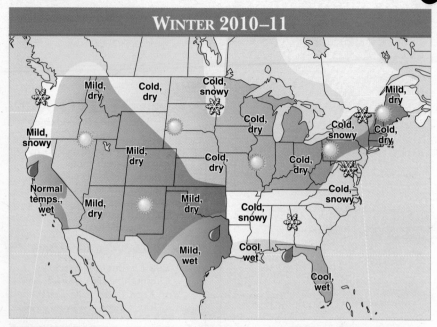

# WINTER 2010–11

These weather maps correspond to the winter (November through March) and summer (June through August) predictions in the General Weather Forecast (opposite).

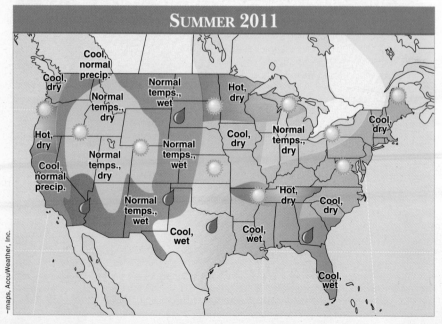

# SUMMER 2011

–maps, AccuWeather, Inc.

# General Weather Forecast and Report

**For regional forecasts, see pages 196–211.**

**T**he prolonged low level of sunspot and space weather activity in the early stages of Solar Cycle 24 reinforces our belief that we are in the midst of a period of significant change. Over the coming years, a gradual cooling of the atmosphere will occur, offset by any warming caused by increased greenhouse gases. We expect that a weak to moderate La Niña will develop for the winter of 2010–11. Most of the eastern portion of the nation will have below-normal winter temperatures, on average (the weaker the La Niña, the colder it will be), with above-normal temperatures in most of the west. Snowfall will be above normal in most of the area from the mid-Atlantic states through the southeast part of the country and below normal in most other regions.

Spring and summer will be relatively cool and dry in most of the country, with the chief exception being above-normal rainfall across most of the southern tier of states. The greatest hurricane threat will be to Florida and the Southeast.

**November through March** temperatures will be above normal, on average, in northern New England and the Texas–Oklahoma, Intermountain, Desert Southwest, and Pacific regions, with below-normal temperatures elsewhere. Precipitation will be above normal from Florida westward to southern Texas and in western New York, northern Minnesota, the eastern Dakotas, and the Pacific Southwest region and below normal elsewhere. Snowfall will be above normal in the mid-Atlantic states, western New York, and the Pacific Northwest region and near or below normal in most other areas that normally receive snow.

**April and May** will be warmer than normal, on average, in the Intermountain, Desert Southwest, and Pacific Southwest regions and cooler than normal elsewhere. Rainfall will be above normal from the Carolinas southward to Florida and westward to New Mexico and in the Heartland region and below normal elsewhere.

**June through August** temperatures will be above normal in the Upper Midwest, Tennessee, northern Arkansas, northern California, and western Oregon and near or cooler than normal elsewhere. Rainfall will be above normal in the High Plains and from South Carolina southward and westward to the Desert Southwest. It will be drier than normal in most other areas.

**September and October** will be cooler than normal in the eastern two-thirds of the country and warmer than normal in the western third. Rainfall will be above normal from Maine southward to Virginia and in southern Florida, the Deep South, the High Plains, and southern California and near or below normal elsewhere.

### How accurate was our forecast last winter?

We predicted that most of the nation would have below-normal winter temperatures and, as shown in the table below, 11 of the 16 regions were indeed below normal. We were also correct in our forecast that snowfall would be above normal in the Atlantic Corridor, Southeast, western Lower Lakes, northern Heartland, and northern High Plains, but we did not predict the above-normal snowfall that also occurred in the Ohio Valley, the southern Heartland, much of the Deep South, and Texas–Oklahoma. Overall, our monthly regional forecasts were 81 percent accurate in predicting the direction of change in precipitation from the previous winter. The accuracy of our temperature forecasts for the winter as a whole is shown in the table below. Overall, we were within 1.9 degrees F, on average, in our temperature forecasts, using a city selected from each region.

| Region/ City | Dec.–Feb. Temp. Variations From Normal (degrees F) | | Region/ City | Dec.–Feb. Temp. Variations From Normal (degrees F) | |
|---|---|---|---|---|---|
| | PREDICTED | ACTUAL | | PREDICTED | ACTUAL |
| 1/Albany | +0.7 | +1.5 | 9/Minneapolis | −3.1 | −1.3 |
| 2/New York | −0.7 | −0.7 | 10/St. Louis | +0.2 | −2.5 |
| 3/Hagerstown | −0.3 | +1.0 | 11/San Antonio | +0.3 | −3.5 |
| 4/Savannah | +0.3 | −3.1 | 12/Billings | −1.2 | −3.1 |
| 5/Miami | +1.7 | −3.0 | 13/Boise | +2.0 | +2.3 |
| 6/Milwaukee | +1.3 | +0.8 | 14/El Paso | −1.5 | −1.5 |
| 7/Pittsburgh | +1.3 | −2.4 | 15/Portland | +1.0 | +1.3 |
| 8/Little Rock | +1.7 | −3.7 | 16/Los Angeles | −0.0 | −0.2 |

# Write Children's Books

### By Patricia Pfitsch

If you've ever dreamed of writing for publication, this may be your best chance to turn that dream into a reality. If you qualify and show promise, we'll teach you—the same way I was taught—how to break into one of the most rewarding of all markets for new writers.

### The $3 billion children's market

The continued success of publications for young people has led to a growing *need* for new writers to help create the $3 billion worth of children's books published each year, plus stories and articles for more than 600 magazines.

### "But am I good enough?"

My dream of writing professionally while raising three kids on a farm once bogged down in the same kind of uncertainty you may have experienced.

Then, an ad for the Institute seemed to offer the writing and selling skills I needed. I passed its test and entered into a richly rewarding relationship with an author-instructor, which was a major turning point in my life—as I hope it will be in yours.

### The at-home training that has launched more successful children's authors than any other school

The Institute of Children's Literature has successfully trained more new writers to meet the needs of this market than any other school. Its unique program turned my dream into reality, and I became one of more than 11,000 Institute graduates who have published children's stories, articles, and books, including prestigious award winners. Now I'm using my skills at the Institute to train promising new writers.

### The promise that paid off

The Institute made exactly the same promise to me that it will make to you if

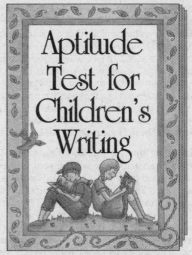

# Aptitude Test for Children's Writing

*Our test and professional evaluation are free*

you demonstrate basic writing aptitude:

*You will complete at least one manuscript suitable to submit to editors by the time you finish the course.*

With skill, empathy, and tough love when needed, my Institute instructor helped me complete and sell three of my course assignments, which, I later discovered, was not unusual.

Now, as a nationally published author of 8 children's books and over 500 stories and articles, I enjoy helping aspiring writers—as *I* was helped—to change their dreams into bright reality.

### A nationally published author or editor is your one-on-one writing and selling coach

If you are accepted, you will be assigned a personal instructor who is a successful author or experienced editor—and who becomes your energizing spark plug and deeply committed writing and selling coach. We all work the same way.

Patricia Pfitsch, a graduate of our course, has published 552 stories and articles, plus 8 books, including 3 award-winning novels and an Edgar nominee. She is also an instructor at the Institute.

When you've finished an assignment at *your* pace, you send it to me. I edit it line-by-line and send you a detailed letter explaining my edits.

I point out your strengths, help eliminate weaknesses, and even show you how to turn bits of your everyday life into saleable writing. You push and I pull, and between us both, you learn how to write—and how to sell what you write.

### From "wannabe" to published author

What I got from my instructor at the Institute changed me from a "wannabe" into a nationally published writer. While there's no guarantee that every student will have the same success, we're praised by students and publishers alike.

"I just wanted to let you know how pleased we are with the work and professionalism of your students, Michelle Barone and Dorothy Heibel," writes Joanne Deitch, editor and former President of Discovery Enterprises. "We just launched a new series entitled Adventures in History. Our first two books were *Out of the Ordinary* by Michelle Barone and *Message for a Spy* by Dorothy Heibel.

"We want to congratulate the writers on their work. Often we read of the struggle to get published, but not so often of the successes, so we just thought you'd like to know how well prepared these students were. Keep up the good work."

Dorothy Heibel, who lives in Wessington Springs, South Dakota, also sent us a note. "I graduated from the Institute 20 years ago. The help I received from your course proved to be a wonderful foundation for writing. You planted the seeds that took root and are now producing the results I had hoped for. In addition to *Message for a Spy*, I currently have two mysteries out making the rounds of publishers."

We also talked to Michelle Barone of Denver, Colorado. She applied to the Institute 25 years ago, was accepted, then "forgot about it." Her careers as a medical worker, real estate agent, curriculum writer, and adoptive mother (before she started teaching 5th grade English and math), came first. "Now," she says, "I grab time for my writing when I can find it. Besides my stories and articles, I've had five books published. You've opened up a whole new world to me."

### Don't let your dream die— send for your free test today!

If a writing life is the one you long for, here's your chance to test that dream. The Institute offers a revealing aptitude test for children's writing based on its 40 years of experience, and it's free.

If you pass, it's because you have the aptitude to make it in the world of writing for children. It takes work, it takes commitment, it takes courage—but you can do it.

Just fill out and mail the coupon below to receive your free test and 32-page introduction to our course, *Writing for Children and Teenagers,* and 80 of our instructors.
*There is no obligation.*

**For faster service, take our test online:
www.WritingForChildren.com/G9870**

Institute of Children's Literature
93 Long Ridge Road
West Redding, CT 06896-0812

Yes, please send me your free *Aptitude Test for Children's Writing* and illustrated brochure. I understand I'm under no obligation, and no salesperson will visit me.

*Please circle one and print name clearly:*

Mr.   Mrs.   Ms.   Miss                                    G9870

_____
Name

_____
Street

_____
City

_____
State                          Zip

Recommended for college credits by the Connecticut Board for State Academic Awards and approved by the Connecticut Commissioner of Higher Education.

COPYRIGHT © ICL 2010, A DIVISION OF WRITER'S INSTITUTE, INC.

# The Old Farmer's Almanac

*Established in 1792 and published every year thereafter*

ROBERT B. THOMAS (1766–1846), *Founder*

YANKEE PUBLISHING INC.

**EDITORIAL AND PUBLISHING OFFICES**

P.O. Box 520, 1121 Main Street, Dublin, NH 03444
Phone: 603-563-8111 • Fax: 603-563-8252

EDITOR *(13th since 1792):* Janice Stillman
ART DIRECTOR: Margo Letourneau
COPY EDITOR: Jack Burnett
SENIOR RESEARCH EDITOR: Mare-Anne Jarvela
SENIOR EDITOR: Heidi Stonehill
ASSOCIATE EDITOR: Sarah Perreault
ASSISTANT EDITOR: Amy Nieskens
INTERN: Sara Shultz
WEATHER GRAPHICS AND CONSULTATION:
AccuWeather, Inc.

V.P., NEW MEDIA AND PRODUCTION:
Paul Belliveau
PRODUCTION DIRECTORS:
Susan Gross, David Ziarnowski
SENIOR PRODUCTION ARTISTS:
Lucille Rines, Rachel Kipka

**WEB SITE: ALMANAC.COM**

WEB EDITOR: Catherine Boeckmann
WEB DESIGNER: Lou S. Eastman
ONLINE MARKETING MANAGER: David Weisberg
PROGRAMMING: Reinvented, Inc.

**CONTACT US**

We welcome your questions and comments about articles in and topics for this Almanac. Mail all editorial correspondence to Editor, The Old Farmer's Almanac, P.O. Box 520, Dublin, NH 03444-0520; fax us at 603-563-8252; or contact us through Almanac.com/Feedback. *The Old Farmer's Almanac* can not accept responsibility for unsolicited manuscripts and will not acknowledge any hard-copy queries or manuscripts that do not include a stamped and addressed return envelope.

All printing inks used in this edition of *The Old Farmer's Almanac* are soy-based. This product is recyclable. Consult local recycling regulations for the right way to do it.

*Thank you for buying this Almanac! We hope that you find it "useful, with a pleasant degree of humor." Thanks, too, to everyone who had a hand in it, including advertisers, distributors, printers, and sales and delivery people.*

## OUR CONTRIBUTORS

**Bob Berman,** our astronomy editor, is the director of Overlook Observatory in Woodstock and Storm King Observatory in Cornwall, both in New York. In 1976, he founded the Catskill Astronomical Society. Bob has led many aurora and eclipse expeditions, venturing as far as the Arctic and Antarctic.

**Tim Clark,** a high school English teacher in New Hampshire, has composed the weather doggerel on the Calendar pages since 1980.

**Bethany E. Cobb,** our astronomer, earned a Ph.D. in astronomy at Yale University and was awarded a National Science Foundation postdoctoral fellowship. She is currently conducting independent research and teaching at George Washington University in Washington, D.C. She has been involved in numerous astronomy programs, including Alien Earths at New Haven's Peabody Museum. When she is not scanning the sky, she enjoys playing the violin and reading science fiction.

**Castle Freeman Jr.,** who lives in southern Vermont, has been writing the Almanac's Farmer's Calendar essays since 1982. The essays come out of his longtime interest in wildlife and the outdoors, gardening, history, and the life of rural New England. His latest book is *All That I Have: A Novel* (Steerforth Press, 2009).

**Celeste Longacre,** our astrologer, often refers to astrology as "a study of timing, and timing is everything." A New Hampshire native, she has been a practicing astrologer for more than 25 years. Her book, *Love Signs* (Sweet Fern Publications, 1999), is available on her Web site, www.yourlovesigns.com.

**Michael Steinberg,** our meteorologist, has been forecasting weather for the Almanac since 1996. In addition to college degrees in atmospheric science and meteorology, he brings a lifetime of experience to the task: He began predicting weather when he attended the only high school in the world with weather Teletypes and radar.

### THE 2011 EDITION OF

# The Old Farmer's Almanac

*Established in 1792 and published every year thereafter*

Robert B. Thomas (1766–1846), *Founder*

YANKEE PUBLISHING INC.
P.O. Box 520, 1121 Main Street, Dublin, NH 03444
Phone: 603-563-8111 • Fax: 603-563-8252

PUBLISHER *(23rd since 1792):* Sherin Pierce
PUBLISHER EMERITUS: John B. Pierce Jr.
EDITOR IN CHIEF: Judson D. Hale Sr.

**FOR DISPLAY ADVERTISING RATES**
Call 800-729-9265, ext. 215
Bob Bernbach • 914-769-0051
Steve Hall • 800-736-1100, ext. 320
Go to Almanac.com/Advertising

**FOR CLASSIFIED ADVERTISING**
Call Gallagher Group • 203-263-7171

AD PRODUCTION COORDINATOR: Janet Grant

**PUBLIC RELATIONS**
Quinn/Brein • 206-842-8922

**TO BUY OR INQUIRE ABOUT
ALMANAC PUBLICATIONS**
Call 800-ALMANAC (800-256-2622)
or go to Almanac.com/Store

**TO SELL ALMANAC PRODUCTS**
RETAIL: Cindy Schlosser, 800-729-9265, ext. 126,
or Stacey Korpi, ext. 160

**FUND-RAISING WITH ALMANAC PRODUCTS**
Sherin Pierce, 800-729-9265, ext. 137

**DISTRIBUTORS**
NATIONAL: Curtis Circulation Company
New Milford, NJ
BOOKSTORE: Houghton Mifflin Harcourt
Boston, MA

The Old Farmer's Almanac publications are available for sales promotions or premiums. Contact Beacon Promotions, info@beaconpromotions.com.

YANKEE PUBLISHING INCORPORATED

Jamie Trowbridge, *President;* Judson D. Hale Sr., *Senior Vice President;* Jody Bugbee, Judson D. Hale Jr., Paul Belliveau, Brook Holmberg, Sherin Pierce, *Vice Presidents.*

# Eclipses

■ There will be six eclipses in 2011, four of the Sun and two of the Moon. Solar eclipses are visible only in certain areas and require eye protection to be viewed safely. Lunar eclipses are technically visible from the entire night side of Earth, but during a penumbral eclipse, the dimming of the Moon's illumination is slight.

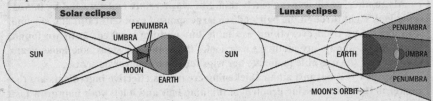

**JANUARY 4: Partial eclipse of the Sun.** This eclipse will not be visible from North America. The eclipse will be visible from Europe, northern Africa, the Middle East, and parts of Asia.

**JUNE 1: Partial eclipse of the Sun.** This eclipse will be visible in North America only from northern Alaska and parts of northern Canada. In Deadhorse, Alaska, for example, the partial eclipse lasts from 12:31 P.M.–1:52 P.M. AKDT.

**JUNE 15: Total lunar eclipse.** This eclipse will not be visible from North America. The eclipse will be visible from South America, Europe, Africa, Asia, and parts of Australia.

**JULY 1: Partial eclipse of the Sun.** This eclipse will not be visible from North America. The eclipse will be visible from only a small area of the southern Indian Ocean.

**NOVEMBER 25: Partial eclipse of the Sun.** This eclipse will not be visible from North America. The eclipse will be visible from Antarctica, southern Africa, southern India, and New Zealand.

**DECEMBER 10: Total lunar eclipse.** This eclipse will be fully visible from Alaska. The Moon will enter the penumbra at 2:32 A.M. AKST and will leave the penumbra at 8:32 A.M. AKST. The eclipse will be partially visible from parts of North America: Central and western areas will be able to observe both a penumbral and

| Full-Moon Dates (Eastern Time) | | | | |
|---|---|---|---|---|
| | 2011 | 2012 | 2013 | 2014 | 2015 |
| Jan. | 19 | 9 | 26 | 15 | 4 |
| Feb. | 18 | 7 | 25 | 14 | 3 |
| Mar. | 19 | 8 | 27 | 16 | 5 |
| Apr. | 17 | 6 | 25 | 15 | 4 |
| May | 17 | 5 | 25 | 14 | 3 |
| June | 15 | 4 | 23 | 13 | 2 |
| July | 15 | 3 | 22 | 12 | 1 & 31 |
| Aug. | 13 | 1 & 31 | 20 | 10 | 29 |
| Sept. | 12 | 29 | 19 | 8 | 27 |
| Oct. | 11 | 29 | 18 | 8 | 27 |
| Nov. | 10 | 28 | 17 | 6 | 25 |
| Dec. | 10 | 28 | 17 | 6 | 25 |

umbral eclipse. The Moon will enter the penumbra at 3:32 A.M. PST and the umbra at 4:45 A.M. PST. A penumbral eclipse will be visible from most of the East Coast, starting at 6:32 A.M. EST, just before the Moon sets.

## The Moon's Path

The Moon's path across the sky changes with the seasons. Full Moons are very high in the sky (at midnight) between November and February and very low between May and July.

## Next Total Eclipse of the Sun

**November 13, 2012: visible from northern Australia and the South Pacific Ocean.**

# Why wait ten months?

## Now you can have rich, dark compost _in just 14 days!_

With the amazing ComposTumbler, you'll have bushels of crumbly, ready-to-use compost — _in just 14 days!_ (And, in the ten months it takes to make compost the old way, your ComposTumbler can produce _hundreds of pounds_ of rich food for your garden!)

Say good-bye to that messy, open compost pile (and to the flies, pests, and odors that come along with it!) Bid a happy farewell to the strain of trying to turn over heavy, wet piles with a pitchfork.

### Compost the Better Way

Compost-making with the ComposTumbler is neat, quick and easy!

Gather up leaves, old weeds, kitchen scraps, lawn clippings, etc. and toss them into the roomy 18-bushel drum. Then, once each day, give the ComposTumbler's _gear-driven_ handle a few easy spins.

### The ComposTumbler's Magic

Inside the ComposTumbler, carefully positioned mixing fins blend materials, pushing fresh mixture to the core where the temperatures are the hottest (up to 160°) and the composting bacteria most active.

After just 14 days, open the door, and you'll find an abundance of dark, sweet-smelling "garden gold" — ready to enrich and feed your garden!

### NEW SMALLER SIZE!

Now there are 2 sizes. The 18-bushel original ComposTumbler and the NEW 9.5-bushel Compact ComposTumbler. Try either size risk-free for 30 days!

See for yourself! Try the ComposTumbler risk-free with our 30-Day Home Trial!

**Call Toll-Free 1-800-880-2345**

Visit us at
www.compostumbler.com

## ComposTumbler®

_The choice of more than 250,000 gardeners_

☐ YES! Please rush FREE information on the ComposTumbler, including special savings and 30-Day Home Trial.

Name _____

Address _____

City _____

State _____ ZIP _____

MAIL TO: **ComposTumbler**
1834 Freedom Road, **Dept. 420111C**
Lancaster, PA 17601

© 2010 PBM Group

# Bright Stars

## Transit Times

■ This table shows the time (EST or EDT) and altitude of a star as it transits the meridian (i.e., reaches its highest elevation while passing over the horizon's south point) at Boston on the dates shown. The transit time on any other date differs from that of the nearest date listed by approximately 4 minutes per day. To find the time of a star's transit for your location, convert its time at Boston using Key Letter C **(see Time Corrections, page 234).**

−Beth Krommes

| Star | Constellation | Magnitude | Time of Transit (EST/EDT) Bold = P.M. Light = A.M. | | | | | | Altitude (degrees) |
|------|--------------|-----------|--------|--------|--------|--------|---------|--------|--------------------|
| | | | **Jan. 1** | **Mar. 1** | **May 1** | **July 1** | **Sept. 1** | **Nov. 1** | |
| Altair | Aquila | 0.8 | **12:51** | 8:59 | 6:00 | 2:00 | **9:52** | **5:52** | 56.3 |
| Deneb | Cygnus | 1.3 | **1:42** | 9:50 | 6:50 | 2:50 | **10:42** | **6:43** | 92.8 |
| Fomalhaut | Psc. Aus. | 1.2 | **3:58** | **12:06** | 9:06 | 5:06 | 1:02 | **8:59** | 17.8 |
| Algol | Perseus | 2.2 | **8:08** | **4:16** | **1:16** | 9:16 | 5:12 | 1:13 | 88.5 |
| Aldebaran | Taurus | 0.9 | **9:35** | **5:43** | **2:43** | 10:44 | 6:40 | 2:40 | 64.1 |
| Rigel | Orion | 0.1 | **10:14** | **6:22** | **3:22** | 11:22 | 7:18 | 3:18 | 39.4 |
| Capella | Auriga | 0.1 | **10:16** | **6:24** | **3:24** | 11:24 | 7:21 | 3:21 | 93.6 |
| Bellatrix | Orion | 1.6 | **10:24** | **6:32** | **3:32** | 11:33 | 7:29 | 3:29 | 54.0 |
| Betelgeuse | Orion | var. 0.4 | **10:54** | **7:02** | **4:02** | **12:03** | 7:59 | 3:59 | 55.0 |
| Sirius | Can. Maj. | −1.4 | **11:44** | **7:52** | **4:52** | **12:52** | 8:49 | 4:49 | 31.0 |
| Procyon | Can. Min. | 0.4 | 12:42 | **8:46** | **5:46** | **1:46** | 9:43 | 5:43 | 52.9 |
| Pollux | Gemini | 1.2 | 12:48 | **8:52** | **5:52** | **1:52** | 9:49 | 5:49 | 75.7 |
| Regulus | Leo | 1.4 | 3:11 | **11:15** | **8:15** | **4:15** | **12:11** | 8:11 | 59.7 |
| Spica | Virgo | var. 1.0 | 6:27 | 2:35 | **11:31** | **7:31** | **3:28** | 11:28 | 36.6 |
| Arcturus | Boötes | −0.1 | 7:17 | 3:25 | 12:25 | **8:22** | **4:18** | **12:18** | 66.9 |
| Antares | Scorpius | var. 0.9 | 9:31 | 5:39 | 2:39 | **10:35** | **6:31** | **2:32** | 21.3 |
| Vega | Lyra | 0 | 11:38 | 7:46 | 4:46 | 12:46 | **8:38** | **4:38** | 86.4 |

## Rise and Set Times

■ To find the time of a star's rising at Boston on any date, subtract the interval shown at right from the star's transit time on that date; add the interval to find the star's setting time. To find the rising and setting times for your city, convert the Boston transit times above using the Key Letter shown at right before applying the interval **(see Time Corrections, page 234).** The directions in which the stars rise and set, shown for Boston, are generally useful throughout the United States. Deneb, Algol, Capella, and Vega are circumpolar stars—they never set but appear to circle the celestial north pole.

| Star | Interval (h. m.) | Rising Key | Dir.* | Setting Key | Dir.* |
|------|------------------|-----------|-------|-------------|-------|
| Altair | 6 36 | B | EbN | E | WbN |
| Fomalhaut | 3 59 | E | SE | D | SW |
| Aldebaran | 7 06 | B | ENE | D | WNW |
| Rigel | 5 33 | D | EbS | B | WbS |
| Bellatrix | 6 27 | B | EbN | D | WbN |
| Betelgeuse | 6 31 | B | EbN | D | WbN |
| Sirius | 5 00 | D | ESE | B | WSW |
| Procyon | 6 23 | B | EbN | D | WbN |
| Pollux | 8 01 | A | NE | E | NW |
| Regulus | 6 49 | B | EbN | D | WbN |
| Spica | 5 23 | D | EbS | B | WbS |
| Arcturus | 7 19 | A | ENE | E | WNW |
| Antares | 4 17 | E | SEbE | A | SWbW |

*b = "by"

*Find more heavenly details at* Almanac.com/Astronomy.

# The Twilight Zone

Twilight is the time preceding sunrise and again following sunset, when the sky is partially illuminated. The three ranges of twilight are defined according to the Sun's position below the horizon. Civil twilight occurs when the Sun is between the horizon and 6 degrees below the horizon (visually, the horizon is clearly defined). Nautical twilight occurs when the Sun is between 6 and 12 degrees below the horizon (the horizon is indistinct). Astronomical twilight occurs when the Sun is between 12 and 18 degrees below the horizon (sky illumination is imperceptible). When the Sun is at 18 degrees (dawn or dark) or below, there is no illumination.

## Length of Twilight (hours and minutes)

| LATITUDE | Jan. 1 to Apr. 10 | Apr. 11 to May 2 | May 3 to May 14 | May 15 to May 25 | May 26 to July 22 | July 23 to Aug. 3 | Aug. 4 to Aug. 14 | Aug. 15 to Sept. 5 | Sept. 6 to Dec. 31 |
|---|---|---|---|---|---|---|---|---|---|
| 25°N to 30°N | 1 20 | 1 23 | 1 26 | 1 29 | 1 32 | 1 29 | 1 26 | 1 23 | 1 20 |
| 31°N to 36°N | 1 26 | 1 28 | 1 34 | 1 38 | 1 43 | 1 38 | 1 34 | 1 28 | 1 26 |
| 37°N to 42°N | 1 33 | 1 39 | 1 47 | 1 52 | 1 59 | 1 52 | 1 47 | 1 39 | 1 33 |
| 43°N to 47°N | 1 42 | 1 51 | 2 02 | 2 13 | 2 27 | 2 13 | 2 02 | 1 51 | 1 42 |
| 48°N to 49°N | 1 50 | 2 04 | 2 22 | 2 42 | — | 2 42 | 2 22 | 2 04 | 1 50 |

**TO DETERMINE THE LENGTH OF TWILIGHT:** The length of twilight changes with latitude and the time of year. Use the **Time Corrections** table, **page 234**, to find the latitude of your city or the city nearest you. Use that figure in the chart above with the appropriate date to calculate the length of twilight in your area.

**TO DETERMINE WHEN DAWN OR DARK WILL OCCUR:** Calculate the sunrise/sunset times for your locality using the instructions in **How to Use This Almanac, page 110.** Subtract the length of twilight from the time of sunrise to determine when dawn breaks. Add the length of twilight to the time of sunset to determine when dark descends.

**EXAMPLE:**

Boston, Mass. (latitude 42°22')

| | |
|---|---|
| Sunrise, August 1 | 5:36 A.M. EDT |
| Length of twilight | − 1 52 |
| Dawn breaks | 3:44 A.M. |
| Sunset, August 1 | 8:04 P.M. EDT |
| Length of twilight | +1 52 |
| Dark descends | 9:56 P.M. |

## Principal Meteor Showers

| SHOWER | BEST VIEWING | POINT OF ORIGIN | DATE OF MAXIMUM* | NO. PER HOUR** | ASSOCIATED COMET |
|---|---|---|---|---|---|
| **Quadrantid** | **Predawn** | N | **Jan. 4** | 25 | — |
| Lyrid | Predawn | S | Apr. 22 | 10 | Thatcher |
| Eta Aquarid | Predawn | SE | May 4 | 10 | Halley |
| Delta Aquarid | Predawn | S | July 30 | 10 | — |
| **Perseid** | **Predawn** | NE | **Aug. 11–13** | 50 | **Swift-Tuttle** |
| Draconid | Late evening | NW | Oct. 9 | 6 | Giacobini-Zinner |
| Orionid | Predawn | S | Oct. 21–22 | 15 | Halley |
| Taurid | Late evening | S | Nov. 9 | 3 | Encke |
| Leonid | Predawn | S | Nov. 18 | 10 | Tempel-Tuttle |
| Andromedid | Late evening | S | Nov. 25–27 | 5 | Biela |
| **Geminid** | **All night** | NE | **Dec. 13–14** | 75 | — |
| Ursid | Predawn | N | Dec. 22 | 5 | Tuttle |

*May vary by one or two days    **Moonless, rural sky    **Bold** = most prominent

# The Visible Planets

■ Listed here for Boston are viewing suggestions for and the rise and set times (EST/EDT) of Venus, Mars, Jupiter, and Saturn on specific days each month, as well as when it is best to view Mercury. Approximate rise and set times for other days can be found by interpolation. Use the Key Letters at the right of each listing to convert the times for other localities **(see pages 110 and 234).** *For all planet rise and set times by zip code, visit* **Almanac.com/Astronomy.**

## Venus

Our nearest planetary neighbor starts off as a dazzling morning star in the east, before dawn. On January 1, Venus gloriously shines at its highest and brightest of the year. Riveting in January, its splendor is short-lived, as it rapidly gets lower and less bright until it is less than 10 degrees high in late March. It scrapes the horizon thereafter, through November. Its conjunction behind the Sun on August 16 doesn't improve things. Finally, December brings a dramatic turnaround, as Venus, at nearly its dimmest, climbs from 10 to 20 degrees high, as seen 40 minutes after sunset. This is the setup for a gorgeous Venus apparition all next winter and through midspring.

| | | | | | | | | | | | |
|---|---|---|---|---|---|---|---|---|---|---|---|
| Jan. 1 | rise | 3:26 | D | Apr. 1 | rise | 5:14 | D | July 1 | rise | 4:17 | A |
| Jan. 11 | rise | 3:36 | E | Apr. 11 | rise | 5:04 | D | July 11 | rise | 4:31 | A |
| Jan. 21 | rise | 3:49 | E | Apr. 21 | rise | 4:53 | C | July 21 | rise | 4:49 | A |
| Feb. 1 | rise | 4:03 | E | May 1 | rise | 4:41 | C | Aug. 1 | rise | 5:13 | B |
| Feb. 11 | rise | 4:14 | E | May 11 | rise | 4:30 | B | Aug. 11 | rise | 5:38 | B |
| Feb. 21 | rise | 4:22 | E | May 21 | rise | 4:20 | B | Aug. 21 | **set** | **7:46** | D |
| Mar. 1 | rise | 4:25 | E | June 1 | rise | 4:12 | B | Sept. 1 | **set** | **7:35** | D |
| Mar. 11 | rise | 4:25 | E | June 11 | rise | 4:08 | B | Sept. 11 | **set** | **7:23** | C |
| Mar. 21 | rise | 5:22 | D | June 21 | rise | 4:10 | A | Sept. 21 | **set** | **7:10** | C |

| | | | | |
|---|---|---|---|---|
| Oct. 1 | **set** | **6:58** | C |
| Oct. 11 | **set** | **6:47** | B |
| Oct. 21 | **set** | **6:39** | B |
| Nov. 1 | **set** | **6:34** | A |
| Nov. 11 | **set** | **5:35** | A |
| Nov. 21 | **set** | **5:43** | A |
| Dec. 1 | **set** | **5:56** | A |
| Dec. 11 | **set** | **6:16** | A |
| Dec. 21 | **set** | **6:39** | A |
| Dec. 31 | **set** | **7:04** | B |

## Mars

Earth and Mars meet every 26 months, so the Red Planet has good years alternating with bad. This one is bad. Mars starts off dim, distant, and almost invisible, passes behind the Sun on February 4, and remains a tiny, inconspicuous, predawn object nearly all year. December finally sees dramatic improvement as Mars rises before midnight and brightens by half a magnitude in that month alone, finishing the year at magnitude 0.4, the seventh brightest "star" in the winter sky, in Leo. At its opposition in March 2012, its most distant meeting with Earth in 17 years, it will attain only magnitude −1.0.

| | | | | | | | | | | | |
|---|---|---|---|---|---|---|---|---|---|---|---|
| Jan. 1 | **set** | **4:55** | A | Apr. 1 | rise | 6:07 | C | July 1 | rise | 3:02 | A |
| Jan. 11 | **set** | **4:54** | A | Apr. 11 | rise | 5:44 | C | July 11 | rise | 2:48 | A |
| Jan. 21 | **set** | **4:55** | B | Apr. 21 | rise | 5:22 | C | July 21 | rise | 2:35 | A |
| Feb. 1 | rise | 7:07 | E | May 1 | rise | 5:00 | B | Aug. 1 | rise | 2:22 | A |
| Feb. 11 | rise | 6:49 | E | May 11 | rise | 4:38 | B | Aug. 11 | rise | 2:11 | A |
| Feb. 21 | rise | 6:30 | D | May 21 | rise | 4:17 | B | Aug. 21 | rise | 2:02 | A |
| Mar. 1 | rise | 6:14 | D | June 1 | rise | 3:55 | B | Sept. 1 | rise | 1:52 | A |
| Mar. 11 | rise | 5:53 | D | June 11 | rise | 3:36 | B | Sept. 11 | rise | 1:44 | A |
| Mar. 21 | rise | 6:31 | C | June 21 | rise | 3:19 | A | Sept. 21 | rise | 1:36 | A |

| | | | | |
|---|---|---|---|---|
| Oct. 1 | rise | 1:27 | A |
| Oct. 11 | rise | 1:18 | B |
| Oct. 21 | rise | 1:08 | B |
| Nov. 1 | rise | 12:55 | B |
| Nov. 11 | **rise** | **11:41** | B |
| Nov. 21 | **rise** | **11:27** | B |
| Dec. 1 | **rise** | **11:11** | B |
| Dec. 11 | **rise** | **10:52** | B |
| Dec. 21 | **rise** | **10:30** | B |
| Dec. 31 | **rise** | **10:04** | C |

☞ **Bold = P.M.**   ☞ Light = A.M.

–illustrations, Beth Krommes

## Jupiter

♃ The Giant Planet has a spectacular year, with a close October 28 opposition that won't be equaled in brilliance until 2022. Jove starts the year as the night's brightest "star," in Pisces, just below aqua-color Uranus, a conjunction easily seen with binoculars. It remains visible albeit lower in February, passes behind the Sun on April 6, and then re-emerges as a morning star in May. This fascinating world rises 2 hours earlier each month, until it starts blazing before midnight beginning in August. It remains glorious for the rest of the year.

| | | | | | | | | | | |
|---|---|---|---|---|---|---|---|---|---|---|
| Jan. 1 | set | 10:42 | C | Apr. 1 | set | 7:24 | D | July 1 | rise | 1:33 | B | Oct. 1 | rise | 7:38 | B |

Jan. 1 .......set 10:42 C | Apr. 1.......set 7:24 D | July 1 ..... rise 1:33 B | Oct. 1 ...... rise 7:38 B
Jan. 11 .....set 10:11 C | Apr. 11... rise 6:09 C | July 11 ... rise 1:01 B | Oct. 11 .... rise 6:56 B
Jan. 21 .....set 9:40 C | Apr. 21... rise 5:35 C | July 21 ... rise 12:22 B | Oct. 21 .... rise 6:13 B
Feb. 1.......set 9:08 C | May 1..... rise 5:01 B | Aug. 1..... rise 11:38 B | Nov. 1......set 7:02 D
Feb. 11.....set 8:39 C | May 11... rise 4:28 B | Aug. 11... rise 11:01 B | Nov. 11....set 5:16 D
Feb. 21.....set 8:11 C | May 21... rise 3:54 B | Aug. 21... rise 10:23 B | Nov. 21....set 4:31 D
Mar. 1 ......set 7:48 C | June 1 .... rise 3:16 B | Sept. 1..... rise 9:40 B | Dec. 1 .....set 3:46 D
Mar. 11 ....set 7:21 C | June 11... rise 2:42 B | Sept. 11... rise 9:00 B | Dec. 11 ....set 3:04 D
Mar. 21 ....set 7:54 C | June 21... rise 2:07 B | Sept. 21... rise 8:19 B | Dec. 21 ....set 2:23 D
| | | | | | | | | | Dec. 31 ....set 1:44 D

## Saturn

♄ The universe's most beautiful planet is at its best from January through August; after that, it is either behind the Sun, low, or a predawn object. Saturn's rings are now "opening up" after their edgewise orientation during the past two years and show up nicely with 30× magnification. In Virgo all year, Saturn rises at around midnight in mid-January, at 9:30 P.M. in mid-February, and at 8 P.M. in mid-March. It is out all night in April. Its opposition and closest approach occur on April 3. Saturn remains high and glorious in May and June, starts setting before midnight in mid-July, and then gets low and finally vanishes behind the Sun on October 13, in conjunction.

Jan. 1 ..... rise 12:20 C | Apr. 1.......rise 7:08 C | July 1 .......set 12:48 C | Oct. 1.......set 6:59 C
Jan. 11 ... rise 11:39 C | Apr. 11......set 6:13 C | July 11 .....set 12:09 C | Oct. 11 .....set 6:23 C
Jan. 21 ... rise 11:00 C | Apr. 21......set 5:32 C | July 21 .....set 11:27 C | Oct. 21 ... rise 6:27 D
Feb. 1...... rise 10:17 C | May 1......set 4:51 C | Aug. 1.....set 10:45 C | Nov. 1.... rise 5:50 D
Feb. 11.... rise 9:36 C | May 11.....set 4:11 C | Aug. 11...set 10:08 C | Nov. 11.. rise 4:17 D
Feb. 21.... rise 8:55 C | May 21.....set 3:30 C | Aug. 21...set 9:30 C | Nov. 21.. rise 3:43 D
Mar. 1 ..... rise 8:21 C | June 1 .....set 2:46 C | Sept. 1.....set 8:50 C | Dec. 1 .... rise 3:09 D
Mar. 11 ... rise 7:39 C | June 11.....set 2:06 C | Sept. 11...set 8:13 C | Dec. 11 .. rise 2:35 D
Mar. 21 ... rise 7:56 C | June 21.....set 1:27 C | Sept. 21...set 7:36 C | Dec. 21 .. rise 2:00 D
| | | | | | | | | | Dec. 31 .. rise 1:24 D

## Mercury

☿ The speedy innermost planet bobs from morning to evening twilight and back again several times during the year. As an evening star in the west, Mercury has its best 2011 appearance in mid-March, when it hovers just to the right of Jupiter. Its runner-up display is in July. The tiny orange planet's best predawn morning appearances occur in the first half of September, especially on the 9th–11th, and in the first half of November. It sits near the blue star Regulus on September 9 and is near Venus in the first weeks of November.

**DO NOT CONFUSE** ■ *Uranus, above Jupiter in the first week of January, with any star. Uranus is blue-green.* ■ *Mercury with Jupiter in mid-March. Jupiter is brighter and whiter.* ■ *Mercury with Regulus on September 9. The planet is orange; the star, blue.* ■ *Venus with Mercury in the first half of November. Venus is higher and brighter.*

# Astronomical Glossary

**Aphelion (Aph.):** The point in a planet's orbit that is farthest from the Sun.

**Apogee (Apo.):** The point in the Moon's orbit that is farthest from Earth.

**Celestial Equator (Eq.):** The imaginary circle around the celestial sphere that can be thought of as the plane of Earth's equator projected out onto the sphere.

**Celestial Sphere:** An imaginary sphere projected into space that represents the entire sky, with an observer on Earth at its center. All celestial bodies other than Earth are imagined as being on its inside surface.

**Circumpolar:** Always visible above the horizon, such as a circumpolar star.

**Conjunction:** The time at which two or more celestial bodies appear closest in the sky. **Inferior (Inf.):** Mercury or Venus is between the Sun and Earth. **Superior (Sup.):** The Sun is between a planet and Earth. Actual dates for conjunctions are given in the **Right-Hand Calendar Pages, 115–141;** the best times for viewing the closely aligned bodies are given in **Sky Watch** on the **Left-Hand Calendar Pages, 114–140.**

**Declination:** The celestial latitude of an object in the sky, measured in degrees north or south of the celestial equator; analogous to latitude on Earth. This Almanac gives the Sun's declination at noon.

**Eclipse, Lunar:** The full Moon enters the shadow of Earth, which cuts off all or part of the sunlight reflected off the Moon. **Total:** The Moon passes completely through the **umbra** (central dark part) of Earth's shadow. **Partial:** Only part of the Moon passes through the umbra. **Penumbral:** The Moon passes through only the **penumbra** (area of partial darkness surrounding the umbra). **See page 88** for more eclipse information.

**Eclipse, Solar:** Earth enters the shadow of the new Moon, which cuts off all or part of the Sun's light. **Total:** Earth passes through the umbra (central dark part) of the Moon's shadow, resulting in totality for observers within a narrow band on Earth. **Annular:** The

Moon appears silhouetted against the Sun, with a ring of sunlight showing around it. **Partial:** The Moon blocks only part of the Sun.

**Ecliptic:** The apparent annual path of the Sun around the celestial sphere. The plane of the ecliptic is tipped 23½° from the celestial equator.

**Elongation:** The difference in degrees between the celestial longitudes of a planet and the Sun. **Greatest Elongation (Gr. Elong.):** The greatest apparent distance of a planet from the Sun, as seen from Earth.

**Epact:** A number from 1 to 30 that indicates the Moon's age on January 1 at Greenwich, England; used for determining the date of Easter.

**Equinox:** When the Sun crosses the celestial equator. This event occurs two times each year: **Vernal** is around March 20 and **Autumnal** is September 22 or 23.

**Evening Star:** A planet that is above the western horizon at sunset and less than 180° east of the Sun in right ascension.

**Golden Number:** A number in the 19-year cycle of the Moon, used for determining the date of Easter. (Approximately every 19 years, the Moon's phases occur on the same dates.) Add 1 to any given year and divide by 19; the remainder is the Golden Number. If there is no remainder, the Golden Number is 19.

**Greatest Illuminated Extent (Gr. Illum. Ext.):** When the maximum surface area of a planet is illuminated as seen from Earth.

**Magnitude:** A measure of a celestial object's brightness. **Apparent** magnitude measures the brightness of an object as see from Earth.

**(continued)**

# The Hand of God

## NOT A RITUAL. NOT A WORD. *THE MOST CHARGED PIECE OF MAGICKAL INFORMATION IN PRINT!*

Elias Raphael writes:

It is a formula.

It's in the Bible – or at least in some translations of it – but only the initiated know its meaning.

EVERYTHING YOU DESIRE CAN BE YOURS WHEN YOU USE THIS FORMULA.

Translated from the original texts the formula means the 'Hand of God'.

The teacher under whom I studied told me (his exact words): 'EVERYTHING BASIC IN THIS PHYSICAL WORLD IS SUBJECT TO THE SACRED POWER OF THIS FORMULA.

'NOTHING PHYSICAL CAN BE ACCOMPLISHED MAGICK-ALLY WITHOUT THE USE OF THIS FORMULA.'

According to him, it was *the bedrock of every magickal operation.*

USE THIS FORMULA AND YOU ARE ASSURED SUCCESS.

You need no previous experience. You only need to learn this formula.

*Learn and use it and everything you seek will be within your grasp.*

*God's hand will open to you.*

*And you can put it into practice within half an hour of reading this booklet.*

I repeat: suddenly *whatever you want will be within your grasp.*

This formula is derived from secret knowledge known only to initiates. It is not new: but it is largely unknown.

*Most people who read the Bible have no idea of its existence!* But it is there, and it is called the 'Hand of God' for a perfectly good reason.

I got the woman I wanted with this formula.

I am not rich, for I don't care for material things. I am not a businessman.

**But when I need money I receive it.**

With the Hand of God I am always provided for.

IT NEVER, EVER, FAILS ME.

What is important to me is good health. I believe that all the health problems I had – and I was a sickly child – disappeared because of the 'Hand of God'.

I find it easy to 'believe' when the results are always apparent.

**BUT THE POINT IS: WHATEVER YOU SEEK OR DESIRE IN THIS WORLD CAN BE YOURS.**

IT CAN BE *AUTOMATICALLY YOURS.*

*Only the 'Hand of God can do this.*

YOU DO NOT HAVE TO BE OF A RELIGIOUS FRAME OF MIND.

You are not asked to believe in the God of the church.

Ever since the scriptures were written they possessed a secret, inner meaning. This meaning is rooted in the magick of ancient Egypt.

The stories people believe in the Bible were written for the public, their true significance concealed.

All you need for this formula to work is to follow the instructions carefully (not difficult).

*Think of the thing you most want now.*

You can have it: it is within your grasp.

But how so? It is not necessary for you to understand, you only have to *do it.*

The 'Hand of God' is not a mere concept or metaphor.

*It has been here since the beginning of time.*

I didn't discover it; I was lucky to be taught by a wise one.

I REALIZE NOW THAT WHAT IS CONCEALED IN THE BIBLE – AS OPPOSED TO WHAT IS OPENLY REVEALED – CONTAINS THE METAPHYSICAL SECRETS OF THE UNI-VERSE AND THE SECRET OF PHYSICAL MATTER ITSELF.

*You only need to know this formula to access this concealed wisdom.*

So few people until now have known about it because of its *deliberate concealment.*

THOSE WITH EYES OPEN, HANDS HELD OUT, *THOSE WHO DESIRE* – IT IS THEY WHO CAN RECEIVE THIS CONCEALED WISDOM.

**Everything you need to know is explained in my monograph.**

You don't need anything else. No candles, rituals, etc.

You don't need to pray.

You don't need to study the Bible; everything you need is in my monograph.

This is based on something *eternal and unchanging.*

I see myself only as a messenger.

Open yourself to this message. Experience the Hand of God. Experience the power of real magick.

*Real magick is the art and practice of creating material events by the invocation of esoteric power.*

As best I know, this information is at present available nowhere else. So, to some extent it still remains hidden.

You don't need positive thinking.

You need only to accept the formula and put it into practice. Tell no one what you are doing.

THINK AGAIN ABOUT WHAT YOU MOST WANT.

*This formula is the one thing that can put it in your grasp.*

WHAT YOU SEEK CAN BE YOURS: AUTOMATICALLY AND ABSOLUTELY.

Within the 'Hand of God' lies all creation and everything that is in it. But this is a *magickal idea*, not a Christian nor a Jewish one. It is an ancient Egyptian concept, found by the Jews in Egypt.

The Hand of God cannot fail you. It epitomizes the inexhaustible law of supply.

YOUR NEED CAN BE SUPPLIED. YOUR DESIRE CAN BE FULFILLED. YOUR DREAM CAN COME TRUE.

Think again seriously about what you most want. A job promotion? The love of another person? The renewed love of someone? Better health? More money? Protection? To get out of trouble? To deal with injustice?

THE PROBLEM CAN BE SOLVED, THE NEED CAN BE FULFILLED.

This booklet contains not only my monograph on the Hand of God, but also the teachings of the Christian Mysteries of the Rosy Cross which will inspire those fascinated by the 'hidden' side of Christianity.

But I reiterate: TO USE THIS FORMULA YOU DO NOT HAVE TO BE A 'BELIEVER'. This is a magickal text, not religious. Open your hand. Open yourself to the power that cannot fail you.

To receive, please send **$22.99**.

**IRON-CLAD GUARANTEE: You must be thrilled with results or return within 45 days for a full refund. Send $22.99 to: FINBARR INTERNATIONAL (OHG), Folkestone, Kent CT20 2QQ, England.** Price includes fast delivery within 16 days. If you are in a real hurry add $5 and we'll guarantee delivery within 12 days. Send personal check or money order. For Canada send $25.99. ALSO AVAILABLE: OUR COMPLETE CATALOG OF BOOKS $3. Please remember to put two first class stamps on your envelope for airmail to England. *Order with confidence – we have advertised in the U.S. since 1982.*

## Astronomical Glossary (continued)

Objects with an apparent magnitude of 6 or less are observable to the naked eye. The lower the magnitude, the greater the brightness. An object with a magnitude of −1, for example, is brighter than an object with a magnitude of +1. **Absolute** magnitude expresses how bright objects would appear if they were all the same distance (about 33 light-years) from Earth.

**Midnight:** Astronomical midnight is the time when the Sun is opposite its highest point in the sky (noon). Midnight is neither A.M. nor P.M., although 12-hour digital clocks typically display midnight as 12:00 A.M. On a 24-hour time cycle, 00:00, rather than 24:00, usually indicates midnight.

**Moon on Equator:** The Moon is on the celestial equator.

**Moon Rides High/Runs Low:** The Moon is highest above or farthest below the celestial equator.

**Moonrise/Moonset:** When the Moon rises above or sets below the horizon.

**Moon's Phases:** The changing appearance of the Moon, caused by the different angles at which it is illuminated by the Sun. **First Quarter:** Right half of the Moon is illuminated. **Full:** The Sun and the Moon are in opposition; the entire disk of the Moon is illuminated. **Last Quarter:** Left half of the Moon is illuminated. **New:** The Sun and the Moon are in conjunction; the entire disk of the Moon is darkened.

**Moon's Place, Astronomical:** The actual position of the Moon within the constellations on the celestial sphere. **Astrological:** The astrological position of the Moon within the zodiac, according to calculations made more than 2,000 years ago. Because of precession of the equinoxes and other factors, this is not the Moon's actual position in the sky.

**Morning Star:** A planet that is above the eastern horizon at sunrise and less than 180° west of the Sun in right ascension.

**Node:** Either of the two points where a celestial body's orbit intersects the ecliptic. **Ascending:** When the body is moving from south to north of the ecliptic. **Descending:** When the body is moving from north to south of the ecliptic.

**Occultation (Occn.):** When the Moon or a planet eclipses a star or planet.

**Opposition:** The Moon or a planet appears on the opposite side of the sky from the Sun (elongation 180°).

**Perigee (Perig.):** The point in the Moon's orbit that is closest to Earth.

**Perihelion (Perih.):** The point in a planet's orbit that is closest to the Sun.

**Precession:** The slowly changing position of the stars and equinoxes in the sky resulting from variations in the orientation of Earth's axis.

**Right Ascension (R.A.):** The celestial longitude of an object in the sky, measured eastward along the celestial equator in hours of time from the vernal equinox; analogous to longitude on Earth.

**Solar Cycle:** In the Julian calendar, a period of 28 years, at the end of which the days of the month return to the same days of the week.

**Solstice, Summer:** When the Sun reaches its greatest declination (23½°) north of the celestial equator, around June 21. **Winter:** When the Sun reaches its greatest declination (23½°) south of the celestial equator, around December 21.

**Stationary (Stat.):** The brief period of apparent halted movement of a planet against the background of the stars shortly before it appears to move backward/westward (retrograde motion) or forward/eastward (direct motion).

**Sun Fast/Slow:** When a sundial reading is ahead of (fast) or behind (slow) clock time.

**Sunrise/Sunset:** The visible rising and setting of the upper edge of the Sun's disk across the unobstructed horizon of an observer whose eyes are 15 feet above ground level.

**Twilight:** For definitions of civil, nautical, and astronomical twilight, **see page 92.** ☐☐

# The Light of the SLIVERY MOON

**The captivating crescent may be the Moon's most fascinating phase.**

BY BOB BERMAN

When first sighted each month, hovering in twilight, the Moon's slender crescent is mesmerizing. Early cave paintings reveal a primitive fascination with the crescent Moon, and its allure continues to this day.

–photo. Antonio M. Rosario/Getty Images

# LOOK FOR A SLY, SLIM SMILE

**THE CRESCENT MOON** is always low in the sky and confined to the hours around dawn or dusk; it is never in darkness. Cartoonists often depict the crescent Moon in a midnight sky, but this is impossible: The night's middle hours are for the broad, or fat, phases of the Moon—gibbous and full.

The crescent Moon's orientation depends on the time of day, the season, and the viewer's location. During evening twilight, from January through March, in all of the northern temperate latitudes (from 25° to 50° north latitude, encompassing Canada, China, all of Europe, Japan, Russia, and the United States; see page 234), the changing angle of the lunar orbit with respect to the horizon orients the crescent with its points, or horns, aimed upward, displaying a benevolent smile.

For the remainder of the year, the crescent appears sideways, like an archer's bow.

At no time of night from any location on Earth does the Moon appear to be frowning; this occurs only around midday, in full sunlight.

The year-round view from the tropics *(near right)* is of a smiling crescent, while in northern polar regions (Alaska, the Yukon, the Northwest Territories, and Nunavut), the crescent always points sideways *(far right)*.

–Alan McKnight, from *Secrets of the Night Sky* by Bob Berman (HarperCollins, 1995)

## NORTH, SOUTH; LEFT, RIGHT—
### *the Same, but Different*

**I**n both the Northern and Southern Hemispheres, the shape and width of the crescent Moon is the same on the same day. However, the angle of the crescent's orientation differs. The crescent's illumination is always aimed at the Sun, while its points, or horns, aim directly away from the Sun. In our hemisphere, the Moon stands above or (more usually) to the upper left of the sunset point. In the Southern Hemisphere, it stands to the upper right of the sunset point. The crescent's "tilt" looks different from each place.

SUN

**CONTINUED**

# What's "NEW," WHAT'S NOT

**NUMEROUS CULTURES OBSERVE** this centuries-old tradition: They call the first sighting of the crescent Moon after its monthly 3-day absence the "new Moon." (The 3 days include the 36 hours before the new Moon and the 36 hours after it.) For example, among Muslims, the first sighting marks the start of each month and determines fast times and holidays.

Today, to astronomers and scientists, "new Moon" means "no Moon." The phrase describes the date and hour when the Moon is closest to the Sun and completely obscured from Earth by solar glare. Two days and 26 degrees later (the Moon appears to move leftward 13 degrees every 24 hours), when the Moon is not in line with the Sun and therefore is only marginally in view, the waxing crescent appears just above the western horizon, setting soon after sunset.

–Stephen V. Loos

## SUN- AND (YES!) EARTHSHINE

**MOON**

**LIGHT RAYS**

**EARTH**

**SUN**

When the crescent Moon appears in evening twilight, a strange but famous feature becomes visible: The dark portion of the Moon (the area unlit by the Sun) seems to glow. Historically called "the new Moon in the old Moon's arms," the phenomenon is now aptly known as **earthshine.**

This occurs because 38 percent of the sunlight that strikes Earth bounces back into space; some of this earthlight bathes the lunar surface. About 10 percent of that light bounces off the lunar surface (which is not very reflective) to create the visible glow (earthshine) on the Moon's dark side.

The thinnest Moon crescents (both waxing and waning) display the brightest earthshine. This is due to the phase reciprocity of the Earth and the Moon: When the Moon appears thinnest from Earth, Earth would look full from the Moon. Conversely, Earth would appear to be unlit, or in its "new" phase, if viewed from the Moon during what we would see as the Moon's full phase.

Don't be fooled: The portion of the crescent Moon that is illuminated by earthshine appears to be part of a smaller orb than the sunlit crescent. This mirage is caused by our eyes' response to the different light levels. It vanishes when you view the crescent through binoculars.

**CONTINUED**

–illustration, Alan McKnight, from *Secrets of the Night Sky* by Bob Berman (HarperCollins, 1995)

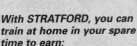

# DID YOU KNOW?

➡ As a result of all of the sun- and earthshine bouncing, the crescent Moon's earthlight is older than its sunlight.

➡ If the Sun were to go dark suddenly, the crescent Moon would disappear at the same time, but earthshine would continue to illuminate the Moon faintly for three seconds.

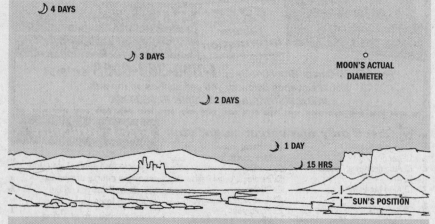

The Moon moves eastward in its orbit around Earth 13 degrees per day, or about its own diameter each hour. The illustration above shows the Moon's position 45 minutes after sunset for 4 days after the new Moon. The size of our Moon has been exaggerated to show how the crescent changes appearance.

## ON THE WAX

**AFTER SUNSET,** the crescent Moon's points, or horns, always aim directly away from the sunset. Imagine the crescent as an archer's bow: The invisible arrow is aimed directly at the Sun, which is below the horizon. Each succeeding night at the same time, the waxing crescent sits higher in the sky and farther left, in an increasingly sideways orientation. The Moon stays out longer before setting and becomes an increasingly nighttime (not twilight) phenomenon.

Simultaneously, the Earth-lit portion shrinks and dims; Earth is shrinking into a thinner phase in the lunar sky. Just 4 or 5 days after the Moon's "new" phase, it opens up more than a 45-degree angle from the Sun and is high in the southwest when twilight ends.

    –illustration, Alan McKnight, from *Secrets of the Night Sky* by Bob Berman (HarperCollins, 1995)

# ON THE WANE

**AT THE AGE OF 23 DAYS** (the time since the last "new" phase), the Moon enters a second crescent cycle. This waning, predawn sliver receives less attention than its waxing evening cousin. Rising only after midnight, it appears monthly for 5 consecutive days. Seen only in the eastern sky, with its points, or horns, aiming rightward (the opposite of the evening form), it heralds the dawn.

Its size foretells the time:

➡ A broad waning crescent normally appears between 1:00 and 2:00 A.M. but occasionally around midnight.

➡ A slim crescent rises in full darkness, just before morning twilight.

➡ A thin sliver of crescent appears only in morning twilight and always low in the sky.

# ONLY TWO OTHERS

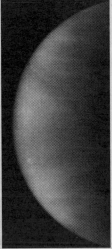

E ven through the world's most powerful telescopes, only two other crescents can be seen from Earth–those of planets Mercury *(near right)* and Venus *(far right)*. The dearth of crescents is because of Earth's location: We can see the crescents only of planets between us and the Sun. If we lived on Pluto, all of the planets in our solar system, as well as the numerous moons of Jupiter, Saturn, and Uranus, would be lit from behind and appear as crescents half of the time.

**In winter, when the Moon's horns are sharp and well-defined, frost is expected.**

*–Scottish proverb*

**CONTINUED**

# Calling All Spotters

**FINDING THE HAIR-THIN LUNAR ARC** each month has become sport. Today, millions of people—amateur astronomers, nature enthusiasts, and casual observers—compete to find the "youngest" Moon. (The lunar age is the number of hours or days that have elapsed since the Moon became new. See the Left-Hand Calendar Pages, 114–140.)

The best crescent-spotting conditions in the Northern Hemisphere occur from January through March, as the Moon's path (its day-to-day change of position) moves nearly vertically up from the sunset point. During the rest of the year, the line follows a horizon-scraping, leftward slant.

Since 1990, the youngest Moon sighted with the naked eye has been 15½ hours old. Thirteen-hour-old crescents have been viewed with binoculars.

A wee 1-day-old Moon (the orb exactly 24 hours after it was officially "new") looks as thin as a wire, is very close to the skyline, and is usually mired in thick horizon haze. It is almost impossible to see in autumn.

A 2-day-old Moon is easy to spot: It is relatively broad, or fat; higher above the horizon (8 degrees, on average) than it was the previous day; and viewable 15 minutes or so after sunset.

□□

**Bob Berman** is the author of six books, including *Biocentrism* (BenBella Books, 2009). He is also director of astronomy for SLOOH, the global online observatory.

**MOON US!**

Would you like to see a slivery Moon? Find its phase time for your location at **Almanac.com/Moon/Calendar**. Take a picture, if possible, and upload it with the details of your location and time to **Almanac.com/Ecard**.

## SALT MAGICK WORKS – THESE UNSOLICITED TESTIMONIALS PROVE IT:

Have already had two wins on the pools' – *M. B. (Fleetwood).* 'In ten minutes my violent son quietened down after I did the salt rite ... I've had no trouble from him since' – *P. E. (Manchester).* 'IT REALLY WORKS! ... I won $1411' – *A. P. (Grimsby).* 'Since I got your book ... money has come into my home in different ways ... my son has paid off his debts ... I bless the day I sent for this book' – *A. L. (Hove)* (This lady wrote again five months later: 'The salt is still working for us ... every day we receive something good'.) *Photo-copies of these actual testimonials available on request. Many more available!*

# NEW SALT MAGICK RITES
# BRING INCREDIBLE RESULTS ... SOMETIMES WITHIN HOURS, EVEN MINUTES!

## NEVER BEFORE MADE PUBLIC. FIRST TIME IN PRINT.
### SIMPLE 1, 2, 3 RITES YOU CAN DO IN THE PRIVACY OF YOUR OWN HOME.

The average New Salt Magick Rite takes only minutes to do. And you can do it in the privacy of your own home.

All you need is common table salt and the wish to make your dreams come true. NEVER HAS SALT MAGICK BEEN SO EASY. This brand new book shows how anyone can do it. You only need a packet of salt – and (apart from this book) nothing else! **No other ingredients are required for most of the salt rites in this new book.**

You will be astonished at their simplicity – and even more astonished at the fast results!

SALT MAGICK WORKS. People have performed it for milenia to solve their problems.

Salt is incorruptible; and it is this quality which has given it a magickal significance in the minds of many people. It has always been used in magick ritual as a *repellent of evil forces.*

From time immemorial those acquainted with salt lore would dare not enter a new home *without first sprink- ling salt outside its door.*

They *would not allow a new baby to leave home without carrying salt; nor would they swear oaths without the presence of salt.*

There are literally hundreds of salt superstitions. No other substance has generated so much magickal fascination. You will read of a few of these superstitions in this new book.

Perhaps the best known salt superstition is the dread of spilling salt, always believed to be a sign of impending disaster. The well known formula for averting disaster is to pick up the spilt salt and cast over the left shoulder. There is more about this in the book.

**Did you know you could keep unwanted persons away from your home by sprinkling salt outside your door?**

Read in this book what exactly it is you have to do.

In his foreword to Mr Pike's book writer Jim Barry explains how using salt in this way has kept unwanted persons out of sight. 'They have never troubled me again', he writes.

SALT MAGICK RITES WORK – AND THEY ARE PROVEN TIME AND AGAIN!

Sprinkle salt on pools and lottery coupons. Carry a pinch of salt when you go to place a bet.

Salt rites are easy, clean, and so simple to perform!

Anyone of any religious faith can do them!

TO PROTECT YOURSELF FROM BAD LUCK USE THESE SIMPLE NEW SALT RITES. You will be astounded at the change in your life!

This brand new book shows how to get results ... over and over again!

These simple rites *have never before been made public!* These are far simpler than the only other salt rituals previously published (in Marcus Bottom-ley's 'Salt Power' book, now out of print).

Jason Pike, the author of this new book has presented these Salt Magick Rites in such a way that even a child can perform!

The magic use of salt is of great antiquity but the new rites in this book are *made simple for today's busy woman and man!*

Mr Pike's own marriage was saved from divorce, thanks to Salt Magick! He writes, 'The end was at hand – we just couldn't live together any longer. I tried the salt rite in desperation ... IT WORKED IMMEDIATELY! The peace that entered our home was unbelievable! 'Now we are happier than ever before!'

In this book you will find *the precise New Salt Magick Rite that saved his marriage.* It takes only minutes to do – and yet what wonders it can bring!

You will find in this book:
● **New Salt Magick Brings Money.** See in Chapter 1 how it can solve your money worries! Receive cash from unexpected sources! Money seemingly out of thin air!
● **Command Another Person's Thoughts And Actions!** This seems unbelievable – but see Chapter 12! (Important: this cannot be used to *harm* someone. Salt Magick cannot be used in this way.)
● **New Salt Magick For Regaining Youth.** This is an age-old formula. Those who have used it swear it works! But it takes 14 days to see results. Chapter 8 explains.
● **New Salt Magick For Protection.** Protect yourself and loved ones from physical injury! See Chapter 7!
● **Salt Rite To Get A Job.** Carry a pinch of salt when you go for an interview. See in Chapter 6 exactly what to do! Incredibly

simple, but those who have tried it swear that this ancient formula works!
● **New Salt Magick For Bringing A Lover!** The person you want in your life can be yours. Also try this on someone you have parted with. See Chapter 2.
● **Diseases And Ailments Healed.** Salt Magick should not be used as a substitute for your doctor; but those who have tried it are convinced it helped them! Even total cures of serious health problems have been reported! See Chapter 11.
● **See Behind Walls; Read Other People's Minds; See The Future.** Chapter 3 reveals what to do!

You can bring love back into your life with this power! The one who doesn't want to know you now can have a change of heart once you use this potent magick! And *you don't need a photo or any article that belongs to this person for the magick to work!*

Also in this remarkable new book are the actual Salt Magick Rites that can help you: TRAVEL OUTSIDE YOUR BODY. An incredibly simple astral projection technique which the author swears by! SUMMON YOUR PERSONAL GUARDIAN ANGEL TO MATERIALIZE BEFORE YOUR VERY EYES. It can happen! See Chapter 5 for creating the salt circle in which to see this phenomenon. *When he appears ask for what you want in life so that he may bring it to you!* ... PROTECT YOUR HOME FROM FIRE AND THEFT. Simple New Salt Magick gives you not only protection but peace of mind ... PSYCHIC DEFENCE. Has someone placed a curse on you? Are you a victim of evil black magick? *Salt magickally dissolves such evil vibrations and sets you free.* See Chapter 14.

Would you believe you can actually *control the weather through Salt Magick?* Author Jason Pike has kept records of using magick to control the elements and is convinced it works. This is the only Salt Magick Rite in the book which needs to be performed outdoors.

The uses of Salt Magick are practi- cally without limit. All the ancient peoples – Egyptians, Hebrews, Greeks, Romans, to name a few – believe in its power; millions still do. Use the amazingly simple new Salt Magick Rites and find out why.

The price of New Salt Magick Rites is **only $22.99.**

**IRON-CLAD GUARANTEE: You must be thrilled with results or return within 45 days for a full refund. Send $22.99 to:** FINBARR INTERNATIONAL (ONS), 5 Godwyn Road, Folkestone, Kent CT20 2QQ, England. Price inc- ludes fast delivery within 16 days. If you are in a real hurry add $3 and we'll guarantee delivery within 12 days. Send personal check or money order. ALSO AVAILABLE: OUR COMPLETE CATALOG OF BOOKS $2. Please remember to put three first class stamps on your envelope for airmail to England. *We have advertised worldwide since 1982.*

# How to Use This Almanac

The calendar pages (114–141) are the heart of *The Old Farmer's Almanac*. They present sky sightings and astronomical data for the entire year and are what make this book a true almanac, a "calendar of the heavens." In essence, these pages are unchanged since 1792, when Robert B. Thomas published his first edition. The long columns of numbers and symbols reveal all of nature's precision, rhythm, and glory, providing an astronomical look at the year 2011.

C A L E N D A R

## Why We Have Seasons

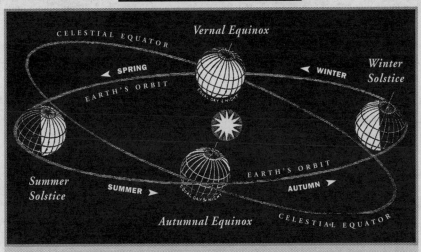

CELESTIAL EQUATOR

Vernal Equinox

SPRING

EARTH'S ORBIT

Winter Solstice

WINTER

Summer Solstice

SUMMER

EARTH'S ORBIT

AUTUMN

Autumnal Equinox

CELESTIAL EQUATOR

### THE SEASONS OF 2011

| | |
|---|---|
| Spring . . . . . . March 20, 7:21 P.M. EDT | Autumn . . . . . September 23, 5:05 A.M. EDT |
| Summer . . . . . . June 21, 1:16 P.M. EDT | Winter . . . . . December 22, 12:30 A.M. EST |

■ The seasons occur because as Earth revolves around the Sun, its axis remains tilted at 23.5 degrees from the perpendicular. This tilt causes different latitudes on Earth to receive varying amounts of sunlight throughout the year.

In the Northern Hemisphere, the summer solstice marks the beginning of summer and occurs when the North Pole is tilted toward the Sun. The winter solstice marks the beginning of winter and occurs when the North Pole is tilted away from the Sun.

The equinoxes occur when the hemispheres equally face the Sun and receive equal amounts (12 hours each) of daylight and darkness. The vernal equinox marks the beginning of spring; the autumnal equinox marks the beginning of autumn. In the Southern Hemisphere, the seasons are the reverse of those in the Northern Hemisphere. **(continued)**

## The Left-Hand Calendar Pages • 114–140

### A SAMPLE MONTH

**SKY WATCH** ☆ *The box at the top of each Left-Hand Calendar Page describes the best times to view celestial highlights, including conjunctions, meteor showers, and planets. (The dates on which select astronomical events occur appear on the Right-Hand Calendar Pages.)*

**1  2  3  4  5  6  7  8**

Purchase these pages with times set to your zip code at MyLocalAlmanac.com.

| Day of Year | Day of Month | Day of Week | ☼ Rises h. m. | Rise Key | ☼ Sets h. m. | Set Key | Length of Day h. m. | Sun Fast m. | Declination of Sun ° ' | High Tide Times Boston | ☾ Rises h. m. | Rise Key | ☾ Sets h. m. | Set Key | ☾ Place | ☾ Age |
|---|---|---|---|---|---|---|---|---|---|---|---|---|---|---|---|---|
| 1 | 1 | Sa. | 7:13 | E | 4:22 | A | 9 09 | 12 | 22 s.59 | 8¼  9 | 4:44 | E | 1:54 | B | SCO | 27 |
| 2 | 2 | **B** | 7:13 | E | 4:23 | A | 9 10 | 12 | 22 54 | 9¼  10 | 5:44 | E | 2:50 | B | OPH | 28 |
| 3 | 3 | M. | 7:13 | E | 4:23 | A | 9 10 | 11 | 22 48 | 10  10¾ | 6:36 | E | 3:51 | B | SAG | 29 |

The **Left-Hand Calendar Pages** (detail above) contain daily Sun and Moon rise and set times, the length of day, high tide times, the Moon's place and age, and more for Boston. Examples of how to calculate astronomical times for your location are shown below.

**1** To calculate the sunrise/sunset times for your locale: Each sunrise/sunset time is assigned a Key Letter whose value is given in minutes in the **Time Corrections** table on **page 234**. Find your city in the table, or the city nearest you, and add or subtract those minutes to/from Boston's sunrise or sunset time given.

### E X A M P L E :

■ To find the time of sunrise in Denver, Colorado, on the first day of the month:

| | |
|---|---|
| Sunrise, Boston, with Key Letter E (above) | 7:13 A.M. EST |
| Value of Key Letter E for Denver (p. 234) | + 7 minutes |
| Sunrise, Denver | 7:20 A.M. MST |

**2** To determine your city's length of day, find the sunrise/sunset Key Letter values for your city on **page 234**. Add or subtract the sunset value to/from Boston's length of day. Then simply *reverse* the sunrise sign (from minus to plus, or plus to minus) and add

or subtract this value to/from the result of the first step.

### E X A M P L E :

■ To find the length of day in Richmond, Virginia:

| | |
|---|---|
| Length of day, Boston (above) | 9h. 09m. |
| Sunset Key Letter A for Richmond (p. 238) | + 41m. |
| Reverse sunrise Key Letter E for Richmond (p. 238, +11 to −11) | 9h. 50m. − 11m. |
| Length of day, Richmond | 9h. 39m. |

**3** Use the Sun Fast column to change sundial time to clock time in Boston or another location. A sundial reads natural time, or Sun time, which is neither Standard nor Daylight time. To get Boston clock time, *subtract* the minutes given in the Sun Fast column (except where the number is preceded by an asterisk [*], in which case *add* the minutes) and use Key Letter C in the table on **page 234** to convert the time to your city.

**ATTENTION, READERS:** *All times given in this edition of the Almanac are for Boston, Massachusetts, and are in Eastern Standard Time (EST), except from 2:00 A.M., March 13, until 2:00 A.M., November 6, when Eastern Daylight Time (EDT) is given. Key Letters (A–E) are provided so that you can calculate times for other localities.*

E X A M P L E :

■ To change sundial time to clock time in Boston, or, for example, in Salem, Oregon:

| | |
|---|---|
| Sundial reading (Boston or Salem) | 12:00 noon |
| Subtract Sun Fast (p. 110) | – 12 minutes |
| Clock time, Boston | 11:48 A.M. EST |
| Use Key Letter C for Salem (p. 237) | + 27 minutes |
| Clock time, Salem | 12:15 P.M. PST |

**4** This column gives the degrees and minutes of the Sun from the celestial equator at noon EST or EDT.

**5** This column gives the approximate times of high tides in Boston. For example, the first high tide occurs at 8:15 A.M. and the second occurs at 9:00 P.M. the same day. (A dash indicates that high tide occurs on or after midnight and is recorded on the next day.) Figures for calculating high tide times and heights for localities other than Boston are given in the **Tide Corrections** table on **page 239**.

**6** To calculate the moonrise/moonset times for localities other than Boston, follow the example in the next column, making a correction for longitude (see table, above right). For the longitude of your city, **see page 234**. (Note: A dash in the moonrise/moonset columns indicates that rise or set times occur on or after midnight and are recorded on the next day.)

Purchase the Left-Hand Calendar pages with times set to your zip code at **MyLocalAlmanac.com.**

–Beth Krommes

| Longitude of city | Correction minutes |
|---|---|
| 58°–76° | 0 |
| 77°–89° | +1 |
| 90°–102° | +2 |
| 103°–115° | +3 |
| 116°–127° | +4 |
| 128°–141° | +5 |
| 142°–155° | +6 |

E X A M P L E :

■ To determine the time of moonrise in Lansing, Michigan:

| | |
|---|---|
| Moonrise, Boston, with Key Letter E (p. 110) | 4:44 A.M. EST |
| Value of Key Letter E for Lansing (p. 236) | + 54 minutes |
| Correction for Lansing longitude, 84° 33' | + 1 minute |
| Moonrise, Lansing | 5:39 A.M. EST |

Use the same procedure to determine the time of moonset.

**7** The Moon's Place is its *astronomical* placement in the heavens at midnight. (This should not be confused with the Moon's *astrological* place in the zodiac. All calculations in this Almanac are based on astronomy, not astrology, except for those on **pages 229–231**.)

In addition to the 12 constellations of the zodiac, this column may indicate others: Auriga **(AUR)**, a northern constellation between Perseus and Gemini; Cetus **(CET)**, which lies south of the zodiac, just south of Pisces and Aries; Ophiuchus **(OPH)**, a constellation primarily north of the zodiac but with a small corner between Scorpius and Sagittarius; Orion **(ORI)**, a constellation whose northern limit first reaches the zodiac between Taurus and Gemini; and Sextans **(SEX)**, which lies south of the zodiac except for a corner that just touches it near Leo.

**8** The last column gives the Moon's Age, which is the number of days since the previous new Moon. (The average length of the lunar month is 29.53 days.) **(continued)**

**CALENDAR**

**A SAMPLE MONTH**

- Weather prediction rhyme.

- The bold letter is the Dominical Letter (from A to G), a traditional ecclesiastical designation for Sunday determined by the date on which the first Sunday falls. For 2011, the Dominical Letter is **B**.

- Sundays and special holy days generally appear in this font.

- Symbols for notable celestial events. (See opposite page for explanations.)

- Proverbs, poems, and adages generally appear in this font.

- Civil holidays and astronomical events appear in this font.

- Noteworthy historical events, folklore, and legends appear in this font.

- High tide heights, in feet, at Boston.

- Religious feasts generally appear in this font. A$^T$ indicates a major feast that the church has this year temporarily transferred to a date other than its usual one.

| Day of Month | Day of Week | Dates, Feasts, Fasts, Aspects, Tide Heights | Weather |
|---|---|---|---|
| 1 | Sa. | New Year's Day • Holy Name • Baseball player Hank Greenberg born, 1911 • Tides {10.7 / 9.1} | Snow's |
| 2 | B | ℂ RUNS LOW • ♂♂ℂ • ♂♍☉ • Tides {10.7 / 9.2} | sporadic, |
| 3 | M. | ℂ AT ☋ • ♂♄ℂ • ⊕ AT PERIHELION • Tides {10.8 / 9.3} | but |
| 4 | Tu. | St. Elizabeth Ann Seton • New ● • Eclipse ☉ • ♂♂ℂ | the |
| 5 | W. | Twelfth Night • A kindly, good Janiveer / Freezeth the pot by the fire. • Tides {10.6 / —} | cold's |
| 6 | Th. | Epiphany • Lion-tailed macaque born, Woodland Park Zoo, Seattle, Wash., 1989 | emphatic! |
| 7 | Fr. | Distaff Day • ♂♅ℂ • Movie "Edison Kinetoscopic Record of a Sneeze" made, 1894 | Flurries |
| 8 | Sa. | ♀ GR. ELONG. (47° WEST) • 15,000+ troops began aid during multiday ice storm, Ont./Que., 1998 | require |
| 9 | B | 1st ♋. af. Ep. • ℂ ON EQ. • ☿ GR. ELONG. (23° WEST) • {9.2 / 9.4} | furries. |
| 10 | M. | Plough Monday • ℂ AT APO. • ♂♍ℂ • ♂♂ℂ • {9.1 / 8.9} | Dogsledders |
| 11 | Tu. | Sir Edmund Hillary (first to summit Mt. Everest) died, 2008 | mush |
| 12 | W. | When the wine is in, the wit is out. • Tides {8.9 / 8.2} | through |
| 13 | Th. | St. Hilary • All in the Family made television debut, 1971 • Tides {8.9 / 8.0} | slop |
| 14 | Fr. | Lethal avalanche near Park City, Utah, 2005 • Tides {9.0 / 7.9} | and |
| 15 | Sa. | −54° to 49°F in 24 hours, Loma, Mont., 1972 • Tides {9.3 / 8.1} | slush. |
| 16 | B | 2nd ♋. af. Ep. • ℂ RIDES HIGH • {9.7 / 8.4} | Bombarded, |
| 17 | M. | Martin Luther King Jr.'s Birthday (observed) • ℂ AT ☋ • ♂♍℞ • Ben Franklin born, 1706 | then |
| 18 | Tu. | 211-lb. striped marlin caught, Red Hill, Hawaii, 1996 | bitter— |
| 19 | W. | Full Wolf ○ • Life is like the Moon, now dark, now full. • {11.1 / 9.8} | this |
| 20 | Th. | JFK sworn in as 35th U.S. president, 1961 • Tides {11.5 / 10.3} | winter's |
| 21 | Fr. | ℂ AT PERIG. • Pittsburgh Steelers won their third Super Bowl, 1979 • Tides {11.6} | no |
| 22 | Sa. | St. Vincent • ℂ ON EQ. • Philosopher Sir Francis Bacon born, 1561 • {10.7 / 11.6} | quitter! |
| 23 | B | 3rd ♋. af. Ep. • Composer Samuel Barber died, 1981 • {10.9 / 11.3} | Storms |
| 24 | M. | Soviet satellite Cosmos 954 crashed in N.W.T., leaking radioactive waste, 1978 • Tides {11.0 / 10.8} | are |
| 25 | Tu. | Conversion of Paul • ♂♄ℂ • Nellie Bly completed around-the-world trip, 1890 | various, |
| 26 | W. | Sts. Timothy & Titus • Raccoons mate now. • Tides {10.7 / 9.5} | but |

☞ **For explanations of Almanac terms, see the glossaries on pages 96, 142, and 241.**

## Predicting Earthquakes

−Beth Krommes

- Note the dates in the **Right-Hand Calendar Pages** when the Moon rides high or runs low. The date of the high begins the most likely 5-day period of earthquakes in the Northern Hemisphere; the date of the low indicates a similar 5-day period in the Southern Hemisphere. Also noted are the 2 days each month when the Moon is on the celestial equator, indicating the most likely time for earthquakes in either hemisphere.

■ Throughout the **Right-Hand Calendar Pages** are groups of symbols that represent notable celestial events. The symbols and names of the principal planets and aspects are:

| | | | |
|---|---|---|---|
| ⊙ | Sun | ♆ | Neptune |
| ○●☽ | Moon | ♇ | Pluto |
| ☿ | Mercury | ♂ | Conjunction (on the |
| ♀ | Venus | | same celestial |
| ⊕ | Earth | | longitude) |
| ♂ | Mars | ☊ | Ascending node |
| ♃ | Jupiter | ☋ | Descending node |
| ♄ | Saturn | ☍ | Opposition (180 |
| ♅ | Uranus | | degrees from Sun) |

**EXAMPLE:**

♂♆☽ on the 7th day of the month (see opposite page) means that on that date a conjunction (♂) of Neptune (♆) and the Moon (☽) occurs: They are aligned along the same celestial longitude and appear to be closest together in the sky.

**EARTH AT PERIHELION AND APHELION**

■ Perihelion: January 3, 2011. Earth will be 91,407,361 miles from the Sun. Aphelion: July 4, 2011. Earth will be 94,512,005 miles from the Sun.

## 2011 Calendar Highlights

### MOVABLE RELIGIOUS OBSERVANCES

| | |
|---|---|
| Septuagesima Sunday. | **February 20** |
| Shrove Tuesday | **March 8** |
| Ash Wednesday | **March 9** |
| Palm Sunday | **April 17** |
| First day of Passover | **April 19** |
| Good Friday | **April 22** |
| Easter | **April 24** |
| Orthodox Easter | **April 24** |
| Rogation Sunday | **May 29** |
| Ascension Day | **June 2** |
| Whitsunday–Pentecost | **June 12** |
| Trinity Sunday | **June 19** |
| Corpus Christi | **June 26** |
| First day of Ramadan | **August 1** |
| Rosh Hashanah | **September 29** |
| Yom Kippur | **October 8** |
| First Sunday of Advent | **November 27** |
| First day of Chanukah | **December 21** |

### CHRONOLOGICAL CYCLES

| | |
|---|---|
| Dominical Letter | **B** |
| Epact | **25** |
| Golden Number (Lunar Cycle) | **17** |
| Roman Indiction | **4** |
| Solar Cycle | **4** |
| Year of Julian Period | **6724** |

–Beth Krommes

**ERAS**

| Era | Year | Begins |
|---|---|---|
| Byzantine | **7520** | September 14 |
| Jewish (A.M.)* | **5772** | September 29 |
| Chinese (Lunar) [Year of the Rabbit] | **4709** | February 3 |
| Roman (A.U.C.) | **2764** | January 14 |
| Nabonassar | **2760** | April 21 |
| Japanese | **2671** | January 1 |
| Grecian (Seleucidae) | **2323** | September 14 (or October 14) |
| Indian (Saka) | **1933** | March 22 |
| Diocletian | **1728** | September 12 |
| Islamic (Hegira) | **1433** | November 26 |

*Year begins at sunset the evening before.*

CALENDAR

CALENDAR

**SKY WATCH** ☆ *A two-ring circus. In the evening sky after sunset, Jupiter has retrograded to the Aquarius–Pisces border, still brilliant and dominant in the south most of the night yet fading ever so slightly to magnitude –2.6. The Moon passes Jupiter on the 16th. In the predawn arena, Saturn and especially Venus speedily return, with Venus rivetingly brilliant as it explosively brightens from magnitude –4.1 to –4.9. At midmonth, 40 minutes before sunrise, UFO-like Venus stands 15 degrees high, with Virgo's blue star Spica just above it and Saturn higher still. While the Ringed World barely exceeds Spica's so-so magnitude 1 brightness, Venus is many times more brilliant than the other two.*

| | | | |
|---|---|---|---|
| ● **New Moon** | 6th day | 0 hour | 52nd minute |
| ◐ **First Quarter** | 13th day | 11th hour | 39th minute |
| ○ **Full Moon** | 21st day | 12th hour | 27th minute |
| ◑ **Last Quarter** | 28th day | 15th hour | 36th minute |

*After 2:00 A.M. on November 7, Eastern Standard Time is given.*

**Purchase these pages with times set to your zip code at MyLocalAlmanac.com.**

| Day of Year | Day of Month | Day of Week | ☼ Rises h. m. | Rise Key | ☼ Sets h. m. | Set Key | Length of Day h. m. | Sun Fast m. | Declination of Sun ° ' | High Tide Times Boston | | ☾ Rises h. m. | Rise Key | ☾ Sets h. m. | Set Key | ☾ Place | ☾ Age |
|---|---|---|---|---|---|---|---|---|---|---|---|---|---|---|---|---|---|
| 305 | 1 | M. | 7:17 | D | **5:37** | B | 10 20 | 32 | 14 s. 32 | 7 | **7½** | 1:43 | D | **2:49** | D | LEO | 25 |
| 306 | 2 | Tu. | 7:18 | D | **5:36** | B | 10 18 | 32 | 14 51 | 8 | **8½** | 2:58 | D | **3:17** | C | LEO | 26 |
| 307 | 3 | W. | 7:19 | D | **5:35** | B | 10 16 | 32 | 15 10 | 9 | **9½** | 4:13 | E | **3:45** | C | VIR | 27 |
| 308 | 4 | Th. | 7:21 | E | **5:33** | B | 10 12 | 32 | 15 29 | 10 | **10½** | 5:29 | E | **4:17** | B | VIR | 28 |
| 309 | 5 | Fr. | 7:22 | E | **5:32** | B | 10 10 | 32 | 15 47 | 10¾ | **11¼** | 6:45 | E | **4:52** | B | VIR | 29 |
| 310 | 6 | Sa. | 7:23 | E | **5:31** | B | 10 08 | 32 | 16 05 | 11½ | — | 8:00 | E | **5:34** | B | LIB | 0 |
| 311 | 7 | **C** | 6:24 | E | **4:30** | B | 10 06 | 32 | 16 23 | 12¼ | 11¼ | 8:11 | E | **5:23** | B | LIB | 1 |
| 312 | 8 | M. | 6:26 | E | **4:29** | B | 10 03 | 32 | 16 40 | 12 | **12¼** | 9:14 | E | **6:19** | B | OPH | 2 |
| 313 | 9 | Tu. | 6:27 | E | **4:28** | B | 10 01 | 32 | 16 57 | 12¾ | **1** | 10:08 | E | **7:20** | B | OPH | 3 |
| 314 | 10 | W. | 6:28 | E | **4:27** | B | 9 59 | 32 | 17 14 | 1¾ | **1¾** | 10:52 | E | **8:24** | B | SAG | 4 |
| 315 | 11 | Th. | 6:29 | E | **4:26** | B | 9 57 | 32 | 17 31 | 2½ | **2¾** | 11:28 | E | **9:27** | B | SAG | 5 |
| 316 | 12 | Fr. | 6:31 | E | **4:25** | B | 9 54 | 32 | 17 47 | 3½ | **3½** | 11:58 | E | **10:30** | C | CAP | 6 |
| 317 | 13 | Sa. | 6:32 | E | **4:24** | B | 9 52 | 31 | 18 03 | 4¼ | **4½** | **12:24** | D | **11:30** | C | AQU | 7 |
| 318 | 14 | **C** | 6:33 | E | **4:23** | B | 9 50 | 31 | 18 19 | 5¼ | **5½** | **12:47** | D | — | - | CAP | 8 |
| 319 | 15 | M. | 6:34 | E | **4:22** | B | 9 48 | 31 | 18 34 | 6 | **6¼** | **1:09** | C | 12:30 | D | AQU | 9 |
| 320 | 16 | Tu. | 6:36 | E | **4:21** | B | 9 45 | 31 | 18 49 | 7 | **7¼** | **1:31** | C | 1:29 | D | PSC | 10 |
| 321 | 17 | W. | 6:37 | E | **4:20** | B | 9 43 | 31 | 19 04 | 7¾ | **8** | **1:54** | C | 2:29 | E | PSC | 11 |
| 322 | 18 | Th. | 6:38 | E | **4:19** | B | 9 41 | 31 | 19 18 | 8½ | **9** | **2:19** | B | 3:30 | E | PSC | 12 |
| 323 | 19 | Fr. | 6:39 | E | **4:19** | B | 9 40 | 30 | 19 32 | 9 | **9¾** | **2:48** | B | 4:33 | E | PSC | 13 |
| 324 | 20 | Sa. | 6:41 | E | **4:18** | B | 9 37 | 30 | 19 46 | 9¾ | **10¼** | **3:22** | B | 5:37 | E | ARI | 14 |
| 325 | 21 | **C** | 6:42 | E | **4:17** | A | 9 35 | 30 | 19 59 | 10½ | **11** | **4:04** | B | 6:42 | E | ARI | 15 |
| 326 | 22 | M. | 6:43 | E | **4:16** | A | 9 33 | 30 | 20 12 | 11 | **11¾** | **4:54** | B | 7:44 | E | TAU | 16 |
| 327 | 23 | Tu. | 6:44 | E | **4:16** | A | 9 32 | 29 | 20 25 | 11¾ | — | **5:53** | B | 8:41 | E | TAU | 17 |
| 328 | 24 | W. | 6:45 | E | **4:15** | A | 9 30 | 29 | 20 37 | 12½ | **12½** | **6:58** | B | 9:32 | E | GEM | 18 |
| 329 | 25 | Th. | 6:46 | E | **4:15** | A | 9 29 | 29 | 20 49 | 1¼ | **1¼** | **8:09** | C | 10:15 | E | GEM | 19 |
| 330 | 26 | Fr. | 6:48 | E | **4:14** | A | 9 26 | 28 | 21 00 | 2 | **2¼** | **9:21** | C | 10:51 | E | CAN | 20 |
| 331 | 27 | Sa. | 6:49 | E | **4:14** | A | 9 25 | 28 | 21 11 | 3 | **3** | **10:34** | D | 11:23 | D | CAN | 21 |
| 332 | 28 | **C** | 6:50 | E | **4:13** | A | 9 23 | 28 | 21 22 | 3¾ | **4** | **11:46** | D | 11:52 | D | LEO | 22 |
| 333 | 29 | M. | 6:51 | E | **4:13** | A | 9 22 | 27 | 21 32 | 4¾ | **5** | — | - | **12:19** | D | SEX | 23 |
| 334 | 30 | Tu. | 6:52 | E | **4:12** | A | 9 20 | 27 | 21 s. 42 | 5¾ | **6¼** | 12:59 | E | **12:46** | C | VIR | 24 |

 **To use this page, see p. 110; for Key Letters, see p. 234.** ☞ **Bold = P.M.** ☞ Light = A.M. 

## NOVEMBER HATH 30 DAYS • 2010

*The autumn is old,*
*The sere leaves are flying.* –Thomas Hood

| Day of Month | Day of Week | Dates, Feasts, Fasts, Aspects, Tide Heights | Weather |
|---|---|---|---|
| 1 | M. | All Saints' • Michelangelo's fresco on Sistine Chapel ceiling unveiled, 1512 • {9.7 10.1 | *Skim* |
| 2 | Tu. | All Souls' • **Election Day** • ☾ ON EQ. • Tides {10.2 10.3 | *ice* |
| 3 | W. | ☾ AT PERIG. • Mary Jacobs granted patent for first modern bra, 1914 • {10.8 10.4 | *cracking,* |
| 4 | Th. | ☌♄☾ • (Royal) Montreal Golf Club, oldest in North America, founded, 1873 • {11.4 10.6 | *snow* |
| 5 | Fr. | ☌♀☾ • *Keep your shop and your shop will keep you.* • Tides {11.7 10.6 | *for* |
| 6 | Sa. | Sadie Hawkins Day • **New** ● • Tides {11.9 — | *tracking.* |
| 7 | C | **Daylight Saving Time ends, 2:00 A.M.** • ☌☿☾ • ☌♂☾ • ♆ STAT. | *Sodden:* |
| 8 | M. | ☾ RUNS LOW • Black bears head to winter dens now. • Tides {10.3 11.5 | *Snow's* |
| 9 | Tu. | ☾ AT ☊ • ☌♇☾ • Worst day of lethal Great Lakes storm, 1913 • {9.9 11.1 | *gone* |
| 10 | W. | Continental Marines (now U.S. Marine Corps) established, 1755 | *but* |
| 11 | Th. | St. Martin of Tours • **Veterans Day** • Tides {9.2 10.0 | *not* |
| 12 | Fr. | Indian Summer • Lobsters move to offshore waters. • Tides {8.9 9.5 | *forgotten.* |
| 13 | Sa. | Ground-breaking ceremony for Martin Luther King Jr. Memorial, Washington, D.C., 2006 • {8.7 9.1 | *Glory* |
| 14 | C | 25th S. af. P. • ☌♆☾ • Actress Veronica Lake born, 1919 | *days* |
| 15 | M. | ☾ ON EQ. • ☾ AT APO. • Crab apples are ripe now. • {8.7 8.7 | *for* |
| 16 | Tu. | ☌♃☾ • ☌⛢☾ • ♀ STAT. • The Philadelphia Orchestra debuted, 1900 | *football* |
| 17 | W. | St. Hugh of Lincoln • First U.S. postage stamp with American eagle issued, 1851 • {9.2 8.7 | *stars,* |
| 18 | Th. | Botanist Asa Gray born, 1810 • Desoto car discontinued, 1960 • Tides {9.5 8.8 | *heavy* |
| 19 | Fr. | ♃ STAT. • *Old friends, old wine, and old gold are best.* | *snow* |
| 20 | Sa. | ☌☿♂ • Skunks hibernate now. • Tides {10.1 9.1 | *buries* |
| 21 | C | 26th S. af. P. • **Full Beaver** ○ • Tides {10.4 9.2 | *our* |
| 22 | M. | ☾ RIDES HIGH • Santa Ana winds in parts of southern Calif. made airborne rubble a hazard, 1957 | *cars.* |
| 23 | Tu. | St. Clement • U.S. president Franklin Pierce born, 1804 • Tides {10.7 — | *Thanks* |
| 24 | W. | ☾ AT ☋ • *The belly carries the legs and not the legs the belly.* • Tides {9.3 10.8 | *for* |
| 25 | Th. | **Thanksgiving Day** • National Independent Party organized, 1874 • Tides {9.3 10.7 | *turkey,* |
| 26 | Fr. | France's first satellite, *Astérix 1,* launched, 1961 • {9.3 10.6 | *bless* |
| 27 | Sa. | 0.5" snow began falling in northern Fla., 1912 • Tides {9.4 10.3 | *the* |
| 28 | C | 1st S. of. Advent • Basketball inventor James Naismith died, 1939 | *sage:* |
| 29 | M. | ☾ ON EQ. • Richard Byrd's expedition first to fly over South Pole, 1929 • Tides {9.8 9.9 | *ice* |
| 30 | Tu. | St. Andrew • ☾ AT PERIG. • Deadly tornado, Simsboro, La., 1996 • {10.1 9.7 | *age!* |

*I never think of the future—it comes soon enough.* –Albert Einstein

## *Farmer's Calendar*

■ The thing to remember about weather signs in nature is that they are highly reliable. In fact, many are never wrong. Consider the celebrated woolly bear caterpillar, larva of the Isabella tiger moth *(Pyrrharctia isabella).* It's a plump, 2-inch worm covered in soft bristles—black at the creature's ends and in its middle the color of a red fox. Everybody knows that the ratio of black bristles to rust on the woolly bear foretells the coming winter: More black bristles mean a hard winter; more rust, a mild one.

Or maybe it's the other way around. It scarcely matters. This is because woolly bears have been predicting the weather for a long time, and they know how to cover themselves. Some years ago, for example, we had an unusual spate of woolly bears in this neighborhood. They appeared late in the fall, after the frosts had set in, and they appeared in numbers. In a half-hour's walk, you'd see hundreds of woolly bears creeping across the road. On examination, they showed a great variety of color proportions, from nearly all-black to rust with the least dip of black at the ends. Evidently, then, there could be no kind of winter that some of them would not accurately predict.

The benefit for the would-be weather-wise is obvious. If you distrust the augury of a given woolly bear, then you simply ignore that caterpillar, take a step, and believe another.

CALENDAR

**SKY WATCH** ☆ *Dazzling in the east during the 2 hours before dawn, Venus attains its greatest brilliancy during the first week of this month, at a shadow-casting magnitude –4.9. This is its best month as a morning star. Venus floats just to the left of the crescent Moon on the mornings of the 2nd and the 31st. Mercury appears far below and to the left of Venus on the 30th and 31st. Brilliant Jupiter is prominent at dusk, setting at around midnight at midmonth. An exceptional total eclipse of the Moon is visible throughout North America early on the 21st. The partial eclipse begins at 1:32 A.M., with totality starting at 2:40 A.M. Winter arrives the same day, with the solstice at 6:38 P.M.*

| | | | |
|---|---|---|---|
| ● **New Moon** | 5th day | 12th hour | 36th minute |
| ◐ **First Quarter** | 13th day | 8th hour | 59th minute |
| ○ **Full Moon** | 21st day | 3rd hour | 13th minute |
| ◑ **Last Quarter** | 27th day | 23rd hour | 18th minute |

*All times are given in Eastern Standard Time.*

**Purchase these pages with times set to your zip code at MyLocalAlmanac.com.**

| Day of Year | Day of Month | Day of Week | ☼ Rises h. m. | Rise Key | ☼ Sets h. m. | Set Key | Length of Day h. m. | Sun Fast m. | Declination of Sun ° ' | High Tide Times Boston | | ☾ Rises h. m. | Rise Key | ☾ Sets h. m. | Set Key | ☾ Place | ☾ Age |
|---|---|---|---|---|---|---|---|---|---|---|---|---|---|---|---|---|---|
| 335 | 1 | W. | 6:53 | E | **4:12** | A | 9 19 | 27 | 21 s. 51 | 6¾ | **7¼** | 2:12 | E | **1:15** | C | VIR | 25 |
| 336 | 2 | Th. | 6:54 | E | **4:12** | A | 9 18 | 26 | 22 00 | 7¾ | **8¼** | 3:25 | E | **1:48** | B | VIR | 26 |
| 337 | 3 | Fr. | 6:55 | E | **4:12** | A | 9 17 | 26 | 22 08 | 8½ | **9¼** | 4:39 | E | **2:26** | B | VIR | 27 |
| 338 | 4 | Sa. | 6:56 | E | **4:11** | A | 9 15 | 26 | 22 17 | 9½ | **10** | 5:51 | E | **3:11** | B | LIB | 28 |
| 339 | 5 | **C** | 6:57 | E | **4:11** | A | 9 14 | 25 | 22 24 | 10¼ | **11** | 6:57 | E | **4:04** | B | SCO | 0 |
| 340 | 6 | M. | 6:58 | E | **4:11** | A | 9 13 | 25 | 22 32 | 11 | **11¾** | 7:55 | E | **5:03** | B | OPH | 1 |
| 341 | 7 | Tu. | 6:59 | E | **4:11** | A | 9 12 | 24 | 22 38 | 11¾ | — | 8:44 | E | **6:06** | B | SAG | 2 |
| 342 | 8 | W. | 7:00 | E | **4:11** | A | 9 11 | 24 | 22 45 | 12½ | **12½** | 9:24 | E | **7:11** | B | SAG | 3 |
| 343 | 9 | Th. | 7:01 | E | **4:11** | A | 9 10 | 23 | 22 51 | 1¼ | **1½** | 9:57 | E | **8:15** | C | SAG | 4 |
| 344 | 10 | Fr. | 7:02 | E | **4:11** | A | 9 09 | 23 | 22 56 | 2 | **2¼** | 10:24 | E | **9:17** | C | AQU | 5 |
| 345 | 11 | Sa. | 7:03 | E | **4:11** | A | 9 08 | 22 | 23 01 | 2¾ | **3** | 10:49 | D | **10:18** | D | CAP | 6 |
| 346 | 12 | **C** | 7:04 | E | **4:11** | A | 9 07 | 22 | 23 06 | 3½ | **3¾** | 11:11 | D | **11:17** | D | AQU | 7 |
| 347 | 13 | M. | 7:04 | E | **4:11** | A | 9 07 | 22 | 23 10 | 4½ | **4¾** | 11:33 | C | — | - | PSC | 8 |
| 348 | 14 | Tu. | 7:05 | E | **4:12** | A | 9 07 | 21 | 23 13 | 5¼ | **5½** | 11:56 | C | 12:16 | D | PSC | 9 |
| 349 | 15 | W. | 7:06 | E | **4:12** | A | 9 06 | 21 | 23 17 | 6 | **6½** | **12:20** | C | 1:16 | E | PSC | 10 |
| 350 | 16 | Th. | 7:07 | E | **4:12** | A | 9 05 | 20 | 23 19 | 6¾ | **7½** | **12:46** | B | 2:18 | E | PSC | 11 |
| 351 | 17 | Fr. | 7:07 | E | **4:12** | A | 9 05 | 20 | 23 21 | 7¾ | **8¼** | **1:18** | B | 3:21 | E | ARI | 12 |
| 352 | 18 | Sa. | 7:08 | E | **4:13** | A | 9 05 | 19 | 23 23 | 8½ | **9** | **1:56** | B | 4:26 | E | ARI | 13 |
| 353 | 19 | **C** | 7:08 | E | **4:13** | A | 9 05 | 19 | 23 25 | 9¼ | **9¾** | **2:43** | B | 5:29 | E | TAU | 14 |
| 354 | 20 | M. | 7:09 | E | **4:14** | A | 9 05 | 18 | 23 25 | 10 | **10¾** | **3:39** | B | 6:30 | E | TAU | 15 |
| 355 | 21 | Tu. | 7:10 | E | **4:14** | A | 9 04 | 18 | 23 26 | 10¾ | **11½** | **4:44** | B | 7:24 | E | TAU | 16 |
| 356 | 22 | W. | 7:10 | E | **4:15** | A | 9 05 | 17 | 23 26 | 11½ | — | **5:55** | B | 8:11 | E | GEM | 17 |
| 357 | 23 | Th. | 7:10 | E | **4:15** | A | 9 05 | 17 | 23 25 | 12¼ | **12¼** | **7:09** | C | 8:51 | E | GEM | 18 |
| 358 | 24 | Fr. | 7:11 | E | **4:16** | A | 9 05 | 16 | 23 24 | 1 | **1** | **8:23** | C | 9:25 | E | CAN | 19 |
| 359 | 25 | Sa. | 7:11 | E | **4:16** | A | 9 05 | 16 | 23 23 | 1¾ | **2** | **9:37** | D | 9:55 | D | LEO | 20 |
| 360 | 26 | **C** | 7:12 | E | **4:17** | A | 9 05 | 15 | 23 21 | 2½ | **2¾** | **10:50** | D | 10:23 | D | SEX | 21 |
| 361 | 27 | M. | 7:12 | E | **4:18** | A | 9 06 | 15 | 23 18 | 3½ | **3¾** | — | - | 10:50 | C | LEO | 22 |
| 362 | 28 | Tu. | 7:12 | E | **4:18** | A | 9 06 | 14 | 23 15 | 4¼ | **4¾** | 12:02 | E | 11:19 | C | VIR | 23 |
| 363 | 29 | W. | 7:12 | E | **4:19** | A | 9 07 | 14 | 23 12 | 5¼ | **5¾** | 1:15 | E | 11:49 | B | VIR | 24 |
| 364 | 30 | Th. | 7:13 | E | **4:20** | A | 9 07 | 13 | 23 08 | 6¼ | **7** | 2:27 | E | **12:25** | B | VIR | 25 |
| 365 | 31 | Fr. | 7:13 | E | **4:21** | A | 9 08 | 13 | 23 s. 04 | 7¼ | **8** | 3:38 | E | **1:06** | B | LIB | 26 |

 **To use this page, see p. 110; for Key Letters, see p. 234.** ☞ **Bold = P.M.** ☞ Light = A.M. 

## DECEMBER HATH 31 DAYS • 2010

*So timely you came, and well you chose,*
*You came when most needed, my winter rose.* –Alfred Austin

| Day of Month | Day of Week | Dates, Feasts, Fasts, Aspects, Tide Heights | Weather |
|---|---|---|---|
| 1 | W. | ☌♄☾ • ☿ GR. ELONG. (21° EAST) • First 12 nations signed Antarctic Treaty, 1959 • {10.5 9.7 | *Mild* |
| 2 | Th. | St. Viviana • First day of Chanukah • ☌♀☾ • {10.9 9.7 | *relief,* |
| 3 | Fr. | Quebec Bridge opened to rail traffic, Quebec City, 1917 • Tides {11.2 9.8 | *briefly—* |
| 4 | Sa. | ♀ GR. ILLUM. EXT. • Actress Deanna Durbin born, 1921 • Tides {11.4 9.8 | *cold* |
| 5 | C | **2nd S. of Advent** • New ● • ☾ RUNS LOW • ☌☿♇ | *and* |
| 6 | M. | St. Nicholas • ☾ AT ☊ • ☌♂☾ • ♅ STAT. • {11.3 9.7 | *snowy,* |
| 7 | Tu. | St. Ambrose • **Nat'l Pearl Harbor Remembrance Day** • ☌☿☾ • ☌♇☾ | *chiefly.* |
| 8 | W. | **Islamic New Year** • Astronaut Robert Lawrence killed during training exercise, 1967 • {9.6 10.8 | *Breath* |
| 9 | Th. | *Visits should be short, like a winter's day.* • Tides {9.4 10.4 | *makes* |
| 10 | Fr. | St. Eulalia • ☿ STAT. • Winterberry fruits especially showy now. • {9.1 9.9 | *vapors* |
| 11 | Sa. | ☌♆☾ • One of earliest recorded sightings of northern lights in North America, 1719 • {9.0 9.4 | *as* |
| 12 | C | **3rd S. of Advent** • 20.4" snow covered Newark, N.J., 1960 • Tides {8.8 9.0 | *we* |
| 13 | M. | St. Lucia • ☾ ON EQ. • ☾ AT APO. • ☌☿♂ • ☌♃☾ • {8.8 8.6 | *wield* |
| 14 | Tu. | Halcyon Days begin. • ☌☿♇ • ☌♅☾ • Tides {8.8 8.3 | *ice* |
| 15 | W. | Ember Day • *Moderate measures succeed best.* • Tides {8.9 8.2 | *scrapers.* |
| 16 | Th. | Colonists dumped British tea in harbor to protest taxation without representation, Boston, 1773 • {9.1 8.2 | *It's* |
| 17 | Fr. | Ember Day • Beware the Pogonip. • Tides {9.4 8.3 | *so wet* |
| 18 | Sa. | Ember Day • *Gifts burst rocks.* • Wind rolled snow into balls, Howe, Ind., 1933 • Tides {9.7 8.5 | *we* |
| 19 | C | **4th S. of Advent** • ☿ IN INF. ☌ • Tides {10.0 8.8 | *look* |
| 20 | M. | ☾ RIDES HIGH • S.C. seceded from Union, 1860 • Tides {10.5 9.0 | *amphibian;* |
| 21 | Tu. | St. Thomas • **Winter Solstice** • **Full Cold ○** • **Eclipse ☾** • ☾ AT ☋ | |
| 22 | W. | *In youth, we believe many things that are not true; in old age, we doubt many truths.* • {11.1 — | *Christmas* |
| 23 | Th. | Marjorie Child Husted, Betty Crocker creator, died, 1986 | *Day* |
| 24 | Fr. | "Stille Nacht" ("Silent Night") first performed, Oberndorf, Austria, 1818 • Tides {9.8 11.1 | *will* |
| 25 | Sa. | **Christmas** • ☾ AT PERIG. • *Santa Maria* abandoned near Hispaniola, 1492 | *feel* |
| 26 | C | **Boxing Day (Canada)** • **First day of Kwanzaa** • ☾ ON EQ. • ☌♇☉ | *Caribbean!* |
| 27 | M. | St. John • Poet Charles Olson born, 1910 • {10.2 10.1 | *Freezin's* |
| 28 | Tu. | Holy Innocents • ☌♄☾ • Iowa became 29th state, 1846 • {10.3 9.6 | *greetings,* |
| 29 | W. | St. Stephen[T] • Patriots' Randy Moss set NFL record with season's 23rd TD catch, 2007 | *everyone!* |
| 30 | Th. | ☿ STAT. • *A red Sun has water in his eye.* • {10.4 9.1 | *Welcome to* |
| 31 | Fr. | St. Sylvester • ☌♀☾ • Tides {10.5 9.1 | *two-oh-one-one!* |

## *Farmer's Calendar*

■ Thirty-one days hath December, as the world knows. In northern New England, this may strike us as a pitiful understatement. This long month can pack a lot into its days. Perhaps nature has given us December as a preview of the winter it inaugurates.

Every part of winter's repertoire is apt to be on offer this month. Hereabouts, the first days of December are really autumn days: There's seldom much snowfall and almost never any lasting snow cover. The days are short, but the sun is often warm, the temperature mild. The oaks and beeches may still bear most of their brown leaves.

By midmonth, things look different. The first snows have come and often, unfortunately, the first ice storms. Pleasant, semiautumnal days are over. The low Sun seems hardly to have risen properly before it's passing behind the western hills, setting in a brief, cold, rosy dusk that is beautiful in its way but that nobody would doubt belonged to winter. The hardwoods are mostly bare.

Then, by month's end, the world is frigid and, often, white. The snow shovel is in use. Daylight dwindles to a mere spark. But now, the solstice has passed. The days are growing longer. In the grand celestial mechanism, spring is inexorably advancing. December's characteristic synopsis of the months to come is complete. By Christmas, we've had a whole winter in a single month.

# JANUARY

## THE FIRST MONTH • 2011

**SKY WATCH** ☆ *Venus, a morning star, rises 3 hours before the Sun at a dazzling magnitude −4.7, its brightest of the year. It now reaches its highest point of 2011. Venus attains its greatest separation from the Sun, 47 degrees, on the 8th. Mercury is a morning star, too, visible at the lower left of Venus during the first 20 days of the month. Mars, however, lurks on the far side of the Sun, lost in its glare. In the evening sky, Jupiter is the brightest "star" at nightfall, in the southwest. Binoculars easily reveal blue-green Uranus just above it during the first week of the month. The Moon is near Mercury on the 2nd and Jupiter on the 9th. Saturn, in Virgo, rises at midnight. Earth reaches perihelion, its closest point to the Sun, on the 3rd.*

| | | | |
|---|---|---|---|
| ● **New Moon** | 4th day | 4th hour | 3rd minute |
| ◐ **First Quarter** | 12th day | 6th hour | 31st minute |
| ○ **Full Moon** | 19th day | 16th hour | 21st minute |
| ◑ **Last Quarter** | 26th day | 7th hour | 57th minute |

*All times are given in Eastern Standard Time.*

**Purchase these pages with times set to your zip code at MyLocalAlmanac.com.**

| Day of Year | Day of Month | Day of Week | ☼ Rises h. m. | Rise Key | ☼ Sets h. m. | Set Key | Length of Day h. m. | Sun Fast m. | Declination of Sun ° ′ | High Tide Times Boston | | ☾ Rises h. m. | Rise Key | ☾ Sets h. m. | Set Key | ☾ Place | ☾ Age |
|---|---|---|---|---|---|---|---|---|---|---|---|---|---|---|---|---|---|
| 1 | 1 | Sa. | 7:13 | E | **4:22** | A | 9 09 | 12 | 22s.59 | 8¼ | **9** | 4:44 | E | **1:54** | B | SCO | 27 |
| 2 | 2 | **B** | 7:13 | E | **4:23** | A | 9 10 | 12 | 22 54 | 9¼ | **10** | 5:44 | E | **2:50** | B | OPH | 28 |
| 3 | 3 | M. | 7:13 | E | **4:23** | A | 9 10 | 11 | 22 48 | 10 | **10¾** | 6:36 | E | **3:51** | B | SAG | 29 |
| 4 | 4 | Tu. | 7:13 | E | **4:24** | A | 9 11 | 11 | 22 42 | 10¾ | **11½** | 7:19 | E | **4:55** | B | SAG | 0 |
| 5 | 5 | W. | 7:13 | E | **4:25** | A | 9 12 | 10 | 22 35 | 11½ | — | 7:55 | E | **6:00** | C | SAG | 1 |
| 6 | 6 | Th. | 7:13 | E | **4:26** | A | 9 13 | 10 | 22 28 | 12¼ | **12¼** | 8:25 | E | **7:03** | C | CAP | 2 |
| 7 | 7 | Fr. | 7:13 | E | **4:27** | A | 9 14 | 10 | 22 21 | 12¾ | **1** | 8:51 | D | **8:05** | C | AQU | 3 |
| 8 | 8 | Sa. | 7:13 | E | **4:28** | A | 9 15 | 9 | 22 13 | 1½ | **1¾** | 9:14 | D | **9:05** | D | AQU | 4 |
| 9 | 9 | **B** | 7:12 | E | **4:29** | A | 9 17 | 9 | 22 04 | 2¼ | **2½** | 9:37 | C | **10:04** | D | PSC | 5 |
| 10 | 10 | M. | 7:12 | E | **4:30** | A | 9 18 | 8 | 21 55 | 3 | **3¼** | 9:59 | C | **11:03** | E | PSC | 6 |
| 11 | 11 | Tu. | 7:12 | E | **4:32** | A | 9 20 | 8 | 21 46 | 3½ | **4** | 10:21 | C | — | – | PSC | 7 |
| 12 | 12 | W. | 7:12 | E | **4:33** | A | 9 21 | 8 | 21 37 | 4½ | **4¾** | 10:47 | B | 12:04 | E | PSC | 8 |
| 13 | 13 | Th. | 7:11 | E | **4:34** | A | 9 23 | 7 | 21 27 | 5¼ | **5¾** | 11:15 | B | 1:05 | E | ARI | 9 |
| 14 | 14 | Fr. | 7:11 | E | **4:35** | A | 9 24 | 7 | 21 16 | 6 | **6¾** | 11:50 | B | 2:08 | E | ARI | 10 |
| 15 | 15 | Sa. | 7:10 | E | **4:36** | A | 9 26 | 6 | 21 05 | 7 | **7¾** | **12:31** | B | 3:11 | E | TAU | 11 |
| 16 | 16 | **B** | 7:10 | E | **4:37** | A | 9 27 | 6 | 20 54 | 7¾ | **8½** | **1:22** | B | 4:12 | E | TAU | 12 |
| 17 | 17 | M. | 7:09 | E | **4:38** | A | 9 29 | 6 | 20 42 | 8¾ | **9½** | **2:22** | B | 5:10 | E | TAU | 13 |
| 18 | 18 | Tu. | 7:09 | E | **4:40** | B | 9 31 | 5 | 20 30 | 9½ | **10¼** | **3:31** | B | 6:01 | E | GEM | 14 |
| 19 | 19 | W. | 7:08 | E | **4:41** | B | 9 33 | 5 | 20 18 | 10¼ | **11** | **4:46** | C | 6:45 | E | GEM | 15 |
| 20 | 20 | Th. | 7:08 | E | **4:42** | B | 9 34 | 5 | 20 05 | 11¼ | **11¾** | **6:02** | C | 7:23 | E | CAN | 16 |
| 21 | 21 | Fr. | 7:07 | E | **4:43** | B | 9 36 | 5 | 19 52 | **12** | — | **7:19** | D | 7:55 | D | LEO | 17 |
| 22 | 22 | Sa. | 7:06 | E | **4:45** | B | 9 39 | 4 | 19 38 | 12½ | **12¾** | **8:35** | D | 8:25 | D | SEX | 18 |
| 23 | 23 | **B** | 7:06 | E | **4:46** | B | 9 40 | 4 | 19 24 | 1¼ | **1¾** | **9:50** | E | 8:54 | C | LEO | 19 |
| 24 | 24 | M. | 7:05 | E | **4:47** | B | 9 42 | 4 | 19 10 | 2¼ | **2½** | **11:05** | E | 9:22 | C | VIR | 20 |
| 25 | 25 | Tu. | 7:04 | E | **4:48** | B | 9 44 | 4 | 18 55 | 3 | **3½** | — | – | 9:53 | B | VIR | 21 |
| 26 | 26 | W. | 7:03 | E | **4:50** | B | 9 47 | 3 | 18 40 | 4 | **4½** | 12:18 | E | 10:27 | B | VIR | 22 |
| 27 | 27 | Th. | 7:02 | E | **4:51** | B | 9 49 | 3 | 18 25 | 5 | **5½** | 1:29 | E | 11:06 | B | LIB | 23 |
| 28 | 28 | Fr. | 7:01 | E | **4:52** | B | 9 51 | 3 | 18 09 | 6 | **6¾** | 2:37 | E | 11:51 | B | LIB | 24 |
| 29 | 29 | Sa. | 7:00 | E | **4:54** | B | 9 54 | 3 | 17 53 | 7 | **7¾** | 3:38 | E | **12:44** | B | OPH | 25 |
| 30 | 30 | **B** | 7:00 | E | **4:55** | B | 9 55 | 3 | 17 37 | 8 | **8¾** | 4:32 | E | **1:42** | B | OPH | 26 |
| 31 | 31 | M. | 6:59 | E | **4:56** | B | 9 57 | 2 | 17s.20 | 9 | **9¾** | 5:17 | E | **2:44** | B | SAG | 27 |

 **To use this page, see p. 110; for Key Letters, see p. 234.** ☞ **Bold = P.M.** ☞ Light = A.M. 

# JANUARY HATH 31 DAYS • 2011

*I hear you, blithe new year,*
*Ring out your laughter.* –Abba Goold Woolson

| Day of Month | Day of Week | Dates, Feasts, Fasts, Aspects, Tide Heights | Weather |
|---|---|---|---|
| 1 | Sa. | New Year's Day • **Holy Name** • Baseball player Hank Greenberg born, 1911 • {10.7 / 9.1 | *Snow's* |
| 2 | **B** | ☾ RUNS LOW • ☌☿☾ • ☌♃♅ • Tides {10.7 / 9.2 | *sporadic,* |
| 3 | M. | ☾ AT ☊ • ☌♇☾ • ⊕ AT PERIHELION • Tides {10.8 / 9.3 | *but* |
| 4 | Tu. | **St. Elizabeth Ann Seton** • **New ●** • **Eclipse ☉** • ☌♂☾ | *the* |
| 5 | W. | Twelfth Night • *A kindly, good Janiveer / Freezeth the pot by the fire.* • Tides {10.6 / — | *cold's* |
| 6 | Th. | **Epiphany** • Lion-tailed macaque born, Woodland Park Zoo, Seattle, Wash., 1989 | *emphatic!* |
| 7 | Fr. | Distaff Day • ☌♆☾ • Movie "Edison Kinetoscopic Record of a Sneeze" made, 1894 | *Flurries* |
| 8 | Sa. | ♀ GR. ELONG. (47° WEST) • 15,000+ troops began aid during multiday ice storm, Ont./Que., 1998 | *require* |
| 9 | **B** | **1st S. af. Ep.** • ☾ ON EQ. • ☿ GR. ELONG. (23° WEST) • {9.2 / 9.4 | *furries.* |
| 10 | M. | Plough Monday • ☾ AT APO. • ☌♃☾ • ☌♅☾ • {9.1 / 8.9 | *Dogsledders* |
| 11 | Tu. | Sir Edmund Hillary (first to summit Mt. Everest) died, 2008 | *mush* |
| 12 | W. | *When the wine is in, the wit is out.* • Tides {8.9 / 8.2 | *through* |
| 13 | Th. | **St. Hilary** • *All in the Family* made television debut, 1971 • Tides {8.9 / 8.0 | *slop* |
| 14 | Fr. | Deadly avalanche near Park City, Utah, 2005 • Tides {9.0 / 7.9 | *and* |
| 15 | Sa. | –54° to 49°F in 24 hours, Loma, Mont., 1972 • Tides {9.3 / 8.1 | *slush.* |
| 16 | **B** | **2nd S. af. Ep.** • ☾ RIDES HIGH • {9.7 / 8.4 | *Bombarded,* |
| 17 | M. | **Martin Luther King Jr.'s Birthday (observed)** • ☾ AT ☋ • ☌☿♇ • Ben Franklin born, 1706 | *then* |
| 18 | Tu. | 211-lb. striped marlin caught, Red Hill, Hawaii, 1996 | *bitter—* |
| 19 | W. | **Full Wolf ○** • *Life is like the Moon, now dark, now full.* • {11.1 / 9.8 | *this* |
| 20 | Th. | JFK sworn in as 35th U.S. president, 1961 • Tides {11.5 / 10.3 | *winter's* |
| 21 | Fr. | ☾ AT PERIG. • Pittsburgh Steelers won their third Super Bowl, 1979 • Tides {11.6 / — | *no* |
| 22 | Sa. | **St. Vincent** • ☾ ON EQ. • Philosopher Sir Francis Bacon born, 1561 • {10.7 / 11.6 | *quitter!* |
| 23 | **B** | **3rd S. af. Ep.** • Composer Samuel Barber died, 1981 • {10.9 / 11.3 | *Storms* |
| 24 | M. | Soviet satellite *Cosmos 954* crashed in N.W.T., leaking radioactive waste, 1978 • Tides {11.0 / 10.8 | *are* |
| 25 | Tu. | **Conversion of Paul** • ☌♄☾ • Nellie Bly completed around-the-world trip, 1890 | *various,* |
| 26 | W. | **Sts. Timothy & Titus** • Raccoons mate now. • Tides {10.7 / 9.5 | *but* |
| 27 | Th. | ♄ STAT. • *From small beginnings come great things.* • {10.4 / 9.0 | *not* |
| 28 | Fr. | **St. Thomas Aquinas** • Christa McAuliffe and six others killed in space shuttle accident, 1986 | *enough* |
| 29 | Sa. | ☾ RUNS LOW • ☌♀☾ • Kansas became 34th state, 1861 | *to* |
| 30 | **B** | ☾ AT ☊ • ☌♇☾ • Two-day storm brought 11" snow, Birmingham, Ala., 1936 • {10.1 / 8.7 | *bury* |
| 31 | M. | *There is no pillow so soft as a clear conscience.* • {10.2 / 8.9 | *us!* |

## *Farmer's Calendar*

■ Why is it that weather, and its associated hardships, should make liars of so many otherwise honest men and women? For certainly there can be no doubt of the effect: The worse, the more adverse, conditions become, the more irresistible is the force with which they push us to mendacity. A snowfall of 4 inches gets reported as half a foot. A thermometer reading of –13°F, in the telling, is rounded to –20°F.

I myself have not been deaf to the weather's call to falsehood, even in a life dedicated to the earnest upholding of truthfulness in all things. A few years ago, an early winter storm knocked out the electric power in this vicinity for days. It was the longest outage that we've had in years.

At this place, we were comparatively lucky. The power was out for 4 days. Well, not exactly. To be sure, 4 days is the length of the ordeal as I have since reported it. But if I consult the record, I find that the power failed in the middle of a Sunday night and was restored late Wednesday afternoon. That's no walk in the park, but it's tough to make an honest 4 days out of it. Two and three quarters would be more factual. No matter: Four days it is and will forever be. So easily is the iron of fact led astray by the magnet of narrative necessity as it concerns the weather.

CALENDAR

**SKY WATCH** ☆ *Mars is in conjunction with the Sun on the 4th and invisible. It will remain dim and on the Sun's side of the sky until December. Jupiter, now lower at nightfall but still conspicuous, is near the Moon on the 6th. Saturn, its rings not as edgewise as last year, rises at 10:30 P.M. on the 1st and 8:30 P.M. at month's end, in Virgo, brightening from magnitude 0.7 to 0.5. It stands to the left of the Moon on the 20th. At least 30× magnification is needed to observe the rings. Meanwhile in the predawn sky, Venus, in Sagittarius, hovers at the right of Pluto early in the month and floats to the left of the crescent Moon on the 28th. Still striking, the morning star is noticeably losing height and dazzle.*

| | | | |
|---|---|---|---|
| ● **New Moon** | 2nd day | 21st hour | 31st minute |
| ◐ **First Quarter** | 11th day | 2nd hour | 18th minute |
| ○ **Full Moon** | 18th day | 3rd hour | 36th minute |
| ◑ **Last Quarter** | 24th day | 18th hour | 26th minute |

*All times are given in Eastern Standard Time.*

**Purchase these pages with times set to your zip code at MyLocalAlmanac.com.**

| Day of Year | Day of Month | Day of Week | ☼ Rises h. m. | Rise Key | ☼ Sets h. m. | Set Key | Length of Day h. m. | Sun Fast m. | Declination of Sun ° ′ | High Tide Times Boston | | ☾ Rises h. m. | Rise Key | ☾ Sets h. m. | Set Key | ☾ Place | ☾ Age |
|---|---|---|---|---|---|---|---|---|---|---|---|---|---|---|---|---|---|
| 32 | 1 | Tu. | 6:58 | E | **4:57** | B | 9 59 | 2 | 17s. 03 | 9¾ | **10½** | 5:55 | E | **3:48** | B | SAG | 28 |
| 33 | 2 | W. | 6:56 | E | **4:59** | B | 10 03 | 2 | 16 46 | 10½ | **11¼** | 6:27 | E | **4:51** | C | CAP | 0 |
| 34 | 3 | Th. | 6:55 | E | **5:00** | B | 10 05 | 2 | 16 28 | 11¼ | **11¾** | 6:54 | D | **5:53** | C | AQU | 1 |
| 35 | 4 | Fr. | 6:54 | D | **5:01** | B | 10 07 | 2 | 16 10 | **12** | — | 7:18 | D | **6:54** | D | CAP | 2 |
| 36 | 5 | Sa. | 6:53 | D | **5:03** | B | 10 10 | 2 | 15 52 | 12½ | **12½** | 7:41 | D | **7:54** | D | AQU | 3 |
| 37 | 6 | **B** | 6:52 | D | **5:04** | B | 10 12 | 2 | 15 34 | 1 | **1¼** | 8:03 | C | **8:53** | E | PSC | 4 |
| 38 | 7 | M. | 6:51 | D | **5:05** | B | 10 14 | 2 | 15 15 | 1½ | **1¾** | 8:26 | C | **9:52** | E | PSC | 5 |
| 39 | 8 | Tu. | 6:50 | D | **5:07** | B | 10 17 | 2 | 14 56 | 2¼ | **2½** | 8:50 | B | **10:53** | E | PSC | 6 |
| 40 | 9 | W. | 6:48 | D | **5:08** | B | 10 20 | 2 | 14 37 | 3 | **3¼** | 9:16 | B | **11:54** | E | PSC | 7 |
| 41 | 10 | Th. | 6:47 | D | **5:09** | B | 10 22 | 2 | 14 18 | 3¾ | **4¼** | 9:48 | B | — | – | ARI | 8 |
| 42 | 11 | Fr. | 6:46 | D | **5:11** | B | 10 25 | 2 | 13 58 | 4½ | **5** | 10:25 | B | 12:55 | E | ARI | 9 |
| 43 | 12 | Sa. | 6:45 | D | **5:12** | B | 10 27 | 2 | 13 38 | 5¼ | **6** | 11:10 | B | 1:56 | E | TAU | 10 |
| 44 | 13 | **B** | 6:43 | D | **5:13** | B | 10 30 | 2 | 13 18 | 6¼ | **7** | **12:04** | B | 2:54 | E | TAU | 11 |
| 45 | 14 | M. | 6:42 | D | **5:14** | B | 10 32 | 2 | 12 58 | 7¼ | **8** | **1:07** | B | 3:47 | E | GEM | 12 |
| 46 | 15 | Tu. | 6:41 | D | **5:16** | B | 10 35 | 2 | 12 37 | 8¼ | **8¾** | **2:18** | B | 4:34 | E | GEM | 13 |
| 47 | 16 | W. | 6:39 | D | **5:17** | B | 10 38 | 2 | 12 16 | 9 | **9¾** | **3:33** | C | 5:15 | E | CAN | 14 |
| 48 | 17 | Th. | 6:38 | D | **5:18** | B | 10 40 | 2 | 11 55 | 10 | **10½** | **4:51** | C | 5:50 | E | CAN | 15 |
| 49 | 18 | Fr. | 6:36 | D | **5:20** | B | 10 44 | 2 | 11 34 | 10¾ | **11¼** | **6:09** | D | 6:22 | D | LEO | 16 |
| 50 | 19 | Sa. | 6:35 | D | **5:21** | B | 10 46 | 2 | 11 13 | 11¾ | — | **7:27** | E | 6:52 | D | SEX | 17 |
| 51 | 20 | **B** | 6:33 | D | **5:22** | B | 10 49 | 2 | 10 52 | 12 | **12½** | **8:45** | E | 7:22 | C | VIR | 18 |
| 52 | 21 | M. | 6:32 | D | **5:23** | B | 10 51 | 2 | 10 30 | 1 | **1¼** | **10:02** | E | 7:53 | B | VIR | 19 |
| 53 | 22 | Tu. | 6:30 | D | **5:25** | B | 10 55 | 2 | 10 08 | 1¾ | **2¼** | **11:16** | E | 8:27 | B | VIR | 20 |
| 54 | 23 | W. | 6:29 | D | **5:26** | B | 10 57 | 3 | 9 46 | 2½ | **3¼** | — | – | 9:06 | B | LIB | 21 |
| 55 | 24 | Th. | 6:27 | D | **5:27** | B | 11 00 | 3 | 9 24 | 3½ | **4¼** | 12:27 | E | 9:50 | B | LIB | 22 |
| 56 | 25 | Fr. | 6:26 | D | **5:28** | B | 11 02 | 3 | 9 02 | 4½ | **5¼** | 1:32 | E | 10:41 | B | OPH | 23 |
| 57 | 26 | Sa. | 6:24 | D | **5:30** | B | 11 06 | 3 | 8 39 | 5½ | **6½** | 2:28 | E | 11:38 | B | OPH | 24 |
| 58 | 27 | **B** | 6:23 | D | **5:31** | C | 11 08 | 3 | 8 17 | 6¾ | **7½** | 3:16 | E | **12:38** | B | SAG | 25 |
| 59 | 28 | M. | 6:21 | D | **5:32** | C | 11 11 | 3 | 7s. 54 | 7¾ | **8½** | 3:56 | E | **1:41** | B | SAG | 26 |

 **To use this page, see p. 110; for Key Letters, see p. 234.** ☞ **Bold = P.M.** ☞ Light = A.M. 

# FEBRUARY HATH 28 DAYS • 2011

*'Tis Cupid come with loving art*
*To honor, worship, and implore.* –Frank Dempster Sherman

| Day of Month | Day of Week | Dates, Feasts, Fasts, Aspects, Tide Heights | Weather |
|---|---|---|---|
| 1 | Tu. | **St. Brigid** • ☌☿☾ • Canadian prime minister Louis Stephen St. Laurent born, 1882 | *Groundhog* |
| 2 | W. | **Candlemas** • Groundhog Day • **New ●** • Tides {10.3 / 9.3} | *cowers:* |
| 3 | Th. | **Chinese New Year** • ☌♂☾ • Journalist Horace Greeley born, 1811 • {10.3 / 9.4} | *sunshine,* |
| 4 | Fr. | ☌♂☉ • ☌♆☾ • –49°F, Calgary, Alta., 1893 • Tides {10.2 / —} | *then* |
| 5 | Sa. | **St. Agatha** • ☾ ON EQ. • Deadly 87-tornado outbreak began, South and Midwest, 2008 | *showers.* |
| 6 | **B** | ☾ AT APO. • ☌♅☾ • U.S. president Ronald Reagan born, 1911 | *Too* |
| 7 | M. | ☌♃☾ • Walt Disney's movie *Pinocchio* debuted, 1940 • Tides {9.5 / 9.4} | *warm* |
| 8 | Tu. | *Under the snow the vegetables purr, Like an old man 'neath a mantle of fur.* • Tides {9.4 / 9.0} | *for* |
| 9 | W. | ☌♀♇ • Britain's Princess Margaret died, 2002 • {9.3 / 8.6} | *storms.* |
| 10 | Th. | Peggy Fleming won Olympic gold medal, figure skating, 1968 • Tides {9.1 / 8.2} | *Mercury* |
| 11 | Fr. | Largest lobster on record (44 lbs. 6 oz.) caught near N.S., 1977 • Tides {9.1 / 7.9} | *plummets,* |
| 12 | Sa. | First Lady Louisa Adams born, 1775 • Tides {9.1 / 7.9} | *fingers* |
| 13 | **B** | ☾ RIDES HIGH • First U.S. quintuplets born, Watertown, Wis., 1875 • Tides {9.3 / 8.0} | *turn* |
| 14 | M. | **Sts. Cyril & Methodius** • **Valentine's Day** • ☾ AT ☋ | *numb: It's* |
| 15 | Tu. | Susan B. Anthony born, 1820 • Tides {10.1 / 9.0} | *frigid air.* |
| 16 | W. | Winter's back breaks. • First fruit tree patent (peach) in U.S., 1932 • {10.7 / 9.7} | *Pleasurable,* |
| 17 | Th. | ☌♆☉ • Confederate *H. L. Hunley* first submarine to sink a warship (USS *Housatonic*), 1864 | *then* |
| 18 | Fr. | **Full Snow ○** • *It is no use going to the goat's house to look for wool.* | *unmeasurable* |
| 19 | Sa. | ☾ ON EQ. • ☾ AT PERIG. • Sen. Carl Hayden honored for 50 years of Congressional service, 1962 | *out* |
| 20 | **B** | **Septuagesima** • ☌☿♂ • ☌☿♆ • ☌♂♆ | *there!* |
| 21 | M. | **Washington's Birthday (observed)** • ☌♄☾ • Tides {11.6 / 11.3} | *Starting* |
| 22 | Tu. | Artist Rembrandt Peale born, 1778 • Tides {11.5 / 10.7} | *to* |
| 23 | W. | Blizzard stranded 750 motorists, Sierra Nevada, Calif., 1936 | *drip—* |
| 24 | Th. | **St. Matthias** • Folklorist Wilhelm Grimm born, 1786 • Tides {10.8 / 9.4} | *it's* |
| 25 | Fr. | ☾ RUNS LOW • ☿ IN SUP. ☌ • First tunnel (railroad) under Hudson River opened, N.J.–N.Y.C., 1908 | *a pip!* |
| 26 | Sa. | ☾ AT ☊ • NASA announced Venus is about 800°F, 1963 • {9.9 / 8.5} | *Wet 'n' wild,* |
| 27 | **B** | **Sexagesima** • ☌♇☾ • Saccharin discovered, 1879 | *but* |
| 28 | M. | ☌♀☾ • *He who goes to bed hungry dreams of pancakes.* • Tides {9.6 / 8.6} | *mild.* |

*One can not manage too many affairs; like pumpkins in water, one pops up while you try to hold down the other.*
–Chinese proverb

## *Farmer's Calendar*

■ The weather is not, like cosmology or the birth and death of stars, a remote system of hypothetical cataclysms describable only by the highest mathematics. It happens to us, it affects us. Therefore, the weather is in our heads as much as it is in the external world. It's in our heads and in our habits—and it's quite remarkable how quickly those habits form.

Several years ago, this district had a uniquely mild and open winter. January temperatures reached the sixties, and the snow held off into February. People were worried. They claimed to find this newfangled, no-snow winter disquieting, impossible to reconcile with the settled order of things. If you can't crank up a real winter in the Green Mountains, then the times really are out of joint.

So they said. As it turned out, many seemed to get used to the open winter more quickly and easily than they let on, judging by their reaction when something like a real winter arrived at last. I know that I did. Around Groundhog Day, we got a couple of inches of fluff. As I went forth to shovel, I found myself aggrieved, insulted. I felt put upon. So quickly had I formed the habit of this snowless winter that the necessity of clearing a quantity of snow negligible in any other year came to me as an affront and seemed to present an unreasonable ordeal.

# THE THIRD MONTH • 2011

**SKY WATCH** ☆ *Venus stands to the right of the crescent Moon on the 1st and is best seen an hour before sunrise. It continues getting lower in the sky and less brilliant. On the 6th, five planets and the Moon all crowd within 22 degrees of the Sun, but only Jupiter is visible in the glare, to the left of the Moon. Mercury, near Jupiter, has its best evening apparition of the year starting around the 11th, 40 minutes after sunset; it's best seen at midmonth, when it hovers just to the right of Jupiter. Saturn rises at 8:00 P.M. at midmonth. The full Moon on the 19th is the closest Moon of the year. It will not again come this close to Earth until 2016. (Expect rare, unusually high tides.) Spring arrives with the vernal equinox on the 20th at 7:21 P.M.*

| | | | | |
|---|---|---|---|---|
| ● | **New Moon** | 4th day | 15th hour | 46th minute |
| ◐ | **First Quarter** | 12th day | 18th hour | 45th minute |
| ○ | **Full Moon** | 19th day | 14th hour | 10th minute |
| ◑ | **Last Quarter** | 26th day | 8th hour | 7th minute |

*After 2:00 A.M. on March 13, Eastern Daylight Time is given.*

**Purchase these pages with times set to your zip code at MyLocalAlmanac.com.**

| Day of Year | Day of Month | Day of Week | ☼ Rises h. m. | Rise Key | ☼ Sets h. m. | Set Key | Length of Day h. m. | Sun Fast m. | Declination of Sun ° ' | High Tide Times Boston | | ☾ Rises h. m. | Rise Key | ☾ Sets h. m. | Set Key | ☾ Place | ☾ Age |
|---|---|---|---|---|---|---|---|---|---|---|---|---|---|---|---|---|---|
| 60 | 1 | Tu. | 6:20 | D | **5:33** | C | 11 13 | 4 | 7 s.31 | 8¾ | **9¼** | 4:29 | E | **2:43** | C | CAP | 27 |
| 61 | 2 | W. | 6:18 | D | **5:34** | C | 11 16 | 4 | 7 09 | 9½ | **10** | 4:58 | E | **3:45** | C | AQU | 28 |
| 62 | 3 | Th. | 6:16 | D | **5:36** | C | 11 20 | 4 | 6 46 | 10¼ | **10¾** | 5:23 | D | **4:46** | D | CAP | 29 |
| 63 | 4 | Fr. | 6:15 | D | **5:37** | C | 11 22 | 4 | 6 23 | 11 | **11¼** | 5:46 | D | **5:45** | D | AQU | 0 |
| 64 | 5 | Sa. | 6:13 | D | **5:38** | C | 11 25 | 4 | 5 59 | 11½ | 12 | 6:08 | C | **6:45** | D | PSC | 1 |
| 65 | 6 | **B** | 6:11 | D | **5:39** | C | 11 28 | 5 | 5 36 | **12¼** | — | 6:31 | C | **7:44** | E | PSC | 2 |
| 66 | 7 | M. | 6:10 | D | **5:40** | C | 11 30 | 5 | 5 13 | 12½ | **12¾** | 6:54 | C | **8:44** | E | PSC | 3 |
| 67 | 8 | Tu. | 6:08 | C | **5:42** | C | 11 34 | 5 | 4 49 | 1 | **1½** | 7:20 | B | **9:44** | E | PSC | 4 |
| 68 | 9 | W. | 6:06 | C | **5:43** | C | 11 37 | 5 | 4 26 | 1¾ | **2** | 7:50 | B | **10:45** | E | ARI | 5 |
| 69 | 10 | Th. | 6:05 | C | **5:44** | C | 11 39 | 6 | 4 02 | 2¼ | **2¾** | 8:24 | B | **11:45** | E | ARI | 6 |
| 70 | 11 | Fr. | 6:03 | C | **5:45** | C | 11 42 | 6 | 3 39 | 3 | **3½** | 9:05 | B | — | - | TAU | 7 |
| 71 | 12 | Sa. | 6:01 | C | **5:46** | C | 11 45 | 6 | 3 15 | 3¾ | **4½** | 9:54 | B | 12:43 | E | TAU | 8 |
| 72 | 13 | **B** | 7:00 | C | **6:48** | C | 11 48 | 6 | 2 52 | 5¾ | **6½** | 11:52 | B | 1:36 | E | TAU | 9 |
| 73 | 14 | M. | 6:58 | C | **6:49** | C | 11 51 | 7 | 2 28 | 6¾ | **7½** | **12:57** | B | 3:24 | E | GEM | 10 |
| 74 | 15 | Tu. | 6:56 | C | **6:50** | C | 11 54 | 7 | 2 04 | 7¾ | **8½** | **2:07** | C | 4:06 | E | GEM | 11 |
| 75 | 16 | W. | 6:54 | C | **6:51** | C | 11 57 | 7 | 1 41 | 8¾ | **9¼** | **3:22** | C | 4:44 | E | CAN | 12 |
| 76 | 17 | Th. | 6:53 | C | **6:52** | C | 11 59 | 8 | 1 17 | 9¾ | **10¼** | **4:39** | D | 5:17 | E | LEO | 13 |
| 77 | 18 | Fr. | 6:51 | C | **6:53** | C | 12 02 | 8 | 0 53 | 10½ | **11** | **5:57** | D | 5:48 | D | SEX | 14 |
| 78 | 19 | Sa. | 6:49 | C | **6:55** | C | 12 06 | 8 | 0 29 | 11½ | 12 | **7:15** | E | 6:18 | C | LEO | 15 |
| 79 | 20 | **B** | 6:47 | C | **6:56** | C | 12 09 | 8 | 0 s.06 | **12¼** | — | **8:34** | E | 6:49 | C | VIR | 16 |
| 80 | 21 | M. | 6:46 | C | **6:57** | C | 12 11 | 9 | 0 N.17 | 12¾ | **1¼** | **9:53** | E | 7:22 | B | VIR | 17 |
| 81 | 22 | Tu. | 6:44 | C | **6:58** | C | 12 14 | 9 | 0 41 | 1½ | **2** | **11:09** | E | 8:00 | B | VIR | 18 |
| 82 | 23 | W. | 6:42 | C | **6:59** | C | 12 17 | 9 | 1 04 | 2¼ | **3** | — | - | 8:44 | B | LIB | 19 |
| 83 | 24 | Th. | 6:41 | C | **7:00** | C | 12 19 | 10 | 1 28 | 3¼ | **3¾** | 12:18 | E | 9:34 | B | SCO | 20 |
| 84 | 25 | Fr. | 6:39 | C | **7:01** | C | 12 22 | 10 | 1 52 | 4¼ | **4¾** | 1:20 | E | 10:31 | B | OPH | 21 |
| 85 | 26 | Sa. | 6:37 | C | **7:03** | C | 12 26 | 10 | 2 15 | 5¼ | **6** | 2:12 | E | 11:32 | B | SAG | 22 |
| 86 | 27 | **B** | 6:35 | C | **7:04** | C | 12 29 | 10 | 2 39 | 6¼ | **7** | 2:55 | E | **12:34** | B | SAG | 23 |
| 87 | 28 | M. | 6:34 | C | **7:05** | D | 12 31 | 11 | 3 02 | 7¼ | **8** | 3:31 | E | **1:37** | B | SAG | 24 |
| 88 | 29 | Tu. | 6:32 | C | **7:06** | D | 12 34 | 11 | 3 25 | 8¼ | **9** | 4:01 | E | **2:39** | C | CAP | 25 |
| 89 | 30 | W. | 6:30 | C | **7:07** | D | 12 37 | 11 | 3 49 | 9¼ | **9¾** | 4:27 | D | **3:40** | C | CAP | 26 |
| 90 | 31 | Th. | 6:28 | C | **7:08** | D | 12 40 | 12 | 4 N.12 | 10¼ | **10½** | 4:51 | D | **4:39** | D | AQU | 27 |

**To use this page, see p. 110; for Key Letters, see p. 234.** ☞ **Bold = P.M.** ☞ Light = A.M.

MARCH HATH 31 DAYS • 2011

*Look all around thee!*
*How the spring advances!* –Ludwig Tieck

| Day of Month | Day of Week | Dates, Feasts, Fasts, Aspects, Tide Heights | Weather |
|---|---|---|---|
| 1 | Tu. | St. David • Johnny Cash married June Carter, 1968 • {9.7 / 8.9 | *Bright* |
| 2 | W. | St. Chad • Hatch Act allowed creation of state agricultural experiment stations, 1887 • {9.8 / 9.1 | *and* |
| 3 | Th. | ☌♆☾ • Fla. admitted to Union as 27th state, 1845 | *chilly,* |
| 4 | Fr. | New ● • ☌♂☾ • Abe Lincoln became 16th U.S. president, 1861 • {10.0 / 9.6 | *then* |
| 5 | Sa. | St. Piran • ☾ ON EQ. • ☌☿☾ • Tides {9.9 / 9.7 | *flakes* |
| 6 | **B** | **Quinquagesima** • ☾ AT APO. • ☌♅☾ • {9.8 / — | *willy-nilly.* |
| 7 | M. | St. Perpetua • **Pure Monday** • ☌♃☾ • TV's Willard Scott born, 1934 | *Clearing,* |
| 8 | Tu. | Shrove Tuesday • 1.6-inch-diameter hail, Erin, Ont., 1879 • Tides {9.8 / 9.3 | *not* |
| 9 | W. | **Ash Wednesday** • ☌☿♅ • Barbie doll debuted, 1959 | *warming;* |
| 10 | Th. | *Chickens are slow in coming from unlaid eggs.* • {9.6 / 8.7 | *milder,* |
| 11 | Fr. | Astronomer Urbain Le Verrier born, 1811 • Tides {9.4 / 8.4 | *but* |
| 12 | Sa. | ☾ RIDES HIGH • Severe flooding began in New England, 1936 • Tides {9.3 / 8.2 | *storming.* |
| 13 | **B** | **1st S. in Lent** • **Sunday of Orthodoxy** • **Daylight Saving Time begins, 2:00 A.M.** • ☾ AT ☋ | |
| 14 | M. | Possible UFO sighted, Healdsburg, Calif., 1958 • {9.4 / 8.4 | *Gray day* |
| 15 | Tu. | Beware the ides of March. • Emperor Julius Caesar died, 44 B.C. | *for* |
| 16 | W. | Ember Day • ☌☿♃ • *A peck of March dust is worth a king's ransom.* • Tides {10.2 / 9.5 | *the* |
| 17 | Th. | St. Patrick • Julie Croteau first woman to play NCAA baseball, 1989 • Tides {10.7 / 10.3 | *Irish:* |
| 18 | Fr. | Ember Day • ☾ ON EQ. • Largest art theft in U.S., Gardner Museum, Boston, 1990 | *damp* |
| 19 | Sa. | St. Joseph • Ember Day • **Full Worm** ○ • ☾ AT PERIG. • Tides {11.5 / 11.6 | *and* |
| 20 | **B** | **2nd S. in Lent** • **Vernal Equinox** • ☌♄☾ • {11.7 / — | *mire-ish.* |
| 21 | M. | ☌♅☉ • MLK began third march from Selma to Montgomery, Ala., 1965 • {12.0 / 11.5 | *Equinox* |
| 22 | Tu. | ☿ GR. ELONG. (19° EAST) • Mt. Redoubt volcano erupted, Alaska, 2009 • Tides {12.1 / 11.1 | *brings* |
| 23 | W. | Chipmunks emerge from hibernation now. • *A change is as good as a rest.* | *snowy* |
| 24 | Th. | Writer Jules Verne died, 1905 • 92°F, St. Louis, Mo., 1929 • Tides {11.4 / 10.0 | *shocks.* |
| 25 | Fr. | Annunciation • ☾ RUNS LOW • ☾ AT ☊ • Triangle Factory fire, N.Y.C., 1911 | *A flash* |
| 26 | Sa. | ☌♀♆ • ☌♇☾ • North West Company merged with Hudson's Bay Company, 1821 | *of sun,* |
| 27 | **B** | **3rd S. in Lent** • X-43A Scramjet flew at Mach 7, 2004 • {9.7 / 8.6 | *a splash* |
| 28 | M. | *Quarrels would not last long if the wrongs were all on one side.* • Tides {9.4 / 8.6 | *of rain:* |
| 29 | Tu. | Washington, D.C., residents allowed to vote in presidential elections, 1961 • Tides {9.3 / 8.8 | *Is it* |
| 30 | W. | ☌♆☾ • ☿ STAT. • Racehorse Secretariat born, 1970 • {9.3 / 9.0 | *spring* |
| 31 | Th. | ☌♀☾ • *Oklahoma!* premiered on Broadway, 1943 | *again?* |

## *Farmer's Calendar*

■ Our farmer forefathers in Vermont ordained Town Meeting to be held on the first Tuesday in March because that date came during a slack time in the agricultural year, a time when a day for the sake of self-government might be spared from the business of living. They may also have sought, in fixing the time of Town Meeting, to demonstrate their hardihood in the face of the kind of weather early March can bring to these parts. Snow, deep cold, and ice storms are common in this period. Town Meeting Day can present a challenge to those who would sally forth each year to polish the medallion of democracy.

And yet, sally forth they do. In my decades hereabouts, only once has our town's annual meeting been canceled due to weather. This was some years back, during an epic snowstorm. The meeting was postponed for a day. Frustration among the civic-minded was deeply felt. But, really, need it have been? After all, Town Meeting democracy is strenuous stuff. Politics is on display, likewise passion, likewise personality. And mostly, there is talk—followed by more talk. On the day of the Town Meeting Storm, we got 2 feet of snow, high winds, and near-zero visibility. In other words, conditions not unlike Town Meeting itself. In a way, we got two Town Meetings that year instead of one.

**SKY WATCH** ☆ *Saturn arrives at opposition on the night of the 3rd, when it is at its closest point to Earth of 2011. It rises at sunset and is visible at magnitude 0.4 all night long as the sole naked-eye planet. Jupiter does the opposite, reaching conjunction behind the Sun on the 6th. It joins Uranus, Mercury, Mars, Venus, and the Moon, all behind the Sun on the 30th and bunched up in Pisces. From far southern locations, such as Miami, this striking gathering may be glimpsed very low in the east, 40 minutes before sunrise. From farther south, below the equator, this group is higher and easier to see.*

| | | | | |
|---|---|---|---|---|
| ● | **New Moon** | 3rd day | 10th hour | 32nd minute |
| ◐ | **First Quarter** | 11th day | 8th hour | 5th minute |
| ○ | **Full Moon** | 17th day | 22nd hour | 44th minute |
| ◑ | **Last Quarter** | 24th day | 22nd hour | 47th minute |

*All times are given in Eastern Daylight Time.*

**Purchase these pages with times set to your zip code at MyLocalAlmanac.com.**

| Day of Year | Day of Month | Day of Week | Rises h. m. | Rise Key | Sets h. m. | Set Key | Length of Day h. m. | Sun Fast m. | Declination of Sun ° ' | High Tide Times Boston | Rises h. m. | Rise Key | Sets h. m. | Set Key | Place | Age |
|---|---|---|---|---|---|---|---|---|---|---|---|---|---|---|---|---|
| 91 | 1 | Fr. | 6:27 | C | 7:09 | D | 12 42 | 12 | 4 N.35 | 10¾ 11¼ | 5:13 | D | 5:38 | D | PSC | 28 |
| 92 | 2 | Sa. | 6:25 | C | 7:10 | D | 12 45 | 12 | 4 58 | 11½ 11¾ | 5:36 | C | 6:37 | E | PSC | 29 |
| 93 | 3 | **B** | 6:23 | C | 7:12 | D | 12 49 | 13 | 5 21 | 12¼ — | 5:59 | C | 7:37 | E | PSC | 0 |
| 94 | 4 | M. | 6:22 | C | 7:13 | D | 12 51 | 13 | 5 44 | 12¼ 12¾ | 6:25 | B | 8:37 | E | PSC | 1 |
| 95 | 5 | Tu. | 6:20 | C | 7:14 | D | 12 54 | 13 | 6 07 | 1 1¼ | 6:53 | B | 9:38 | E | ARI | 2 |
| 96 | 6 | W. | 6:18 | B | 7:15 | D | 12 57 | 13 | 6 30 | 1½ 2 | 7:26 | B | 10:38 | E | ARI | 3 |
| 97 | 7 | Th. | 6:16 | B | 7:16 | D | 13 00 | 14 | 6 52 | 2 2¾ | 8:05 | B | 11:36 | E | TAU | 4 |
| 98 | 8 | Fr. | 6:15 | B | 7:17 | D | 13 02 | 14 | 7 15 | 2¾ 3¼ | 8:51 | B | — | - | TAU | 5 |
| 99 | 9 | Sa. | 6:13 | B | 7:18 | D | 13 05 | 14 | 7 37 | 3½ 4¼ | 9:45 | B | 12:30 | E | TAU | 6 |
| 100 | 10 | **B** | 6:11 | B | 7:19 | D | 13 08 | 14 | 8 00 | 4¼ 5 | 10:46 | B | 1:19 | E | GEM | 7 |
| 101 | 11 | M. | 6:10 | B | 7:21 | D | 13 11 | 15 | 8 22 | 5¼ 6 | 11:52 | B | 2:02 | E | GEM | 8 |
| 102 | 12 | Tu. | 6:08 | B | 7:22 | D | 13 14 | 15 | 8 44 | 6¼ 7 | 1:02 | C | 2:40 | E | CAN | 9 |
| 103 | 13 | W. | 6:06 | B | 7:23 | D | 13 17 | 15 | 9 05 | 7¼ 8 | 2:15 | C | 3:13 | E | CAN | 10 |
| 104 | 14 | Th. | 6:05 | B | 7:24 | D | 13 19 | 15 | 9 27 | 8¼ 8¾ | 3:30 | D | 3:44 | D | LEO | 11 |
| 105 | 15 | Fr. | 6:03 | B | 7:25 | D | 13 22 | 16 | 9 49 | 9¼ 9¾ | 4:46 | E | 4:14 | D | LEO | 12 |
| 106 | 16 | Sa. | 6:02 | B | 7:26 | D | 13 24 | 16 | 10 10 | 10¼ 10½ | 6:04 | E | 4:44 | C | VIR | 13 |
| 107 | 17 | **B** | 6:00 | B | 7:27 | D | 13 27 | 16 | 10 31 | 11 11½ | 7:23 | E | 5:16 | C | VIR | 14 |
| 108 | 18 | M. | 5:58 | B | 7:28 | D | 13 30 | 16 | 10 52 | 12 — | 8:41 | E | 5:52 | B | VIR | 15 |
| 109 | 19 | Tu. | 5:57 | B | 7:30 | D | 13 33 | 17 | 11 13 | 12¼ 1 | 9:56 | E | 6:33 | B | LIB | 16 |
| 110 | 20 | W. | 5:55 | B | 7:31 | D | 13 36 | 17 | 11 34 | 1 1¾ | 11:03 | E | 7:22 | B | SCO | 17 |
| 111 | 21 | Th. | 5:54 | B | 7:32 | D | 13 38 | 17 | 11 54 | 2 2¾ | — | - | 8:17 | B | OPH | 18 |
| 112 | 22 | Fr. | 5:52 | B | 7:33 | D | 13 41 | 17 | 12 14 | 2¾ 3½ | 12:02 | E | 9:19 | B | SAG | 19 |
| 113 | 23 | Sa. | 5:51 | B | 7:34 | D | 13 43 | 17 | 12 34 | 3¾ 4½ | 12:50 | E | 10:23 | B | SAG | 20 |
| 114 | 24 | **B** | 5:49 | B | 7:35 | D | 13 46 | 18 | 12 54 | 4¾ 5½ | 1:29 | E | 11:27 | B | SAG | 21 |
| 115 | 25 | M. | 5:48 | B | 7:36 | D | 13 48 | 18 | 13 14 | 5¾ 6½ | 2:02 | E | 12:31 | C | CAP | 22 |
| 116 | 26 | Tu. | 5:46 | B | 7:37 | D | 13 51 | 18 | 13 33 | 6¾ 7½ | 2:30 | E | 1:32 | C | AQU | 23 |
| 117 | 27 | W. | 5:45 | B | 7:39 | D | 13 54 | 18 | 13 52 | 7¾ 8¼ | 2:55 | D | 2:32 | D | AQU | 24 |
| 118 | 28 | Th. | 5:43 | B | 7:40 | E | 13 57 | 18 | 14 11 | 8¾ 9¼ | 3:18 | D | 3:31 | D | AQU | 25 |
| 119 | 29 | Fr. | 5:42 | B | 7:41 | E | 13 59 | 18 | 14 30 | 9½ 10 | 3:40 | C | 4:30 | E | PSC | 26 |
| 120 | 30 | Sa. | 5:41 | B | 7:42 | E | 14 01 | 18 | 14 N.49 | 10¼ 10½ | 4:03 | C | 5:29 | E | PSC | 27 |

# APRIL HATH 30 DAYS • 2011

*April is in:*
*New loves begin!* –John Addington Symonds

| Day of Month | Day of Week | Dates, Feasts, Fasts, Aspects, Tide Heights | Weather |
|---|---|---|---|
| 1 | Fr. | **All Fools'** • ☾ ON EQ. • Nunavut territory created, 1999 • { 9.6 / 9.6 | *Fools* |
| 2 | Sa. | ☾ AT APO. • ☌♂☾ • ☌♅☾ • Tides { 9.6 / 9.8 | *schuss* |
| 3 | **B** | **New** ● • ☌♂♅ • ☌♃☾ • ♄ AT ☍ • { 9.6 / — | *in,* |
| 4 | M. | ☌☿☾ • John Tyler first V.P. to take over after a president died, 1841 • Tides { 10.0 / 9.6 | *then* |
| 5 | Tu. | *Teeth placed before the tongue give good advice.* • Tides { 10.0 / 9.4 | *a* |
| 6 | W. | ☌♃☉ • Mormon leader Brigham Young married last wife (27th), 1868 • { 10.1 / 9.3 | *breather:* |
| 7 | Th. | Circus owner P. T. Barnum died, 1891 • Tides { 10.0 / 9.0 | *We* |
| 8 | Fr. | ☾ RIDES HIGH • Fire tornadoes, 2nd day, San Luis Obispo, Calif., 1926 • Tides { 9.9 / 8.8 | *don't* |
| 9 | Sa. | ☾ AT ☋ • ☿ IN INF. ☌ • ♇ STAT. • Dust storm, Colo./Wyo., 1895 | *mean* |
| 10 | **B** | **5th S. in Lent** • ☌☿♃ • Tides { 9.7 / 8.6 | *a short* |
| 11 | M. | *He who is shipwrecked the second time, can not lay the blame on Neptune.* • Tides { 9.7 / 8.7 | *one,* |
| 12 | Tu. | Civil War began, 1861 • First baseball game in indoor stadium, Houston, Tex., 1965 • { 9.7 / 9.0 | *either!* |
| 13 | W. | U.S. president Thomas Jefferson born, 1743 • { 9.9 / 9.5 | *Daffodils* |
| 14 | Th. | 51-lb. 4-oz. monkfish caught, Stellwagen Bank, Mass., 2008 • Tides { 10.2 / 10.2 | *and* |
| 15 | Fr. | ☾ ON EQ. • Chesapeake Bay Bridge-Tunnel opened, Va.–Delmarva Penin., 1964 • { 10.6 / 10.9 | *rippling* |
| 16 | Sa. | Agricultural College founded, Guelph, Ont., 1874 • { 10.9 / 11.6 | *rills* |
| 17 | **B** | **Palm Sunday** • **Full Pink** ○ • ☾ AT PERIG. • ☌♄☾ | *arrive* |
| 18 | M. | *No killing frost after martins.* • Tides { 11.2 / — | *together!* |
| 19 | Tu. | **First day of Passover** • ☌☿♂ • 59" snow, Lead, S.Dak., 2006 • { 12.2 / 11.1 | *Even* |
| 20 | W. | Upset swamp rabbit approached U.S. president Carter's fishing boat, Plains, Ga., 1979 • { 12.2 / 10.8 | *chills* |
| 21 | Th. | **Maundy Thursday** • ☾ RUNS LOW • ☾ AT ☊ • Battle of San Jacinto, Tex., 1836 | *and* |
| 22 | Fr. | **Good Friday** • ☌♀♅ • ☌♇☾ • ☿ STAT. • { 11.3 / 9.9 | *snow* |
| 23 | Sa. | Natalie Wood accepted "Worst Actress of the Year" award from *Harvard Lampoon,* 1966 • { 10.7 / 9.4 | *on* |
| 24 | **B** | **Easter** • Robert B. Thomas born, 1766 • Hubble space telescope launched, 1990 | *northern* |
| 25 | M. | **Easter Monday** • *A drop of ink may make a million think.* • Tides { 9.6 / 8.8 | *hills* |
| 26 | Tu. | First U.S. weather report broadcast, WEW, St. Louis, Mo., 1921 • Tides { 9.2 / 8.8 | *can't* |
| 27 | W. | ☌♆☾ • 94°F, Hartford, Conn., 1962 • Tides { 9.0 / 9.0 | *still the* |
| 28 | Th. | ☾ ON EQ. • Vaccine for yellow fever announced, 1932 • Tides { 9.0 / 9.2 | *thrill of* |
| 29 | Fr. | ☾ AT APO. • Poplars leaf out about now. • Tides { 9.0 / 9.5 | *vernal* |
| 30 | Sa. | ☌♀☾ • ☌♅☾ • *When folly passes by, reason draws back.* • { 9.1 / 9.7 | *weather.* |

*The plow that works is always shiny.* –Greek proverb

## *Farmer's Calendar*

■ So you're tooling along the dirt road, without a care in the world, when you hit a washboard. Suddenly your vehicle begins to bounce and shake uncontrollably. You slow down, but you can't stop, because your wheels aren't fully in contact with the road. For the same reason, you can't steer. You watch helplessly as your car bounces over the road in the direction of the ditch. With luck, you come to a stop before you get there.

Washboards are sections of unpaved roads that develop regularly spaced ridges or corrugations. They cause accidents, beat up your car, blow your tires, and can seem to loosen the fillings in your teeth. They're also quite an interesting phenomenon.

Many assume that washboards are caused, like potholes, by water in and on the road. In fact, their origin is more abstruse. Washboards are an inevitable mechanical consequence of wheels running over a particulate surface. When a wheel crosses even a slight irregularity in the dirt, it bounces, compacting the dirt directly beneath it and displacing some of it forward. The result is a ridge. As succeeding wheels encounter the same ridge, it grows, producing the washboard. The effect depends on the mass of the wheel and the speed at which it's turning. When you enter a washboard, then, you're a victim not of erosion, but of physics. Does that help?

## MAY

### THE FIFTH MONTH • 2011

**SKY WATCH** ☆ *Saturn is now nicely up in the east at nightfall, glorious all night long. From the 10th–13th, 35 minutes before sunrise, the residual planet party in Pisces is now more easily seen in southern locations: 10 degrees high from Miami but a very low 4 degrees up from middle America. On the 21st, in the same predawn location, Venus, still fading, forms a challengingly low acute triangle with Mercury and dim Mars. The Moon passes a good distance below Saturn on the 13th, stands near Scorpius's famous orange star Antares on the night of the 16th, and, as a crescent, floats just above the five-planet grouping in the predawn east on the 30th.*

| | | | | |
|---|---|---|---|---|
| ● | **New Moon** | 3rd day | 2nd hour | 51st minute |
| ◐ | **First Quarter** | 10th day | 16th hour | 33rd minute |
| ○ | **Full Moon** | 17th day | 7th hour | 9th minute |
| ◑ | **Last Quarter** | 24th day | 14th hour | 52nd minute |

*All times are given in Eastern Daylight Time.*

**Purchase these pages with times set to your zip code at MyLocalAlmanac.com.**

| Day of Year | Day of Month | Day of Week | ☼ Rises h. m. | Rise Key | ☼ Sets h. m. | Set Key | Length of Day h. m. | Sun Fast m. | Declination of Sun ° ' | High Tide Times Boston | | ☾ Rises h. m. | Rise Key | ☾ Sets h. m. | Set Key | ☾ Place | ☾ Age |
|---|---|---|---|---|---|---|---|---|---|---|---|---|---|---|---|---|---|
| 121 | 1 | **B** | 5:39 | B | **7:43** | E | 14 04 | 19 | 15 N. 07 | 11 | **11¼** | 4:28 | B | **6:29** | E | PSC | 28 |
| 122 | 2 | M. | 5:38 | B | **7:44** | E | 14 06 | 19 | 15 25 | 11¾ | **11¾** | 4:56 | B | **7:30** | E | PSC | 29 |
| 123 | 3 | Tu. | 5:37 | B | **7:45** | E | 14 08 | 19 | 15 42 | **12¼** | — | 5:28 | B | **8:31** | E | ARI | 0 |
| 124 | 4 | W. | 5:35 | B | **7:46** | E | 14 11 | 19 | 16 00 | 12½ | **1** | 6:05 | B | **9:30** | E | ARI | 1 |
| 125 | 5 | Th. | 5:34 | B | **7:48** | E | 14 14 | 19 | 16 17 | 1 | **1¾** | 6:50 | B | **10:26** | E | TAU | 2 |
| 126 | 6 | Fr. | 5:33 | B | **7:49** | E | 14 16 | 19 | 16 34 | 1¾ | **2¼** | 7:41 | B | **11:17** | E | TAU | 3 |
| 127 | 7 | Sa. | 5:32 | B | **7:50** | E | 14 18 | 19 | 16 51 | 2½ | **3** | 8:40 | B | — | – | GEM | 4 |
| 128 | 8 | **B** | 5:30 | B | **7:51** | E | 14 21 | 19 | 17 07 | 3¼ | **3¾** | 9:44 | B | 12:01 | E | GEM | 5 |
| 129 | 9 | M. | 5:29 | B | **7:52** | E | 14 23 | 19 | 17 23 | 4 | **4¾** | 10:52 | C | 12:40 | E | CAN | 6 |
| 130 | 10 | Tu. | 5:28 | B | **7:53** | E | 14 25 | 19 | 17 39 | 4¾ | **5½** | **12:02** | C | 1:14 | E | CAN | 7 |
| 131 | 11 | W. | 5:27 | B | **7:54** | E | 14 27 | 19 | 17 55 | 5¾ | **6½** | **1:14** | D | 1:44 | D | LEO | 8 |
| 132 | 12 | Th. | 5:26 | B | **7:55** | E | 14 29 | 19 | 18 10 | 6¾ | **7½** | **2:26** | D | 2:13 | D | SEX | 9 |
| 133 | 13 | Fr. | 5:25 | B | **7:56** | E | 14 31 | 19 | 18 25 | 8 | **8½** | **3:41** | E | 2:42 | C | LEO | 10 |
| 134 | 14 | Sa. | 5:24 | B | **7:57** | E | 14 33 | 19 | 18 39 | 9 | **9¼** | **4:56** | E | 3:12 | C | VIR | 11 |
| 135 | 15 | **B** | 5:23 | B | **7:58** | E | 14 35 | 19 | 18 54 | 9¾ | **10¼** | **6:14** | E | 3:45 | C | VIR | 12 |
| 136 | 16 | M. | 5:22 | B | **7:59** | E | 14 37 | 19 | 19 07 | 10¾ | **11** | **7:30** | E | 4:23 | B | VIR | 13 |
| 137 | 17 | Tu. | 5:21 | B | **8:00** | E | 14 39 | 19 | 19 21 | 11¾ | 12 | **8:41** | E | 5:08 | B | LIB | 14 |
| 138 | 18 | W. | 5:20 | A | **8:01** | E | 14 41 | 19 | 19 34 | **12½** | — | **9:45** | E | 6:01 | B | SCO | 15 |
| 139 | 19 | Th. | 5:19 | A | **8:02** | E | 14 43 | 19 | 19 47 | 12¾ | **1½** | **10:39** | E | 7:00 | B | OPH | 16 |
| 140 | 20 | Fr. | 5:18 | A | **8:03** | E | 14 45 | 19 | 20 00 | 1¾ | **2¼** | **11:24** | E | 8:05 | B | SAG | 17 |
| 141 | 21 | Sa. | 5:17 | A | **8:04** | E | 14 47 | 19 | 20 12 | 2½ | **3¼** | — | – | 9:11 | B | SAG | 18 |
| 142 | 22 | **B** | 5:16 | A | **8:05** | E | 14 49 | 19 | 20 24 | 3¼ | **4** | 12:00 | E | 10:17 | C | CAP | 19 |
| 143 | 23 | M. | 5:15 | A | **8:06** | E | 14 51 | 19 | 20 36 | 4¼ | **5** | 12:30 | E | 11:20 | C | AQU | 20 |
| 144 | 24 | Tu. | 5:15 | A | **8:07** | E | 14 52 | 19 | 20 47 | 5¼ | **5¾** | 12:57 | D | **12:22** | D | CAP | 21 |
| 145 | 25 | W. | 5:14 | A | **8:08** | E | 14 54 | 19 | 20 58 | 6 | **6¾** | 1:21 | D | **1:22** | D | AQU | 22 |
| 146 | 26 | Th. | 5:13 | A | **8:09** | E | 14 56 | 19 | 21 09 | 7 | **7½** | 1:44 | C | **2:21** | D | PSC | 23 |
| 147 | 27 | Fr. | 5:12 | A | **8:10** | E | 14 58 | 19 | 21 19 | 8 | **8¼** | 2:07 | C | **3:20** | E | PSC | 24 |
| 148 | 28 | Sa. | 5:12 | A | **8:11** | E | 14 59 | 18 | 21 28 | 8¾ | **9¼** | 2:31 | C | **4:20** | E | PSC | 25 |
| 149 | 29 | **B** | 5:11 | A | **8:11** | E | 15 00 | 18 | 21 38 | 9¾ | **9¾** | 2:57 | B | **5:20** | E | PSC | 26 |
| 150 | 30 | M. | 5:11 | A | **8:12** | E | 15 01 | 18 | 21 47 | 10½ | **10½** | 3:28 | B | **6:22** | E | ARI | 27 |
| 151 | 31 | Tu. | 5:10 | A | **8:13** | E | 15 03 | 18 | 21 N. 56 | 11¼ | **11¼** | 4:03 | B | **7:22** | E | ARI | 28 |

 To use this page, see p. 110; for Key Letters, see p. 234. ☞ **Bold** = P.M. ☞ Light = A.M. 

## MAY HATH 31 DAYS • 2011

*Birds are noisy, bees are humming,*
*All because the May's a-coming.* –William Cox Bennett

| Day of Month | Day of Week | Dates, Feasts, Fasts, Aspects, Tide Heights | Weather |
|---|---|---|---|
| 1 | B | May Day • ☌☿☾ • ☌♂♃ • ☌♂☾ • ☌♃☾ • { 9.2 10.0 | *We* |
| 2 | M. | First drawing sent by radio across Atlantic, 1926 • { 9.3 10.1 | *demand* |
| 3 | Tu. | New ● • Iconic "Old Man of the Mountain" fell, Franconia Notch, N.H., 2003 • { 9.3 — | *an* |
| 4 | W. | Haymarket Affair, Chicago, Ill., 1886 • { 10.2 9.3 | *explanation* |
| 5 | Th. | Cinco de Mayo • ☾ RIDES HIGH • *Every wind has its weather.* • { 10.3 9.2 | *for* |
| 6 | Fr. | ☾ AT ☋ • Psychiatrist Sigmund Freud born, 1856 • { 10.3 9.1 | *this* |
| 7 | Sa. | ☿ GR. ELONG. (27° WEST) • 10" snow, Rochester, N.Y., 1989 • { 10.3 9.1 | *wintry* |
| 8 | B | 3rd Sunday of Easter • Train robbed near Kamloops, B.C., 1906 | *precipitation!* |
| 9 | M. | St. Gregory of Nazianzus • *Hindenburg* completed its first flight to U.S., 1936 | *That's* |
| 10 | Tu. | ☌☿♃ • Cranberries in bud now. • Tides { 10.0 9.4 | *better!* |
| 11 | W. | ☌♀♃ • Siamese twins Chang and Eng Bunker born, 1811 • Three • { 10.0 9.7 | *Wetter,* |
| 12 | Th. | ☾ ON EQ. • Montreal chosen as site for 1976 Summer Olympics, 1970 • Chilly • { 10.0 10.2 | *but* |
| 13 | Fr. | *A man who always wears his best kimono has no Sunday clothes.* • Saints • { 10.1 10.8 | *suddenly* |
| 14 | Sa. | ☌♄☾ • Physicist Gabriel Daniel Fahrenheit born, 1686 | *tropic!* |
| 15 | B | 4th S. of Easter • ☾ AT PERIG. • Tides { 10.4 11.7 | *Heat's* |
| 16 | M. | Grand League of the American Horseshoe Pitchers Association organized, Kansas City, Kans., 1914 • { 10.6 12.0 | *the* |
| 17 | Tu. | Vesak • Full Flower ○ • *If you have the Moon, ignore the stars.* • { 10.6 12.1 | *topic* |
| 18 | W. | ☾ RUNS LOW • Violent storm wrecked several vessels, Lake Michigan, 1894 • Tides { 10.5 — | *of* |
| 19 | Th. | St. Dunstan • ☾ AT ☊ • ☌☿♂ • Anne Boleyn beheaded, 1536 | *every* |
| 20 | Fr. | ☌♇☾ • D. Hyde patented the fountain pen, 1830 • Tides { 11.6 10.1 | *conversation.* |
| 21 | Sa. | *A kiss without a hug is like a flower without fragrance.* | *Mildness* |
| 22 | B | 5th S. of Easter • ☌♀♂ • 101°F, Lewiston, Maine, 1911 | *and* |
| 23 | M. | Victoria Day (Canada) • Bandleader Artie Shaw born, 1910 • Tides { 10.0 9.2 | *mist,* |
| 24 | Tu. | ☌♆☾ • Milton Shedd, cofounder of Sea World, died, 2002 • Tides { 9.5 9.1 | *then* |
| 25 | W. | St. Bede • ☾ ON EQ. • Stephen Badin first Catholic priest ordained in U.S., 1793 • { 9.1 9.1 | *beaming* |
| 26 | Th. | Actor Jay Silverheels ("Tonto") born, 1912 • Tides { 8.8 9.1 | *and* |
| 27 | Fr. | ☾ AT APO. • ☌♅☾ • USS *John F. Kennedy* christened by Caroline Kennedy, 1967 | *brisk—* |
| 28 | Sa. | *Mars 3* orbiter and lander launched, 1971 • Tides { 8.6 9.5 | *rumors* |
| 29 | B | Rogation S. • ☌♃☾ • Supreme Court affirmed state blue laws OK, 1961 | *of* |
| 30 | M. | Memorial Day (observed) • ☌♂☾ • *The first wealth Is health.* • { 8.8 10.0 | *thunder-* |
| 31 | Tu. | Visit. of Mary • ☌☿☾ • ☌♀☾ • Social worker Emily Bissell born, 1861 | *boomers!* |

### *Farmer's Calendar*

■ Nature is a bountiful giver, but she has two hands. With one she gives the good news, with the other she gives the . . . other.

Consider the bluet *(Houstonia),* high among everybody's favorite early wildflowers. This single, tiny, four-petal bloom appears in lawns, fields, and barrens before the leaves on the trees have grown and spread to shade them. Bluets spread over the ground in patches. In color, they are commonly a true, pure, light blue that, as the densely crowded little flowers cover the ground in their drifts, gives them a look almost as though someone had broken a mirror on the grass and left its bright fragments to reflect the mild spring sky. After the long winter, there is no sight that is viewed more gratefully.

Or it would be so, save for the other half of nature's springtime gift to those who would enjoy the outdoors: the blackfly. Bluets and blackflies arrive on the same bus. The same spring sun, rain, and warming temperatures that bring the heaven-reflecting flower bring, in far greater numbers, the clouds of swarming, buzzing, biting flies—evidently fetched from quite other regions. To admire the bluets, you must peer at them through a veil of torment. This is unfortunate, but it seems that there is no other way: So many of the gifts of the seasons are gifts of ambivalence.

**SKY WATCH** ☆ *Venus has dropped and faded so much that it's almost a lost viewing cause very low in the eastern dawn at its minimum light, magnitude –3.8. Mars is technically visible there, too, but don't bother: The Red Planet is tiny, dim, and distant. Jupiter, now in Aries, is rising rapidly out of dawn's twilight, coming up 3 hours before sunrise at midmonth. The Moon's path this year is unextreme, with its highest and lowest positions pretty much matching the Sun's. It passes far beneath Saturn—the month's best planet—on the 9th and 10th and is near Jupiter on the 26th. The solstice brings summer to the Northern Hemisphere on the 21st, at 1:16 P.M.*

| | | | |
|---|---|---|---|
| ● New Moon | 1st day | 17th hour | 3rd minute |
| ◐ First Quarter | 8th day | 22nd hour | 11th minute |
| ○ Full Moon | 15th day | 16th hour | 14th minute |
| ◑ Last Quarter | 23rd day | 7th hour | 48th minute |

*All times are given in Eastern Daylight Time.*

Purchase these pages with times set to your zip code at MyLocalAlmanac.com.

| Day of Year | Day of Month | Day of Week | ☼ Rises h. m. | Rise Key | ☼ Sets h. m. | Set Key | Length of Day h. m. | Sun Fast m. | Declination of Sun ° ' | High Tide Times Boston | | ☾ Rises h. m. | Rise Key | ☾ Sets h. m. | Set Key | ☾ Place | ☾ Age |
|---|---|---|---|---|---|---|---|---|---|---|---|---|---|---|---|---|---|
| 152 | 1 | W. | 5:10 | A | 8:14 | E | 15 04 | 18 | 22 N.04 | **12** | 12 | 4:46 | B | **8:20** | E | TAU | 0 |
| 153 | 2 | Th. | 5:09 | A | 8:15 | E | 15 06 | 18 | 22 12 | **12½** | — | 5:36 | B | **9:13** | E | TAU | 1 |
| 154 | 3 | Fr. | 5:09 | A | 8:15 | E | 15 06 | 18 | 22 19 | 12½ | 1¼ | 6:33 | B | **10:00** | E | TAU | 2 |
| 155 | 4 | Sa. | 5:08 | A | 8:16 | E | 15 08 | 17 | 22 26 | 1¼ | 2 | 7:37 | B | **10:41** | E | GEM | 3 |
| 156 | 5 | **B** | 5:08 | A | 8:17 | E | 15 09 | 17 | 22 33 | 2 | 2¾ | 8:44 | C | **11:16** | E | GEM | 4 |
| 157 | 6 | M. | 5:08 | A | 8:17 | E | 15 09 | 17 | 22 39 | 2¾ | 3½ | 9:54 | C | **11:48** | D | CAN | 5 |
| 158 | 7 | Tu. | 5:07 | A | 8:18 | E | 15 11 | 17 | 22 45 | 3¾ | 4¼ | 11:04 | D | — | – | LEO | 6 |
| 159 | 8 | W. | 5:07 | A | 8:19 | E | 15 12 | 17 | 22 51 | 4½ | 5¼ | **12:16** | D | 12:17 | D | SEX | 7 |
| 160 | 9 | Th. | 5:07 | A | 8:19 | E | 15 12 | 16 | 22 56 | 5½ | 6 | **1:27** | E | 12:45 | C | LEO | 8 |
| 161 | 10 | Fr. | 5:07 | A | 8:20 | E | 15 13 | 16 | 23 01 | 6½ | 7 | **2:40** | E | 1:13 | C | VIR | 9 |
| 162 | 11 | Sa. | 5:06 | A | 8:20 | E | 15 14 | 16 | 23 05 | 7½ | 8 | **3:55** | E | 1:44 | C | VIR | 10 |
| 163 | 12 | **B** | 5:06 | A | 8:21 | E | 15 15 | 16 | 23 09 | 8½ | 9 | **5:09** | E | 2:19 | B | VIR | 11 |
| 164 | 13 | M. | 5:06 | A | 8:21 | E | 15 15 | 15 | 23 12 | 9½ | 9¾ | **6:21** | E | 2:59 | B | LIB | 12 |
| 165 | 14 | Tu. | 5:06 | A | 8:22 | E | 15 16 | 15 | 23 16 | 10½ | 10¾ | **7:28** | E | 3:47 | B | SCO | 13 |
| 166 | 15 | W. | 5:06 | A | 8:22 | E | 15 16 | 15 | 23 18 | 11½ | 11¾ | **8:27** | E | 4:43 | B | OPH | 14 |
| 167 | 16 | Th. | 5:06 | A | 8:23 | E | 15 17 | 15 | 23 21 | 12¼ | — | **9:15** | E | 5:46 | B | SAG | 15 |
| 168 | 17 | Fr. | 5:06 | A | 8:23 | E | 15 17 | 15 | 23 22 | 12½ | 1¼ | **9:56** | E | 6:52 | B | SAG | 16 |
| 169 | 18 | Sa. | 5:06 | A | 8:23 | E | 15 17 | 15 | 23 24 | 1¼ | 2 | **10:29** | E | 7:59 | C | SAG | 17 |
| 170 | 19 | **B** | 5:07 | A | 8:24 | E | 15 17 | 14 | 23 25 | 2 | 2¾ | **10:58** | D | 9:05 | C | AQU | 18 |
| 171 | 20 | M. | 5:07 | A | 8:24 | E | 15 17 | 14 | 23 26 | 3 | 3½ | **11:23** | D | 10:08 | C | CAP | 19 |
| 172 | 21 | Tu. | 5:07 | A | 8:25 | E | 15 18 | 14 | 23 26 | 3¾ | 4¼ | **11:46** | D | 11:09 | D | AQU | 20 |
| 173 | 22 | W. | 5:07 | A | 8:24 | E | 15 17 | 14 | 23 26 | 4½ | 5 | — | – | **12:09** | D | PSC | 21 |
| 174 | 23 | Th. | 5:07 | A | 8:24 | E | 15 17 | 14 | 23 25 | 5½ | 6 | 12:09 | C | **1:09** | E | PSC | 22 |
| 175 | 24 | Fr. | 5:08 | A | 8:25 | E | 15 17 | 13 | 23 24 | 6¼ | 6¾ | 12:33 | C | **2:08** | E | PSC | 23 |
| 176 | 25 | Sa. | 5:08 | A | 8:25 | E | 15 17 | 13 | 23 22 | 7¼ | 7½ | 12:59 | B | **3:08** | E | PSC | 24 |
| 177 | 26 | **B** | 5:08 | A | 8:25 | E | 15 17 | 13 | 23 21 | 8 | 8¼ | 1:27 | B | **4:09** | E | ARI | 25 |
| 178 | 27 | M. | 5:09 | A | 8:25 | E | 15 16 | 13 | 23 18 | 9 | 9¼ | 2:00 | B | **5:10** | E | ARI | 26 |
| 179 | 28 | Tu. | 5:09 | A | 8:25 | E | 15 16 | 13 | 23 16 | 9¾ | 10 | 2:40 | B | **6:09** | E | TAU | 27 |
| 180 | 29 | W. | 5:09 | A | 8:25 | E | 15 16 | 12 | 23 13 | 10¾ | 10¾ | 3:27 | B | **7:05** | E | TAU | 28 |
| 181 | 30 | Th. | 5:10 | A | 8:25 | E | 15 15 | 12 | 23 N.09 | 11½ | 11½ | 4:22 | B | **7:55** | E | TAU | 29 |

Name:

Address:

City/Town: State: Zip:

☛ *RUSH Order Enclosed!*

NO POSTAGE
NECESSARY
IF MAILED
IN THE
UNITED STATES

# BUSINESS REPLY MAIL

FIRST-CLASS MAIL PERMIT NO. 132 DES MOINES IA

POSTAGE WILL BE PAID BY ADDRESSEE

The Old Farmer's Almanac
Subscriptions

PO Box 4002828
Des Moines, IA 50340-4828

Name:

Address:

City/Town: State: Zip:

☛ *RUSH Order Enclosed!*

NO POSTAGE
NECESSARY
IF MAILED
IN THE
UNITED STATES

BUSINESS REPLY MAIL

FIRST-CLASS MAIL PERMIT NO. 132 DES MOINES IA

POSTAGE WILL BE PAID BY ADDRESSEE

The Old Farmer's Almanac
Subscriptions

PO Box 4002828
Des Moines, IA 50340-4828

CALENDAR

*Mine is the Month of Roses; yes, and mine*
*The Month of Marriages!* –Henry Wadsworth Longfellow

## Farmer's Calendar

■ In 1627, John Donne, one of the great poets of our language, reflected on the miraculous in the everyday. We experience the world around us, Donne observed, as made up of mundane occurrences that we hardly notice but which, if they were rare, would be accounted prodigies. "Nay, the ordinary things in Nature would be greater miracles than the extraordinary, which we admire most, if they were done but once."

How many events of a June afternoon bear him out? The sky darkens, thunder sounds, rain arrives, passes. A rainbow appears in the east, a vast shimmering arch of light above the valley. We pause to enjoy it, we don't fail to notice it; but then we go on about our business. We've seen rainbows before. If that rainbow were the only rainbow, if it "were done but once," we would be astonished.

As the shower passes, a hummingbird returns to the delphiniums, hovering, feeding, zooming off, circling, zooming back, halting, poised on invisible wings. Its movements are so quick that they can be hard to follow, and its brilliant colors make it look like a high-speed gemstone. As with the rainbow, however, though we admire the hummingbird, we don't marvel: It's familiar. If, as Donne reminds us, this hummingbird were unique, we would behold it with wonder.

| Day of Month | Day of Week | Dates, Feasts, Fasts, Aspects, Tide Heights | Weather |
|---|---|---|---|
| 1 | W. | New ● ● Eclipse ☉ ● *Sesame Street*'s Oscar the Grouch born, 1969 ● { 9.0 / 10.4 | *Fine* |
| 2 | Th. | **Ascension** ● ☾ RIDES HIGH ● ☾ AT ☍ ● Tides { 9.1 | *for* |
| 3 | Fr. | ♆ STAT. ● Golfball-size hail, northeast Colo., 2002 ● Tides { 10.5 / 9.3 | *outdoor* |
| 4 | Sa. | *When the mouse laughs at the cat, there is a hole nearby.* | *puttering,* |
| 5 | **B** | **1st ♅. af. Asc.** ● Bananas sold as novelty at Centennial Exhibition, Philadelphia, 1876 | *but* |
| 6 | M. | D-Day, 1944 ● Astronomer Regiomontanus born, 1436 ● { 10.6 / 9.7 | *what's* |
| 7 | Tu. | Physician James Young Simpson born, 1811 ● Tides { 10.5 / 9.9 | *that* |
| 8 | W. | **Shavuot** ● ☾ ON EQ. ● First U.S. ad for commercial ice cream, N.Y.C., 1786 | *muttering,* |
| 9 | Th. | *The Philadelphia Spelling Book* first copyrighted book in U.S., 1790 ● Tides { 10.1 / 10.4 | *those* |
| 10 | Fr. | ♂ ♄ ☾ ● United States War Dogs Memorial dedicated, Holmdel, N.J., 2006 ● { 9.9 / 10.7 | *ominous* |
| 11 | Sa. | **St. Barnabas** ● ☾ AT PERIG. ● *Advice when most needed Is least heeded.* | *flashes?* |
| 12 | **B** | **Whit ♅. ● Pentecost** ● ☿ IN SUP. ♂ ● { 9.8 / 11.3 | *Pull* |
| 13 | M. | Musician Benny Goodman died, 1986 ● Tides { 9.8 / 11.5 | *down* |
| 14 | Tu. | **St. Basil** ● ♄ STAT. ● 106°F, San Francisco, Calif., 1961 ● Tides { 9.9 / 11.6 | *your* |
| 15 | W. | Ember Day ● **Full Strawberry** ● Eclipse ☾ ● ☾ RUNS LOW ● ☾ AT ☍ | *sashes!* |
| 16 | Th. | ♂ ♇ ☾ ● Alfred Hitchcock's film *Psycho* released, 1960 ● Tides { 10.0 | *Impatient* |
| 17 | Fr. | Ember Day ● Tornado struck Iowa College, Grinnell, Iowa, 1882 ● Tides { 11.5 / 9.9 | *scholars* |
| 18 | Sa. | Ember Day ● First fly-casting tournament in U.S., Utica, N.Y., 1861 ● Tides { 11.2 / 9.8 | *are* |
| 19 | **B** | **Trinity ● Orthodox All Saints'** ● Baseball player Lou Gehrig born, 1903 | *hot* |
| 20 | M. | ♂ ♀ ☾ ● First "Baby Bonus" checks sent to Canadian families, 1945 ● Tides { 10.4 / 9.5 | *under* |
| 21 | Tu. | **Summer Solstice** ● *Summer comes with a bound; winter comes yawning.* ● Tides { 9.9 / 9.4 | *their* |
| 22 | W. | **St. Alban** ● ☾ ON EQ. ● Chess master Paul Morphy born, 1837 ● Tides { 9.4 / 9.3 | *collars.* |
| 23 | Th. | ♂ ♄ ☾ ● First practical typewriter patented, 1868 | *Graduation* |
| 24 | Fr. | **Nativ. John the Baptist** ● Midsummer Day ● ☾ AT APO. | *days* |
| 25 | Sa. | 19-year-old cellist Arturo Toscanini filled in as conductor for *Aida*, Rio de Janeiro, Brazil, 1886 ● { 8.4 / 9.3 | *blaze* |
| 26 | **B** | **Corpus Christi** ● ♂ ♃ ☾ ● Coney Island's Cyclone roller coaster debuted, N.Y., 1927 ● { 8.3 / 9.5 | *with* |
| 27 | M. | *If it rains on June 27th, it will rain seven weeks.* ● { 8.3 / 9.7 | *Thor's* |
| 28 | Tu. | **St. Irenaeus** ● ♂ ♂ ☾ ● ♇ AT ☍ ● U.S. president James Madison died, 1836 | *tympani:* |
| 29 | W. | **Sts. Peter & Paul** ● ☾ RIDES HIGH ● Actor Slim Pickens born, 1919 | *summer's* |
| 30 | Th. | ☾ AT ☍ ● ♂ ♀ ☾ ● Gadsden Purchase Treaty signed, 1854 ● { 8.9 / 10.6 | *symphony!* |

*The heart has its reasons of which reason knows nothing.* –B. Pascal

# THE SEVENTH MONTH • 2011



**SKY WATCH** ☆ *Earth reaches aphelion, its farthest point from the Sun, on the 4th. Saturn, in the southwest at nightfall, stands above the Moon on the 7th and sets at around midnight at month's end. Mercury has a so-so evening-sky showing during the first 3 weeks of the month, 8 degrees high in fading twilight, in Cancer. It's brightest on the 2nd–4th. Jupiter rises at around 1:00 A.M. at midmonth. Dim Mars, near the Moon on the night of the 26th, still beats the dawn by only 2 hours. Month's end brings an unusually close visit by the asteroid Vesta, which is faintly visible to the naked eye at magnitude 5.7 in the lower central part of Capricornus.*

| | | | | |
|---|---|---|---|---|
| ● | **New Moon** | 1st day | 4th hour | 54th minute |
| ◐ | **First Quarter** | 8th day | 2nd hour | 29th minute |
| ○ | **Full Moon** | 15th day | 2nd hour | 40th minute |
| ◑ | **Last Quarter** | 23rd day | 1st hour | 2nd minute |
| ● | **New Moon** | 30th day | 14th hour | 40th minute |

*All times are given in Eastern Daylight Time.*

**Purchase these pages with times set to your zip code at MyLocalAlmanac.com.**

| Day of Year | Day of Month | Day of Week | ☼ Rises h. m. | Rise Key | ☼ Sets h. m. | Set Key | Length of Day h. m. | Sun Fast m. | Declination of Sun ° ' | High Tide Times Boston | | ☾ Rises h. m. | Rise Key | ☾ Sets h. m. | Set Key | ☾ Place | ☾ Age |
|---|---|---|---|---|---|---|---|---|---|---|---|---|---|---|---|---|---|
| 182 | 1 | Fr. | 5:10 | A | **8:24** | E | 15 14 | 12 | 23 N.05 | **12** | — | 5:24 | B | **8:39** | E | GEM | 0 |
| 183 | 2 | Sa. | 5:11 | A | **8:24** | E | 15 13 | 12 | 23 01 | 12¼ | **12¾** | 6:32 | C | **9:17** | E | GEM | 1 |
| 184 | 3 | **B** | 5:12 | A | **8:24** | E | 15 12 | 12 | 22 56 | 1 | **1½** | 7:43 | C | **9:50** | E | CAN | 2 |
| 185 | 4 | M. | 5:12 | A | **8:24** | E | 15 12 | 11 | 22 51 | 1¾ | **2¼** | 8:54 | C | **10:21** | D | CAN | 3 |
| 186 | 5 | Tu. | 5:13 | A | **8:24** | E | 15 11 | 11 | 22 46 | 2½ | **3** | 10:06 | D | **10:49** | D | SEX | 4 |
| 187 | 6 | W. | 5:13 | A | **8:23** | E | 15 10 | 11 | 22 40 | 3¼ | **4** | 11:18 | D | **11:17** | C | LEO | 5 |
| 188 | 7 | Th. | 5:14 | A | **8:23** | E | 15 09 | 11 | 22 33 | 4¼ | **4¾** | **12:31** | E | **11:47** | C | VIR | 6 |
| 189 | 8 | Fr. | 5:15 | A | **8:23** | E | 15 08 | 11 | 22 27 | 5¼ | **5¾** | **1:44** | E | — | – | VIR | 7 |
| 190 | 9 | Sa. | 5:15 | A | **8:22** | E | 15 07 | 11 | 22 20 | 6¼ | **6¾** | **2:57** | E | 12:20 | B | VIR | 8 |
| 191 | 10 | **B** | 5:16 | A | **8:22** | E | 15 06 | 10 | 22 12 | 7¼ | **7¾** | **4:08** | E | 12:57 | B | LIB | 9 |
| 192 | 11 | M. | 5:17 | A | **8:21** | E | 15 04 | 10 | 22 04 | 8¼ | **8¾** | **5:16** | E | 1:41 | B | LIB | 10 |
| 193 | 12 | Tu. | 5:18 | A | **8:21** | E | 15 03 | 10 | 21 56 | 9½ | **9¾** | **6:16** | E | 2:33 | B | OPH | 11 |
| 194 | 13 | W. | 5:18 | A | **8:20** | E | 15 02 | 10 | 21 48 | 10¼ | **10½** | **7:08** | E | 3:31 | B | OPH | 12 |
| 195 | 14 | Th. | 5:19 | A | **8:20** | E | 15 01 | 10 | 21 39 | 11¼ | **11½** | **7:51** | E | 4:35 | B | SAG | 13 |
| 196 | 15 | Fr. | 5:20 | A | **8:19** | E | 14 59 | 10 | 21 29 | **12** | — | **8:28** | E | 5:42 | B | SAG | 14 |
| 197 | 16 | Sa. | 5:21 | A | **8:18** | E | 14 57 | 10 | 21 20 | 12¼ | **12¾** | **8:58** | E | 6:48 | C | CAP | 15 |
| 198 | 17 | **B** | 5:22 | A | **8:18** | E | 14 56 | 10 | 21 10 | 1 | **1½** | **9:25** | D | 7:53 | C | AQU | 16 |
| 199 | 18 | M. | 5:22 | A | **8:17** | E | 14 55 | 10 | 20 59 | 1¾ | **2¼** | **9:49** | D | 8:56 | D | AQU | 17 |
| 200 | 19 | Tu. | 5:23 | A | **8:16** | E | 14 53 | 9 | 20 48 | 2½ | **3** | **10:13** | C | 9:57 | D | AQU | 18 |
| 201 | 20 | W. | 5:24 | A | **8:15** | E | 14 51 | 9 | 20 37 | 3¼ | **3¾** | **10:36** | C | 10:56 | D | PSC | 19 |
| 202 | 21 | Th. | 5:25 | A | **8:15** | E | 14 50 | 9 | 20 26 | 4 | **4½** | **11:01** | C | 11:56 | E | PSC | 20 |
| 203 | 22 | Fr. | 5:26 | A | **8:14** | E | 14 48 | 9 | 20 14 | 4¾ | **5¼** | **11:28** | B | **12:56** | E | PSC | 21 |
| 204 | 23 | Sa. | 5:27 | A | **8:13** | E | 14 46 | 9 | 20 02 | 5½ | **6** | **11:58** | B | **1:56** | E | ARI | 22 |
| 205 | 24 | **B** | 5:28 | A | **8:12** | E | 14 44 | 9 | 19 49 | 6½ | **6¾** | — | – | **2:56** | E | ARI | 23 |
| 206 | 25 | M. | 5:29 | A | **8:11** | E | 14 42 | 9 | 19 37 | 7¼ | **7¾** | 12:35 | B | **3:55** | E | ARI | 24 |
| 207 | 26 | Tu. | 5:30 | B | **8:10** | E | 14 40 | 9 | 19 23 | 8¼ | **8½** | 1:18 | B | **4:52** | E | TAU | 25 |
| 208 | 27 | W. | 5:31 | B | **8:09** | E | 14 38 | 9 | 19 10 | 9¼ | **9¼** | 2:08 | B | **5:45** | E | TAU | 26 |
| 209 | 28 | Th. | 5:32 | B | **8:08** | E | 14 36 | 9 | 18 56 | 10 | **10¼** | 3:08 | B | **6:32** | E | GEM | 27 |
| 210 | 29 | Fr. | 5:33 | B | **8:07** | E | 14 34 | 9 | 18 42 | 10¾ | **11** | 4:13 | B | **7:13** | E | GEM | 28 |
| 211 | 30 | Sa. | 5:34 | B | **8:06** | E | 14 32 | 9 | 18 28 | 11¾ | **11¾** | 5:24 | C | **7:49** | E | CAN | 0 |
| 212 | 31 | **B** | 5:35 | B | **8:05** | E | 14 30 | 9 | 18 N.13 | **12½** | — | 6:37 | C | **8:22** | D | CAN | 1 |

 **To use this page, see p. 110; for Key Letters, see p. 234.** ☞ **Bold = P.M.** ☞ Light = A.M. 

# JULY HATH 31 DAYS • 2011

*O so drowsy! In a daze*
*Sweating 'mid the golden haze.* –Robert Buchanan

| Day of Month | Day of Week | Dates, Feasts, Fasts, Aspects, Tide Heights | Weather |
|---|---|---|---|
| 1 | Fr. | **Canada Day** • **New ●** • **Eclipse ☉** • Tides { 9.2 / — | *These* |
| 2 | Sa. | ☌☿☾ • Actor Jimmy Stewart died, 1997 • Tides { 10.8 / 9.5 | *are* |
| 3 | **B** | **3rd S. af. P.** • Dog Days begin. • Tides { 11.0 / 9.8 | *the* |
| 4 | M. | **Independence Day** • ⊕ AT APHELION • 106°F, Nashua, N.H., 1911 | *times* |
| 5 | Tu. | Japanese destroyer *Arare* sunk, Kiska Harbor, Alaska, 1942 • Tides { 11.0 / 10.4 | *that* |
| 6 | W. | ☾ ON EQ. • Nuclear test caused largest manmade crater in U.S. (Sedan Crater), Nevada Test Site, 1962 | *fry* |
| 7 | Th. | ☾ AT PERIG. • ☌♄☾ • *Take time while time is, for time will away.* • { 10.5 / 10.7 | *men's* |
| 8 | Fr. | Last bare-knuckles heavyweight championship boxing match, 1889 • Tides { 10.1 / 10.8 | *soles.* |
| 9 | Sa. | Samuel Latham Mitchill first agriculture professor, Columbia College, N.Y., 1792 • { 9.7 / 10.8 | *A peach:* |
| 10 | **B** | **4th S. af. P.** • ♅ STAT. • Tides { 9.4 / 10.9 | *Hit* |
| 11 | M. | U.S. Marine Band established, 1798 • Tides { 9.3 / 11.0 | *the* |
| 12 | Tu. | ☾ RUNS LOW • ☾ AT ☊ • 112°F, Emerson, Man., 1936 | *beach!* |
| 13 | W. | ☌♇☾ • Cornscateous air is everywhere. • Tides { 9.4 / 11.1 | *Cool* |
| 14 | Th. | **Bastille Day** • Armadillos mate now. • *Cloudy mornings turn to clear evenings.* • { 9.5 / 11.1 | *and* |
| 15 | Fr. | **St. Swithin** • **Full Buck ○** • Tides { 9.7 / — | *rumbly—* |
| 16 | Sa. | 135 pilot whales beached, Point au Gaul, N.L., 1979 • Explorer Pierre Le Moyne born, 1661 | *picnickers* |
| 17 | **B** | **5th S. af. P.** • Black-eyed Susans bloom now. • { 10.8 / 9.7 | *are* |
| 18 | M. | ☌♆☾ • Writer William Makepeace Thackeray born, 1811 • { 10.5 / 9.7 | *grumbly.* |
| 19 | Tu. | ☾ ON EQ. • Third hurricane within a month hit northern Florida, 1886 • Tides { 10.1 / 9.6 | *A* |
| 20 | W. | ☿ GR. ELONG. (27° EAST) • B.C. joined Canadian Confed., 1871 • { 9.7 / 9.5 | *rainy* |
| 21 | Th. | ☾ AT APO. • ☌♅☾ • Gus Grissom became 2nd American to orbit Earth, 1961 • { 9.3 / 9.4 | *spell,* |
| 22 | Fr. | **St. Mary Magdalene** • *Life is for one generation; a good name is forever.* • { 8.9 / 9.3 | *then* |
| 23 | Sa. | ☌♃☾ • Copyright for "America the Beautiful" by Katharine Lee Bates registered, 1906 • { 8.5 / 9.2 | *swell.* |
| 24 | **B** | **6th S. af. P.** • Lightning measured 345,000 amperes, Pittsburgh, Pa., 1947 | *Skies* |
| 25 | M. | **St. James & Christopher** • Gypsy moths emerge. • { 8.1 / 9.4 | *blacken,* |
| 26 | Tu. | **St. Anne** • ☾ RIDES HIGH • SS *Andrea Doria* sank near Nantucket, Mass., 1956 | *lightning* |
| 27 | W. | ☾ AT ☋ • ☌♂☾ • Basketball player Reggie Lewis died, 1993 | *crackin'.* |
| 28 | Th. | *The frog who has never seen the sea thinks the well a fine stretch of water.* • Tides { 8.7 / 10.4 | *Hot* |
| 29 | Fr. | **St. Martha** • 5.4 earthquake, Los Angeles, Calif., 2008 | *as* |
| 30 | Sa. | **New ●** • ☌♀☾ • Artist Giorgio Vasari born, 1511 • { 9.6 / 11.1 | *Hades,* |
| 31 | **B** | **7th S. af. P.** • Alys McKey Bryant first woman to fly plane in Canada, 1913 | *ladies!* |

## *Farmer's Calendar*

■ Around midsummer, as the nights grow cooler and heavy dews begin to fall, meadows and lawns are the sites of mysterious nocturnal gatherings whose signs we find on starting our day in the morning. Scattered over the grass are small scraps or patches of material, gray or white fragments a few inches square. Did messy elvish picnickers leave behind their dirty napkins?

No. The patches are evidence of little funnel-web spiders (family *Agelenidae*). They are dime-size creatures that live in the grasses and spin their flat, dense, sheetlike webs close to the ground, like tiny carpets woven among the grass stems. The family includes more than 400 species in North America.

Funnel-web spiders prey on insects caught on their webs. Examine a web closely, and you'll find a small funnel in one corner or side, where the spider lies in wait. The webs are virtually invisible by day, except when the dew, falling in early morning, collects on them. By midmorning, the webs will have disappeared. Now, however, they lie everywhere on the fields and lawns. They look like hundreds of soiled handkerchiefs, as though a fairy audience the night before had assembled on your lawn to enjoy, with plentiful tears, an expert, highly pathetic, deeply moving performance of *Romeo and Juliet.*

# THE EIGHTH MONTH • 2011



**SKY WATCH** ☆ *Asteroid Vesta is closest to Earth in the first week of the month, dimly visible to the unaided eye and highest at midnight. This is its brightest visit for the next decade. Saturn stands above the Moon on the 3rd; it is low at nightfall in the west. Venus is gone, passing behind the Sun on the 16th. Jupiter, the sky's brightest current object, improves from magnitude –2.4 to –2.6. It rises at about midnight on the 1st and at 10:00 P.M. by the 31st. Mars is still inconspicuous, rising at midmonth at 3:00 A.M. Mercury is a faint morning star at the end of the month but will soon improve. The famous Perseid meteor shower on the 11th–13th will be washed out by a nearly full Moon.*

| | | | |
|---|---|---|---|
| ◐ **First Quarter** | 6th day | 7th hour | 8th minute |
| ○ **Full Moon** | 13th day | 14th hour | 57th minute |
| ◑ **Last Quarter** | 21st day | 17th hour | 54th minute |
| ● **New Moon** | 28th day | 23rd hour | 4th minute |

*All times are given in Eastern Daylight Time.*

**Purchase these pages with times set to your zip code at MyLocalAlmanac.com.**

| Day of Year | Day of Month | Day of Week | ☼ Rises h. m. | Rise Key | ☼ Sets h. m. | Set Key | Length of Day h. | m. | Sun Fast m. | Declination of Sun ° | ' | High Tide Times Boston | | ☾ Rises h. m. | Rise Key | ☾ Sets h. m. | Set Key | ☾ Place | ☾ Age |
|---|---|---|---|---|---|---|---|---|---|---|---|---|---|---|---|---|---|---|---|
| 213 | 1 | M. | 5:36 | B | **8:04** | E | 14 | 28 | 9 | 17 N. | 58 | 12½ | **1¼** | 7:51 | D | **8:52** | D | LEO | 2 |
| 214 | 2 | Tu. | 5:37 | B | **8:02** | E | 14 | 25 | 10 | 17 | 43 | 1½ | **2** | 9:05 | D | **9:21** | C | SEX | 3 |
| 215 | 3 | W. | 5:38 | B | **8:01** | E | 14 | 23 | 10 | 17 | 27 | 2¼ | **2¾** | 10:19 | E | **9:51** | C | VIR | 4 |
| 216 | 4 | Th. | 5:39 | B | **8:00** | E | 14 | 21 | 10 | 17 | 11 | 3 | **3½** | 11:34 | E | **10:23** | B | VIR | 5 |
| 217 | 5 | Fr. | 5:40 | B | **7:59** | E | 14 | 19 | 10 | 16 | 55 | 4 | **4½** | **12:47** | E | **10:59** | B | VIR | 6 |
| 218 | 6 | Sa. | 5:41 | B | **7:58** | E | 14 | 17 | 10 | 16 | 39 | 5 | **5¼** | **1:59** | E | **11:41** | B | LIB | 7 |
| 219 | 7 | **B** | 5:42 | B | **7:56** | E | 14 | 14 | 10 | 16 | 22 | 6 | **6¼** | **3:07** | E | — | – | LIB | 8 |
| 220 | 8 | M. | 5:43 | B | **7:55** | E | 14 | 12 | 10 | 16 | 05 | 7 | **7½** | **4:09** | E | 12:29 | B | OPH | 9 |
| 221 | 9 | Tu. | 5:44 | B | **7:54** | E | 14 | 10 | 10 | 15 | 48 | 8¼ | **8½** | **5:03** | E | 1:24 | B | OPH | 10 |
| 222 | 10 | W. | 5:45 | B | **7:52** | D | 14 | 07 | 10 | 15 | 30 | 9¼ | **9½** | **5:49** | E | 2:26 | B | SAG | 11 |
| 223 | 11 | Th. | 5:46 | B | **7:51** | D | 14 | 05 | 11 | 15 | 13 | 10¼ | **10¼** | **6:27** | E | 3:30 | B | SAG | 12 |
| 224 | 12 | Fr. | 5:47 | B | **7:49** | D | 14 | 02 | 11 | 14 | 55 | 11 | **11¼** | **6:59** | E | 4:35 | C | CAP | 13 |
| 225 | 13 | Sa. | 5:48 | B | **7:48** | D | 14 | 00 | 11 | 14 | 37 | 11¾ | 12 | **7:27** | D | 5:40 | C | AQU | 14 |
| 226 | 14 | **B** | 5:49 | B | **7:47** | D | 13 | 58 | 11 | 14 | 18 | **12½** | — | **7:53** | D | 6:43 | C | CAP | 15 |
| 227 | 15 | M. | 5:50 | B | **7:45** | D | 13 | 55 | 11 | 14 | 00 | 12¾ | **1** | **8:16** | C | 7:45 | D | AQU | 16 |
| 228 | 16 | Tu. | 5:52 | B | **7:44** | D | 13 | 52 | 12 | 13 | 41 | 1¼ | **1¾** | **8:40** | C | 8:45 | D | PSC | 17 |
| 229 | 17 | W. | 5:53 | B | **7:42** | D | 13 | 49 | 12 | 13 | 22 | 2 | **2¼** | **9:04** | C | 9:45 | E | PSC | 18 |
| 230 | 18 | Th. | 5:54 | B | **7:41** | D | 13 | 47 | 12 | 13 | 02 | 2¾ | **3** | **9:30** | B | 10:44 | E | PSC | 19 |
| 231 | 19 | Fr. | 5:55 | B | **7:39** | D | 13 | 44 | 12 | 12 | 43 | 3¼ | **3¾** | **9:59** | B | 11:44 | E | PSC | 20 |
| 232 | 20 | Sa. | 5:56 | B | **7:38** | D | 13 | 42 | 12 | 12 | 23 | 4 | **4½** | **10:32** | B | **12:43** | E | ARI | 21 |
| 233 | 21 | **B** | 5:57 | B | **7:36** | D | 13 | 39 | 13 | 12 | 03 | 5 | **5¼** | **11:12** | B | **1:42** | E | ARI | 22 |
| 234 | 22 | M. | 5:58 | B | **7:35** | D | 13 | 37 | 13 | 11 | 43 | 5¾ | **6** | **11:58** | B | **2:39** | E | TAU | 23 |
| 235 | 23 | Tu. | 5:59 | B | **7:33** | D | 13 | 34 | 13 | 11 | 23 | 6¾ | **7** | — | – | **3:33** | E | TAU | 24 |
| 236 | 24 | W. | 6:00 | B | **7:31** | D | 13 | 31 | 13 | 11 | 03 | 7¾ | **8** | 12:52 | B | **4:22** | E | ORI | 25 |
| 237 | 25 | Th. | 6:01 | B | **7:30** | D | 13 | 29 | 14 | 10 | 42 | 8½ | **8¾** | 1:54 | B | **5:05** | E | GEM | 26 |
| 238 | 26 | Fr. | 6:02 | B | **7:28** | D | 13 | 26 | 14 | 10 | 21 | 9½ | **9¾** | 3:02 | C | **5:44** | E | GEM | 27 |
| 239 | 27 | Sa. | 6:03 | B | **7:27** | D | 13 | 24 | 14 | 10 | 00 | 10¼ | **10½** | 4:13 | C | **6:18** | E | CAN | 28 |
| 240 | 28 | **B** | 6:04 | B | **7:25** | D | 13 | 21 | 15 | 9 | 39 | 11 | **11½** | 5:28 | D | **6:50** | D | LEO | 0 |
| 241 | 29 | M. | 6:05 | B | **7:23** | D | 13 | 18 | 15 | 9 | 18 | **12** | — | 6:43 | D | **7:20** | D | SEX | 1 |
| 242 | 30 | Tu. | 6:06 | B | **7:22** | D | 13 | 16 | 15 | 8 | 56 | 12¼ | **12¾** | 7:59 | E | **7:51** | C | LEO | 2 |
| 243 | 31 | W. | 6:07 | B | **7:20** | D | 13 | 13 | 15 | 8 N. | 35 | 1 | **1½** | 9:16 | E | **8:23** | C | VIR | 3 |

 To use this page, see p. 110; for Key Letters, see p. 234. ☞ **Bold = P.M.** ☞ Light = A.M. 

## AUGUST HATH 31 DAYS • 2011

*There's a baby Moon rocking far up in the sky,*
*And the night-wind is blowing a soft lullaby.* –Pauline F. Camp

| Day of Month | Day of Week | Dates, Feasts, Fasts, Aspects, Tide Heights | Weather |
|---|---|---|---|
| 1 | M. | **First day of Ramadan** • Lammas Day • ☌☿☾ • Tides { 11.4 10.5 | *Ben* |
| 2 | Tu. | ☾ ON EQ. • ☾ AT PERIG. • ☿ STAT. • First cable car tested, San Francisco, 1873 | *Franklin* |
| 3 | W. | *Vision without action is a daydream; action without vision is a nightmare.* • Tides { 11.3 11.1 | *would* |
| 4 | Th. | ☌♄☾ • 108°F, Spokane, Wash., 1961 • Tides { 10.9 11.2 | *get a* |
| 5 | Fr. | Brown booby spotted, Virginia Beach, Va., 2006 • { 10.5 11.1 | *charge* |
| 6 | Sa. | **Transfiguration** • Sonic boom broke windows, Kelowna, B.C., 1969 • { 9.9 10.9 | *if* |
| 7 | **B** | **8th S. af. P.** • Love Canal, N.Y., declared disaster area, 1978 • { 9.5 10.7 | *he* |
| 8 | M. | **St. Dominic** • ☾ RUNS LOW • Gray squirrels have second litters now. • { 9.1 10.6 | *and* |
| 9 | Tu. | ☾ AT ☊ • Jesse Owens won his 4th gold medal, Summer Olympics, Berlin, Germany, 1936 | *his* |
| 10 | W. | **St. Lawrence** • ☌♇☾ • Canadian Bill of Rights took effect, 1960 • { 9.0 10.5 | *kite* |
| 11 | Th. | **St. Clare** • Dog Days end. • First baseball game televised in color, 1951 • { 9.2 10.6 | *were* |
| 12 | Fr. | *The handsomest flower is not the sweetest.* • Tides { 9.4 10.6 | *at* |
| 13 | Sa. | **Full Sturgeon** ○ • Small tornado hit Meredith, N.H., 2004 • Tides { 9.6 10.5 | *large.* |
| 14 | **B** | **9th S. af. P.** • ☌♆☾ • Social Security Act signed into law, 1935 | *Cooler* |
| 15 | M. | **Assumption** • ☾ ON EQ. • ☌☿♀ • Tides { 10.4 9.8 | *and* |
| 16 | Tu. | ☿ IN INF. ☌ • ♀ IN SUP. ☌ • *Sports Illustrated* debuted, 1954 • { 10.2 9.8 | *drier* |
| 17 | W. | Cat Nights commence. • ☌♅☾ • Tides { 9.9 9.8 | *out,* |
| 18 | Th. | ☾ AT APO. • Begole, Johnson, and Lucas summited Mt. Whitney, Sierra Nevada, Calif., 1873 | *with* |
| 19 | Fr. | Ragweed in bloom. • Aviator Orville Wright born, 1871 • { 9.2 9.5 | *less* |
| 20 | Sa. | ☌♃☾ • Hurricane and fire destroyed Indianola, Tex., 1886 • { 8.8 9.4 | *heavenly* |
| 21 | **B** | **10th S. af. P.** • *Gemini V* launched, 1965 • Tides { 8.4 9.3 | *fire* |
| 22 | M. | ♆ AT ☍ • Version of *The Scream* painting stolen from Munch Museum, Oslo, Norway, 2004 | *about.* |
| 23 | Tu. | ☾ RIDES HIGH • ☾ AT ☋ • Ornithologist Alexander Wilson died, 1813 • { 8.1 9.3 | *Say* |
| 24 | W. | **St. Bartholomew** • *St. Bartlemy's mantle wipes dry, All the tears that St. Swithin can cry.* | *farewell* |
| 25 | Th. | ☌♂☾ • First parachute wedding, N.Y.C., 1940 • Tides { 8.5 10.0 | *to* |
| 26 | Fr. | ☿ STAT. • Hummingbirds migrate south. • First Ford Edsel produced, 1957 • { 9.0 10.5 | *school* |
| 27 | Sa. | ☌☿☾ • Composer Tomás Luis de Victoria died, 1611 • Tides { 9.6 10.9 | *vacation* |
| 28 | **B** | **11th S. af. P.** • New ● • 18" rain, Saint George, Ga., 1911 | *with* |
| 29 | M. | **St. John the Baptist** • ☾ ON EQ. • ☌♀☾ • Tides { 10.8 — | *a* |
| 30 | Tu. | ☾ AT PERIG. • ♃ STAT. • *Never fish in troubled waters.* • { 11.5 11.3 | *thunderous* |
| 31 | W. | ☌♄☾ • Honolulu declared capital of Hawaiian Islands, 1850 • Tides { 11.6 11.6 | *ovation.* |

### *Farmer's Calendar*

■ It can be a hard thing to know how to help a fellow being, even when you have the ability to do so and the best of intentions. Misunderstanding thwarts goodwill.

Recently, a blue jay became trapped in the dusty attic room above our woodshed. The roof soffits are open, and there is an open staircase from the ground floor. The jay simply flew up. It might have simply flown back down, as well—but no. It flapped and fluttered around up there, banging into the closed window, occasionally uttering a cluck of perplexity.

I went to help. I found the bird perched on a rafter tie, out of reach. When I approached, it flew off and crashed into the window, after which it sat on the sill. I tried to catch it there to release it, but it flew back to the rafter. This went on for some time. The bird wouldn't help itself, and it wouldn't be helped. I didn't know what my part was in breaking the impasse.

At last I realized that I didn't have a part. I opened the shut window and went about my business. A couple of hours later, the jay was gone. It occurred to me that here we have an image of helping relationships, an image with broad application. When we would be of use but are not, we might reflect that if doing nothing is the only thing to do, then doing nothing is the best thing to do.

# THE NINTH MONTH • 2011



**SKY WATCH** ☆ *Mercury's best morning apparition of 2011 occurs during the first 2 weeks of the month, with its optimum brightness/height combination on the 9th–11th. The tiny orange planet is very close to the blue star Regulus on the 9th. Saturn is still very low in the sky, but Jupiter keeps brightening and rises by 9:00 P.M. at midmonth. The Moon joins Jupiter on the 15th and 16th. Uranus, in Pisces, is closest to Earth on the 25th, its first opposition north of the equator in 42 years. Virgo hosts a party on the 27th: The Moon, Mercury, Venus, and Saturn crowd invisibly near the Sun. Fall arrives with the autumnal equinox on the 23rd, at 5:05 A.M.*

| | | | | |
|---|---|---|---|---|
| ◐ | **First Quarter** | 4th day | 13th hour | 39th minute |
| ○ | **Full Moon** | 12th day | 5th hour | 27th minute |
| ◑ | **Last Quarter** | 20th day | 9th hour | 39th minute |
| ● | **New Moon** | 27th day | 7th hour | 9th minute |

*All times are given in Eastern Daylight Time.*

**Purchase these pages with times set to your zip code at MyLocalAlmanac.com.**

| Day of Year | Day of Month | Day of Week | ☼ Rises h. m. | Rise Key | ☼ Sets h. m. | Set Key | Length of Day h. m. | Sun Fast m. | Declination of Sun ° ' | High Tide Times Boston | | ☾ Rises h. m. | Rise Key | ☾ Sets h. m. | Set Key | ☾ Place | ☾ Age |
|---|---|---|---|---|---|---|---|---|---|---|---|---|---|---|---|---|---|
| 244 | 1 | Th. | 6:09 | B | **7:18** | D | 13 09 | 16 | 8 N.13 | 2 | **2¼** | 10:32 | E | **8:59** | B | VIR | 4 |
| 245 | 2 | Fr. | 6:10 | B | **7:17** | D | 13 07 | 16 | 7 51 | 2¾ | **3¼** | 11:47 | E | **9:40** | B | VIR | 5 |
| 246 | 3 | Sa. | 6:11 | C | **7:15** | D | 13 04 | 16 | 7 29 | 3¾ | **4** | **12:58** | E | **10:27** | B | LIB | 6 |
| 247 | 4 | **B** | 6:12 | C | **7:13** | D | 13 01 | 17 | 7 07 | 4¾ | **5** | **2:03** | E | **11:21** | B | SCO | 7 |
| 248 | 5 | M. | 6:13 | C | **7:11** | D | 12 58 | 17 | 6 45 | 5¾ | **6** | **3:00** | E | — | – | OPH | 8 |
| 249 | 6 | Tu. | 6:14 | C | **7:10** | D | 12 56 | 17 | 6 23 | 6¾ | **7¼** | **3:47** | E | 12:20 | B | SAG | 9 |
| 250 | 7 | W. | 6:15 | C | **7:08** | D | 12 53 | 18 | 6 00 | 8 | **8¼** | **4:27** | E | 1:23 | B | SAG | 10 |
| 251 | 8 | Th. | 6:16 | C | **7:06** | D | 12 50 | 18 | 5 38 | 9 | **9¼** | **5:01** | E | 2:28 | C | SAG | 11 |
| 252 | 9 | Fr. | 6:17 | C | **7:04** | D | 12 47 | 18 | 5 15 | 10 | **10¼** | **5:30** | D | 3:32 | C | AQU | 12 |
| 253 | 10 | Sa. | 6:18 | C | **7:03** | D | 12 45 | 19 | 4 52 | 10¾ | **11** | **5:56** | D | 4:34 | C | CAP | 13 |
| 254 | 11 | **B** | 6:19 | C | **7:01** | D | 12 42 | 19 | 4 30 | 11¼ | **11½** | **6:21** | D | 5:36 | D | AQU | 14 |
| 255 | 12 | M. | 6:20 | C | **6:59** | C | 12 39 | 20 | 4 07 | **12** | — | **6:44** | C | 6:36 | D | PSC | 15 |
| 256 | 13 | Tu. | 6:21 | C | **6:57** | C | 12 36 | 20 | 3 44 | 12¼ | **12½** | **7:08** | C | 7:36 | E | PSC | 16 |
| 257 | 14 | W. | 6:22 | C | **6:56** | C | 12 34 | 20 | 3 21 | 1 | **1¼** | **7:34** | C | 8:35 | E | PSC | 17 |
| 258 | 15 | Th. | 6:23 | C | **6:54** | C | 12 31 | 21 | 2 58 | 1½ | **1¾** | **8:02** | B | 9:34 | E | PSC | 18 |
| 259 | 16 | Fr. | 6:24 | C | **6:52** | C | 12 28 | 21 | 2 35 | 2¼ | **2½** | **8:33** | B | 10:34 | E | ARI | 19 |
| 260 | 17 | Sa. | 6:25 | C | **6:50** | C | 12 25 | 21 | 2 12 | 2¾ | **3** | **9:10** | B | 11:32 | E | ARI | 20 |
| 261 | 18 | **B** | 6:26 | C | **6:49** | C | 12 23 | 22 | 1 48 | 3½ | **3¾** | **9:53** | B | **12:29** | E | TAU | 21 |
| 262 | 19 | M. | 6:27 | C | **6:47** | C | 12 20 | 22 | 1 25 | 4¼ | **4½** | **10:43** | B | **1:23** | E | TAU | 22 |
| 263 | 20 | Tu. | 6:29 | C | **6:45** | C | 12 16 | 22 | 1 02 | 5¼ | **5½** | **11:40** | B | **2:13** | E | TAU | 23 |
| 264 | 21 | W. | 6:30 | C | **6:43** | C | 12 13 | 23 | 0 38 | 6¼ | **6½** | — | – | **2:57** | E | GEM | 24 |
| 265 | 22 | Th. | 6:31 | C | **6:42** | C | 12 11 | 23 | 0 N.15 | 7 | **7¼** | 12:43 | B | **3:37** | E | GEM | 25 |
| 266 | 23 | Fr. | 6:32 | C | **6:40** | C | 12 08 | 23 | 0 S.07 | 8 | **8¼** | 1:51 | C | **4:13** | E | CAN | 26 |
| 267 | 24 | Sa. | 6:33 | C | **6:38** | C | 12 05 | 24 | 0 31 | 9 | **9¼** | 3:02 | C | **4:45** | D | CAN | 27 |
| 268 | 25 | **B** | 6:34 | C | **6:36** | C | 12 02 | 24 | 0 54 | 9¾ | **10** | 4:16 | D | **5:16** | D | LEO | 28 |
| 269 | 26 | M. | 6:35 | C | **6:34** | C | 11 59 | 24 | 1 17 | 10½ | **11** | 5:32 | D | **5:47** | C | LEO | 29 |
| 270 | 27 | Tu. | 6:36 | C | **6:33** | C | 11 57 | 25 | 1 41 | 11½ | **11¾** | 6:49 | E | **6:19** | C | VIR | 0 |
| 271 | 28 | W. | 6:37 | C | **6:31** | C | 11 54 | 25 | 2 04 | **12¼** | — | 8:07 | E | **6:54** | B | VIR | 1 |
| 272 | 29 | Th. | 6:38 | C | **6:29** | C | 11 51 | 25 | 2 27 | 12¾ | **1** | 9:26 | E | **7:35** | B | VIR | 2 |
| 273 | 30 | Fr. | 6:39 | C | **6:27** | C | 11 48 | 26 | 2 S.51 | 1½ | **1¾** | 10:41 | E | **8:21** | B | LIB | 3 |

 To use this page, see p. 110; for Key Letters, see p. 234. ☞ Bold = P.M. ☞ Light = A.M. 

# SEPTEMBER HATH 30 DAYS • 2011

*O sweet September rain!*
*I hear it fall upon the garden beds.* –Mortimer Collins

| Day of Month | Day of Week | Dates, Feasts, Fasts, Aspects, Tide Heights | Weather |
|---|---|---|---|
| 1 | Th. | Missionary Narcissa Whitman arrived at Walla Walla, Wash., 1836 • Tides { 11.3 / 11.7 | *Days* |
| 2 | Fr. | *A fog from the hills / Brings corn to the mills.* • { 10.9 / 11.6 | *bright* |
| 3 | Sa. | ☿ GR. ELONG. (18° WEST) • World record set by auto averaging 301.13 mph for 1 mile, Bonneville Salt Flats, Utah, 1935 | *as a* |
| 4 | **B** | **12th S. af. P.** • 127-pound cabbage won prize at Alaska State Fair, 2009 | *'Golden* |
| 5 | M. | **Labor Day** • ☾ RUNS LOW • ☾ AT ☊ • 102°F, Portland, Oreg., 1944 | *Delicious',* |
| 6 | Tu. | ☌♇☾ • Clergyman Heinrich Muhlenberg born, 1711 • Tides { 9.0 / 10.2 | *nights* |
| 7 | W. | Entertainment and Sports Programming Network (ESPN) debuted, 1979 • Tides { 8.9 / 10.1 | *crisp* |
| 8 | Th. | Writer Euell Gibbons born, 1911 • Cranberry harvest begins, Cape Cod, Mass. • { 9.0 / 10.1 | *as a* |
| 9 | Fr. | **St. Omer** • USS *Long Beach*, first nuclear-powered surface warship, commissioned, 1961 | *'Granny* |
| 10 | Sa. | ☌♆☾ • *There are three friends in this world: courage, sense, and insight.* • { 9.5 / 10.1 | *Smith':* |
| 11 | **B** | **13th S. af. P.** • **Patriot Day** • Tides { 9.7 / 10.1 | *Apples* |
| 12 | M. | **Full Harvest** ○ • ☾ ON EQ. • Whale followed boat to Montreal harbor, 1823 • { 9.8 / — | *make* |
| 13 | Tu. | ☌♅☾ • World's hottest temperature, 136°F, recorded, Al'Aziziyah, Libya, 1922 • { 10.0 / 9.9 | *our* |
| 14 | W. | **Holy Cross** • Launch of *Zond 5*, eventual first spacecraft to orbit Moon, 1968 • { 9.9 / 10.0 | *favorite* |
| 15 | Th. | ☾ AT APO. • Milch goat show started, Rochester Industrial Exposition, N.Y., 1913 • { 9.6 / 9.9 | *dishes* |
| 16 | Fr. | ☌♃☾ • ♇ STAT. • *Sweet is the memory of past labor.* • { 9.4 / 9.8 | *tempt* |
| 17 | Sa. | 17-lb. 4-oz. white catfish caught, Humboldt River, Nev., 2005 • Tides { 9.0 / 9.7 | *us* |
| 18 | **B** | **14th S. af. P.** • Cornerstone for U.S. Capitol laid, Wash., D.C., 1793 • { 8.7 / 9.5 | *as the* |
| 19 | M. | ☾ RIDES HIGH • ☾ AT ☋ • Anti-AIDS drug AZT first available, 1986 • { 8.4 / 9.3 | *serpent* |
| 20 | Tu. | **St. Eustace** • 4.88" rain, Berne, Ind., 1957 • { 8.3 / 9.3 | *did.* |
| 21 | W. | **St. Matthew** • Ember Day • Canada's "toonie" coin unveiled, 1995 • { 8.2 / 9.4 | *Rain* |
| 22 | Th. | *Teachers open the door, but you must enter by yourself.* | *brings* |
| 23 | Fr. | Ember Day • Harvest Home • **Autumnal Equinox** • ☌♂☾ • { 8.9 / 10.0 | *warning,* |
| 24 | Sa. | Ember Day • James Henry Fleming first to band a bird in Canada, 1905 • { 9.5 / 10.5 | *frost* |
| 25 | **B** | **15th S. af. P.** • ♅ AT ☍ • Tides { 10.2 / 11.0 | *belief:* |
| 26 | M. | ☾ ON EQ. • 111°F, San Diego, Calif., 1963 • Tides { 10.9 / 11.3 | *Every* |
| 27 | Tu. | **St. Vincent de Paul** • **New** ● • ☾ AT PERIG. • ☌☿☾ | *garden* |
| 28 | W. | ☌♀☾ • ☌♄☾ • ☿ IN SUP. ☌ • Tides { 12.0 / — | *comes* |
| 29 | Th. | **St. Michael** • **Rosh Hashanah** • Woodchucks hibernate now. • { 11.4 / 12.2 | *to* |
| 30 | Fr. | **St. Sophia** • ☌♀♄ • *Better a bad harvest than a bad neighbor.* • { 11.2 / 12.1 | *grief.* |

*If you surrender to the wind, you can ride it.* –Toni Morrison

## *Farmer's Calendar*

■ The belted kingfisher *(Ceryle alcyon)* is a bird of manic high spirits. It appears to enjoy its life hugely. In fishing, it leaves its waterside branch or other perch and strikes out in a rapid, swooping flight like a woodpecker's, uttering a loud, cackling chatter. Spotting a minnow in the water below, it hits the brakes and hovers over the surface, helicopter-like, then drops headfirst into the water in a kind of corkscrew dive, splashing mightily, to emerge with its meal held fast in its bill. The bird then repairs to another perch where it dines, not without further bursts of self-satisfied laughter.

Common near rivers and ponds across the country, the kingfisher nests in tunnels it makes in vertical faces of shoreline banks. It seems to stake out certain stretches of water to patrol, using the same perches regularly to watch for small fish, tadpoles, and the like. Maybe its characteristic rattling cry is used in part to proclaim its territory.

Or, perhaps the kingfisher has a big personality to compensate for other disadvantages. It is, frankly, a rather peculiar-looking bird. Not much larger than a robin, it has an outsized head carried on a stubby body. This busy, talkative bird looks like nothing so much as a figure in an old-fashioned political cartoon.

# THE TENTH MONTH • 2011



**SKY WATCH** ☆ *Saturn reaches its unseen conjunction behind the Sun on the 13th. The month belongs to Jupiter, which rises at sunset in Aries, is near the Moon on the 13th, and is closest to Earth on the 27th at a blazing magnitude –2.9. Appearing almost 50 arcseconds in width and looking wonderful through telescopes, Jupiter makes its closest visit until 2022. No other planet is worthwhile this month. Mars is still not bright, as it rises at 1:30* A.M. *at midmonth. The 27th brings a close conjunction of the Moon, Venus, and Mercury, but it can be seen only from the far south, below Miami.*

| | | | | |
|---|---|---|---|---|
| ◐ | **First Quarter** | 3rd day | 23rd hour | 15th minute |
| ○ | **Full Moon** | 11th day | 22nd hour | 6th minute |
| ◑ | **Last Quarter** | 19th day | 23rd hour | 30th minute |
| ● | **New Moon** | 26th day | 15th hour | 56th minute |

*All times are given in Eastern Daylight Time.*

**Purchase these pages with times set to your zip code at MyLocalAlmanac.com.**

| Day of Year | Day of Month | Day of Week | ☼ Rises h. m. | Rise Key | ☼ Sets h. m. | Set Key | Length of Day h. m. | Sun Fast m. | Declination of Sun ° ' | High Tide Times Boston | | ☾ Rises h. m. | Rise Key | ☾ Sets h. m. | Set Key | ☾ Place | ☾ Age |
|---|---|---|---|---|---|---|---|---|---|---|---|---|---|---|---|---|---|
| 274 | 1 | Sa. | 6:40 | C | **6:26** | C | 11 46 | 26 | 3 s.14 | 2½ | **2¾** | 11:51 | E | **9:14** | B | SCO | 4 |
| 275 | 2 | **B** | 6:41 | C | **6:24** | C | 11 43 | 26 | 3 37 | 3½ | **3¾** | **12:52** | E | **10:13** | B | OPH | 5 |
| 276 | 3 | M. | 6:43 | C | **6:22** | C | 11 39 | 27 | 4 00 | 4½ | **4¾** | **1:44** | E | **11:17** | B | SAG | 6 |
| 277 | 4 | Tu. | 6:44 | D | **6:21** | C | 11 37 | 27 | 4 24 | 5½ | **5¾** | **2:27** | E | — | – | SAG | 7 |
| 278 | 5 | W. | 6:45 | D | **6:19** | C | 11 34 | 27 | 4 47 | 6½ | **6¾** | **3:03** | E | 12:21 | B | SAG | 8 |
| 279 | 6 | Th. | 6:46 | D | **6:17** | C | 11 31 | 28 | 5 10 | 7½ | **8** | **3:33** | E | 1:25 | C | CAP | 9 |
| 280 | 7 | Fr. | 6:47 | D | **6:15** | C | 11 28 | 28 | 5 33 | 8½ | **9** | **4:00** | D | 2:28 | C | AQU | 10 |
| 281 | 8 | Sa. | 6:48 | D | **6:14** | C | 11 26 | 28 | 5 56 | 9½ | **9¾** | **4:25** | D | 3:29 | D | AQU | 11 |
| 282 | 9 | **B** | 6:49 | D | **6:12** | C | 11 23 | 28 | 6 18 | 10¼ | **10½** | **4:49** | C | 4:29 | D | PSC | 12 |
| 283 | 10 | M. | 6:50 | D | **6:10** | C | 11 20 | 29 | 6 41 | 10¾ | **11¼** | **5:13** | C | 5:29 | D | PSC | 13 |
| 284 | 11 | Tu. | 6:52 | D | **6:09** | C | 11 17 | 29 | 7 04 | 11½ | **11¾** | **5:38** | C | 6:28 | E | PSC | 14 |
| 285 | 12 | W. | 6:53 | D | **6:07** | B | 11 14 | 29 | 7 26 | **12** | — | **6:05** | B | 7:27 | E | PSC | 15 |
| 286 | 13 | Th. | 6:54 | D | **6:05** | B | 11 11 | 30 | 7 49 | 12½ | **12½** | **6:36** | B | 8:26 | E | ARI | 16 |
| 287 | 14 | Fr. | 6:55 | D | **6:04** | B | 11 09 | 30 | 8 11 | 1 | **1¼** | **7:11** | B | 9:25 | E | ARI | 17 |
| 288 | 15 | Sa. | 6:56 | D | **6:02** | B | 11 06 | 30 | 8 33 | 1¾ | **1¾** | **7:52** | B | 10:23 | E | TAU | 18 |
| 289 | 16 | **B** | 6:57 | D | **6:01** | B | 11 04 | 30 | 8 56 | 2½ | **2½** | **8:39** | B | 11:17 | E | TAU | 19 |
| 290 | 17 | M. | 6:58 | D | **5:59** | B | 11 01 | 30 | 9 18 | 3¼ | **3¼** | **9:32** | B | **12:07** | E | TAU | 20 |
| 291 | 18 | Tu. | 7:00 | D | **5:57** | B | 10 57 | 31 | 9 39 | 4 | **4** | **10:31** | B | **12:53** | E | GEM | 21 |
| 292 | 19 | W. | 7:01 | D | **5:56** | B | 10 55 | 31 | 10 01 | 4¾ | **5** | **11:35** | C | **1:33** | E | GEM | 22 |
| 293 | 20 | Th. | 7:02 | D | **5:54** | B | 10 52 | 31 | 10 23 | 5½ | **5¾** | — | – | **2:09** | E | CAN | 23 |
| 294 | 21 | Fr. | 7:03 | D | **5:53** | B | 10 50 | 31 | 10 44 | 6½ | **6¾** | 12:43 | C | **2:42** | E | CAN | 24 |
| 295 | 22 | Sa. | 7:04 | D | **5:51** | B | 10 47 | 31 | 11 05 | 7½ | **7¾** | 1:53 | C | **3:12** | D | LEO | 25 |
| 296 | 23 | **B** | 7:06 | D | **5:50** | B | 10 44 | 31 | 11 26 | 8½ | **8¾** | 3:05 | D | **3:42** | C | SEX | 26 |
| 297 | 24 | M. | 7:07 | D | **5:48** | B | 10 41 | 32 | 11 47 | 9¼ | **9¾** | 4:20 | E | **4:13** | C | LEO | 27 |
| 298 | 25 | Tu. | 7:08 | D | **5:47** | B | 10 39 | 32 | 12 08 | 10 | **10¾** | 5:37 | E | **4:47** | C | VIR | 28 |
| 299 | 26 | W. | 7:09 | D | **5:46** | B | 10 37 | 32 | 12 29 | 11 | **11½** | 6:55 | E | **5:25** | B | VIR | 0 |
| 300 | 27 | Th. | 7:10 | D | **5:44** | B | 10 34 | 32 | 12 49 | 11¾ | — | 8:14 | E | **6:09** | B | LIB | 1 |
| 301 | 28 | Fr. | 7:12 | D | **5:43** | B | 10 31 | 32 | 13 09 | 12½ | **12¾** | 9:29 | E | **7:00** | B | LIB | 2 |
| 302 | 29 | Sa. | 7:13 | D | **5:41** | B | 10 28 | 32 | 13 29 | 1¼ | **1½** | 10:36 | E | **7:59** | B | OPH | 3 |
| 303 | 30 | **B** | 7:14 | D | **5:40** | B | 10 26 | 32 | 13 49 | 2¼ | **2½** | 11:35 | E | **9:03** | B | OPH | 4 |
| 304 | 31 | M. | 7:15 | D | **5:39** | B | 10 24 | 32 | 14 s.08 | 3 | **3¼** | **12:23** | E | **10:10** | B | SAG | 5 |

 **To use this page, see p. 110; for Key Letters, see p. 234.** ☞ **Bold = P.M.** ☞ Light = A.M. 

# OCTOBER HATH 31 DAYS • 2011

*The maples in the forest glow;*
*On the lawn the fall flowers blaze.* –Sylvester Baxter

| Day of Month | Day of Week | Dates, Feasts, Fasts, Aspects, Tide Heights | Weather |
|---|---|---|---|
| 1 | Sa. | St. Gregory • Panama gained sovereignty over Canal, 1979 • Tides {10.8 11.8 | *Warm* |
| 2 | B | 16th S. af. P. • ☾ runs low • ☾ at ☊ | *reception's* |
| 3 | M. | ☌♇☾ • "October Gale" hit southern New England, 1841 • {9.7 10.7 | *misdirection:* |
| 4 | Tu. | St. Francis of Assisi • Ruth Allen won L.I. horseshoe championship, 1942 | *damp* |
| 5 | W. | Pumpkin Flood, Susquehanna and Delaware Rivers, Pa., 1786 | *and* |
| 6 | Th. | *No one is more afraid of ghosts than those who don't believe in them.* • Tides {9.0 9.7 | *raw.* |
| 7 | Fr. | ☌☿♄ • ☌♆☾ • Frank Sinatra's first TV show debuted, 1950 • {9.2 9.6 | *Milder,* |
| 8 | Sa. | Yom Kippur • California Desert Bill passed, 1994 • {9.4 9.6 | *briefly,* |
| 9 | B | 17th S. af. P. • ☾ on Eq. • Tides {9.6 9.7 | *then* |
| 10 | M. | Columbus Day (observed) • Thanksgiving Day (Canada) • ☌♅☾ • {9.8 9.7 | *beware:* |
| 11 | Tu. | Full Hunter's ○ • X-15 rocket plane ascended to 217,000', setting record, 1961 | *williwaws!* |
| 12 | W. | ☾ at apo. • Al Gore cowinner of Nobel Peace Prize, 2007 • Tides {10.1 — | *A* |
| 13 | Th. | Sukkoth • ☌♃☾ • ☌♄☉ • Tides {9.5 10.1 | *perfect* |
| 14 | Fr. | *The darkness of night can not stop the light of morning.* | *week:* |
| 15 | Sa. | Veterans Memorial Bridge opened, Port Arthur–Bridge City, Tex., 1991 • Tides {9.2 10.0 | *The* |
| 16 | B | 18th S. af. P. • ☾ rides high • ☾ at ☋ • Tides {8.9 9.8 | *peaks* |
| 17 | M. | St. Ignatius of Antioch • Stunt motorcyclist Evel Knievel born, 1938 • {8.7 9.7 | *are* |
| 18 | Tu. | St. Luke • St. Luke's little summer. • Baseball manager Connie Mack announced retirement, 1950 | *showy.* |
| 19 | W. | Watertown Senior High School first to fingerprint students, S.Dak., 1936 • Tides {8.5 9.5 | *Seize* |
| 20 | Th. | Last day of Prince of Wales's North American tour, Portland, Maine, 1860 • Tides {8.6 9.5 | *the* |
| 21 | Fr. | ☌♂☾ • Timber rattlesnakes move to winter dens. | *day!* |
| 22 | Sa. | Margaret Meagher became Canada's first female ambassador (to Israel), 1958 • {9.4 10.0 | *Showers* |
| 23 | B | 19th S. af. P. • ☾ on Eq. • 1' snow, Haverhill, N.H., 1843 • {10.1 10.3 | *(some* |
| 24 | M. | First transcontinental telegraph message, Calif. to D.C., 1861 • Last passenger flight of Concorde jet, 2003 | *snowy)* |
| 25 | Tu. | Archibald J. Turner granted patent for a football shoulder pad, 1960 • Tides {11.5 11.0 | *make* |
| 26 | W. | New ● • ☾ at perig. • ☌♄☾ • Little brown bats hibernate now. | *colors* |
| 27 | Th. | ☌☿☾ • Inventor Isaac Singer born, 1811 • Tides {12.3 — | *duller.* |
| 28 | Fr. | Sts. Simon & Jude • ☌♀☾ • ♃ at ☍ • {11.1 12.4 | *Trick-or-* |
| 29 | Sa. | ☾ runs low • ☾ at ☊ • John Glenn returned to space at age 77, 1998 • {10.9 12.2 | *treaters'* |
| 30 | B | 20th S. af. P. • ☌♇☾ • First Lamborghini car debuted, 1963 | *rain* |
| 31 | M. | All Hallows' Eve • Reformation Day • *Nothing sharpens sight like envy.* • {10.1 11.1 | *delay!* |

## *Farmer's Calendar*

■ Harvest figures, scarecrow-like effigies, appear on porches and in dooryards. They sprawl like last night's revelers who didn't quite make it home. They're a louche and disreputable lot, intended mainly to display their creators' wit. Harvest figures are improvised and more or less crude. A pumpkin head, a stuffed suit of long underwear, a cast-off Red Sox jacket will do very well. We're not talking about high art here.

Or are we? In his work *The Golden Bough,* British scholar J. G. Frazer surveyed the world's art, literature, myth, and folkways to discover themes that replicate the cycle of the year from planting to ripening to harvest. For Frazer, the annual decline and renewal of the land's vegetation was the symbolic foundation of much of human behavior, crucially in literature, art, and religion.

In the world of *The Golden Bough,* the construction of the harvest figure was more than a reliable seasonal joke. It was a mystery, a solemn ritual intended to be enacted with devotion, faith, and awe. The harvest figure itself was a sacrificial symbol whose demise would magically ensure the rebirth of nature by which, precariously, all men lived. The drunken yokels who populate our lawns this month may not look like much, but they come of a very old family.

# NOVEMBER

## THE ELEVENTH MONTH • 2011

**SKY WATCH** ☆ *Venus slowly emerges from behind the Sun at its faintest of the year, moving next to and in sync with Mercury just below it, from the 1st to the 15th. By midmonth, the duo stands 6 degrees high, 35 minutes after sunset. The changing angle of the zodiac to the horizon carries Venus higher by month's end, where it meets the crescent Moon 10 degrees up on the 26th in fading twilight. The month's real standout remains Jupiter. At a brilliant magnitude –2.9, this is the brightest it ever gets. It's already up in the east at nightfall, then out all night. In most places, the length of night grows by 3 minutes daily at the start of November but falls to just 1 minute by month's end.*

| | | | | |
|---|---|---|---|---|
| ◐ | **First Quarter** | 2nd day | 12th hour | 38th minute |
| ○ | **Full Moon** | 10th day | 15th hour | 16th minute |
| ◑ | **Last Quarter** | 18th day | 10th hour | 9th minute |
| ● | **New Moon** | 25th day | 1st hour | 10th minute |

*After 2:00 A.M. on November 6, Eastern Standard Time is given.*

**Purchase these pages with times set to your zip code at MyLocalAlmanac.com.**

| Day of Year | Day of Month | Day of Week | ☼ Rises h. m. | Rise Key | ☼ Sets h. m. | Set Key | Length of Day h. | m. | Sun Fast m. | Declination of Sun ° | ' | High Tide Times Boston | | ☾ Rises h. m. | Rise Key | ☾ Sets h. m. | Set Key | ☾ Place | ☾ Age |
|---|---|---|---|---|---|---|---|---|---|---|---|---|---|---|---|---|---|---|---|
| 305 | 1 | Tu. | 7:17 | D | **5:38** | B | 10 | 21 | 32 | 14 s. | 28 | 4 | **4¼** | **1:02** | E | **11:16** | C | SAG | 6 |
| 306 | 2 | W. | 7:18 | D | **5:36** | B | 10 | 18 | 32 | 14 | 47 | 5 | **5¼** | **1:35** | E | — | - | CAP | 7 |
| 307 | 3 | Th. | 7:19 | D | **5:35** | B | 10 | 16 | 32 | 15 | 06 | 6 | **6¼** | **2:03** | D | 12:20 | C | AQU | 8 |
| 308 | 4 | Fr. | 7:20 | D | **5:34** | B | 10 | 14 | 32 | 15 | 24 | 7 | **7½** | **2:29** | D | 1:22 | C | AQU | 9 |
| 309 | 5 | Sa. | 7:22 | E | **5:33** | B | 10 | 11 | 32 | 15 | 43 | 8 | **8¼** | **2:53** | C | 2:23 | D | AQU | 10 |
| 310 | 6 | **B** | 6:23 | E | **4:31** | B | 10 | 08 | 32 | 16 | 01 | 7¾ | **8¼** | **2:17** | C | 2:22 | D | PSC | 11 |
| 311 | 7 | M. | 6:24 | E | **4:30** | B | 10 | 06 | 32 | 16 | 18 | 8½ | **9** | **2:42** | C | 3:21 | E | PSC | 12 |
| 312 | 8 | Tu. | 6:25 | E | **4:29** | B | 10 | 04 | 32 | 16 | 36 | 9¼ | **9¾** | **3:08** | B | 4:20 | E | PSC | 13 |
| 313 | 9 | W. | 6:27 | E | **4:28** | B | 10 | 01 | 32 | 16 | 53 | 10 | **10½** | **3:38** | B | 5:19 | E | PSC | 14 |
| 314 | 10 | Th. | 6:28 | E | **4:27** | B | 9 | 59 | 32 | 17 | 10 | 10½ | **11** | **4:12** | B | 6:18 | E | ARI | 15 |
| 315 | 11 | Fr. | 6:29 | E | **4:26** | B | 9 | 57 | 32 | 17 | 27 | 11¼ | **11¾** | **4:51** | B | 7:17 | E | ARI | 16 |
| 316 | 12 | Sa. | 6:30 | E | **4:25** | B | 9 | 55 | 32 | 17 | 43 | 11¾ | — | **5:36** | B | 8:12 | E | TAU | 17 |
| 317 | 13 | **B** | 6:32 | E | **4:24** | B | 9 | 52 | 32 | 17 | 59 | 12¼ | **12½** | **6:28** | B | 9:04 | E | TAU | 18 |
| 318 | 14 | M. | 6:33 | E | **4:23** | B | 9 | 50 | 31 | 18 | 15 | 1 | **1** | **7:26** | B | 9:51 | E | ORI | 19 |
| 319 | 15 | Tu. | 6:34 | E | **4:22** | B | 9 | 48 | 31 | 18 | 30 | 1¾ | **1¾** | **8:27** | B | 10:33 | E | GEM | 20 |
| 320 | 16 | W. | 6:35 | E | **4:21** | B | 9 | 46 | 31 | 18 | 45 | 2½ | **2½** | **9:33** | C | 11:09 | E | GEM | 21 |
| 321 | 17 | Th. | 6:37 | E | **4:20** | B | 9 | 43 | 31 | 19 | 00 | 3¼ | **3½** | **10:40** | C | 11:42 | E | CAN | 22 |
| 322 | 18 | Fr. | 6:38 | E | **4:19** | B | 9 | 41 | 31 | 19 | 15 | 4¼ | **4¼** | **11:49** | D | **12:12** | D | LEO | 23 |
| 323 | 19 | Sa. | 6:39 | E | **4:19** | B | 9 | 40 | 30 | 19 | 29 | 5 | **5¼** | — | - | **12:41** | D | SEX | 24 |
| 324 | 20 | **B** | 6:40 | E | **4:18** | B | 9 | 38 | 30 | 19 | 42 | 6 | **6¼** | 12:59 | D | **1:10** | C | LEO | 25 |
| 325 | 21 | M. | 6:41 | E | **4:17** | B | 9 | 36 | 30 | 19 | 56 | 7 | **7½** | 2:12 | E | **1:41** | C | VIR | 26 |
| 326 | 22 | Tu. | 6:43 | E | **4:17** | B | 9 | 34 | 30 | 20 | 09 | 7¾ | **8¼** | 3:27 | E | **2:16** | B | VIR | 27 |
| 327 | 23 | W. | 6:44 | E | **4:16** | B | 9 | 32 | 29 | 20 | 22 | 8¾ | **9¼** | 4:44 | E | **2:56** | B | VIR | 28 |
| 328 | 24 | Th. | 6:45 | E | **4:15** | A | 9 | 30 | 29 | 20 | 34 | 9½ | **10¼** | 6:00 | E | **3:43** | B | LIB | 29 |
| 329 | 25 | Fr. | 6:46 | E | **4:15** | A | 9 | 29 | 29 | 20 | 46 | 10½ | **11¼** | 7:13 | E | **4:39** | B | SCO | 0 |
| 330 | 26 | Sa. | 6:47 | E | **4:14** | A | 9 | 27 | 29 | 20 | 57 | 11¼ | — | 8:17 | E | **5:42** | B | OPH | 1 |
| 331 | 27 | **B** | 6:48 | E | **4:14** | A | 9 | 26 | 28 | 21 | 08 | 12 | **12¼** | 9:11 | E | **6:50** | B | SAG | 2 |
| 332 | 28 | M. | 6:50 | E | **4:14** | A | 9 | 24 | 28 | 21 | 19 | 1 | **1** | 9:56 | E | **7:58** | C | SAG | 3 |
| 333 | 29 | Tu. | 6:51 | E | **4:13** | A | 9 | 22 | 27 | 21 | 29 | 1¾ | **2** | 10:33 | E | **9:05** | C | SAG | 4 |
| 334 | 30 | W. | 6:52 | E | **4:13** | A | 9 | 21 | 27 | 21 s. | 39 | 2¾ | **2¾** | 11:04 | D | **10:10** | C | AQU | 5 |

 **To use this page, see p. 110; for Key Letters, see p. 234.** ☞ **Bold = P.M.** ☞ Light = A.M. 

# NOVEMBER HATH 30 DAYS • 2011

*Old Frost, the silversmith, has come:*
*His crisping touch is on the weeds.* –Charles Dawson Shanly

| Day of Month | Day of Week | Dates, Feasts, Fasts, Aspects, Tide Heights | Weather |
|---|---|---|---|
| 1 | Tu. | **All Saints'** • Hurricane battered Union fleet, Cape Hatteras, N.C., 1861 | *Remember,* |
| 2 | W. | **All Souls'** • N.Dak. and S.Dak. became 39th and 40th states, 1889 • {9.3 / 9.9} | *remember* |
| 3 | Th. | *In the eyes of its mother, every turkey is a swan.* | *Gunpowder* |
| 4 | Fr. | ☌♆☾ • Earthquake rang bells in Notre Dame basilica, Montreal, 1877 • {9.1 / 9.2} | *Treason!* |
| 5 | Sa. | Sadie Hawkins Day • ☾ ON EQ. • Actor Roy Rogers born, 1911 • {9.2 / 9.1} | *It's* |
| 6 | **B** | **21st S. af. P.** • **Daylight Saving Time ends, 2:00 A.M.** • ☌♅☾ | *cool* |
| 7 | M. | Magic Johnson announced retirement from basketball, 1991 | *for* |
| 8 | Tu. | **Election Day** • ☾ AT APO. • Black bears head to winter dens now. • {9.8 / 9.1} | *the* |
| 9 | W. | ☌♃☾ • ♆ STAT. • 70°F, Manchester, N.H., 2009 | *season.* |
| 10 | Th. | **Full Beaver** ○ • National Book Week (U.S.) first observed, 1919 • {10.1 / 9.2} | *Snowball* |
| 11 | Fr. | **St. Martin of Tours** • **Veterans Day** • Deadly Armistice Day Storm in central U.S., 1940 | *fights* |
| 12 | Sa. | Indian Summer • ☾ AT ☋ • Lobsters move to offshore waters. • {10.2 / —} | *and* |
| 13 | **B** | **22nd S. af. P.** • ☾ RIDES HIGH • Ginger Rogers married Lew Ayres, 1934 | *chilly* |
| 14 | M. | ☿ GR. ELONG. (23° EAST) • *Ice in November Brings mud in December.* • {8.9 / 10.1} | *nights* |
| 15 | Tu. | Crab apples are ripe now. • Astronomer Johannes Kepler died, 1630 • {8.8 / 10.0} | *give* |
| 16 | W. | Radio commentator Mary Margaret McBride born, 1899 • UNESCO established, 1945 | *way* |
| 17 | Th. | **St. Hugh of Lincoln** • Turkey plucked in 1 minute 30 seconds, setting world record, 1980 | *to* |
| 18 | Fr. | Composer Carl Maria von Weber born, 1786 • {9.1 / 9.7} | *rising* |
| 19 | Sa. | ☾ ON EQ. • ☌♂☾ • Skunks hibernate now. | *temperature;* |
| 20 | **B** | **23rd S. af. P.** • Alcan Highway dedicated, Soldier's Summit, Y.T., 1942 | *snow* |
| 21 | M. | Verrazano-Narrows Bridge opened, N.Y.C., 1964 | *whitens,* |
| 22 | Tu. | ☌♄☾ • Storm caused deadly mudslide, Prince Rupert, B.C., 1957 • Tides {11.1 / 10.2} | *sun* |
| 23 | W. | **St. Clement** • ☾ AT PERIG. • Intercollegiate Football Association formed, 1876 | *brightens* |
| 24 | Th. | **Thanksgiving Day** • ☿ STAT. • Transit of Venus first observed, 1639 • {12.0 / 10.5} | *for* |
| 25 | Fr. | **Eclipse** ⊙ • **New** ● • ☾ AT ☊ • 1st door to Tut's tomb opened, 1922 | *Turkey* |
| 26 | Sa. | **Islamic New Year** • ☾ RUNS LOW • ☌☿☾ • ☌♀☾ • Tides {12.2 / —} | *Day,* |
| 27 | **B** | **1st S. of Advent** • ☌♇☾ • Tides {10.5 / 11.9} | *we're* |
| 28 | M. | *Plenty sits still; Hunger is a wanderer.* • Tides {10.3 / 11.5} | *sure.* |
| 29 | Tu. | Enos became first chimp to orbit Earth, 1961 • {10.0 / 10.9} | *Pelting,* |
| 30 | W. | **St. Andrew** • British prime minister Sir Winston Churchill born, 1874 | *then melting!* |

*He who slings mud generally loses ground.* –Adlai Stevenson

## *Farmer's Calendar*

■ The psychrometer is a scientific instrument for the exact measurement of relative humidity. It's a clever little rig, invented around 1890 by a German physician and meteorologist, that works because of the different rates at which wet and dry objects cool. Two thermometers are mounted in a tube, protected against outside heat and cold. The bulb of one thermometer is dry; the other, wet. Because the moisture on the wet bulb evaporates and cools the bulb more quickly than the dry bulb cools, a comparison of their readings indicates the water content of the ambient air.

Today's humidity meters rely on electronics to measure the air's moisture. Those who prefer their psychrometry low-tech, however, need not despond, at least not in this house. We measure humidity by a device so simple it has only one moving part—the old plank door leading to the cellar. Each year, on a day in November, this door, which has been stuck tight since late spring, suddenly opens easily. All summer, the damp air has been swelling the door's pine planks, causing it to expand into its frame and jam. Now, with cooler, drier air outdoors and heating indoors, the boards give up their moisture and shrink. In June the door will jam up again, but for now it's back in business, and furnishes as good a humidity gauge as we will ever need.

## THE TWELFTH MONTH • 2011



**SKY WATCH** ☆ *Earth's two nearest neighbors finally show dramatic improvement. In fading evening twilight, Venus stands 10 degrees up on the 1st but twice that height by the 31st. It's at the left of the Moon on the 26th. This is the start of a glorious apparition that will peak in late winter and spring. Mars finally rises before midnight and gains a half magnitude from 0.7 to a conspicuous 0.2, in Leo. Jupiter fades a bit but still dominates the night on the Aries–Pisces border. December 10 brings a total lunar eclipse just before dawn, visible from everywhere except eastern North America. A nearly full Moon washes out the usually reliable Geminid meteor shower on the 13th–14th. Winter begins with the solstice on the 22nd, at 12:30* A.M.

| | | | | |
|---|---|---|---|---|
| ◐ | **First Quarter** | 2nd day | 4th hour | 52nd minute |
| ○ | **Full Moon** | 10th day | 9th hour | 36th minute |
| ◑ | **Last Quarter** | 17th day | 19th hour | 48th minute |
| ● | **New Moon** | 24th day | 13th hour | 6th minute |

*All times are given in Eastern Standard Time.*

**Purchase these pages with times set to your zip code at MyLocalAlmanac.com.**

| Day of Year | Day of Month | Day of Week | ☼ Rises h. m. | Rise Key | ☼ Sets h. m. | Set Key | Length of Day h. | m. | Sun Fast m. | Declination of Sun ° | ' | High Tide Times Boston | | ☾ Rises h. m. | Rise Key | ☾ Sets h. m. | Set Key | ☾ Place | ☾ Age |
|---|---|---|---|---|---|---|---|---|---|---|---|---|---|---|---|---|---|---|---|
| 335 | 1 | Th. | 6:53 | E | **4:12** | A | 9 | 19 | 27 | 21 s. | 49 | 3½ | **3¾** | 11:31 | D | **11:13** | D | CAP | 6 |
| 336 | 2 | Fr. | 6:54 | E | **4:12** | A | 9 | 18 | 26 | 21 | 58 | 4½ | **4¾** | 11:56 | D | — | – | AQU | 7 |
| 337 | 3 | Sa. | 6:55 | E | **4:12** | A | 9 | 17 | 26 | 22 | 06 | 5½ | **5¾** | **12:20** | C | 12:13 | D | PSC | 8 |
| 338 | 4 | **B** | 6:56 | E | **4:11** | A | 9 | 15 | 26 | 22 | 15 | 6¼ | **6¾** | **12:45** | C | 1:12 | E | PSC | 9 |
| 339 | 5 | M. | 6:57 | E | **4:11** | A | 9 | 14 | 25 | 22 | 22 | 7 | **7½** | **1:11** | C | 2:11 | E | PSC | 10 |
| 340 | 6 | Tu. | 6:58 | E | **4:11** | A | 9 | 13 | 25 | 22 | 30 | 8 | **8½** | **1:39** | B | 3:11 | E | PSC | 11 |
| 341 | 7 | W. | 6:59 | E | **4:11** | A | 9 | 12 | 24 | 22 | 37 | 8¾ | **9¼** | **2:11** | B | 4:10 | E | ARI | 12 |
| 342 | 8 | Th. | 7:00 | E | **4:11** | A | 9 | 11 | 24 | 22 | 43 | 9¼ | **10** | **2:49** | B | 5:09 | E | ARI | 13 |
| 343 | 9 | Fr. | 7:01 | E | **4:11** | A | 9 | 10 | 23 | 22 | 49 | 10 | **10¾** | **3:32** | B | 6:06 | E | TAU | 14 |
| 344 | 10 | Sa. | 7:02 | E | **4:11** | A | 9 | 09 | 23 | 22 | 55 | 10¾ | **11¼** | **4:22** | B | 7:00 | E | TAU | 15 |
| 345 | 11 | **B** | 7:02 | E | **4:11** | A | 9 | 09 | 23 | 23 | 00 | 11¼ | — | **5:19** | B | 7:49 | E | TAU | 16 |
| 346 | 12 | M. | 7:03 | E | **4:11** | A | 9 | 08 | 22 | 23 | 04 | 12 | **12** | **6:20** | B | 8:33 | E | GEM | 17 |
| 347 | 13 | Tu. | 7:04 | E | **4:11** | A | 9 | 07 | 22 | 23 | 09 | 12¼ | **12¾** | **7:25** | C | 9:11 | E | GEM | 18 |
| 348 | 14 | W. | 7:05 | E | **4:12** | A | 9 | 07 | 21 | 23 | 12 | 1¼ | **1½** | **8:32** | C | 9:45 | E | CAN | 19 |
| 349 | 15 | Th. | 7:06 | E | **4:12** | A | 9 | 06 | 21 | 23 | 16 | 2 | **2¼** | **9:40** | D | 10:16 | D | CAN | 20 |
| 350 | 16 | Fr. | 7:06 | E | **4:12** | A | 9 | 06 | 20 | 23 | 19 | 2¾ | **3** | **10:48** | D | 10:44 | D | LEO | 21 |
| 351 | 17 | Sa. | 7:07 | E | **4:13** | A | 9 | 06 | 20 | 23 | 21 | 3¾ | **4** | **11:58** | E | 11:13 | C | LEO | 22 |
| 352 | 18 | **B** | 7:08 | E | **4:14** | A | 9 | 06 | 19 | 23 | 23 | 4½ | **5** | — | – | 11:42 | C | VIR | 23 |
| 353 | 19 | M. | 7:08 | E | **4:14** | A | 9 | 06 | 19 | 23 | 24 | 5½ | **6** | 1:10 | E | **12:13** | C | VIR | 24 |
| 354 | 20 | Tu. | 7:09 | E | **4:14** | A | 9 | 05 | 18 | 23 | 25 | 6½ | **7** | 2:23 | E | **12:49** | B | VIR | 25 |
| 355 | 21 | W. | 7:09 | E | **4:14** | A | 9 | 05 | 18 | 23 | 26 | 7½ | **8** | 3:37 | E | **1:32** | B | LIB | 26 |
| 356 | 22 | Th. | 7:10 | E | **4:15** | A | 9 | 05 | 17 | 23 | 26 | 8½ | **9** | 4:50 | E | **2:22** | B | LIB | 27 |
| 357 | 23 | Fr. | 7:10 | E | **4:16** | A | 9 | 06 | 17 | 23 | 25 | 9¼ | **10** | 5:57 | E | **3:20** | B | OPH | 28 |
| 358 | 24 | Sa. | 7:11 | E | **4:17** | A | 9 | 06 | 16 | 23 | 24 | 10¼ | **11** | 6:56 | E | **4:26** | B | OPH | 0 |
| 359 | 25 | **B** | 7:11 | E | **4:17** | A | 9 | 06 | 16 | 23 | 23 | 11 | **11¾** | 7:46 | E | **5:35** | B | SAG | 1 |
| 360 | 26 | M. | 7:12 | E | **4:18** | A | 9 | 06 | 15 | 23 | 21 | **12** | — | 8:27 | E | **6:44** | C | SAG | 2 |
| 361 | 27 | Tu. | 7:12 | E | **4:19** | A | 9 | 07 | 15 | 23 | 19 | 12½ | **12¾** | 9:02 | E | **7:52** | C | CAP | 3 |
| 362 | 28 | W. | 7:12 | E | **4:19** | A | 9 | 07 | 14 | 23 | 16 | 1¼ | **1½** | 9:31 | D | **8:57** | D | AQU | 4 |
| 363 | 29 | Th. | 7:13 | E | **4:20** | A | 9 | 07 | 14 | 23 | 13 | 2¼ | **2¼** | 9:58 | D | **10:00** | D | AQU | 5 |
| 364 | 30 | Fr. | 7:13 | E | **4:21** | A | 9 | 08 | 13 | 23 | 09 | 3 | **3¼** | 10:23 | C | **11:00** | D | PSC | 6 |
| 365 | 31 | Sa. | 7:13 | E | **4:22** | A | 9 | 09 | 13 | 23 s. | 05 | 3¾ | **4** | 10:47 | C | — | – | PSC | 7 |

 **To use this page, see p. 110; for Key Letters, see p. 234.** ☞ **Bold = P.M.** ☞ Light = A.M. 

## DECEMBER HATH 31 DAYS • 2011

*The quiet day in winter beauty closes,*
*And sunset clouds are tinged with crimson dye.* –Sarah Doudney

| Day of Month | Day of Week | Dates, Feasts, Fasts, Aspects, Tide Heights | Weather |
|---|---|---|---|
| 1 | Th. | ☌♀♇ • ☌♆☾ • New York's Erie Canal closed due to weather, 1831 • {9.4 / 9.7} | *It's* |
| 2 | Fr. | St. Viviana • ☾ ON EQ. • Ambrose Small sold Canadian theater chain and disappeared, 1919 | *sopping* |
| 3 | Sa. | Johann Ludwig Krapf and Johannes Rebmann first Europeans to see Mt. Kenya, 1849 • {9.1 / 8.8} | *for* |
| 4 | **B** | **2nd S. of Advent** • ☌♅☾ • ☿ IN INF. ☌ | *shopping.* |
| 5 | M. | ☾ AT APO. • *When snow falls dry, / It means to lie; / But flakes light and soft / Bring rain oft.* • {9.2 / 8.5} | *Snow* |
| 6 | Tu. | St. Nicholas • ☌♃☾ • Wind toppled national Christmas tree, White House, D.C., 1970 | *spits* |
| 7 | W. | St. Ambrose • **Nat'l Pearl Harbor Remembrance Day** • Tides {9.6 / 8.6} | *give* |
| 8 | Th. | First concert by San Francisco Symphony, 1911 • Musician John Lennon died, 1980 | *us* |
| 9 | Fr. | Frozen-food tycoon Clarence Birdseye born, 1886 • {10.0 / 8.8} | *fits,* |
| 10 | Sa. | St. Eulalia • **Full Cold** ○ • **Eclipse** ☾ • ☾ RIDES HIGH • ☾ AT ☋ • ♅ STAT. | *then* |
| 11 | **B** | **3rd S. of Advent** • Winterberry fruits especially showy now. • {10.3 / —} | *mix* |
| 12 | M. | **Our Lady of Guadalupe** • Joseph Hayne Rainey first African-American to serve as a U.S. rep., 1870 | *with* |
| 13 | Tu. | St. Lucia • ☿ STAT. • *The fuel in the lamp consumes itself but lights others.* | *rain—* |
| 14 | W. | Ember Day • Prince Albert, Prince Consort of Queen Victoria, died, 1861 • Tides {9.2 / 10.3} | *what a* |
| 15 | Th. | Halcyon Days begin. • Fire at the U.S. Patent Office, 1836 • Tides {9.3 / 10.2} | *pain.* |
| 16 | Fr. | Ember Day • 8.1 earthquake, northeast Ark., 1811 • {9.5 / 10.0} | *Snowmageddon!* |
| 17 | Sa. | Ember Day • ☾ ON EQ. • ☌♂☾ • {9.7 / 9.8} | *Skies* |
| 18 | **B** | **4th S. of Advent** • Beware the Pogonip. • {10.0 / 9.6} | *are* |
| 19 | M. | First conversation between Britain and Canada over CANTAT-1 transatlantic cable, 1961 • {10.3 / 9.4} | *leaden,* |
| 20 | Tu. | ☌♄☾ • First successful water-powered cotton spinning mill in U.S., Pawtucket, R.I., 1790 | *each* |
| 21 | W. | St. Thomas • First day of Chanukah • ☾ AT PERIG. • {11.0 / 9.5} | *road's* |
| 22 | Th. | **Winter Solstice** • ☌☿☾ • ☿ GR. ELONG. (22° WEST) • Tides {11.3 / 9.7} | *a rink!* |
| 23 | Fr. | ☾ RUNS LOW • ☾ AT ☊ • –50°F, Williston, N.Dak., 1983 • {11.6 / 9.9} | *Santa's* |
| 24 | Sa. | **New** ● • ☌♇☾ • Jason Varitek named captain of Boston Red Sox, 2004 • {11.7 / 10.1} | *team* |
| 25 | **B** | **Christmas** • *Words that come from the heart stay warm three winters long.* • {11.7 / 10.1} | *needs* |
| 26 | M. | St. Stephen • **Boxing Day (Canada)** • **First day of Kwanzaa** • ♃ STAT. | *skates,* |
| 27 | Tu. | St. John • ☌♀☾ • Canadian prime minister Lester Pearson died, 1972 • {10.1 / 11.2} | *we think!* |
| 28 | W. | Holy Innocents • ☌♆☾ • U.S. patent #4,000,000 issued, 1976 | *We're* |
| 29 | Th. | ☌♇☉ • Actress Mary Tyler Moore born, 1936 • {9.7 / 10.1} | *overdue* |
| 30 | Fr. | ☾ ON EQ. • *Many drops will fill the pot.* • Tides {9.5 / 9.5} | *for* |
| 31 | Sa. | St. Sylvester • ☌♅☾ • 15" snow, Meridian, Miss., 1963 | *two-oh-one-two!* |

## *Farmer's Calendar*

■ *December 22.* First day of winter. Feels like the hundredth. Snow came early, and now the roads are covered with semi-frozen slush, the Sun is hardly to be seen, and a keen little north wind cuts down out of a sky the color of a prison wall.

Despite the chill, I decide to take the dogs down the road. They need the outing. So do I. The difference is, they don't believe it. They're dachshunds, which is to say, independent thinkers. They're also old. Time was, they couldn't wait for their walk. They surged ahead, quartering avidly back and forth across the road. Today, however, they plod gloomily along, dragging their feet, pulling up lame, feeling sorry for themselves. You can't blame them, they're 15. By one formula, this makes them 90 in human years; by another, 105.

Now, the fact is, I'm no longer young in human years myself, and so, short of our normal halfway point, I stop and prepare to turn back. And here, a miraculous rejuvenation is seen to bless the dogs. Human years, dog years, years in general fall away. They perk right up. Their lameness vanishes. They commence trotting briskly on the return leg of our walk. I follow. Perhaps I, too, feel a certain lightening. For all of us, however we count our years, when they begin to accumulate, the shortest way is the way home.

■ Many readers have expressed puzzlement over the rather obscure notations that appear on our **Right-Hand Calendar Pages, 115–141.** These "oddities" have long been fixtures in the Almanac, and we are pleased to provide some definitions. (Once explained, they may not seem so odd after all!)

–Beth Krommes

**Ember Days:** The four periods formerly observed by the Roman Catholic and Anglican churches for prayer, fasting, and the ordination of clergy are called Ember Days. Specifically, these are the Wednesdays, Fridays, and Saturdays that follow in succession following (1) the First Sunday in Lent; (2) Whitsunday–Pentecost; (3) the Feast of the Holy Cross, September 14; and (4) the Feast of St. Lucia, December 13. The word *ember* is perhaps a corruption of the Latin *quatuor tempora,* "four times."

Folklore has it that the weather on each of the three days foretells the weather for the next three months; that is, for September's Ember Days, Wednesday forecasts the weather for October, Friday for November, and Saturday for December.

**Distaff Day (January 7):** This was the first day after Epiphany (January 6), when women were expected to return to their spinning following the Christmas holiday. A distaff is the staff that women used

for holding the flax or wool in spinning. (Hence the term "distaff" refers to women's work or the maternal side of the family.)

**Plough Monday (January):** Traditionally, the first Monday after Epiphany was called Plough Monday because it was the day when men returned to their plough, or daily work, following the Christmas holiday. (Every few years, Plough Monday and Distaff Day fall on the same day.) It was customary at this time for farm laborers to draw a plough through the village, soliciting money for a "plough light," which was kept burning in the parish church all year. One proverb notes that

> *"Yule is come and Yule is gone,*
> *and we have feasted well;*
> *so Jack must to his flail again*
> *and Jenny to her wheel."*

**Three Chilly Saints (May):** Mamertus, Pancras, and Gervais were three early Christian saints. Because their feast days, on May 11, 12, and 13, respectively, are traditionally cold, they have come to be known as the Three Chilly Saints. An old French saying translates to: "St. Mamertus, St. Pancras, and St. Gervais do not pass without a frost."

**Midsummer Day (June 24):** To the farmer, this day is the midpoint of the growing season, halfway between planting and harvest. (Midsummer Eve is an occasion for festivity and celebrates fertility.) The Anglican church considered it a "Quarter Day," one of the four major divisions of the liturgical year. It also marks the feast day of St. John the Baptist.

**(continued)**

C
A
L
E
N
D
A
R

**Cornscateous Air (July):** First used by early almanac makers, this term signifies warm, damp air. Though it signals ideal climatic conditions for growing corn, it poses a danger to those affected by asthma and other respiratory problems.

**Dog Days (July 3–August 11):** These are the hottest and most unhealthy days of the year. Also known as Canicular Days, their name derives from the Dog Star, Sirius. The traditional 40-day period of Dog Days coincides with the heliacal (at sunrise) rising of Sirius.

**Lammas Day (August 1):** Derived from the Old English *hlaf maesse*, meaning "loaf mass," Lammas Day marked the beginning of the harvest. Traditionally, loaves of bread were baked from the first-ripened grain and brought to the churches to be consecrated. Eventually, "loaf mass" became "Lammas." In Scotland, Lammastide fairs became famous as the time when trial marriages could be made. These marriages could end after a year with no strings attached.

**Cat Nights Begin (August 17):** This term harks back to the days when people believed in witches. An Irish legend says that a witch could turn into a cat and regain herself eight times, but on the ninth time (August 17), she couldn't change back, hence the saying: "A cat has nine lives." Because August is a "yowly" time for cats, this may have initially prompted the speculation about witches on the prowl.

**Harvest Home (September):** In Europe and Britain, the conclusion of the harvest each autumn was once marked by festivals of fun, feasting, and thanksgiving known as "Harvest Home." It was also a time to hold elections, pay workers, and collect rents. These festivals usually took place around the autumnal equinox.

Certain groups in this country, particularly the Pennsylvania Dutch, have kept the tradition alive.

**St. Luke's Little Summer (October):** This is a spell of warm weather that occurs on or near St. Luke's feast day (October 18) and is sometimes called Indian summer.

**Indian Summer (November):** A period of warm weather following a cold spell or a hard frost, Indian summer can occur between St. Martin's Day (November 11) and November 20. Although there are differing dates for its occurrence, for more than 200 years the Almanac has adhered to the saying "If All Saints' brings out winter, St. Martin's brings out Indian summer." Some say that the term comes from the early Native Americans, who believed that the condition was caused by a warm wind sent from the court of their southwestern god, Cautantowwit.

**Halcyon Days (December):** This refers to about 2 weeks of calm weather often follow the blustery winds of autumn's end. Ancient Greeks and Romans experienced this weather around the time of the winter solstice, when the halcyon, or kingfisher, was brooding. In a nest floating on the sea, the bird was said to have charmed the wind and waves so that the waters were especially calm during this period.

**Beware the Pogonip (December):** The word *pogonip* is a meteorological term used to describe an uncommon occurrence—frozen fog. The word was coined by Native Americans to describe the frozen fogs of fine ice needles that occur in the mountain valleys of the western United States and Canada. According to their tradition, breathing the fog is injurious to the lungs. □□

**For Movable Religious Observances, see page 113. Federal holidays listed in bold.**

| | |
|---|---|
| **Jan. 1** | New Year's Day |
| **Jan. 17** | **Martin Luther King Jr.'s Birthday** *(observed)* |
| **Jan. 19** | Robert E. Lee Day *(Fla., Ky., La., S.C.)* |
| **Feb. 2** | Groundhog Day |
| **Feb. 12** | Abraham Lincoln's Birthday |
| **Feb. 14** | Valentine's Day |
| **Feb. 15** | Susan B. Anthony's Birthday *(Fla., Wis.)* National Flag of Canada Day |
| **Feb. 21** | **Washington's Birthday** *(observed)* |
| **Mar. 1** | Town Meeting Day *(Vt.)* |
| **Mar. 2** | Texas Independence Day |
| **Mar. 8** | Mardi Gras *(Baldwin & Mobile counties, Ala.; La.)* |
| **Mar. 15** | Andrew Jackson Day *(Tenn.)* |
| **Mar. 17** | St. Patrick's Day Evacuation Day *(Suffolk Co., Mass.)* |
| **Mar. 28** | Seward's Day *(Alaska)* |
| **Apr. 2** | Pascua Florida Day |
| **Apr. 18** | Patriots Day *(Maine, Mass.)* |
| **Apr. 21** | San Jacinto Day *(Tex.)* |
| **Apr. 22** | Earth Day |
| **Apr. 29** | National Arbor Day |
| **May 5** | Cinco de Mayo |
| **May 8** | Mother's Day Truman Day *(Mo.)* |
| **May 21** | Armed Forces Day |
| **May 22** | National Maritime Day |
| **May 23** | Victoria Day *(Canada)* |
| **May 30** | **Memorial Day** *(observed)* |
| **June 5** | World Environment Day |
| **June 11** | King Kamehameha I Day *(Hawaii)* |
| **June 14** | Flag Day |
| **June 17** | Bunker Hill Day *(Suffolk Co., Mass.)* |
| **June 19** | Father's Day Emancipation Day *(Tex.)* |
| **June 20** | West Virginia Day |
| **July 1** | Canada Day |
| **July 4** | **Independence Day** |
| **July 24** | Pioneer Day *(Utah)* |
| **Aug. 1** | Colorado Day Civic Holiday *(Canada)* |
| **Aug. 16** | Bennington Battle Day *(Vt.)* |
| **Aug. 19** | National Aviation Day |
| **Aug. 26** | Women's Equality Day |
| **Sept. 5** | **Labor Day** |
| **Sept. 9** | Admission Day *(Calif.)* |
| **Sept. 11** | Patriot Day Grandparents Day |
| **Sept. 17** | Constitution Day |
| **Sept. 21** | International Day of Peace |
| **Oct. 3** | Child Health Day |
| **Oct. 9** | Leif Eriksson Day |
| **Oct. 10** | **Columbus Day** *(observed)* Native Americans' Day *(S.Dak.)* Thanksgiving Day *(Canada)* |
| **Oct. 18** | Alaska Day |
| **Oct. 24** | United Nations Day |
| **Oct. 28** | Nevada Day |
| **Oct. 31** | Halloween |
| **Nov. 4** | Will Rogers Day *(Okla.)* |
| **Nov. 8** | Election Day |
| **Nov. 11** | **Veterans Day** Remembrance Day *(Canada)* |
| **Nov. 19** | Discovery Day *(Puerto Rico)* |
| **Nov. 24** | **Thanksgiving Day** |
| **Nov. 25** | Acadian Day *(La.)* |
| **Dec. 7** | National Pearl Harbor Remembrance Day |
| **Dec. 15** | Bill of Rights Day |
| **Dec. 17** | Wright Brothers Day |
| **Dec. 25** | **Christmas Day** |
| **Dec. 26** | Boxing Day *(Canada)* First day of Kwanzaa |

# 2010

## January
| S | M | T | W | T | F | S |
|---|---|---|---|---|---|---|
|   |   |   |   |   | 1 | 2 |
| 3 | 4 | 5 | 6 | 7 | 8 | 9 |
| 10 | 11 | 12 | 13 | 14 | 15 | 16 |
| 17 | 18 | 19 | 20 | 21 | 22 | 23 |
| 24 | 25 | 26 | 27 | 28 | 29 | 30 |
| 31 |   |   |   |   |   |   |

## February
| S | M | T | W | T | F | S |
|---|---|---|---|---|---|---|
|   | 1 | 2 | 3 | 4 | 5 | 6 |
| 7 | 8 | 9 | 10 | 11 | 12 | 13 |
| 14 | 15 | 16 | 17 | 18 | 19 | 20 |
| 21 | 22 | 23 | 24 | 25 | 26 | 27 |
| 28 |   |   |   |   |   |   |

## March
| S | M | T | W | T | F | S |
|---|---|---|---|---|---|---|
|   | 1 | 2 | 3 | 4 | 5 | 6 |
| 7 | 8 | 9 | 10 | 11 | 12 | 13 |
| 14 | 15 | 16 | 17 | 18 | 19 | 20 |
| 21 | 22 | 23 | 24 | 25 | 26 | 27 |
| 28 | 29 | 30 | 31 |   |   |   |

## April
| S | M | T | W | T | F | S |
|---|---|---|---|---|---|---|
|   |   |   |   | 1 | 2 | 3 |
| 4 | 5 | 6 | 7 | 8 | 9 | 10 |
| 11 | 12 | 13 | 14 | 15 | 16 | 17 |
| 18 | 19 | 20 | 21 | 22 | 23 | 24 |
| 25 | 26 | 27 | 28 | 29 | 30 |   |

## May
| S | M | T | W | T | F | S |
|---|---|---|---|---|---|---|
|   |   |   |   |   |   | 1 |
| 2 | 3 | 4 | 5 | 6 | 7 | 8 |
| 9 | 10 | 11 | 12 | 13 | 14 | 15 |
| 16 | 17 | 18 | 19 | 20 | 21 | 22 |
| 23 | 24 | 25 | 26 | 27 | 28 | 29 |
| 30 | 31 |   |   |   |   |   |

## June
| S | M | T | W | T | F | S |
|---|---|---|---|---|---|---|
|   |   | 1 | 2 | 3 | 4 | 5 |
| 6 | 7 | 8 | 9 | 10 | 11 | 12 |
| 13 | 14 | 15 | 16 | 17 | 18 | 19 |
| 20 | 21 | 22 | 23 | 24 | 25 | 26 |
| 27 | 28 | 29 | 30 |   |   |   |

## July
| S | M | T | W | T | F | S |
|---|---|---|---|---|---|---|
|   |   |   |   | 1 | 2 | 3 |
| 4 | 5 | 6 | 7 | 8 | 9 | 10 |
| 11 | 12 | 13 | 14 | 15 | 16 | 17 |
| 18 | 19 | 20 | 21 | 22 | 23 | 24 |
| 25 | 26 | 27 | 28 | 29 | 30 | 31 |

## August
| S | M | T | W | T | F | S |
|---|---|---|---|---|---|---|
| 1 | 2 | 3 | 4 | 5 | 6 | 7 |
| 8 | 9 | 10 | 11 | 12 | 13 | 14 |
| 15 | 16 | 17 | 18 | 19 | 20 | 21 |
| 22 | 23 | 24 | 25 | 26 | 27 | 28 |
| 29 | 30 | 31 |   |   |   |   |

## September
| S | M | T | W | T | F | S |
|---|---|---|---|---|---|---|
|   |   |   | 1 | 2 | 3 | 4 |
| 5 | 6 | 7 | 8 | 9 | 10 | 11 |
| 12 | 13 | 14 | 15 | 16 | 17 | 18 |
| 19 | 20 | 21 | 22 | 23 | 24 | 25 |
| 26 | 27 | 28 | 29 | 30 |   |   |

## October
| S | M | T | W | T | F | S |
|---|---|---|---|---|---|---|
|   |   |   |   |   | 1 | 2 |
| 3 | 4 | 5 | 6 | 7 | 8 | 9 |
| 10 | 11 | 12 | 13 | 14 | 15 | 16 |
| 17 | 18 | 19 | 20 | 21 | 22 | 23 |
| 24 | 25 | 26 | 27 | 28 | 29 | 30 |
| 31 |   |   |   |   |   |   |

## November
| S | M | T | W | T | F | S |
|---|---|---|---|---|---|---|
|   | 1 | 2 | 3 | 4 | 5 | 6 |
| 7 | 8 | 9 | 10 | 11 | 12 | 13 |
| 14 | 15 | 16 | 17 | 18 | 19 | 20 |
| 21 | 22 | 23 | 24 | 25 | 26 | 27 |
| 28 | 29 | 30 |   |   |   |   |

## December
| S | M | T | W | T | F | S |
|---|---|---|---|---|---|---|
|   |   |   | 1 | 2 | 3 | 4 |
| 5 | 6 | 7 | 8 | 9 | 10 | 11 |
| 12 | 13 | 14 | 15 | 16 | 17 | 18 |
| 19 | 20 | 21 | 22 | 23 | 24 | 25 |
| 26 | 27 | 28 | 29 | 30 | 31 |   |

# 2011

## January
| S | M | T | W | T | F | S |
|---|---|---|---|---|---|---|
|   |   |   |   |   |   | 1 |
| 2 | 3 | 4 | 5 | 6 | 7 | 8 |
| 9 | 10 | 11 | 12 | 13 | 14 | 15 |
| 16 | 17 | 18 | 19 | 20 | 21 | 22 |
| 23 | 24 | 25 | 26 | 27 | 28 | 29 |
| 30 | 31 |   |   |   |   |   |

## February
| S | M | T | W | T | F | S |
|---|---|---|---|---|---|---|
|   |   | 1 | 2 | 3 | 4 | 5 |
| 6 | 7 | 8 | 9 | 10 | 11 | 12 |
| 13 | 14 | 15 | 16 | 17 | 18 | 19 |
| 20 | 21 | 22 | 23 | 24 | 25 | 26 |
| 27 | 28 |   |   |   |   |   |

## March
| S | M | T | W | T | F | S |
|---|---|---|---|---|---|---|
|   |   | 1 | 2 | 3 | 4 | 5 |
| 6 | 7 | 8 | 9 | 10 | 11 | 12 |
| 13 | 14 | 15 | 16 | 17 | 18 | 19 |
| 20 | 21 | 22 | 23 | 24 | 25 | 26 |
| 27 | 28 | 29 | 30 | 31 |   |   |

## April
| S | M | T | W | T | F | S |
|---|---|---|---|---|---|---|
|   |   |   |   |   | 1 | 2 |
| 3 | 4 | 5 | 6 | 7 | 8 | 9 |
| 10 | 11 | 12 | 13 | 14 | 15 | 16 |
| 17 | 18 | 19 | 20 | 21 | 22 | 23 |
| 24 | 25 | 26 | 27 | 28 | 29 | 30 |

## May
| S | M | T | W | T | F | S |
|---|---|---|---|---|---|---|
| 1 | 2 | 3 | 4 | 5 | 6 | 7 |
| 8 | 9 | 10 | 11 | 12 | 13 | 14 |
| 15 | 16 | 17 | 18 | 19 | 20 | 21 |
| 22 | 23 | 24 | 25 | 26 | 27 | 28 |
| 29 | 30 | 31 |   |   |   |   |

## June
| S | M | T | W | T | F | S |
|---|---|---|---|---|---|---|
|   |   |   | 1 | 2 | 3 | 4 |
| 5 | 6 | 7 | 8 | 9 | 10 | 11 |
| 12 | 13 | 14 | 15 | 16 | 17 | 18 |
| 19 | 20 | 21 | 22 | 23 | 24 | 25 |
| 26 | 27 | 28 | 29 | 30 |   |   |

## July
| S | M | T | W | T | F | S |
|---|---|---|---|---|---|---|
|   |   |   |   |   | 1 | 2 |
| 3 | 4 | 5 | 6 | 7 | 8 | 9 |
| 10 | 11 | 12 | 13 | 14 | 15 | 16 |
| 17 | 18 | 19 | 20 | 21 | 22 | 23 |
| 24 | 25 | 26 | 27 | 28 | 29 | 30 |
| 31 |   |   |   |   |   |   |

## August
| S | M | T | W | T | F | S |
|---|---|---|---|---|---|---|
|   | 1 | 2 | 3 | 4 | 5 | 6 |
| 7 | 8 | 9 | 10 | 11 | 12 | 13 |
| 14 | 15 | 16 | 17 | 18 | 19 | 20 |
| 21 | 22 | 23 | 24 | 25 | 26 | 27 |
| 28 | 29 | 30 | 31 |   |   |   |

## September
| S | M | T | W | T | F | S |
|---|---|---|---|---|---|---|
|   |   |   |   | 1 | 2 | 3 |
| 4 | 5 | 6 | 7 | 8 | 9 | 10 |
| 11 | 12 | 13 | 14 | 15 | 16 | 17 |
| 18 | 19 | 20 | 21 | 22 | 23 | 24 |
| 25 | 26 | 27 | 28 | 29 | 30 |   |

## October
| S | M | T | W | T | F | S |
|---|---|---|---|---|---|---|
|   |   |   |   |   |   | 1 |
| 2 | 3 | 4 | 5 | 6 | 7 | 8 |
| 9 | 10 | 11 | 12 | 13 | 14 | 15 |
| 16 | 17 | 18 | 19 | 20 | 21 | 22 |
| 23 | 24 | 25 | 26 | 27 | 28 | 29 |
| 30 | 31 |   |   |   |   |   |

## November
| S | M | T | W | T | F | S |
|---|---|---|---|---|---|---|
|   |   | 1 | 2 | 3 | 4 | 5 |
| 6 | 7 | 8 | 9 | 10 | 11 | 12 |
| 13 | 14 | 15 | 16 | 17 | 18 | 19 |
| 20 | 21 | 22 | 23 | 24 | 25 | 26 |
| 27 | 28 | 29 | 30 |   |   |   |

## December
| S | M | T | W | T | F | S |
|---|---|---|---|---|---|---|
|   |   |   |   | 1 | 2 | 3 |
| 4 | 5 | 6 | 7 | 8 | 9 | 10 |
| 11 | 12 | 13 | 14 | 15 | 16 | 17 |
| 18 | 19 | 20 | 21 | 22 | 23 | 24 |
| 25 | 26 | 27 | 28 | 29 | 30 | 31 |

# 2012

## January
| S | M | T | W | T | F | S |
|---|---|---|---|---|---|---|
| 1 | 2 | 3 | 4 | 5 | 6 | 7 |
| 8 | 9 | 10 | 11 | 12 | 13 | 14 |
| 15 | 16 | 17 | 18 | 19 | 20 | 21 |
| 22 | 23 | 24 | 25 | 26 | 27 | 28 |
| 29 | 30 | 31 |   |   |   |   |

## February
| S | M | T | W | T | F | S |
|---|---|---|---|---|---|---|
|   |   |   | 1 | 2 | 3 | 4 |
| 5 | 6 | 7 | 8 | 9 | 10 | 11 |
| 12 | 13 | 14 | 15 | 16 | 17 | 18 |
| 19 | 20 | 21 | 22 | 23 | 24 | 25 |
| 26 | 27 | 28 | 29 |   |   |   |

## March
| S | M | T | W | T | F | S |
|---|---|---|---|---|---|---|
|   |   |   |   | 1 | 2 | 3 |
| 4 | 5 | 6 | 7 | 8 | 9 | 10 |
| 11 | 12 | 13 | 14 | 15 | 16 | 17 |
| 18 | 19 | 20 | 21 | 22 | 23 | 24 |
| 25 | 26 | 27 | 28 | 29 | 30 | 31 |

## April
| S | M | T | W | T | F | S |
|---|---|---|---|---|---|---|
| 1 | 2 | 3 | 4 | 5 | 6 | 7 |
| 8 | 9 | 10 | 11 | 12 | 13 | 14 |
| 15 | 16 | 17 | 18 | 19 | 20 | 21 |
| 22 | 23 | 24 | 25 | 26 | 27 | 28 |
| 29 | 30 |   |   |   |   |   |

## May
| S | M | T | W | T | F | S |
|---|---|---|---|---|---|---|
|   |   | 1 | 2 | 3 | 4 | 5 |
| 6 | 7 | 8 | 9 | 10 | 11 | 12 |
| 13 | 14 | 15 | 16 | 17 | 18 | 19 |
| 20 | 21 | 22 | 23 | 24 | 25 | 26 |
| 27 | 28 | 29 | 30 | 31 |   |   |

## June
| S | M | T | W | T | F | S |
|---|---|---|---|---|---|---|
|   |   |   |   |   | 1 | 2 |
| 3 | 4 | 5 | 6 | 7 | 8 | 9 |
| 10 | 11 | 12 | 13 | 14 | 15 | 16 |
| 17 | 18 | 19 | 20 | 21 | 22 | 23 |
| 24 | 25 | 26 | 27 | 28 | 29 | 30 |

## July
| S | M | T | W | T | F | S |
|---|---|---|---|---|---|---|
| 1 | 2 | 3 | 4 | 5 | 6 | 7 |
| 8 | 9 | 10 | 11 | 12 | 13 | 14 |
| 15 | 16 | 17 | 18 | 19 | 20 | 21 |
| 22 | 23 | 24 | 25 | 26 | 27 | 28 |
| 29 | 30 | 31 |   |   |   |   |

## August
| S | M | T | W | T | F | S |
|---|---|---|---|---|---|---|
|   |   |   | 1 | 2 | 3 | 4 |
| 5 | 6 | 7 | 8 | 9 | 10 | 11 |
| 12 | 13 | 14 | 15 | 16 | 17 | 18 |
| 19 | 20 | 21 | 22 | 23 | 24 | 25 |
| 26 | 27 | 28 | 29 | 30 | 31 |   |

## September
| S | M | T | W | T | F | S |
|---|---|---|---|---|---|---|
|   |   |   |   |   |   | 1 |
| 2 | 3 | 4 | 5 | 6 | 7 | 8 |
| 9 | 10 | 11 | 12 | 13 | 14 | 15 |
| 16 | 17 | 18 | 19 | 20 | 21 | 22 |
| 23 | 24 | 25 | 26 | 27 | 28 | 29 |
| 30 |   |   |   |   |   |   |

## October
| S | M | T | W | T | F | S |
|---|---|---|---|---|---|---|
|   | 1 | 2 | 3 | 4 | 5 | 6 |
| 7 | 8 | 9 | 10 | 11 | 12 | 13 |
| 14 | 15 | 16 | 17 | 18 | 19 | 20 |
| 21 | 22 | 23 | 24 | 25 | 26 | 27 |
| 28 | 29 | 30 | 31 |   |   |   |

## November
| S | M | T | W | T | F | S |
|---|---|---|---|---|---|---|
|   |   |   |   | 1 | 2 | 3 |
| 4 | 5 | 6 | 7 | 8 | 9 | 10 |
| 11 | 12 | 13 | 14 | 15 | 16 | 17 |
| 18 | 19 | 20 | 21 | 22 | 23 | 24 |
| 25 | 26 | 27 | 28 | 29 | 30 |   |

## December
| S | M | T | W | T | F | S |
|---|---|---|---|---|---|---|
|   |   |   |   |   |   | 1 |
| 2 | 3 | 4 | 5 | 6 | 7 | 8 |
| 9 | 10 | 11 | 12 | 13 | 14 | 15 |
| 16 | 17 | 18 | 19 | 20 | 21 | 22 |
| 23 | 24 | 25 | 26 | 27 | 28 | 29 |
| 30 | 31 |   |   |   |   |   |

# What a Difference

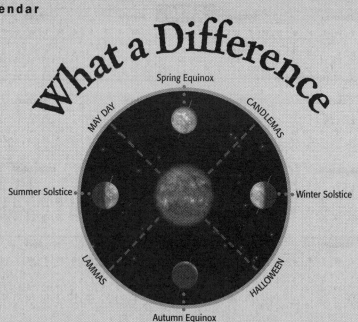

Spring Equinox

CANDLEMAS

MAY DAY

Summer Solstice

Winter Solstice

LAMMAS

HALLOWEEN

Autumn Equinox

# a Quarter Day Makes!

*Ever wonder why June is the month for weddings, how Groundhog Day got started, or why we hold elections in the fall?*

The ancient Celtic peoples who first inhabited the British Isles divided the year into four major periods and then halved each of these to make an eight-part year that followed the natural procession of the seasons.

Long after the Anglo-Saxon culture became dominant and the 12-month Roman calendar

by Andrew E. Rothovius

was adopted, the Celtic division of the year continued, especially in rural societies. It lingers on in the timing of some of our holidays, as noted in the Right-Hand Calendar Pages (115–141). All of these days became occasions for community gatherings and feasts.

# QUARTER DAYS

"Quarter Days" (or more accurately, its Celtic translation) was the name given by the Celts to the days marking the four major divisions of the year (the solstices and equinoxes). Gradually, to conform more closely to the liturgical year of the Christian church, these days became identified with its high seasonal festivals, which occurred close to the astronomical dates. These days also fit readily into the rhythm of the farming year.

**MARCH 25, Lady Day** (Annunciation) in the church calendar, marked the Angel Gabriel's annunciation to the Virgin Mary that she would be the mother of Christ. Among farmers, it became the traditional day for hiring laborers for the planting season ahead.

**JUNE 24,** or **Midsummer Day,** was, to the farmer, the midpoint of the growing season, halfway between planting and harvest, and therefore an occasion for festivity. The English church celebrated the day as the birthday of John the Baptist, who had foretold the birth of Jesus exactly 6 months later.

**SEPTEMBER 29, Michaelmas,*** was, in the church, the feast of the Archangel Michael, slayer of that old dragon, the Devil. In the country, this was the day on which farmers customarily paid rents to the landowners. Because market fairs, or Harvest Home festivals, were held on the preceding days, the farmers had money. This was also a convenient time for people to elect mayors and magistrates, hence, the custom of autumnal general elections. In North America, which has a longer harvest season, these events shifted to November.

**DECEMBER 25, Christmas,** was the first festival of the new year for the Celts. It originated as a solstice festival and celebrated a time of resting and gathering fertility for a new round of sowing and reaping. This merged easily with the Christian celebration of the birth of Jesus. Farmworkers, who were largely itinerant, usually received pay for the year's labor on this day. During the next 3 months, they looked for work, securing it on Lady Day.

(CONTINUED)

# CROSS-QUARTER DAYS ·······························

These days marked the midpoint of each season and came to be identified with other religious festivals. The Celts invested them with gender characteristics.

**FEBRUARY 2** acquired its English name, **Candlemas,** from the candles lighted in churches to celebrate the presentation of the Christ Child in the temple at Jerusalem. Originally it was called Imbolc ("lamb's milk") because it signaled the beginning of the lambing season. Celts also knew it as Brigantia, named for their female deity of light and in recognition of the Sun being halfway between the winter solstice and the spring equinox. A sunny day betokened unwelcome snow and frost until Lady Day. Clouds portended warmth and rain that would thaw out the fields and have them ready for planting. Our Groundhog Day is a remote survivor of this belief.

**MAY 1, May Day** or **Beltane,** being halfway to summer, was a day for dance and song to hail the sown fields starting to sprout, a time of male fertility that would yield fecundity. It was also the day for young couples to pair— although not in marriage. In the earlier ages, a wedding would occur on the next Cross-Quarter Day, after 3 months of courting. For impatient ones, the waiting period would be shortened to 6 weeks, concluding on Midsummer Day—hence our tradition of June bridals.

**AUGUST 1,** or, to the Celts, **Lughnasadh,** the wedding of the Sun god, Lugh, to the Earth goddess now fecund with ripening crops, marked the beginning of the harvest. (Despite its male name, this festival was held to be a female one.) The church transformed the day into an offering of first fruit: On this day, the first loaves baked from new wheat were offered at the Loaf Mass, which became corrupted in pronunciation to **Lammas.***

**OCTOBER 31,** or **Samhain,*** known today as **Halloween,** was the death-night of the old year. It came to be associated with ghosts, ghouls, and graveyards, as well as with apple bobbing, which was a form of telling fortunes for the new year. It was also the day when cattle were brought in from summer pasture, where they had grazed since May 1. Those needed for the winter's meat would be slaughtered in 10 days. This was a male task; thus, this day was considered masculine.   □□

*The unequal intervals between Lammas, Michaelmas, and Samhain (pronounced SAW-wen) resulted from a complicated attempt to reconcile the ancient Celtic lunar year with the 12-month solar year.*

**Andrew E. Rothovius,** who passed away in 2009, was a frequent contributor to this Almanac.

# Best Fishing Days and Times

The best times to fish are when the fish are naturally most active. The Sun, Moon, tides, and weather all influence fish activity. For example, fish tend to feed more at sunrise and sunset. During a full Moon, tides are higher than average and fish tend to feed more. However, most of us go fishing when we can get the time off, not because it is the best time. But there *are* best times, according to fishing lore:

**The Best Fishing Days for 2011, when the Moon is between new and full:**

January 4–19

February 2–18

March 4–19

April 3–17

May 3–17

June 1–15

July 1–15

July 30–August 13

August 28–September 12

September 27–October 11

October 26–November 10

November 25–December 10

December 24–31

- One hour before and one hour after high tides, and one hour before and one hour after low tides. (The times of high tides for Boston are given on pages 114–140; also see pages 239–240. Inland, the times for high tides correspond with the times when the Moon is due south. Low tides are halfway between high tides.)

- During the "morning rise" (after sunup for a spell) and the "evening rise" (just before sundown and the hour or so after).

- When the barometer is steady or on the rise. (But even during stormy periods, the fish aren't going to give up feeding. The smart fisherman will find just the right bait.)

- When there is a hatch of flies—caddis flies or mayflies, commonly. (The fisherman will have to match *his* fly with the hatching flies or go fishless.)

- When the breeze is from a westerly quarter rather than from the north or east.

- When the water is still or rippled, rather than during a wind.

## How to Estimate the Weight of a Fish

Measure the fish from the tip of its nose to the tip of its tail. Then measure its girth at the thickest portion of its midsection.

The weight of a fat-bodied fish (bass, salmon) = (length x girth x girth)/800

The weight of a slender fish (trout, northern pike) = (length x girth x girth)/900

**Example:** If a fish is 20 inches long and has a 12-inch girth, its estimated weight is (20 x 12 x 12)/900 = 2,880/900 = 3.2 pounds

salmon

trout

catfish

# New electronic lure may catch too many fish; one state bans it.

## A bass every seven minutes.

### by Mike Butler

YALESVILLE, CT– A new fishing technology that set a record for catching bass in Mexico is now showing its stuff in the U. S. It has out-fished shrimp bait in Washington State and beat top-selling U. S. lures three to one in Florida. The new technology is so effective one state, Wyoming, has banned its use.

The breakthrough is a tiny, battery-powered electrical system that flashes a blood-red light down a lure's tail when it's moved in water. Fish think it's an injured prey and strike. Some fishing authorities, like those in Wyoming, think that gives fishermen too much of an advantage.

They may be right. Three fishermen using a flashing lure in Mexico caught 650 large-mouth bass in just 25 hours. That's a bass every seven minutes for each person, and a record for the lake they were fishing. They said the bass struck with such ferocity they hardly lost a strike.

In Florida two professionals fished for four hours from the same boat. One used a flashing-red lure; the other used top-selling U. S. lures. The new, "bleed-ing" lure caught three times as many fish.

Before reporting this, I asked a veter-an fisherman in my office for his opin-ion. Monday morning he charged into my office yelling "I caught six monster fish in an hour with this thing! Where did you get it?"

Then I phoned an ichthyologist (fish expert).

"Predators - lions, sharks," he said, "will always go for the most vulnerable prey. Fish are predators, so if a fish sees a smaller fish bleeding, it knows it's

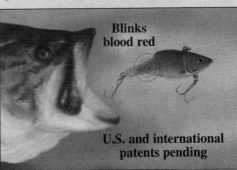

**Blinks blood red**

**U.S. and international patents pending**

New Bite Light® lure uses a blinking red light to create appearance of a live, bleeding prey. Triggers strikes.

weakened and will strike.

"If a lure could appear to be a live, bleeding fish, a few fishermen could probably empty a lake with it."

I told him three almost did.

### Fishes top, middle and deep

There is a U.S. company that offers a kit of three blinking lures (one each for shallow, middle and deep water) called the Bite Light®. Each lure is a different color. They work in fresh or salt water, contain rattle attractants inside and last 300 hours in the water.

One kit of three Bite Lights® costs $29.95, two or more kits cost $25.00 each. Each kit has the same three mod-els, but in different colors: S/h is only $7.00 no matter how many kits you buy.

To order, go to **www.ngcsports.com /gear** or call **1-800-873-4415** anytime of day and ask for the Bite Light® lure (Item #kbl). Or send your name, address and a check (or cc and exp. date) to NGC Sports (Dept. BL-268), 60 Church Street, Yalesville, CT 06492.

The company gives your money back, if you don't catch more fish and return your purchase within 30 days.

BL-14 © NGC Worldwide, Inc. 2011 **Dept. BL-268**

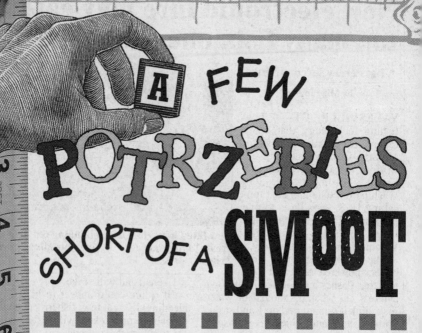

# A FEW POTRZEBIES SHORT OF A SMOOT

... and other strange, funny, and esoteric units of measure

BY JEFF BAKER

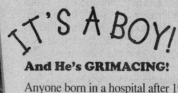

## IT'S A BOY!

### And He's GRIMACING!

Anyone born in a hospital after 1962 was likely to have been given an **Apgar score** not long after being slapped and swaddled as a newborn. Devised by anesthesiologist Dr. Virginia Apgar (1909–74), the score, which ranges from 0 to 10, measures the health of a baby based on criteria of Appearance, Pulse, Grimace, Activity, and Respiration.

# Were You Raised in a $10^{-28}$ m²?

Who says that nuclear physicists don't have a sense of humor? They refer to the size of a tiny cross section of the nucleus of an atom ($10^{-28}$ m²) as a **barn.** The term was wryly adapted from the phrase "can't hit the broad side of a barn." An **outhouse** and a **shed** are defined as $10^{-6}$ (one millionth) and $10^{-24}$ (one septillionth) of a barn, respectively.

## Watch Where You POINT That Thing

Ah, the BB gun—the Christmas wish of boys everywhere. But what, exactly, does **"BB"** mean? Surprisingly, it doesn't stand for "ball bearing" or "bullet ball," but instead refers to a BB's size. With a diameter of 0.18 inch (4.57 mm), a BB is between sizes B and BBB.

## How Much Is the QUARTER £ER?

*The Economist* magazine isn't known for its lightheartedness, but one of its

editors, Pam Woodall, did come up with an amusing (and effective) way to analyze exchange rates. The **Big Mac Index** compares the relative purchasing power of different currencies using the cost of a McDonald's Big Mac hamburger, which is available in more than 120 countries.

> We find no sense in talking about something unless we specify how we measure it; a definition by the method of measuring a quantity is the one sure way of avoiding talking nonsense . . .
>
> –Sir Hermann Bondi,
> *Anglo-Austrian
> mathematician and
> cosmologist
> (1919–2005)*

## A Close Shave

American physicist Theodore Maiman (1927–2007), who produced the first working laser, measured a laser's power by the **Gillette,** the number of stacked Gillette razor blades it could burn a hole through. Early prototypes were in the 2- to 4-Gillette range.

CONTINUED ➡

## A Whole Lot of
# NOTHING

In 1938, mathematician Edward Kasner asked his 9-year-old nephew, Milton Sirotta, to name a truly huge number. Perhaps inspired by the popular comic strip "Barney Google," the boy suggested the word "google." However you spell it, a **googol** is an impressive amount: It is 1 followed by 100 zeroes. (Yes, the search engine Google is named after this number.) A year later, Kasner came up with another number, the **googolplex,** which is equal to

$$10^{\text{googol}} \text{ or } 10^{10^{100}}$$

Cosmologist Carl Sagan (1934–96) claimed that it would be impossible to write out all of the zeroes of the googolplex, since it would take more space than exists in the known universe.

# HOUSTON,
## WE HAVE . . .

We all have to be known for something, and Jake Garn (b. 1932) is triply blessed: He made a reputation as an astronaut, a U.S. senator, and the man who became extremely "spacesick" during an orbital flight in 1985. The **Garn,** therefore, is NASA's unit of measure for the symptoms of space adaptation syndrome, the body's response to weightlessness in space. If an astronaut is completely incapacitated, he or she is experiencing 1 Garn, the highest possible level of sickness.

## THE ULTIMATE
# Star Registry

Speaking of Carl Sagan, he was so famously fond of saying "billions and billions of stars" that in his honor a **Sagan** is defined by astronomers to mean "at least 4 billion."

–NASA/Cosmos Studios

# IT'S ABOUT TIME

When someone says that he'll be "back in a jiffy," he'd better move fast. To computer scientists, a **jiffy** is one cycle (one "tick," so to speak) of a computer's system clock, equal to 0.01 second (10 milliseconds). American physical chemist Gilbert Lewis (1875–1946) proposed that a jiffy was the time required for light to travel 1 centimeter, or 33.3564 picoseconds (a picosecond is one trillionth of a second).

If someone won't "wait a second" for you, ask them to wait a **microfortnight,** or 1.21 seconds. If you're asked to "hold on for a moment," cool your heels; a **moment** is a medieval unit of time equal to ¹⁄₄₀ of an hour, or 1.5 minutes.

It has been proposed over the years that a day should be broken into units of 10 instead of 24. One day would be divided into 10 hours, each hour into 100 minutes, and each minute into 100 metric seconds, or blinks. A **blink** would be 0.864 second—about twice the time it takes to blink your eye.

## WHAT, Me Worry?

−Timothy Archibald

In June 1957, *MAD* magazine published the "Potrzebie System of Weights and Measures," created by 19-year-old Donald E. Knuth, who later became a celebrated computer scientist. Knuth's system of measurement was based on the **potrzebie,** a unit that he claimed equaled the exact thickness of *MAD* issue #26: 2.263348517438173216473 millimeters. Knuth's basic unit of power was the **whatmeworry;** volume was measured in **ngogns;** and the unit for mass was the **blintz.** The system also featured such units as the **cowznofski,** the **vreeble,** the **hoo,** and the **hah.**

CONTINUED ➡

# Between a DASH and a SPLASH

When your grandmother told you to add a "smidgen" of an ingredient to a recipe, she wasn't being vague. A **smidgen** is exactly ¹/₂ of a pinch, or ¹/₃₂ of a teaspoon.

## WHAT ABOUT MINNIE?

Walt Disney would be proud: A **mickey** is the smallest detectable movement of a computer mouse. About ¹/₂₀₀ of an inch, or 0.1 millimeter, it is named for the beloved cartoon M-O-U-S-E. Incidentally, another computer measurement is something mice love to do: A **nybble** is half a byte.

## THE TRUE MEASURE OF A MAN

Asked to name a ruler, you could say Queen Victoria, King Tut, or Oliver R. Smoot. Of these, however, only Smoot would qualify for one sense of the word.

In 1958, Smoot's MIT fraternity brothers decided that as a prank they would measure the Harvard Bridge between Boston and Cambridge, Massachusetts, by the **Smoot**—or his height, which was 5 feet 7 inches. They had him lie down, painted a mark, and repeated the process until they had determined that the bridge was 364.4 Smoots long, "plus or minus an ear." To this day, the Cambridge Police Department uses the Smoot marks to indicate the location of accidents on the bridge. (For good measure, Smoot later became the president of the International Organization for Standardization.) □□

**Jeff Baker's** work has appeared in *The New York Times Magazine, The Oxford American,* and other publications.

# Table of Measures

## APOTHECARIES'
1 scruple = 20 grains
1 dram = 3 scruples
1 ounce = 8 drams
1 pound = 12 ounces

## AVOIRDUPOIS
1 ounce = 16 drams
1 pound = 16 ounces
1 hundredweight = 100 pounds
1 ton = 2,000 pounds
1 long ton = 2,240 pounds

## LIQUID
4 gills = 1 pint
63 gallons = 1 hogshead
2 hogsheads = 1 pipe or butt
2 pipes = 1 tun

## DRY
2 pints = 1 quart
4 quarts = 1 gallon
2 gallons = 1 peck
4 pecks = 1 bushel

## LINEAR
1 hand = 4 inches
1 link = 7.92 inches

1 span = 9 inches
1 foot = 12 inches
1 yard = 3 feet
1 rod = 5½ yards
1 mile = 320 rods = 1,760 yards = 5,280 feet
1 Int. nautical mile = 6,076.1155 feet
1 knot = 1 nautical mile per hour
1 fathom = 2 yards = 6 feet
1 furlong = ⅛ mile = 660 feet = 220 yards
1 league = 3 miles = 24 furlongs
1 chain = 100 links = 22 yards

## SQUARE
1 square foot = 144 square inches
1 square yard = 9 square feet
1 square rod = 30¼ square yards = 272¼ square feet
1 acre = 160 square rods = 43,560 square feet
1 square mile = 640 acres = 102,400 square rods
1 square rod = 625 square links

1 square chain = 16 square rods
1 acre = 10 square chains

## CUBIC
1 cubic foot = 1,728 cubic inches
1 cubic yard = 27 cubic feet
1 cord = 128 cubic feet
1 U.S. liquid gallon = 4 quarts = 231 cubic inches
1 imperial gallon = 1.20 U.S. gallons = 0.16 cubic foot
1 board foot = 144 cubic inches

## KITCHEN
3 teaspoons = 1 tablespoon
16 tablespoons = 1 cup
1 cup = 8 ounces
2 cups = 1 pint
2 pints = 1 quart
4 quarts = 1 gallon

### TO CONVERT CELSIUS AND FAHRENHEIT:
$°C = (°F - 32)/1.8$
$°F = (°C \times 1.8) + 32$

## Metric Conversions

### LINEAR
1 inch = 2.54 centimeters
1 centimeter = 0.39 inch
1 meter = 39.37 inches
1 yard = 0.914 meter
1 mile = 1.61 kilometers
1 kilometer = 0.62 mile

### SQUARE
1 square inch = 6.45 square centimeters
1 square yard = 0.84 square meter

1 square mile = 2.59 square kilometers
1 square kilometer = 0.386 square mile
1 acre = 0.40 hectare
1 hectare = 2.47 acres

### CUBIC
1 cubic yard = 0.76 cubic meter
1 cubic meter = 1.31 cubic yards

### HOUSEHOLD
½ teaspoon = 2 mL
1 teaspoon = 5 mL
1 tablespoon = 15 mL

¼ cup = 60 mL
⅓ cup = 75 mL
½ cup = 125 mL
⅔ cup = 150 mL
¾ cup = 175 mL
1 cup = 250 mL
1 liter = 1.057 U.S. liquid quarts
1 U.S. liquid quart = 0.946 liter
1 U.S. liquid gallon = 3.78 liters
1 gram = 0.035 ounce
1 ounce = 28.349 grams
1 kilogram = 2.2 pounds
1 pound = 0.45 kilogram

## WINNERS in the 2010 Essay Contest

## The Kindest Thing Anyone Ever Did for Me

### FIRST PRIZE

In 1966, a friend and I completed Navy boot camp. Our first duty was to go to New York City and board our ship. We were to fly out of [Chicago's] Midway Airport that day, so we never received any pay for food or lodging. The weather got bad and the airport was shut down, so our flight was routed to Rochester, New York. We were rebooked on a 9:30 A.M. flight the next day. We couldn't stay at the airport, so we hitchhiked into town and found a bowling alley that was open 24/7. We had only a few cents between us—enough for one hamburger and a soda. When the lady working the counter brought our order, she noticed that we split it. She asked what a couple of sailors were doing in Rochester. We told her and asked if we could spend the night at the bowling alley. She talked with her husband, and then they invited us home with them. They fed us and put us in their son's room. Her husband brought us to the airport in the morning. We couldn't thank them enough. Both said that if their son was in our situation, they hoped someone would do the same for him. I don't remember their names but I'll never forget their kindness.

*—Bob Dowell, Terre Haute, Indiana*

### SECOND PRIZE

As a youth growing up in northeast Texas, this son of a twice-divorced single mother of seven and an alcoholic, stay-away dad had a life that wasn't always pine trees and sunshine. Random acts of kindness were few and far between. Little did I know that I was on someone's radar to receive an act of kindness. A bicycle had always been out of reach. One quiet night, days before Christmas, I heard a rap, rap, rap at the front door and opened it to a middle-age man looking for my mother. Calling my mother's attention, I slipped back. Silently, I gathered information from their whispers: This man was Santa's helper, disguised as my teacher's husband. He was there to surprise yours truly with a brand-new bike. Happily, my mother accepted. Kindness is contagious. When he left, we all owned smiles. I owned a smile and a bike that I couldn't ride until Christmas day.

*–Matthew Sparks, Henderson, Texas*

*Editor's note:* Mr. Sparks is passing his prize money forward to his aunt, in further demonstration that "kindness is contagious."

## THIRD PRIZE

Sixty-five years ago, I was 5 years old and had recently arrived in Atlantic City from Baltimore with my older sister and younger brother. Our mother had traveled by train with us and then walked out of our lives, leaving us in our father's care. My sister boarded with a family, and my brother and I spent our days and nights in a garage where my father worked as a mechanic. Come the end of a day, father would leave until the next morning. One night, as he was about to go, a friend of his who happened to be there said, "Let me take your boys home. It's awfully cold tonight." We were given a warm place to sleep and a bowlful of oatmeal with a delicious cinnamon bun the next morning by this stranger. That simple act of caring opened my eyes to the meaning of human kindness.

*–Daniel Walters, Margate City, New Jersey*

**Thanks to all of our readers who submitted stories of kindness. Here are a few more:**

■ One Saturday in 1943, while I was driving in the family truck to my cello lesson, the cello bounced out of the back of the truck and was run over by a bunch of teenage boys in a station wagon. I sobbed uncontrollably while my mother told them that it hadn't been their fault. On Monday, there was a loud knock on the door. It was the six boys with a new cello. They had each given $35 to buy it for me. Today, I still play that cello.

*–Patricia Gibbs Scoggin, Rochester, Minnesota*

■ In the summer of 2006, I was unable to pay my college tuition—about $2,000. On the last day to pay it, I was substitute teaching. One of the office personnel came into the room and handed me a receipt. I looked at it twice before I realized what it said: Someone had paid my bill, in one of the kindest acts I could imagine.

*–Fonda Bean, Russellville, Alabama*

■ One day in 2009, when the cashier subtotaled my grocery order, I realized that I didn't have enough money. I removed the items I could not afford and paid my bill. As I was putting my groceries into my car, a young girl and her mom came over and handed me two grocery bags. They had overheard my conversation with the cashier and paid for the items I had left behind.

*–Irene Freni, Flanders, New Jersey*

□□

**ANNOUNCING THE
2011 ESSAY CONTEST TOPIC**

**My Best Original
Money-Saving Habit**

In 200 words or less, please tell us about your best money-saving practice. See page 178 for contest rules.

# 23
# CURIOUS · CU

If shocking news
really works,
these folk ways will
do wonders.

*by Martha Deeringer*

■

**Scrape moss from a skull,
pound it into a powder, and
sniff it up your nose.**

**Apply tobacco leaves
to your temples.**

■

**Rub your forehead with a
lodestone.**

■

**Weave a match into your hair.**

On April 9, 1865, General Ulysses S. Grant struggled with two problems. The first was what to do about Confederate general Robert E. Lee and his soldiers, who were cornered near Appomattox, Virginia; the second was how to get rid of his excruciating headache. (This was a chronic affliction. Grant mentioned "those terrible headaches which I am subject to" in his diary.)

Earlier in the day, Grant had undergone a hot mustard footbath, but it had provided no relief. Later, in the midst of his agony, he received word that General Lee was planning to surrender. Only then did his headache disappear.

Coincidence . . . or catharsis? Perhaps Grant's relief came from realizing what he would now not have to do—wage battle.

We may never know, but if this was the case, consider the following remedies practiced by people of the 18th and 19th centuries the next time you get a headache. Knowing that you don't have to try one could make you feel better fast.

# RES **FOR A** Headache

Place sliced raw potatoes on your forehead.

Tie your aching head in a red bandanna.

■

Soak a brown paper bag in vinegar and apply it to your head.

■

Pick up a sharp knife, make a cross in the air in front of your face, and throw the knife on the floor.

Have someone blow smoke into your ear.

Paste a leaf of cottonwood on each temple and do not remove it until it falls off on its own, taking the skin with it.

Gargle with mustard.

Mix a beaver gland with olive oil and beeswax, shape it into a pill, and swallow it.

■

Tie a salt herring around your throat.

■

Apply collard greens to your head.

CONTINUED

Boil cottonweed in lye and smoke it.

**Apply cobwebs across the bridge of your nose.**

Wrap the skin of a rattlesnake tightly around your head.

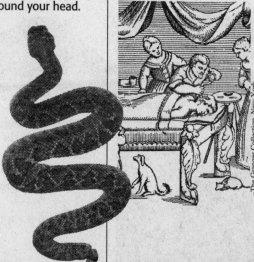

Form fresh cow manure into a heat-producing poultice and put it on your head.

Rub an even number of mashed earthworms into your forehead and temples.

**Use a trephine to drill a small hole in your skull to release demons and other ailments that have taken up residence there.**

–The Granger Collection, New York

## Real REMEDIES

Folklore is fun, but headaches are a pain. Try these solutions for real relief:

Squeeze the flesh between the thumb and first finger of either hand for 30 seconds. Repeat two or three times.

Drink tart cherry juice.

Soak your feet in hot water for about 15 minutes, or until the water gets lukewarm. Put on warm, cotton socks and lie down for 15 minutes.

□□

Writer **Martha Deeringer** of McGregor, Texas, is grateful that she has never had a headache requiring one of these cures.

# Pain-Killing Cream Reduces <u>Arthritis</u> Pain! *Works*...On Contact!

## If You Suffer from Pain – Read this Very Carefully:

NEW JERSEY: Arthritis pain sufferers will be amazed by the uniquely formulated pain relief cream that could help them live normal and active lives. **PAIN BUST-R II®** is a fast acting therapeutic cream developed in the fight against arthritis pain. Upon application, it penetrates deep to the areas most affected – the joints themselves, to help bring fast relief where it's needed most.

### 2 of the Most Effective Topical Painkillers!

**PAIN BUST-R II** combines two active pain-killing powerhouses in one concentrated formula. These pain-relieving agents are known to work, providing analgesic relief at the site of arthritis pain. **PAIN BUST-R II** provides deep penetrating heat to help relieve stiffness and improve mobility. And it's greaseless so it won't stain or smear clothes or sheets.

- ❶ Knees  ❹ Hands  ❼ Fingers
- ❷ Shoulders  ❺ Wrists  ❽ Ankles
- ❸ Legs  ❻ Feet

## Effective on Even the Toughest Cases

Many of our customers with chronic arthritis and joint pain swear by **PAIN BUST-R II**. It's recommended by users who have resumed daily activities and can enjoy life again. **PAIN BUST-R II** can help put an end to agonizing days and sleepless nights.

"**PAIN BUST-R II** is the best there is. I have tried other pain meds – there is no comparison. It has gotten me through many, many nights of pain in my back and legs from arthritis. Where I go, it goes!" H.W.

"Thank you for a wonderful product!! **PAIN BUST-R II** gives the ultimate relief of pain due to arthritis. Since I started using it, I have been getting soothing sleep at night that I just wasn't getting before." M.B.

## NO-RISK FREE TRIAL - We Trust You – Send No Money!

**TO ORDER THE FREE TRIAL:** Just write **"PAIN BUST-R II"** on a sheet of paper and send it along with your name, address, phone number, and indicate that you would like to try our trial tube of **PAIN BUST-R II.** We will promptly ship you 1 large tube for $9.90, which includes shipping and handling. We will enclose an invoice and if for any reason you don't agree that **PAIN BUST-R II** relieves pain more effectively than anything you've tried, simply return the invoice to us with the word "cancel" written on it and there will be no charge to you. You don't even have to bother returning the merchandise. Act quickly – this offer may not be repeated. **CALL NOW! TOLL FREE 1-800-451-5773** and ask for offer OLF-11 or write to: CCA Industries, Inc., Dept. OLF-11, 200 Murray Hill Parkway, E. Rutherford, NJ 07073.

**TO BUY NOW:** If you would like to purchase **PAIN BUST-R II** directly without the trial period, please send a check or money order written out to **"PAIN BUST-R II"** for either $9.90 for 1 tube, $16.80 for 2 tubes, or $21.90 for 3 tubes. All prices include shipping and handling.

©2010 CCA Industries, Inc

# GOOD MANNERS:

## WHAT'S CHANGED,
## WHAT HASN'T,
## & What to Do Now

I t is, was, and always will be impolite to imply (or, heaven forbid, say directly) to a friend that he is ugly, overweight, or unintelligent.

Similarly, you should never tell your host or hostess that you do not like any of his or her friends. Doing so would be rude because it implies that the host has bad taste in friends, with one notable exception—you.

Some "best" behaviors, like these, never go out of fashion, but many others do. Brush up on these now . . . so that you don't get the brush-off later.

● ● ● ● ● ● ● ● ●

### JUST THE TICKET

- The word *étiquette*, which means "ticket" in French, dates from 1750 as a term for the conduct prescribed by authority to be observed in social life.

# MAKING
## (and Unmaking)
# FRIENDS

Introductions followed a specific protocol until around 1950. A mutual friend confirmed that each party desired to make the other's acquaintance. The friend then presented the man to the woman, the younger person to

the older, or the less prestigious person to the more important. Once two people were introduced, expectations (and, often, expenses) mounted as they now had to return each other's social calls and invitations.

TODAY, introductions tend to be casual because we have few, if any, expectations or obligations.

Ironically, technology has adopted some traditional protocols; one is the preapproval. Social Web sites, such as Facebook and LinkedIn, give users the ability to accept or decline individuals as new members of their networks.

Online social networks also have a modern version of the "cut." In the past, one acquaintance could "cut" another by ignoring him or her in the street and ceasing to return visits. Now, "unfriending" someone on Facebook accomplishes the same thing.

## WE DON'T NEED TO BE
# TOLD
## NOT TO DO THIS
### (Do we?)

●

**English diners in the 16th century grabbed food from common dishes with their hands and buttered their bread with their thumbs.**

●

**In 1558, a book by Italian poet Giovanni Della Casa cautioned readers to keep their hands off excrement found on the side of the road and desist from "insisting upon holding it up to their [friends'] noses."**

*(continued)*

## BY ANDREA CURRY

**169**

# Waisted Efforts

- The stately bow was on its way out by the 1920s.

By the 1960s, bending at the waist had morphed into a simple nod.

TODAY, nodding while shaking someone's hand is acceptable, but most people don't do it. Nix the nod to a foreign dignitary, too, and, if you're a U.S. citizen, don't even think about bowing. We should not bow or curtsy to leaders of other nations; only that leader's subjects should bow to him or her. It is proper for Canadians to bow or curtsy to the monarch of the Commonwealth of Nations.

●●●●●●●●●

## GET A GRIP

A good, firm handshake never goes out of style, but nobody wants to shake a "dead fish." Etiquette heiress Peggy Post says that a proper handshake should last 3 seconds and involve two to three good pumps.

## QUICKER PICKER UPPERS RANKED
# MOST POLITE

Recently, reporters in 35 major cities tested residents' courtesy in three sets of circumstances, including a staged "accident" in which a reporter dropped a folder full of papers. Would the person behind him stop to help pick them up?

Eight in 10 New Yorkers and 7 in 10 Torontonians

did, making these two cities, at least by this standard, the first and third most polite places in the world, respectively. (In case you're wondering: Zurich came in second; and Berlin; São Paulo, Brazil; and Zagreb, Croatia, tied for fourth.)

# YOU DON'T SAY . . .

No one should ever monopolize conversation, unless he wishes to win for himself the name of bore, and to be avoided as such.

–Margaret E. Sangster, American writer (1838–1912)

The ability to chat with both friends and strangers is crucial to good manners, but what to talk about? Weather has been so much maligned and politicized that many of us decline to bring it up. There were good reasons to talk about the weather in the past; for one, it steered the conversation away from the following forbidden topics:

## ● RELIGION AND POLITICS.

These were never discussed with strangers or in "small talk" situations. **TODAY,** hot topics and headlines are fair game, although that's not to say that everyone will come out of a conversation on speaking terms.

## ● MONEY. For

centuries, this was forbidden in polite conversation; no one liked to hear people bragging about their savings or their stuff.

**TODAY,** Americans talk about money constantly, on the theory that it really doesn't matter—"it's just money."

## ● YOURSELF.

Talking on and on about yourself and your accomplishments (or your children and theirs) was and is rude.

**TODAY,** it's only really rude in person. On their own blogs, people can "talk" about themselves as much as they like, letting everyone (or no one) know everything.

## ● TRIVIAL MATTERS. Lord

Chesterfield, in his letters to his son (published in a series of best-selling American editions from 1775 to 1860), sternly warned against "frivolous curiosity about trifles."

**TODAY,** "trifles" are fodder for stand-up comedy and a steady stream of Twitter and Facebook updates—and most definitely for conversation. Funnily enough, the mundane details of life that Chesterfield once scorned now serve the same purpose that weather once did. They keep the conversation going and steer it clear of personal, controversial, or offensive topics.

*(continued)*

## LEAVE 'EM LAUGHING

In the 1700s, Lord Chesterfield declared, "There is nothing so illiberal, and so ill bred, as audible laughter."

**TODAY,** sincere, hearty laughter is a sure sign of a conversation that's going well.

● ● ● ● ● ● ● ● ● ●

# Eat, Blink, AND RUN

At dinner, which was often a formal affair of five to nine courses, colonial Americans observed strict rules of "precedence": The host led guests from the drawing room to the dining room, with the most prestigious female guest on his arm. The other guests followed in pairs, in order of social importance (as indicated by the hostess); the hostess went last, escorted by the man of highest social standing. Precedence also affected seating and the order in which guests departed.

As recently as the early 20th century, hostesses were still parading guests to the table, but by then, age, not rank, was the main criterion for precedence. Until quite recently, a hostess would never seat a married couple together.

During the meal, it was unbecoming of a lady to ask for wine, to take more than a small helping, to eat any of the cheese, or to partake of anything rich or messy, such as artichokes with butter sauce.

TODAY, few meals include more than three courses and diners often gather in the kitchen—territory once reserved for servers. Arrivals are casual, but departures can be conspiratorial. According to *New York Times* etiquette writer Philip Galanes, between couples, two blinks of the eyes mean, "Can we leave now?"

## Too Free Speech?

**Verbal abuse "is becoming accepted as the quickest and smartest way of dealing with criticism in all areas of life."**

*–Lynne Truss, author of* Talk to the Hand

In 2009, 75 percent of Americans said that the nation was growing ruder and less civilized. Examples are easy to find:

- rants on the "Comments" pages of news and political blogs

- passive-aggressive remarks ("Well, there would be room—if somebody would carry a smaller bag")

- salesclerks who ignore customers while they talk on the phone or to each other—and customers who ignore salesclerks and carry on phone conversations while checking out

## THE CHANGED FATE OF
# LATE DATES

Before the cell phone, a fellow who kept a lady waiting more than 15 minutes had "stood her up"—and seldom got a second date.

TODAY, tardy people keep their companions waiting, but with status reports, phoning or texting updates on their progress every few minutes ("Now I'm stuck behind a bus . . .").

● ● ● ● ● ● ● ● ●

# WEDDING BELLS
## AND WHISTLES

Centuries ago, weddings involved a minimum of fuss and expense, and the bride chose a dress that she could wear again (unlike today's white ball gowns). By the 1880s, weddings were becoming more luxurious, and etiquette expert Mary Elizabeth Wilson Sherwood criticized showy weddings as well as "absurdly gorgeous" gifts.

*(continued)*

173

TODAY, a wedding dress costs $1,000, on average, and can't be worn again because it is much too fancy. Couples often "register" for thousands of dollars in gifts, which they may exchange for cash later. Engraved reception invitations have never gone out of style, but in addition to "RSVP," some declare, "No wrapped gifts, please" (code for "just bring money").

## WRITE AWAY, DEAR

● In major cities in the 19th and early 20th centuries, people sent so many letters that mail was delivered up to seven times a day. Invitations and replies, congratulations, thanks, and condolences sped in every direction across the nation.

Traditionally written correspondence began with a salutation ("My dear Mr. So-and-so") and ended with a complimentary closing—"Cordially yours," "Sincerely yours," or the like.

TODAY, if you want to receive a handwritten letter, send a gift—and include a self-addressed stamped envelope: Only half of us report that we always write a thank-you note.

If you write a letter, start it with "Dear." Paper correspondence that doesn't include that word still seems curt. Omitting such niceties on e-mail and instant messaging, however, is perfectly acceptable.

### NEVER "NEVER . . ."

"All letters that begin 'Never in my life have I been subjected to such . . .' fit into the category of letters that ought not to be written."

–Miss Manners' Guide to Excruciatingly Correct Behavior, 2005

## ENOUGH, ALREADY!

In 2000, people who phoned home with anxious questions from the grocery aisle were the butt of jokes, while those without cell phones couldn't decide which annoyed them more: loud, public conversations about private matters or

the frequent phone chatter about nothing (like groceries).

TODAY, nearly everyone is on the phone talking, texting, and e-mailing; in Philip Galanes's words, "typing in the street has become a basic human right." Although we are generally tolerant of people's phone calls from the grocery aisle, coffee shop, or airport, 9 in 10 people find other instances of "mobile manners" annoying. High on the list:

- texting while driving (which is now illegal in many places)
- conducting too loud or too personal phone conversations in public
- phoning from a bathroom stall while others wait
- encroaching on face-to-face family time by using a mobile device

# LOOKING BUSY IS LOOKING GOOD

Among office workers, 9 in 10 say that it's rude to text or answer e-mails during meetings, yet 3 in 10 say that this is accepted practice and makes a worker seem more productive. (For the record: They're probably all doing it, but the 7 in 10 who don't think that it's accepted practice still feel guilty about it.)

## THE ONLY GOOD MANNERS THAT REALLY MATTER

Even if you don't do anything else . . .

Remember that he who corrects others will soon do something perfectly awful himself.
–Miss Manners

And as ye would that [others] should do to you, do ye also to them likewise.
–Luke 6:31

S P E C I A L   R E P O R T

**Andrea Curry** writes from North Carolina and is a frequent contributor to *The Old Farmer's Almanac*. When she told a few people that she was writing on this topic, they said things like, "Oh, right, manners—people used to have those."

175

# WINNERS
## in the 2010
# Pumpkin Recipe Contest

---

**FIRST PRIZE**

## Pumpkin Harvest Soup

1 pound boneless chicken breasts
1 tablespoon olive oil
3 stalks celery, chopped
3 medium carrots, chopped
1 medium onion, chopped
1 tablespoon minced garlic
1 can (15 ounces) low sodium chicken broth
1 can (15 ounces) pumpkin
1 can (15 ounces) Great Northern or
    cannellini beans, drained
1 teaspoon nutmeg
¼ teaspoon white pepper
salt, to taste
sour cream (optional)

**C**ut the chicken into bite-size pieces. Heat the oil in a large pan, add the chicken, and cook until it is no longer pink. Add the celery, carrots, onion, and garlic and sauté until the vegetables are tender. Add the chicken broth, pumpkin, beans, nutmeg, pepper, and salt. Simmer on low for 30 minutes. Season to taste. Top the soup or individual servings with sour cream, if desired. **Makes 6 to 8 servings.**

*–Tessa Bowers, Noblesville, Indiana*

---

**SECOND PRIZE**

## Southwestern Pumpkin Hummus

6 to 8 cloves garlic
¼ cup fresh cilantro
¼ cup lime juice
¼ cup tahini
2 tablespoons pumpkin or olive oil
1 can (15 ounces) pumpkin
3 teaspoons cumin
1 teaspoon salt, or to taste
½ teaspoon chili powder
½ teaspoon chipotle pepper (ground or
    flakes)
pumpkin seeds, for garnish

**P**ut the garlic cloves into a food processor and pulse to chop fine. Add the remaining ingredients (except pumpkin seeds) and blend until smooth. Transfer to a bowl, cover, and refrigerate overnight. Garnish with pumpkin seeds and drizzle with additional oil before serving. Serve with vegetables, crackers, or plain tortilla chips. **Makes approximately 2¼ cups.**

*–Sharon Ricci, Mendon, New York*

*(continued)*

## Pumpkin Nutmeg Knots

1 package (¼ ounce) active dry yeast
⅓ cup sugar, divided
¾ cup lukewarm milk
7 to 8 cups all-purpose flour
1 teaspoon freshly grated nutmeg
1 teaspoon kosher salt
¾ cup (1½ sticks) butter
1 egg, lightly beaten
2 cups fresh or 1 can (15 ounces) pumpkin
1 large egg yolk

**C**ombine the yeast, 1 teaspoon of sugar, and the lukewarm milk. Set aside for 5 minutes, or until the mixture becomes frothy. In a large bowl, combine 7 cups of flour and the nutmeg, salt, and remaining sugar.

Cut in the butter until the mixture resembles coarse meal. Add the egg, pumpkin, and yeast mixture. Stir to blend well.

Turn the dough out onto a floured surface and knead for about 10 minutes, or until the dough is smooth and elastic and no longer sticky, using as much of the remaining flour as necessary. Form the dough into a ball, place it in a large, well-buttered bowl, and turn it to coat in butter. Cover with plastic wrap and set aside in a warm place for 1 hour, or until doubled in size.

Turn the dough out onto the work surface and divide it into 14 pieces. Roll each piece in your palm until it is 5 inches in length. Fold the dough into a knot. Place the knots onto a cookie sheet lined with parchment paper and cover with a kitchen towel. Set the knots in a warm place for 45 minutes, or until doubled in size.

Preheat the oven to 350°F. Combine the egg yolk with 1 tablespoon of water, whisking to blend. Brush each knot with the egg wash and bake for 40 to 50 minutes, or until golden brown. Cool slightly before serving with butter. **Makes 14 knots.**

*–Michele Weiser, Albany, New York*

Thank you to everyone who sent pumpkin recipes—we received hundreds. Two runners-up—*Pumpkin Waffles With Butter Pecan Butter* by Jackie Hardin and *Ginger Thai Pumpkin Bisque* by Sally Sibthorpe—are available along with dozens more in the existing recipe collection at **Almanac.com/RecipeContest.**

### ANNOUNCING THE 2011 RECIPE CONTEST: COFFEE

**Send us your favorite recipe using coffee (not in beverages). It must be yours, original, and unpublished. Amateur cooks only, please. See below for contest rules.**

### RECIPE AND ESSAY CONTEST RULES

Cash prizes (first, $250; second, $150; third, $100) will be awarded for the best recipe using coffee and the best essay on the subject "My Best Original Money-Saving Habit" (see page 163). All entries become the property of Yankee Publishing, which reserves all rights to the material. The deadline for entries is Friday, January 28, 2011. Label "Recipe Contest" or "Essay Contest" and mail to The Old Farmer's Almanac, P.O. Box 520, Dublin, NH 03444. You can also enter at Almanac.com/RecipeContest or /EssayContest. Include your name, mailing address, and e-mail address. Winners will appear in *The 2012 Old Farmer's Almanac* and on those Web pages.

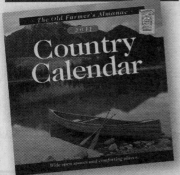

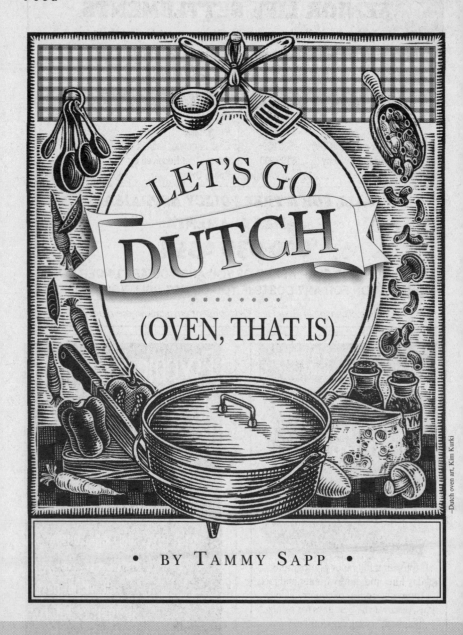

# LET'S GO

## DUTCH

### (OVEN, THAT IS)

• BY TAMMY SAPP •

–Dutch oven art, Kim Kurki

**Cooking in cast-iron pots is not just for campers**

Among outdoor chefs, DUTCH OVENS are now hotter than Five-Alarm Chili. Whether this is because food seems to taste better when cooked in them, because they're easy to use with a campfire, or because they harken back to mountain men, cowboys, and Civil War soldiers, many folks agree that Dutch ovens are, well, cool.

Getting started in Dutch oven cooking requires some gear. At minimum, you'll need a lid lifter, tongs, heavy gloves made especially for camp cooking, wooden utensils, charcoal briquettes, and a Dutch oven, which can range from 5 to 22 inches in diameter and be purchased new or used.

## What Makes It "Dutch"?

Ideas abound about how the flat-bottom cast-iron kettle got its name. John G. Ragsdale, author of *Dutch Ovens Chronicled, Their Use in the United States* (University of Arkansas Press, 1991), floats three theories:

♦ In 1704, Englishman Abraham Darby visited a Dutch foundry and observed the process for casting brass in dry sand molds. Later, he perfected the method for iron and attributed it to the Dutch.

♦ The pots became associated with the early Dutch traders who peddled them.

♦ Dutch settlers in the Pennsylvania area used similar cast-iron cooking vessels.

## From HEARTHS to HEARTS

Cast-iron pots have a long history in American kitchens:

♦ They first appeared in the 1700s.

♦ The Lewis and Clark Expedition (1804–06) probably carried Dutch ovens at least on the first part of its journey.

♦ The ovens were regular passengers on the wagon trains that traversed the West.

continued

and cast-iron stomachs are not needed.

◆ During the California gold rush, "Forty-niners" baked sourdough bread in them.

◆ With the invention of the electric stove in the 1890s, interest in Dutch oven cooking waned.

◆ In the early 1940s, Boy Scouts at the Philmont (N.Mex.) Scout Ranch began learning how to cook in Dutch ovens, a program that continues to this day.

◆ The International Dutch Oven Society (IDOS; www.idos.com) now has 48 chapters in 27 states, and the number continues to grow. Canada (www.idoscanada.com) has two chapters, in Alberta and Ontario.

## A Colonist's Crock?

A popular myth suggests that Paul Revere—the excellent metalsmith who made the famous 1775 Midnight Ride—adapted the Dutch oven's lid to include the flanged lip that holds the coals on top. In fact, the Dutch oven's lip and three legs—which allow the pot to sit over (not in) coals—appeared in the early 1700s.

## HOW TO ARRANGE YOUR BRIQUETTES

◆ To bake: approx. 2:1 ratio, above to underneath
◆ To stew or simmer: approx. 1:1 ratio, above to underneath
◆ To broil: checkerboard pattern, approx. 2:1 ratio, above to underneath
◆ To fry or boil: checkerboard pattern, all underneath

–Robert Kemper

## It's Pot SKILL, Not Pot LUCK

Anyone can cook almost anything in a Dutch oven, as long as the pot has a well-sealing lid and the temperature is controlled.

A secure lid allows heat and internal pressure to build, while preserving moisture so that the food is gently steamed from the inside out.

Controlling the temperature takes practice. To attain the 325° to 350°F temperatures required by many recipes, cooks apply a simple formula: In general, use twice as many charcoal briquettes as the size of the Dutch oven. A 12-inch oven would use about 24 briquettes. As a general rule, to increase the temperature 25 degrees, add three briquettes. Place one underneath the pot and two on top.

Briquette placement, both on the lid and under the pot, is crucial, too.

To prevent hot spots, rotate the lid and pot 90 degrees every 15 minutes, depending on sun, wind, and altitude.

Seasoned veterans believe that the nose knows when food is done. Lifting the lid to peek inside can release moisture and lengthen the cooking time.

## The Cook's Affliction

A common "disease" among Dutch oven enthusiasts is "castironitis." Don Tinney, a member of Alberta's Chinook Winds IDOS chapter, has it bad. He owns 156 Dutch ovens from three continents, dating from the 1800s.

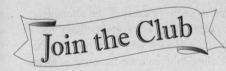

◆ IDOS chapters host cook-offs, seminars, demonstrations, and events for the entire family, including Dutch Oven Gatherings (DOGs), where people get together to cook, chat, trade recipes, and eat. Kids have their own cooking event—a Puppy.

Each spring, IDOS hosts the World Championship Dutch Oven Cook-Off, where teams compete with main courses, breads, and desserts. Cash awards range from $2,500 to $5,000, but the real prize is bragging rights.

Most Dutch oven recipes can be made on the stove, in the oven, or in a slow cooker. See how to adapt this recipe and get more from IDOS members at **Almanac.com/DutchOven.**

## BACON AND CHEESE TATERS

one 10-inch Dutch oven
25 briquettes

1 pound bacon
1 onion, finely diced
2 jalapeños, seeded and chopped
6 medium potatoes, finely diced
1 package (8 ounces) cream cheese, cubed
1 cup shredded Monterey Jack cheese, divided
salt and pepper, to taste

In a Dutch oven over eight briquettes, cook the bacon until crisp. Remove the bacon, set aside, and drain off most of the fat. Add the onions and peppers to the oven and cook for 5 minutes. Add the potatoes and cook, covered, for 5 minutes more. Crumble the bacon and add to the oven, then add the cream cheese, half of the shredded cheese, salt, and pepper. Cover and bake with 17 briquettes on the lid for 45 minutes, stirring every 10 minutes. Top with the remaining shredded cheese before serving. **Makes 10 servings.**

–*International Dutch Oven Society*
□□

Award-winning author **Tammy Sapp** has been writing for 24 years about conservation and the outdoors.

# SCYTHE MATTERS

## All about the best cutting-edge tool ever

BY JANET WALLACE

*There was never a sound beside the wood but one, and that was my long scythe whispering to the ground.*

–Robert Frost, American poet (1874–1963)

**THE SCYTHE,** an ages-old tool for mowing grass, is enjoying new popularity as a truly "green" machine.

"Interest in the scythe is coming from the new generation, the alternative crowd that didn't grow up as farmers," says Peter Vido, 60, a self-declared "missionary" for scything who teaches the practice and whose family operates the Web site www.scytheconnection.com. He is seeing increased interest in hand mowing from homesteaders and small farmers. "In relation to interest in organic things in general, scything is lagging in North America," he says, "but it is picking up among people who leave the city to live in the country."

Typical new adopters of this ancient exercise are farmers who have 2 acres of hay or 5 acres of pasture or a field of grain to cut for personal use. The tool is a multitasker: It is useful both for mowing a lawn or hay and for wacking weeds. It is quiet, does not require fossil fuels, and emits no exhaust.

**CONTINUED**

## Cutting a Swath

Romans introduced the scythe to Europeans as a tool for cutting grass during the 12th and 13th centuries.

By the 16th century, the scythe had replaced the sickle (a curved metal blade with a short handle) for gathering crops.

Early settlers brought the scythe

# Through History

to North America, but the art of making a scythe seems to have been lost in the journey. In Europe, scythe blades had been hammered by hand. In the New World, they were stamped out of sheets of steel and then sharpened by grinding.

Today, many descendants of early Austrian, German, Dutch, and Scandinavian users prefer the scythe to mechanical tools.

# Cutting Words

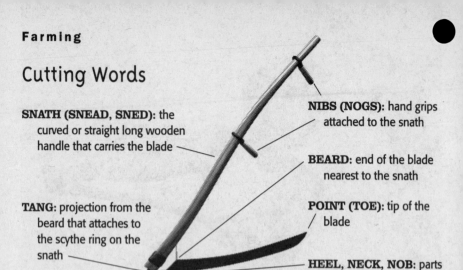

**SNATH (SNEAD, SNED):** the curved or straight long wooden handle that carries the blade

**TANG:** projection from the beard that attaches to the scythe ring on the snath

**NIBS (NOGS):** hand grips attached to the snath

**BEARD:** end of the blade nearest to the snath

**POINT (TOE):** tip of the blade

**HEEL, NECK, NOB:** parts of the tang

## A Butter Knife vs. a Brute

**HAND MOWERS,** the term for people who use scythes, can be divided into two camps: those who use the European, or Austrian, scythe and those who favor its American counterpart.

The first type of tool is lightweight and highly efficient. Its delicate blade requires frequent sharpening but cuts through lush grass like a knife through butter when the edge is freshly honed and peened (sharpened and hammered).

The American scythe, the sort often found in hardware stores, is more of a brute—a sturdy blade on a heavy snath. It requires more strength than fine technique and is best suited for rough brush.

Both tools can employ different blades for different tasks: short and heavy ones for brush; long and slender ones for grass and hay; and general purpose ones that do a fair job on grass, grain, and weedy areas. A 28-inch grass blade is also suitable for weeds, briars, and small trees.

# GETTING INTO THE SWING

*The mechanics of mowing,*
*The grass will teach you.*

–David Tresemer, American scythe expert

**IF A SCYTHE IS SHARP** and the mower is adept, hand mowing has a peaceful, meditative quality. The scythe and body move as one, gracefully forming an arc.

Perhaps the best (and only) book on using this tool is by David Tresemer, who designed and sold scythes and other implements as Green River Tools in the 1980s. In *The Scythe Book: Mowing Hay, Cutting Weeds, and Harvesting Small Grains With Hand Tools* (Alan C. Hood & Company, Inc., 2005), his advice to beginners is simple: "Mowing is a twisting movement."

He advises standing up straight, twisting the body from right to left, and ending the stroke with the left elbow almost touching the backbone. Power the movement with the legs, not the arms. Stand with your feet aligned with your shoulders, with your knees slightly bent and back relaxed. Lean into the task; if the stance becomes a stoop, stop and return to an upright position.

Finally, remember that the goal is a clean cut, not the widest swath.

## Needles Really Did Get Lost in the Haystack

**LOOSE HAY** that is cut with a scythe is stored in stacks rather than in bales. In the past, stacks were held together with long thin pieces of metal—hay pins, similar to hairpins. When one went missing, it was difficult to find.

■ Traditionally, it was believed that a man could mow an acre in a day. The actual square footage varied, depending on the nature of the vegetation and/or the work ethic and strength of the mower.

■ Dawn is the best time to hand mow. The high moisture content of grass at that hour makes it stand up and the dew keeps the blade wet, making cutting easier.

■ Turn to page 231 for the "Best Days" for cutting hay.

□□

**Janet Wallace** is an organic farmer in New Brunswick and editor of *The Canadian Organic Grower*.

# Moo-o-o-ve Over,

## Heritage breeds, descendants of old-time livestock, put the fun back in farming.

Our farming ancestors were practical people. For example, they usually owned a single breed of cattle that tilled the fields, fertilized the pasture, and provided both milk and beef. By contrast, modern commercial farmers and ranchers raise different breeds of livestock for different purposes—milk, eggs, meat, or wool.

Today, the descendants of old-time livestock are called heritage breeds, and descendants of our forebears—especially those who operate small farms—appreciate the convenience and value of these heritage breeds:

- They have a natural foraging ability and thus require less feed.
- They adapt easily to their environments.
- They have high reproduction rates and good mothering skills.
- They have even temperaments and long lives.

As Dan Singletary, a cattle farmer in Jefferson, New York, and member of the American Livestock Breeds Conservancy (ALBC), says, "These heritage breeds, they practically raise themselves."

It doesn't get any better than that—or these, if you want to put the fun back in the farm.

## A PIG'S TALE

**THE TAMWORTH PIG** descended from wild boars in Europe and was imported to America in the 1800s. Today's heritage breed, like previous generations, has sturdy feet that enable it to wander long distances in search of food. Its prominent snout is perfect for foraging (especially for acorns in a forest), and its red coloring offers protection

—The Accidental Smallholder/www.accidentalsmallholder.net

# Holsteins!

## by Martie Majoros

against sunburn. The Tamworth is a hardy animal that has a good disposition and is able to adapt to great temperature variations. Plus, the sows are good mothers—important to the breed's continuity.

Gail Burns and her husband Allan raise Tamworth pigs on their 33-acre farm near Perth, Ontario. "These old breeds, it's the temperament that gets you," says Gail. She claims that when one of their Tamworths contracted pneumonia, Gail brought it into the house, where it camped out on an extra bed it had discovered and stayed there even after Gail's 3-year-old daughter began to read to it.

*Successful farming is based upon stock.*

–*Facts for Farmers*, 1868

# UDDER PLEASURE

**THE AMERICAN MILKING DEVON** traveled from Devonshire, England, to the New World with colonists. George Washington bred American Milking Devons with other cattle at Mount Vernon to improve the endurance of his stock. Ironically, modern-day crossbreeding has diluted the characteristic qualities of the breed, and today purebred Milking Devons —known for producing rich Devon cream—are becoming a rarity in their own homeland.

Dan Singletary raises about 50 red-color American Milking Devons on his farm in the Catskill Mountains. "God's greatest gift is the ruminant," Singletary

says. "You can put them on the crummiest grass and they make it into milk, meat, protein."

Singletary chose to raise Milking Devons because he wanted to preserve the breed's genetic qualities—disease resistance, foraging skill, success in calving, long life expectancy, and the production of great milk, which is excellent for butter and cheese. Typically, Milking Devons produce about 4 gallons of milk per day. (Commercial breeds such as Guernseys, Jerseys, and Holsteins produce from 6 to 10 gallons a day.)

Singletary could increase his herd's milk production if he increased the protein (corn, grain, and silage) in their diet. However, this would lead to digestive problems that eventually might require antibiotics, which would compromise the animals' natural disease resistance.

## CHICK MAGNETS

**THE DOMINIQUE CHICKEN** (right) was a popular backyard bird in the early 20th century, especially during the Depression. In the late 1940s, when commercial livestock production increased, it fell out of favor.

Today, the Dominique is a favorite

**Want to show your chicken?** To get it blue ribbon–ready, wash it with mild dish detergent and then rinse with a lemon juice–and–water solution. Rub canola oil on its legs to make them shine.

190

because it is hardy and easy to maintain. Its tightly arranged feathers act as natural insulation to keep it warm in winter and cool in summer. (As pillow and mattress stuffing, the feathers give people comfort, too.) The bird's small comb is less susceptible to frostbite than a larger one would be.

Another heritage breed getting a big welcome back into the henhouse is the sturdy Java—one of the oldest chicken breeds, if not the oldest. With striking, black-green, iridescent feathers and a red comb, it is a good forager and reliable layer. Even the rooster has a pleasant temperament!

–The Fraser family

# SHEEP TO KEEP

**GULF COAST SHEEP** are believed to be descended from sheep that roamed wild in the U.S. Southeast after having been brought to the New World by Spanish settlers in the 1500s.

–Andrew Bassett/American Livestock Breeds Conservancy

The breed is remarkably hardy, adapting easily to temperatures ranging from –60° to 100°F. It has a natural resistance to foot rot, a disease common to sheep, and is not readily susceptible to the parasitic worm *Haemonchus contortus,* which is prevalent in the Southeast and attacks many other breeds.

David James and his wife Tammy raise heritage Gulf Coast sheep on their farm in Spruce Pine, Alabama. He praises the attributes of heritage breeds and claims that "their natural foraging ability makes them a smart choice for low-input, sustainable, grass-based agriculture."

**(continued)**

Husbandry

# PERPETUATING THE HERITAGE

*When the last individual of a race of living things breathes no more, another Heaven and another Earth must pass before such a one can be again.*

—William Beebe, American naturalist (1877–1962)

## A Foundation for Future Success

Newport, Rhode Island, long home to some of the best-bred members of high society, is also the site of a preeminent heritage animal breeding program.

Nestled in 35 acres of rolling hills along Ocean Drive are the renovated stone barns of the Swiss Village Farm (SVF) Foundation. Scientists there work with the American Livestock Breeds Conservancy (ALBC) and rare-breed animals from across the country to preserve endangered breeds.

When an animal arrives, it is quarantined. SVF, in partnership with Tufts University's Cummings School of Veterinary Medicine, performs tests for nearly a dozen diseases. Once the animal has a clean bill of health, SVF collects and preserves its sperm or eggs. The Foundation's goal is to preserve 3,000 straws of semen and 300 embryos from targeted breeds on the ALBC endangered list.

The Foundation has an eye to the future. The embryos may be transferred to a parent animal of a different breed to produce an offspring with the genetic characteristics of the heritage breed. Or, if an infectious disease were to decimate a popular commercial breed, the preserved genetic material could be used to breed animals that might be resistant to the disease.

There is also the possibility that the study and preservation of the germplasm from heritage breeds with specific disease-resistant qualities could prove valuable in preventing or treating diseases in humans.  □□

Lab supervisor Dr. Dorothy Roof and Tufts University veterinarian Kevin Lindell analyze bovine embryos in the main lab at SFV.

---

**BREEDS THAT ARE OUTSTANDING IN THE FIELD**

For complete lists of endangered heritage breeds, visit the Web sites of the American Livestock Breeds Conservancy, www.albc-usa.org, and Rare Breeds Canada, www.rarebreedscanada.ca.

# Gestation and Mating Tables

| | Proper Age for First Mating | Period of Fertility (yrs.) | Number of Females for One Male | Period of Gestation (days) AVERAGE | RANGE |
|---|---|---|---|---|---|
| **Ewe** | 90 lbs. or 1 yr. | 6 | | 147 / 151[1] | 142–154 |
| **Ram** | 12–14 mos., well matured | 7 | 50–75[2] / 35–40[3] | | |
| **Mare** | 3 yrs. | 10–12 | | 336 | 310–370 |
| **Stallion** | 3 yrs. | 12–15 | 40–45[4] / Record 252[5] | | |
| **Cow** | 15–18 mos.[6] | 10–14 | | 283 | 279–290[7] 262–300[8] |
| **Bull** | 1 yr., well matured | 10–12 | 50[4] / Thousands[5] | | |
| **Sow** | 5–6 mos. or 250 lbs. | 6 | | 115 | 110–120 |
| **Boar** | 250–300 lbs. | 6 | 50[2] / 35–40[3] | | |
| **Doe goat** | 10 mos. or 85–90 lbs. | 6 | | 150 | 145–155 |
| **Buck goat** | Well matured | 5 | 30 | | |
| **Bitch** | 16–18 mos. | 8 | | 63 | 58–67 |
| **Male dog** | 12–16 mos. | 8 | 8–10 | | |
| **Queen cat** | 12 mos. | 6 | | 63 | 60–68 |
| **Tom cat** | 12 mos. | 6 | 6–8 | | |
| **Doe rabbit** | 6 mos. | 5–6 | | 31 | 30–32 |
| **Buck rabbit** | 6 mos. | 5–6 | 30 | | |

[1]For fine wool breeds. [2]Hand-mated. [3]Pasture. [4]Natural. [5]Artificial. [6]Holstein and beef: 750 lbs.; Jersey: 500 lbs. [7]Beef; 8–10 days shorter for Angus. [8]Dairy.

### Incubation Period of Poultry (days)

Chicken . . . . . . . . . . . . . . . . . .21
Duck . . . . . . . . . . . . . . . . .26–32
Goose. . . . . . . . . . . . . . . .30–34
Guinea . . . . . . . . . . . . . .26–28

### Average Life Span of Animals in Captivity (years)

Cat (domestic) . . . . . . . . . . . 14
Chicken (domestic) . . . . . . . . 8
Dog (domestic) . . . . . . . . . . 13
Duck (domestic) . . . . . . . . 10
Goat (domestic) . . . . . . . . . . 14
Goose (domestic). . . . . . . . . 20
Horse. . . . . . . . . . . . . . . . . . . 22
Rabbit (domestic) . . . . . . . . . 6

| | Estral/Estrous Cycle (including heat period) AVERAGE | RANGE | Length of Estrus (heat) AVERAGE | RANGE | Usual Time of Ovulation | When Cycle Recurs If Not Bred |
|---|---|---|---|---|---|---|
| **Mare** | 21 days | 10–37 days | 5–6 days | 2–11 days | 24–48 hours before end of estrus | 21 days |
| **Sow** | 21 days | 18–24 days | 2–3 days | 1–5 days | 30–36 hours after start of estrus | 21 days |
| **Ewe** | 16½ days | 14–19 days | 30 hours | 24–32 hours | 12–24 hours before end of estrus | 16½ days |
| **Goat** | 21 days | 18–24 days | 2–3 days | 1–4 days | Near end of estrus | 21 days |
| **Cow** | 21 days | 18–24 days | 18 hours | 10–24 hours | 10–12 hours after end of estrus | 21 days |
| **Bitch** | 24 days | 16–30 days | 7 days | 5–9 days | 1–3 days after first acceptance | Pseudo-pregnancy |
| **Cat** | | 15–21 days | 3–4 days, if mated | 9–10 days, in absence of male | 24–56 hours after coitus | Pseudo-pregnancy |

# How We Predict the Weather

W e derive our forecasts from a se-cret formula that was devised by the founder of this Almanac, Robert B. Thomas, in 1792. He believed that climate and weather on Earth are influenced by sunspots. (Galileo discovered sunspots in 1610.)

Sunspots are magnetic storms on the surface of the Sun. They and numerous other factors affect the Sun's irradiance. Sunspots occur in cycles of 11 years, on average, and vary in size, number, and frequency. The current solar cycle, 24, began in January 2008.

Over the years, we have refined and enhanced Mr. Thomas's formula with state-of-the-art technology and modern scientific calculations. Today, we employ three scientific disciplines to make our long-range forecasts:

- solar science, the study of the activity on the Sun, including sunspots

- climatology, the study of prevailing weather patterns and conditions over time

- meteorology, the study of the atmosphere

We predict weather trends and events by comparing solar patterns and historical weather conditions with current solar activity.

Our forecasts emphasize temperature and precipitation deviations from averages, or normals. These are based on 30-year statistical averages prepared by government meteorological agencies and updated every 10 years. The most recent tabulations span the period 1971 to 2000.

Our winter forecasts cover the winter season (November through March), not the astronomical winter (from the winter solstice to the vernal equinox). The weather region configurations define areas of relatively similar weather, based upon climatology and typical storm tracks.

We also observe weather lore involving animal behavior, plants, and other elements in nature that indicate a change in the weather. Most have a degree of truth (see page 74). However, we do not employ weather lore in making our predictions.

### The Accuracy of Our Forecasts

We believe that nothing in the universe happens haphazardly, that there is a cause-and-effect pattern to all phenomena. However, although neither we nor any other forecasters have yet gained sufficient insight into the mysteries of the universe to predict the weather with total accuracy, our results are almost always very close to our traditional claim of 80 percent. For details on our predictions for last year, see page 81.

**GET MORE WEATHER**

For additional information on solar activity, sunspots, and weather patterns, as well as alternative forecasting methods (such as with a pig spleen or woolly bear caterpillar), go to **Almanac.com/Weather.**

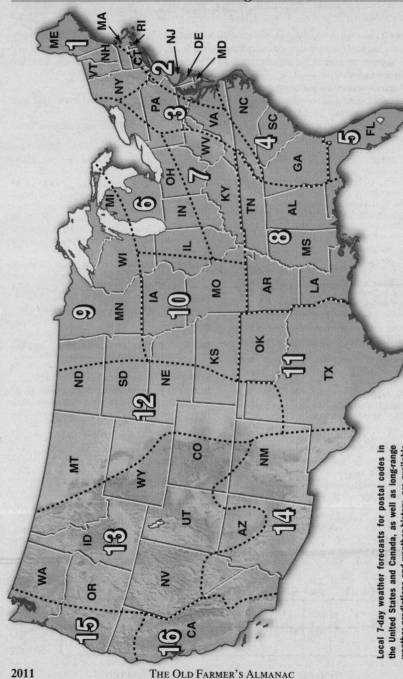

Local 7-day weather forecasts for postal codes in the United States and Canada, as well as long-range weather predictions and weather history, are available at Almanac.com/Weather.

# Northeast

**SUMMARY:** Winter will be milder than normal across the north but colder across the south, with the coldest periods in early and mid-December, early and mid-January, and mid-February. Precipitation will be below normal, with near- to below-normal snowfall. The snowiest periods will be in late December, mid- and late January, mid- to late February, and early March.

April and May will be cooler and drier than normal.

Summer temperatures will be near normal in New York and cooler than normal elsewhere, with below-normal rainfall. The hottest periods will be in late June and early and late July.

September and October will be cooler than normal, with precipitation above normal in the north and below normal in the south.

**NOV. 2010:** Temp. 34.5° (4° above avg. north, 1° below south); precip. 4" (2" above avg. north, 1" below south). 1–4 Rain and snow, then sunny, cold. 5–7 Showers, seasonable. 8–16 Periods of rain and snow, chilly. 17–25 Rain and snow, then sunny, cool. 26–30 Showers, mild.

**DEC. 2010:** Temp. 26° (avg.); precip. 2" (1" below avg.). 1–2 Sunny, cool. 3–5 Snow showers, cold. 6–12 Snow north; showers, mild south. 13–15 Flurries, cold. 16–19 Rain and snow, mild. 20–25 Sunny; cold, then mild. 26–31 Snowy periods, seasonable.

**JAN. 2011:** Temp. 19° (1° above avg. north, 3° below south); precip. 2" (1" below avg.). 1–5 Snow showers, then sunny, cold. 6–9 Flurries, cold. 10–15 Snowy periods, mild. 16–19 Snowstorm, then sunny, very cold. 20–25 Snowy periods. 26–31 Snow showers; mild east, cold west.

**FEB. 2011:** Temp. 20° (1° below avg.); precip. 3.5" (0.5" above avg. north, 1.5" above south). 1–4 Sunny, mild. 5–8 Rain and snow, mild. 9–14 Snow showers, turning bitterly cold. 15–17 Snow showers. 18–21 Heavy snow. 22–25 Rain, then sunny, mild. 26–28 Heavy rain, mild.

**MAR. 2011:** Temp. 33° (2° above avg. north, 2° below south); precip. 1" (2" below avg.). 1–4 Sunny, cool. 5–10 Snow, then sunny, cool. 11–15 Rainy periods, mild. 16–22 Rain to snow, turning cold. 23–28 Snow showers, then sunny, seasonable. 29–31 Sprinkles, mild.

**APR. 2011:** Temp. 41.5° (3.5° below avg.); precip. 1.5" (1.5" below avg.). 1–8 Rain and snow, then sunny. 9–12 Sunny, nice. 13–18 Showers, warm. 19–22 Sunny, cool. 23–30 Showers, cool; wet snow north.

**MAY 2011:** Temp. 54.5° (1.5° below avg.); precip. 2.5" (1" below avg.). 1–4 Rain and snow, then sunny, chilly. 5–6 Rainy, raw. 7–10 Sunny, seasonable. 11–20 Rain, then sunny, very warm. 21–27 Showers, then sunny, cool. 28–31 T-storms, warm.

**JUNE 2011:** Temp. 66° (avg. east, 2° above west); precip. 2" (2" below avg. north, 1" below south). 1–5 Showers, then sunny, cool. 6–14 Scattered t-storms. 15–21 Sunny, hot. 22–26 T-storms, then sunny, hot. 27–30 T-storms, warm.

**JULY 2011:** Temp. 68° (2° below avg.); precip. 3.5" (0.5" below avg.). 1–2 Sunny, hot. 3–8 T-storms, then sunny, cool. 9–11 Sunny, hot. 12–15 T-storms, cool. 16–19 T-storms north, sunny south. 20–23 Showers, then sunny, cool. 24–28 Scattered t-storms, cool. 29–31 Sunny, hot.

**AUG. 2011:** Temp. 66° (2° below avg. north, avg. south); precip. 4" (avg.). 1–8 T-storms, then sunny, cool. 9–12 T-storms, then sunny, warm. 13–20 A few t-storms, cool. 21–25 Sunny, warm. 26–31 T-storms, cool.

**SEPT. 2011:** Temp. 55° (4° below avg.); precip. 3" (0.5" below avg.). 1–2 Sunny, warm. 3–6 T-storms, then sunny, cool. 7–13 T-storms, then sunny, cool. 14–21 Rain, then sunny, chilly. 22–28 Rainy periods, cool. 29–30 Sunny.

**OCT. 2011:** Temp. 48.5° (0.5° above avg.); precip. 4" (2" above avg. north, 1" below south). 1–2 Sunny, warm. 3–8 Rainy, raw, then sunny, mild. 9–13 Rainy periods, cool. 14–21 Sunny, pleasant. 22–24 Rain and snow showers, cool. 25–27 Rainy, mild. 28–31 Showers, cool.

W E A T H E R

Caribou

Augusta

Burlington

Concord

Albany

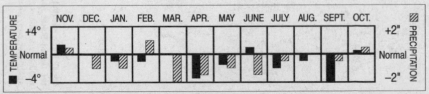

# Atlantic Corridor

**SUMMARY:** Winter will be colder and drier than normal, on average, with below-normal snowfall in New England and above-normal snowfall elsewhere. The coldest periods will be in mid-December, January, and mid-February. The snowiest periods will be in early January and mid- and late February.

April and May will be cooler and drier than normal.

Summer will be drier and slightly cooler than normal, with the hottest periods in mid- and late June, early July, and early to mid-August.

September and October will be much cooler and rainier than normal.

**NOV. 2010:** Temp. 47° (avg.); precip. 1.5" (2" below avg.). 1–3 Sunny, cold. 4–8 Showers, then sunny, cold. 9–13 Rain, then sunny, mild. 14–18 Showers, then sunny, cool. 19–25 Rain, then sunny, cold. 26–30 Showers, then sunny, cold.

**DEC. 2010:** Temp. 37° (1° below avg.); precip. 2.0" (1" below avg.). 1–6 Sunny, then rain, mild. 7–10 Snow north, showers south. 11–16 Sunny, cold. 17–19 Rainy, mild. 20–25 Sunny; cold, then mild. 26–28 Rain, then sunny, mild. 29–31 Rain, mild.

**JAN. 2011:** Temp. 30° (3° below avg.); precip. 2.5" (1" below avg.). 1–5 Snow, then sunny, very cold. 6–11 Snow showers, then sunny, cold. 12–17 Rain and snow, seasonable. 18–21 Snowstorm, then sunny, very cold. 22–24 Snow, then sunny, cold. 25–31 Snow, then sunny, very cold.

**FEB. 2011:** Temp. 35° (2° above avg.); precip. 4" (1" above avg.). 1–3 Sunny, turning mild. 4–6 Heavy rain, mild. 7–10 Rain to snow. 11–16 Snow showers, then sunny, very cold. 17–20 Snowstorm, then sunny. 21–24 Rain, then sunny, mild. 25–26 Rain, mild. 27–28 Sunny, mild.

**MAR. 2011:** Temp. 39° (2° below avg.); precip. 1.5" (2.5" below avg.). 1–4 Sunny, cold. 5–10 Rain and snow, seasonable. 11–16 Showers, mild. 17–22 Rain, then sunny, cool. 23–26 Showers, then sunny, cool. 27–31 Rainy periods.

**APR. 2011:** Temp. 49° (3° below avg.); precip. 3" (0.5" below avg.). 1–4 Drizzle, cool. 5–10 Sunny, cool. 11–17 Rainy periods; cool north, warm south. 18–19 Sunny, warm. 20–26 Rainy periods, cool. 27–30 Sunny, turning warm.

**MAY 2011:** Temp. 65° (1° below avg.); precip. 3" (avg. north, 2" below south). 1–4 Rain, then sunny, cool. 5–7 Showers, cool. 8–11 Showers, cool north; sunny, warm south. 12–17 T-storms, then sunny, warm. 18–22 Showers, warm. 23–26 Cloudy, cool. 27–31 Sunny, turning hot.

**JUNE 2011:** Temp. 70° (1° below avg.); precip. 2.5" (1" below avg.). 1–5 T-storms, then sunny, cool. 6–12 Scattered showers. 13–16 Sunny, hot. 17–19 T-storms north; sunny, hot south. 20–30 Scattered t-storms, hot.

**JULY 2011:** Temp. 75° (1° below avg.); precip. 3" (1" below avg.). 1–7 Scattered t-storms, hot. 8–11 Sunny; cool nights. 12–17 Sunny, comfortable. 18–22 Scattered t-storms, warm and humid. 23–27 Scattered t-storms, seasonable. 28–31 Sunny, cool north; rain south.

**AUG. 2011:** Temp. 75.5° (1.5° above avg.); precip. 2.5" (1.5" below avg.). 1–7 Scattered t-storms, seasonable. 8–14 Sunny, then sunny, hot. 15–22 T-storms, then sunny, seasonable. 23–25 Sunny, warm. 26–29 T-storms, cool north; sunny, warm south. 30–31 Showers, cool.

**SEPT. 2011:** Temp. 63° (4° below avg.); precip. 7.5" (4" above avg.). 1–5 Sunny, nice. 6–11 Heavy t-storms, then sunny, cool. 12–17 Rain, then sunny, cool. 18–21 Sunny north, rain south. 22–26 Rain, then sunny, chilly. 27–30 Showers.

**OCT. 2011:** Temp. 55.5° (0.5° above avg. north, 2° below south): precip. 4.5" (1" above avg.). 1–3 Sunny, warm. 4–8 Showers, then sunny, seasonable. 9–10 Showers, cool. 11–14 Heavy rain, then sunny, cool. 15–22 Sunny, warm north; a few showers south. 23–25 Showers, cool. 26–31 Heavy rain, then sunny, cool.

Boston
Hartford
New York
Philadelphia
Baltimore
Washington
Atlantic City
Richmond

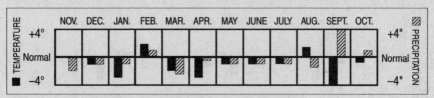

# Appalachians

**SUMMARY:** Winter will be colder and drier than normal, with near- to below-normal snowfall in the north and above-normal snowfall in the south. The coldest periods will be in mid- and late January and mid- and late February. The snowiest periods will be in mid- to late November, mid-December, and mid-February.

April and May will be cooler and drier than normal across most of the area, with near-normal rainfall across the north.

Summer will be drier and slightly cooler than normal, with the hottest periods in late June, early and mid-July, and mid- to late August.

September and October will be much cooler than normal, with rainfall below normal in the north and above normal in the south.

**NOV. 2010:** Temp. 42.5° (avg.); precip. 1.5" (2" below avg.). 1–4 Rain, then sunny, cool. 5–7 Showers, cool. 8–12 Rain and snow, then sunny, cool. 13–17 Rain to snow, then sunny, cool. 18–24 Rain, then sunny, cold. 25–30 Rain and snow, then sunny, cold.

**DEC. 2010:** Temp. 33° (1° below avg.); precip. 1.5" (1.5" below avg.). 1–2 Sunny. 3–10 Rainy periods, mild. 11–14 Snow showers, cold. 15–20 Rainy, mild, then sunny, cold. 21–24 Sunny, unseasonably mild. 25–31 Periods of rain and snow, mild.

**JAN. 2011:** Temp. 23° (5° below avg.); precip. 3" (1" below avg. north, 0.5" above south). 1–5 Sunny, cold. 6–9 Snowy periods, cold. 10–14 Snow showers, cold. 15–18 Snowstorm, then sunny, cold. 19–26 Snowy periods, very cold. 27–31 Snow showers, very cold.

**FEB. 2011:** Temp. 28.5° (2° above avg. north, 1° below south); precip. 3.5" (avg. north, 2" above south). 1–2 Sunny, seasonable. 3–8 Rainy periods, quite mild. 9–10 Sunny, mild. 11–15 Snow showers, cold. 16–19 Snowstorm, then sunny, cold. 20–24 Rain, then sunny, mild. 25–28 Rain to snow, turning cold.

**MAR. 2011:** Temp. 37° (2° below avg.); precip. 1.5" (1.5" below avg.). 1–4 Sunny; cold, then mild. 5–10 Rain, then sunny, cool. 11–16 Showers north, sunny south; warm. 17–22 Rain, then sunny, cold. 23–27 Rain and snow showers, chilly. 28–31 Snow showers north, sunny south; cool.

**APR. 2011:** Temp. 47° (3° below avg.); precip. 3.5" (avg.). 1–9 Sunny, then rainy periods; cool. 10–14 Sunny, turning warm. 15–18 Showers, warm. 19–28 Rainy periods, then sunny, cool. 29–30 Rainy, cool north; sunny, warm south.

**MAY 2011:** Temp. 58.5° (1.5° below avg.); precip. 3.5" (avg. north, 1.5" below south). 1–4 Rain, then sunny, quite cool. 5–8 Rainy periods, cool. 9–20 Scattered t-storms, turning warm. 21–26 T-storms, then sunny, cool. 27–31 Sunny, warm.

**JUNE 2011:** Temp. 66° (2° below avg.); precip. 1.5" (2.5" below avg.). 1–2 Sunny, warm. 3–6 T-storms, then sunny, cool. 7–16 T-storms, then sunny, seasonable. 17–27 T-storms, then sunny, hot. 28–30 Scattered t-storms, hot.

**JULY 2011:** Temp. 73.5° (0.5° above avg.); precip. 2.5" (2" below avg. north, avg. south). 1–7 Sunny, hot. 8–12 Scattered t-storms, warm. 13–19 Sunny; cool, then hot. 20–25 T-storms, then sunny, cooler. 26–31 T-storms, then sunny, warm.

**AUG. 2011:** Temp. 72° (1° above avg.); precip. 4.5" (2" above avg. north, avg. south). 1–4 Scattered t-storms, warm. 5–15 Scattered t-storms; cool, then warm. 16–19 Sunny, cool. 20–26 T-storms, then sunny, hot. 27–31 T-storms, then sunny, cool.

**SEPT. 2011:** Temp. 60° (4° below avg.); precip. 5" (avg. north, 3" above south). 1–5 Sunny, pleasant. 6–11 T-storms, then sunny, cool. 12–24 Frequent rainy periods, cool. 25–30 Sunny, cool.

**OCT. 2011:** Temp. 51.5° (1.5° below avg.); precip. 2" (2" below avg. north, 0.5" above south). 1–3 Sunny, warm. 4–7 Showers, then sunny, mild. 8–13 Rainy periods, turning cool. 14–22 Sunny, seasonable. 23–24 Showers, cool. 25–29 Rain, then sunny, cool. 30–31 Showers, cool.

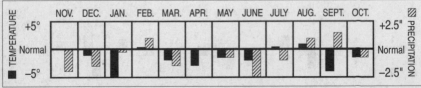

# Southeast

**SUMMARY:** Winter will be colder than normal, with below-normal precipitation and near- to above-normal snowfall. The coldest periods will be in January, especially the mid- to late part of the month, and mid- and late February. The snowiest periods will be in mid- to late January.

April and May will be cooler than normal, with rainfall slightly below normal in the north and above normal in the south.

Summer will be cooler than normal, with rainfall below normal in the north and slightly above normal in the south. The hottest temperatures will be in early July and mid-August. Expect a hurricane in the second week of June.

September and October will be cooler and drier than normal.

**NOV. 2010:** Temp. 54° (1° below avg.); precip. 1.5" (1.5" below avg.). 1–2 Sunny, warm. 3–6 Showers, cool. 7–13 Sunny; warm, then cool. 14–17 Rain, then sunny, cool. 18–25 Showers, then sunny, cold. 26–30 Showers, then sunny, cold.

**DEC. 2010:** Temp. 46° (1° below avg.); precip. 2.5" (1" below avg.). 1–4 Sunny, turning warm. 5–10 Rainy periods, mild. 11–16 Sunny, cool. 17–20 Showers, then sunny, cool. 21–25 Sunny, warm. 26–31 Rainy periods, turning cooler.

**JAN. 2011:** Temp. 43° (2° below avg.); precip. 5" (0.5" above avg.). 1–5 Sunny, cold. 6–9 Heavy rain, cool. 10–13 Sunny, cold. 14–17 Periods of rain and snow, cold. 18–25 Snowstorm north, rain to snow south; turning very cold. 26–31 Sunny, cold.

**FEB. 2011:** Temp. 47° (1° above avg.); precip. 7" (3" above avg.). 1–11 Sunny, then rainy periods, turning warm. 12–15 Sunny, cold. 16–19 Rain, then sunny, cool. 20–23 Heavy rain, then sunny, mild. 24–28 Heavy rain, then sunny, cold.

**MAR. 2011:** Temp. 53° (2° below avg.); precip. 2" (2.5" below avg.). 1–5 Sunny; cold, then mild. 6–11 Rain, then sunny, seasonable. 12–16 Sunny, turning warm. 17–24 Showers, then sunny, cold. 25–31 Rainy periods, cool.

**APR. 2011:** Temp. 63° (avg.); precip. 2.5" (0.5" below avg.). 1–4 Sunny, cool. 5–9 Rainy periods, cool. 10–12 Sunny, turning warmer. 13–20 Some scattered t-storms, warm. 21–23

T-storms, then sunny, cooler. 24–30 T-storms, then sunny, seasonable.

**MAY 2011:** Temp. 69° (2° below avg.); precip. 5" (avg. north, 3" above south). 1–4 Rain, then sunny, cool. 5–10 T-storms, then sunny, seasonable. 11–13 Scattered t-storms, very warm. 14–24 Rainy periods, seasonable. 25–31 Sunny, cool.

**JUNE 2011:** Temp. 76° (1° above avg. north, 3° below south); precip. 7" (avg. north, 5" above south). 1–7 T-storms, then sunny, cool. 8–12 Hurricane threat. 13–19 Sunny; cool, then warm. 20–30 Scattered t-storms, seasonable.

**JULY 2011:** Temp. 79° (2° below avg.); precip. 4" (1" below avg.). 1–5 T-storms, hot. 6–9 Scattered t-storms, warm. 10–15 Sunny, cool. 16–22 Scattered t-storms, seasonable. 23–26 T-storms, then sunny, cool. 27–31 Heavy t-storms, cool.

**AUG. 2011:** Temp. 79° (avg.); precip. 2" (3" below avg.). 1–8 Scattered t-storms, humid. 9–13 Sunny, hot. 14–19 Scattered t-storms, turning cooler. 20–26 Sunny, seasonable. 27–31 Sunny, warm.

**SEPT. 2011:** Temp. 72° (2° below avg.); precip. 2.5" (2" below avg.). 1–3 Sunny, cool. 4–10 Showers, then sunny, cool. 11–19 Heavy rain, then sunny, seasonable. 20–23 Rain, then sunny, warm. 24–30 T-storms, then sunny, cool.

**OCT. 2011:** Temp. 62° (2° below avg.); precip. 2.5" (1.5" below avg.). 1–4 Showers, warm. 5–7 Sunny; cool, then warm. 8–12 T-storms, warm. 13–16 Sunny; cool, then warm. 17–24 T-storms, then sunny, cool. 25–31 Rain, then sunny, cold.

Raleigh · Columbia · Atlanta · Savannah

WEATHER

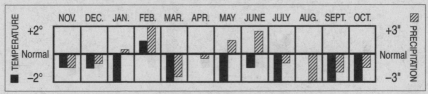

# Florida

**SUMMARY:** Winter will be slightly colder than normal, on average, with the coldest temperatures in mid-December, mid- and late January, and mid-February. Rainfall will be above normal, with the best chance for any snow in the north in mid- to late January.

April and May will be rainier than normal, with temperatures above normal in the north and below normal elsewhere.

Summer will be cooler and much rainier than normal, with the hottest periods in early and mid-July and mid- and late August. Expect hurricane threats in June and early October.

September and October will be slightly cooler than normal, with rainfall below normal in the north and above normal in the south.

**NOV. 2010:** Temp. 70° (1° above avg.); precip. 0.5" (2" below avg.). 1–5 Sunny, warm. 6–14 Showers, then sunny, seasonable. 15–21 T-storms, then sunny, warm. 22–26 T-storms, then sunny, cool. 27–30 Showers, then sunny, cool.

**DEC. 2010:** Temp. 62° (1° below avg.); precip. 2.5" (avg.). 1–4 Sunny, cool. 5–11 T-storms, then sunny, warm. 12–21 T-storms, then sunny, cool. 22–31 A few t-storms, warm.

**JAN. 2011:** Temp. 59° (2° below avg.); precip. 3.5" (1" above avg.). 1–6 Sunny north, showers south; turning cool. 7–12 T-storms, then sunny, cool. 13–17 Rain, then sunny, cool. 18–21 T-storms, then sunny, cool. 22–24 T-storms, then sunny, cold. 25–31 Sunny, very cool.

**FEB. 2011:** Temp. 62.5° (1.5° above avg.); precip. 6.5" (4" above avg.). 1–10 Scattered t-storms north, sunny south; warm. 11–14 Heavy t-storms, then sunny, cool. 15–19 Heavy rain, then sunny, cool. 20–25 Showers, turning warm. 26–28 T-storms, then sunny, cool.

**MAR. 2011:** Temp. 66° (1° below avg.); precip. 3" (1" below avg. north, 1" above south). 1–2 Sunny, cool. 3–11 Occasional rain, seasonable. 12–16 Sunny, warm. 17–27 Showers, then sunny, cool. 28–31 Rain, cool.

**APR. 2011:** Temp. 71° (2° above avg. north, 2° below south); precip. 1.5" (1" below avg.). 1–4 Sunny north, t-storms south; cool. 5–7 Sunny, warm. 8–12 Showers, then sunny, pleasant. 13–19 Showers, then sunny, warm. 20–27 Scattered t-storms, seasonable. 28–30 T-storms, cool.

**MAY 2011:** Temp. 76° (1° below avg.); precip. 6.5" (2.5" above avg.). 1–7 Scattered t-storms, seasonable. 8–9 Sunny, warm. 10–13 T-storms, then sunny, warm. 14–24 Daily t-storms, seasonable. 25–31 Sunny north, t-storms south; cool.

**JUNE 2011:** Temp. 79° (2° below avg.); precip. 14.5" (8" above avg.). 1–3 Heavy t-storms, cool. 4–9 Sunny north, a few t-storms south. 10–13 Hurricane threat. 14–20 Sunny north, t-storms south; cool. 21–24 Hurricane threat. 25–30 Scattered t-storms, warm.

**JULY 2011:** Temp. 81° (1° below avg.); precip. 8.5" (avg. north, 4" above south). 1–5 Sunny, hot north; t-storms, cool south. 6–14 Scattered t-storms, seasonable. 15–18 T-storms, cool. 19–23 Sunny, hot north; t-storms, cool south. 24–26 Sunny north, t-storms south; cool. 27–31 Scattered t-storms, seasonable.

**AUG. 2011:** Temp. 81° (avg.); precip. 6.5" (1" below avg.). 1–8 Scattered t-storms, slightly cooler than normal. 9–12 Sunny, warm. 13–19 Scattered t-storms, hot. 20–26 Sunny, seasonable. 27–31 Scattered t-storms, hot.

**SEPT. 2011:** Temp. 79° (1° below avg.); precip. 7.5" (2" below avg. north, 3" above south). 1–8 Scattered t-storms, slightly cooler than normal. 9–10 Sunny, warm. 11–13 T-storms north, sunny south; warm. 14–18 Sunny north, t-storms south; cool. 19–24 Sunny, warm north; t-storms south. 25–30 Scattered t-storms, warm.

**OCT. 2011:** Temp. 73.5° (1.5° below avg.); precip. 3" (1" below avg.). 1–3 Hurricane threat. 4–10 Sunny, warm. 11–13 Sunny, cool north; showers south. 14–18 Sunny north, t-storms south; warm. 19–25 Sunny, seasonable. 26–31 Showers, then sunny, chilly.

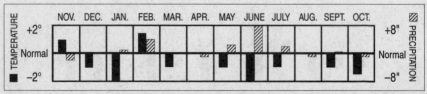

## Lower Lakes

**SUMMARY:** Winter will be colder than normal, with the coldest periods in late December, mid- and late January, and mid- and late February. Snowfall and precipitation will be near or slightly above normal in New York and below normal elsewhere. The snowiest periods will be in mid-December, January, and mid-February.

April and May will be cooler and drier than normal.

Summer temperatures will be near normal, on average, with below-normal rainfall. The hottest periods will be in mid- to late June and early and mid-July.

September and October will be cooler and drier than normal.

**NOV. 2010:** Temp. 39.5° (0.5° below avg.); precip. 2.5" (1" above avg. east, 2" below west). 1–3 Rain, then sunny, cold. 4–8 Showers; cool east, mild west. 9–13 Rain to snow, then sunny, seasonable. 14–19 Rainy periods, turning warmer. 20–24 Rain and snow, then flurries, cold. 25–30 Rain and snow showers, seasonable.

**DEC. 2010:** Temp. 29° (avg.); precip. 4" (0.5" below avg. east, 2.5" above west). 1–7 Sunny, then rain, mild. 8–14 Rain and snow showers, seasonable. 15–18 Rain to snow, mild. 19–23 Snow showers, then sunny, warm. 24–28 T-storms, then sunny, mild. 29–31 Rain to snow, turning cold.

**JAN. 2011:** Temp. 22° (2° below avg.); precip. 2.5" (1" above avg. east, 1" below west). 1–3 Snow showers, turning milder. 4–8 Snow showers east, snowstorm west; seasonable. 9–14 Snow showers, seasonable. 15–22 Snowstorm, then lake snows, bitter cold. 23–31 Snowstorm, then lake snows, very cold.

**FEB. 2011:** Temp. 25° (1° above avg.); precip. 2" (avg.). 1–4 Rainy periods, unseasonably mild. 5–9 Snow showers, seasonable. 10–15 Lake snows, bitter cold. 16–20 Snow showers, seasonable. 21–23 Snow to rain, then mild. 24–28 Rain to snow, turning cold.

**MAR. 2011:** Temp. 34° (2° below avg.); precip. 2" (1" below avg.). 1–3 Sunny, mild. 4–10 Rainy, mild, then sunny, cold. 11–16 Showers, mild. 17–21 T-storms, then snow showers, cold. 22–31 Rain and snow showers, chilly.

**APR. 2011:** Temp. 45° (2° below avg.); precip. 3" (0.5" below avg.). 1–10 Showers, then sunny, seasonable. 11–18 A few t-storms, warm. 19–27 Rain, then sunny, cool. 28–30 T-storms, warm.

**MAY 2011:** Temp. 56° (2° below avg.); precip. 2.5" (1" below avg.). 1–3 Sunny, cool. 4–8 Rain and wet snow, then sunny, cool. 9–14 Showers, seasonable. 15–17 Sunny, turning warm. 18–20 Showers, then sunny, warm. 21–26 Sunny, cool. 27–31 Scattered t-storms, hot.

**JUNE 2011:** Temp. 69° (2° above avg.); precip. 2.5" (1" below avg.). 1–5 T-storms, then sunny, cool. 6–10 Showers, cool. 11–20 Sunny, turning very warm. 21–26 Scattered t-storms, hot. 27–30 T-storms, then sunny, seasonable.

**JULY 2011:** Temp. 71° (1° below avg.); precip. 3.5" (1" above avg. east, 1" below west). 1–6 Scattered t-storms, hot. 7–10 Sunny, comfortable. 11–15 T-storms, then sunny, cool. 16–20 Scattered t-storms, hot. 21–24 T-storms, then sunny, cool. 25–31 T-storms, then sunny, cool.

**AUG. 2011:** Temp. 69° (1° below avg.); precip. 3" (1" below avg.). 1–6 A few t-storms; warm, then cool. 7–12 Scattered t-storms east, sunny west; seasonable. 13–18 T-storms, cool. 19–25 Sunny, warm. 26–31 T-storms, then sunny, cool.

**SEPT. 2011:** Temp. 60° (3° below avg.); precip. 2.5" (1" below avg.). 1–6 Sunny, turning warm. 7–11 T-storms, then sunny, pleasant. 12–15 T-storms, mild. 16–21 Showers, then sunny, cool. 22–25 Showers, then sunny, cool. 26–30 Scattered showers, cool.

**OCT. 2011:** Temp. 50° (2° below avg.); precip. 2" (0.5" below avg.). 1–2 Sunny, warm. 3–5 Showers, cool. 6–8 T-storms, warm. 9–17 Showers, then sunny, cooler. 18–21 Sunny, warm. 22–25 Showers, cool. 26–31 Rain and snow, chilly.

WEATHER

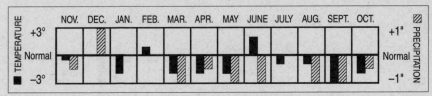

# Ohio Valley

**WEATHER**

**SUMMARY:** Winter will be colder and drier than normal, on average, with below-normal snowfall. Most days in January will be cold, with other cold periods in early to mid-December and mid-February. The snowiest periods will occur in mid-January and mid-February.

April and May will continue cooler and drier than normal, on average.

Summer will be drier and slightly cooler than normal, with the hottest periods in mid- to late June, early July, and mid-July.

September and October will be much cooler and slightly drier than normal.

**NOV. 2010:** Temp. 44° (1° below avg.); precip. 2.5" (1" below avg.). 1–4 Rain, then sunny, cold. 5–8 Rain, then sunny, cold. 9–13 Rain, then sunny, cold. 14–20 Rainy periods, mild. 21–30 Snow showers, cold.

**DEC. 2010:** Temp. 35° (avg.); precip. 4" (1" above avg.). 1–8 Sunny, then showers, mild. 9–14 Snow showers, cold. 15–17 Sunny, warm. 18–22 Rain and snow, then sunny, seasonable. 23–31 Rainy periods, mild.

**JAN. 2011:** Temp. 29° (2° below avg.); precip. 2" (1" below avg.). 1–5 Snow showers, cold. 6–14 Rain to snow, then snow showers, cold. 15–21 Snowstorm, then snow showers, very cold. 22–25 Snow squalls, bitter cold. 26–31 Snow showers, cold.

**FEB. 2011:** Temp. 34° (2° above avg.); precip. 2.5" (0.5" below avg.). 1–2 Sunny, warm. 3–9 Rainy periods, mild. 10–16 Sunny, cold. 17–22 Snow, then rainy periods, turning mild. 23–25 Sunny, then rain, warm. 26–28 Snow showers, cold.

**MAR. 2011:** Temp. 43° (1° below avg.); precip. 2.5" (1.5" below avg.). 1–2 Sunny, cold. 3–10 Rain, then sunny, warm. 11–14 Showers, cooler. 15–16 Sunny, warm, then t-storms. 17–22 Rain to snow, then snow showers, cold. 23–31 Rain and snow showers, chilly.

**APR. 2011:** Temp. 53.5° (0.5° below avg.); precip. 4.5" (1" above avg.). 1–3 Rain and snow showers, chilly. 4–10 Rain, then sunny, cool. 11–15 Scattered showers, turning warm. 16–23 A few t-storms, warm. 24–30 Sunny, cool.

**MAY 2011:** Temp. 61° (2° below avg.); precip. 3" (1.5" below avg.). 1–4 Rain to snow, then sunny, cold. 5–10 Rain, then sunny, seasonable. 11–14 Showers, warm. 15–20 Sunny, warm. 21–26 T-storms, then sunny, cool. 27–31 Sunny, then t-storms, warm.

**JUNE 2011:** Temp. 73° (1° above avg.); precip. 2" (2" below avg.). 1–5 T-storms, then sunny, cool. 6–13 T-storms, then sunny, seasonable. 14–20 Sunny, hot. 21–25 T-storms, then sunny, hot. 26–30 Scattered t-storms, warm.

**JULY 2011:** Temp. 75° (1° below avg.); precip. 3.5" (0.5" below avg.). 1–7 Scattered t-storms, hot. 8–11 Sunny, warm. 12–15 T-storms, then sunny, cool. 16–21 Scattered t-storms, very warm. 22–25 Sunny, pleasant. 26–31 T-storms, then sunny, seasonable.

**AUG. 2011:** Temp. 73° (1° below avg.); precip. 4" (0.5" above avg.). 1–3 T-storms, warm. 4–9 Scattered t-storms; cool, then warm. 10–12 Sunny, warm. 13–15 T-storms, warm. 16–25 Sunny; cool, then warm. 26–31 T-storms, then sunny, cool.

**SEPT. 2011:** Temp. 63° (4° below avg.); precip. 3" (avg.). 1–5 Sunny, pleasant. 6–11 Rain, then sunny, cool. 12–17 Rain, then sunny, cool. 18–24 Rainy periods, cool. 25–30 Sunny, cool.

**OCT. 2011:** Temp. 53° (3° below avg.); precip. 2" (0.5" below avg.). 1–7 Rain, then sunny, warm. 8–13 Rainy periods, cool. 14–23 Sunny, cool. 24–28 Rain and snow, then sunny, cold. 29–31 Snow to rain, then sunny, warm.

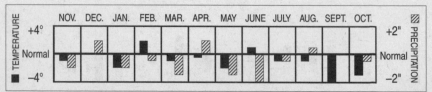

# Deep South

**SUMMARY:** Winter will be colder than normal, with precipitation below normal in the north and above normal in the south. Most days in January will be cold, with other cold periods in early to mid-February. Snowfall will generally be above normal, with the snowiest periods in mid- and late January and mid-February.

April and May will bring near-normal temperatures and rainfall.

Summer will be warmer and drier than normal across the north but cooler and rainier than normal across the south. The hottest periods will occur in late June and early and mid-July. Expect a hurricane in late July.

September and October will be much cooler and slightly rainier than normal.

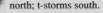

**NOV. 2010:** Temp. 55.5° (1° above avg.); precip. 2" (3" below avg.). 1–9 Scattered t-storms, warm. 10–13 Sunny; cool, then warm. 14–20 Warm, then a few t-storms. 21–25 Sunny, cold. 26–30 T-storms, then sunny, cold.

**DEC. 2010:** Temp. 47° (avg.); precip. 7" (1" below avg. north, 5" above south). 1–4 Sunny, turning warm. 5–9 T-storms, warm. 10–12 Sunny, cool north; heavy rain south. 13–16 Sunny; cool, then warm. 17–21 Rain, then sunny, seasonable. 22–26 Scattered t-storms, warm. 27–31 Heavy rain, mild.

**JAN. 2011:** Temp. 42° (2° below avg.); precip. 4" (1" below avg.). 1–4 Sunny, cold. 5–10 Rain, then sunny, cold. 11–22 Periods of rain and snow north, rain south; cold. 23–24 Sunny, cold. 25–31 Rain and snow, then sunny, cold.

**FEB. 2011:** Temp. 46° (1° above avg. north, 1° below south); precip. 7" (avg. north, 4" above south). 1–7 Rainy periods, warm. 8–15 T-storms, then sunny, cold. 16–18 Rain to snow, then sunny, cold. 19–23 Rainy periods, seasonable. 24–28 T-storms, then sunny, cold.

**MAR. 2011:** Temp. 54° (2° below avg.); precip. 3" (3" below avg.). 1–4 Sunny, turning warm. 5–10 T-storms, then sunny, warm. 11–16 Scattered t-storms, warm. 17–21 Sunny, cold. 22–26 Showers, then sunny, warm. 27–31 T-storms, then sunny, cool.

**APR. 2011:** Temp. 65° (2° above avg.); precip. 5.5" (1" above avg.). 1–3 T-storms, then sunny, cool. 4–10 Scattered t-storms, cool. 11–25 Several t-storms, warm. 26–30 Sunny, warm

north; t-storms south.

**MAY 2011:** Temp. 69° (2° below avg.); precip. 4.5" (2" below avg. north, 1" above south). 1–4 Sunny, cool. 5–8 T-storms; cool north, warm south. 9–15 Scattered t-storms, seasonable. 16–19 Sunny north, t-storms south; warm. 20–28 Sunny, cool. 29–31 T-storms, warm.

**JUNE 2011:** Temp. 77.5° (2° above avg. north, 3° above south); precip. 3" (2" below avg.). 1–5 T-storms, then sunny, nice. 6–14 Scattered t-storms, then sunny, cool. 15–21 Sunny, warm north; scattered t-storms south. 22–30 Scattered t-storms; hot north, cool south.

**JULY 2011:** Temp. 82.5° (0.5° above avg.); precip. 5.5" (1" below avg. north, 2" above south). 1–7 Sunny, hot. 8–11 T-storms, hot. 12–20 Sunny north, scattered t-storms south; seasonable. 21–23 Scattered t-storms, hot. 24–27 Hurricane threat. 28–31 Sunny, cool.

**AUG. 2011:** Temp. 80° (1° below avg.); precip. 5.5" (1" above avg.). 1–13 Scattered t-storms, seasonable. 14–20 T-storms, then sunny, cool. 21–31 Scattered t-storms, cool.

**SEPT. 2011:** Temp. 73° (3° below avg.); precip. 4.5" (avg.). 1–2 Sunny, warm. 3–5 T-storms, seasonable. 6–10 T-storms, then sunny, cool. 11–17 T-storms, then sunny, cool. 18–23 T-storms, warm. 24–30 Sunny, cool.

**OCT. 2011:** Temp. 62° (3° below avg.); precip. 3.5" (0.5° above avg.). 1–5 T-storms, then sunny, cool. 6–15 T-storms, then sunny, cool. 16–23 T-storms, then sunny, cool. 24–28 Rain to snow north, rain south, then sunny, cold. 29–31 Rain, then sunny, warm.

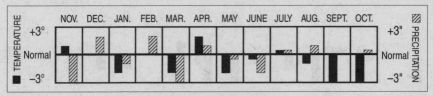

# Upper Midwest

**SUMMARY:** Winter will be colder than normal, especially in the west, where temperatures will be 2 to 3 degrees below normal, on average. Most days in January will be cold, especially in the west, with other cold periods in mid-December and early to mid-February. Precipitation and snowfall will be near normal, with the snowiest periods in mid-December, late February, and mid-March.

April and May will be much cooler and a bit drier than normal, with a chance for significant snowfall in mid-April.

Summer will be hotter and drier than normal. The hottest periods will occur in mid- to late June, early July, and mid-August.

September and October will be much cooler and slightly drier than normal.

**NOV. 2010:** Temp. 27° (avg. east, 2° below west); precip. 2.5" (0.5" above avg.). 1–3 Rain, then sunny, cold. 4–7 Rain to snow, cold. 8–11 Snow east, flurries west; cold. 12–17 Snow showers, milder. 18–24 Snow and ice, then flurries, cold. 25–30 Rain and snow east, sunny west; mild.

**DEC. 2010:** Temp. 15° (1° above avg.); precip. 1.5" (0.5" above avg.). 1–6 Periods of rain and snow, mild. 7–11 Snow showers, cold. 12–15 Sunny, mild. 16–20 Snow, then flurries, turning cold. 21–27 Snowy periods; mild, then cold. 28–31 Snow showers; mild east, cold west.

**JAN. 2011:** Temp. 5° (4° below avg.); precip. 0.5" (0.5" below avg.). 1–3 Flurries, cold. 4–11 Snow, then flurries, very cold. 12–15 Flurries; mild east, very cold west. 16–23 Flurries, bitter cold. 24–27 Snow, milder east; flurries, very cold west. 28–31 Flurries, milder.

**FEB. 2011:** Temp. 9° (1° above avg. east, 5° below west); precip. 1" (1" below avg. east, 1" above west). 1–5 Rain and snow, then sunny, mild. 6–14 Snow showers, then sunny, bitter cold. 15–19 Flurries, milder. 20–22 Rain and snow showers, mild. 23–28 Snowstorm, then sunny, cold.

**MAR. 2011:** Temp. 25° (2° below avg.); precip. 1" (0.5" below avg.). 1–8 Sunny, warm. 9–14 Showers, mild. 15–21 Snowstorm, then sunny, cold. 22–25 Showers, mild east; snowy, cold west. 26–31 Snow showers, cold.

**APR. 2011:** Temp. 37° (4° below avg.); precip.

1" (1" below avg.). 1–8 Sunny, cool. 9–10 Sunny, warm. 11–14 Rain to snow, then sunny, cold. 15–17 Showers, mild. 18–30 Rain to snow, then sunny, cool.

**MAY 2011:** Temp. 51° (4° below avg.); precip. 2.5" (0.5" below avg.). 1–8 Rainy periods, cool. 9–11 Showers, seasonable. 12–17 A few t-storms, turning warm. 18–23 T-storms, then sunny, chilly. 24–31 Scattered t-storms, seasonable.

**JUNE 2011:** Temp. 66° (2° above avg.); precip. 2.5" (1.5" below avg.). 1–3 Sunny, cool. 4–6 T-storms, warm. 7–12 Sunny, cool. 13–20 Scattered t-storms, very warm. 21–24 Sunny, hot. 25–30 T-storms, then sunny, seasonable.

**JULY 2011:** Temp. 71.5° (2.5° above avg.); precip. 4" (0.5" above avg.). 1–6 Scattered t-storms, hot. 7–14 Sunny, warm. 15–23 T-storms, then sunny, warm. 24–31 Scattered t-storms, warm.

**AUG. 2011:** Temp. 65° (2° below avg.); precip. 3.5" (avg.). 1–8 Scattered t-storms, cool. 9–12 Sunny, cool. 13–17 T-storms, then sunny, cool. 18–24 Sunny, very warm. 25–31 T-storms, then sunny, cool.

**SEPT. 2011:** Temp. 56° (2° below avg.); precip. 2" (1" below avg.). 1–6 A few showers, warm. 7–13 Sunny, seasonable. 14–19 Showers, then sunny, cool. 20–28 Rainy periods, cool. 29–30 Sunny, warm.

**OCT. 2011:** Temp. 43° (3° below avg.); precip. 2.5" (avg.). 1–4 Rain, then sunny, cool. 5–12 Rain to snow, then sunny, cool. 13–15 Showers, warm. 16–20 Sunny; cool, then warm. 21–31 Rain to snow, then flurries, cold.

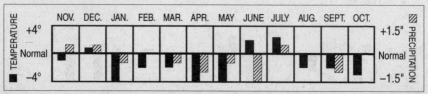

*Get your local forecast at Almanac.com/Weather.*

# Heartland

**SUMMARY:** Winter will be slightly colder than normal, on average, with below-normal precipitation and near- to below-normal snowfall. The coldest periods will be in mid-January and mid-February, with other cold periods in mid- to late December and early February. The snowiest periods will be the last 2 weeks of January, early and late February, and mid-March.

April and May will be much cooler than normal. Precipitation will be slightly below normal in Kansas and Nebraska and above normal elsewhere.

Summer will be drier and slightly cooler than normal, on average, despite hot spells in mid-June, early July, and mid- to late August.

September and October will be much cooler and drier than normal.

**NOV. 2010:** Temp. 49° (1° above avg.); precip. 0.5" (2" below avg.). 1–3 Sunny, cool. 4–7 Rain, then sunny, cool. 8–9 T-storms, warm. 10–12 Sunny, cool. 13–19 Rainy periods, mild. 20–23 Flurries, cold. 24–30 Showers, then sunny, mild.

**DEC. 2010:** Temp. 33° (3° above avg.); precip. 2.5" (1" above avg.). 1–5 Sunny, then t-storms; quite mild. 6–9 Rain and snow showers, seasonable. 10–15 Sunny, mild. 16–21 Rain to snow, then sunny, cold. 22–26 Sunny, then rain, mild. 27–31 Sunny, turning colder.

**JAN. 2011:** Temp. 23° (3° below avg.); precip. 0.5" (0.5" below avg.). 1–3 Sunny, turning mild. 4–8 Rain to snow, then sunny, seasonable. 9–13 Flurries, very cold. 14–19 Snow showers, very cold. 20–24 Snow, then sunny, bitter cold. 25–31 Snow, then sunny, turning milder.

**FEB. 2011:** Temp. 28° (1° below avg.); precip. 2" (2" above avg. east, 1" below west). 1–5 Rain, then sunny, mild. 6–10 Snow, then sunny, cold. 11–16 Snow showers, then sunny, very cold. 17–19 Sunny, seasonable. 20–24 Rainy periods, turning mild. 25–28 Snow, then sunny, cold.

**MAR. 2011:** Temp. 42° (1° below avg.); precip. 1" (1.5" below avg.). 1–3 Sunny, warmer. 4–9 T-storms, then sunny, warm. 10–14 Rainy periods, warm. 15–19 Snow, then sunny, cold. 20–24 Snow, then sunny, warm. 25–31 Showers, chilly.

**APR. 2011:** Temp. 52° (2° above avg.); precip. 4" (2" above avg. east, 1" below west). 1–5 Rainy periods, chilly. 6–12 Scattered t-storms, turning warm. 13–15 Showers, cool. 16–18 Sunny, warm. 19–25 Showers, cool. 26–30 Sunny, turning hot.

**MAY 2011:** Temp. 60° (4° below avg.); precip. 5" (0.5" above avg.). 1–8 T-storms, chilly. 9–16 Scattered t-storms, cool. 17–21 Sunny, warm. 22–26 T-storms, then sunny, cool. 27–31 T-storms, then sunny, cool.

**JUNE 2011:** Temp. 73° (avg.); precip. 3.5" (1" below avg.). 1–3 T-storms, cool. 4–10 Scattered t-storms, seasonable. 11–18 Sunny, turning hot. 19–27 T-storms, then sunny, hot. 28–30 T-storms, then sunny, cool.

**JULY 2011:** Temp. 79° (1° above avg.); precip. 3" (1" below avg.). 1–7 Sunny, hot. 8–11 T-storms, warm. 12–16 Scattered t-storms, cool. 17–22 Scattered t-storms, humid. 23–29 Sunny, cool. 30–31 T-storms, humid.

**AUG. 2011:** Temp. 74° (2° below avg.); precip. 3.5" (avg.). 1–5 T-storms, then sunny, cool. 6–10 T-storms, warm and humid. 11–18 T-storms, sunny, cool. 19–25 Sunny, very warm. 26–31 T-storms, then sunny, cool.

**SEPT. 2011:** Temp. 63° (4° below avg.); precip. 2" (1.5" below avg.). 1–3 Sunny, warm. 4–10 T-storms, then sunny, cool. 11–16 T-storms, then sunny, seasonable. 17–21 Rain, then sunny, cool. 22–28 Showers, then sunny, chilly. 29–30 Sunny, warm.

**OCT. 2011:** Temp. 54° (2° below avg.); precip. 1.5" (1.5" below avg.). 1–4 Sunny, then sunny, cool. 5–7 T-storms, warm. 8–12 Sunny, then rain, cool. 13–21 Sunny, turning warm. 22–27 Showers and flurries, then sunny, cold. 28–31 Rain, then sunny, mild.

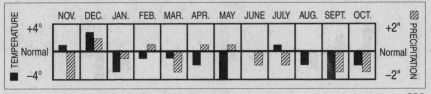

# Texas–Oklahoma

**SUMMARY:** Winter temperatures will be slightly milder than normal, on average, with the coldest periods in late December, mid-January, and early and mid-February. Precipitation will be above normal in Texas and below normal in Oklahoma. Snowfall will be near to above normal, with the most significant snow and ice occurring in mid-January and mid-February.

April and May will be rainier than normal, with temperatures above normal in Oklahoma and below normal in Texas.

Summer will be a bit cooler and rainier than normal, with the hottest periods from late June through the first half of July and in mid-August. The hurricane risk is slightly below normal.

September and October will be much cooler and drier than normal.

**NOV. 2010:** Temp. 59° (3° above avg.); precip. 3.5" (2" below avg. north, 3" above south). 1–9 Sunny north, t-storms south; warm. 10–20 Sunny, warm. 21–24 T-storms, then sunny, cool. 25–30 Sunny, warm north; t-storms south.

**DEC. 2010:** Temp. 50° (2° above avg.); precip. 3.5" (1" above avg.). 1–6 Scattered t-storms, warm. 7–12 Sunny north, t-storms south; seasonable. 13–15 Sunny, mild. 16–20 T-storms, then sunny, cool. 21–23 Sunny, warm. 24–27 T-storms, then sunny, cold. 28–31 Showers, mild.

**JAN. 2011:** Temp. 44° (2° below avg.); precip. 1.5" (0.5" below avg.). 1–5 Sunny, mild. 6–9 Sunny north, showers south; seasonable. 10–14 Snow north, rain south; cold. 15–17 Sunny, cold. 18–23 Snow, then sunny, very cold. 24–27 Snow showers north, sunny south; cold. 28–31 Sunny, mild.

**FEB. 2011:** Temp. 47° (1° below avg.); precip. 3" (1" above avg.). 1–4 Rain, then sunny, cold. 5–10 Snow, then sunny north; rain south; cold. 11–13 Sunny, cool. 14–17 Rain to snow, then sunny, cold. 18–23 Rain, then sunny, mild. 24–28 T-storms, then sunny, cold.

**MAR. 2011:** Temp. 57° (1° below avg.); precip. 1.5" (1" below avg.). 1–5 Rainy periods, mild. 6–14 Sunny, warm. 15–18 T-storms, then sunny, cool. 19–23 Showers, then sunny, cool. 24–26 Sunny, warm. 27–31 T-storms, then sunny, cool.

**APR. 2011:** Temp. 65° (1° below avg.); precip. 7" (4" above avg.). 1–3 Sunny. 4–9 T-storms, then sunny, cool. 10–14 T-storms then sunny, cool. 15–24 T-storms; cool north, warm south. 25–30 Sunny, warm north; t-storms, cool south.

**MAY 2011:** Temp. 73° (2° above avg. north, 2° below south); precip. 3" (2" below avg.). 1–6 T-storms, then sunny, cool. 7–10 Sunny, hot. 11–20 T-storms, then sunny, cool. 21–25 Sunny north, scattered t-storms south. 26–31 T-storms north, sunny south; warm.

**JUNE 2011:** Temp. 79° (1° above avg. north, 3° below south); precip. 3" (1" below avg.). 1–4 Sunny, warm. 5–8 Sunny, hot north; t-storms south. 9–17 T-storms, then sunny north; sunny, then t-storms south; seasonable. 18–22 Sunny; hot north, cooler south. 23–27 Sunny, hot. 28–30 Sunny, hot north; t-storms south.

**JULY 2011:** Temp. 84° (1° above avg.); precip. 2.5" (0.5" above avg.). 1–4 Sunny, hot. 5–12 Scattered t-storms, hot. 13–20 T-storms, then sunny, seasonable. 21–31 Scattered t-storms, cooler north; sunny, hot south.

**AUG. 2011:** Temp. 80° (2° below avg.); precip. 4.5" (2" above avg.). 1–7 Scattered t-storms, seasonable. 8–10 Sunny, hot. 11–16 T-storms, turning cool north; sunny, hot south. 17–23 T-storms, then sunny, comfortable. 24–28 T-storms, then sunny, warm. 29–31 Sunny north, t-storms south.

**SEPT. 2011:** Temp. 73° (3° below avg.); precip. 3" (0.5" below avg.). 1–8 T-storms, then sunny, cool. 9–17 T-storms, then sunny, cool. 18–22 Scattered t-storms, seasonable. 23–26 Sunny, warm. 27–30 Sunny north, t-storms south; cool.

**OCT. 2011:** Temp. 64° (3° below avg.); precip. 2" (2" below avg.). 1–2 Sunny, warm. 3–7 Sunny north, t-storms south; warm. 8–15 T-storms, then sunny, cool. 16–23 Sunny, warm north; t-storms, then sunny, cool south. 24–28 T-storms, then sunny, very cool. 29–31 Sunny, warm.

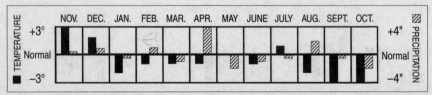

# High Plains

**SUMMARY:** Winter will be colder than normal, on average, from Nebraska northward, with above-normal temperatures in the south. The coldest periods will occur in mid-December, mid-January, and the first half of February. Precipitation and snowfall will be slightly below normal, with the snowiest periods in mid-December, mid-January, and early February.

April and May will be cooler and drier than normal, especially in the north.

Summer temperatures will be near normal, with slightly above-normal rainfall. The hottest periods will be from late June through the first half of July.

September and October will be slightly warmer and wetter than normal.

**NOV. 2010:** Temp. 37° (1° below avg. north, 3° above south); precip. 0.5" (0.5" below avg.). 1–3 Sunny, mild. 4–6 Snow north, showers south, then sunny, cooler. 7–9 Snowy periods north; sunny, warm south. 10–15 Sunny, mild. 16–21 Snow, then sunny, colder. 22–30 Sunny, mild.

**DEC. 2010:** Temp. 29° (2° above avg.); precip. 0.5" (avg.). 1–5 Sunny north, showers south; mild. 6–9 Rain to snow, then sunny, cold. 10–14 Flurries, then sunny, mild. 15–20 Snow, then sunny, cold. 21–22 Sunny, mild. 23–28 Rain to snow, then sunny, cold. 29–31 Rain and snow, then sunny, mild.

**JAN. 2011:** Temp. 25° (2° below avg. north, 2° above south); precip. 0.2" (0.3" below avg.). 1–6 Sunny, mild. 7–10 Snow, then sunny, very cold. 11–18 Snowstorm, then sunny, bitter cold. 19–23 Snow showers, then sunny, very cold. 24–31 Snow showers, then sunny, mild.

**FEB. 2011:** Temp. 26° (3° below avg. north, 1° above south); precip. 1.5" (1" above avg.). 1–4 Snowstorm, then sunny, cold. 5–12 Snow and flurries, then sunny, very cold. 13–18 Snow showers, then sunny, not as cold. 19–28 Snowy periods, then sunny, cold.

**MAR. 2011:** Temp. 37° (1° below avg.); precip. 0.5" (0.5" below avg.). 1–8 Sunny, mild. 9–13 Rain and snow, then sunny, mild. 14–17 Snow, then sunny, cold. 18–25 Sunny, turning warm. 26–31 Rain and snow showers, cool.

**APR. 2011:** Temp. 45° (3° below avg.); precip. 1.5" (0.5" below avg.). 1–6 Periods of rain and snow, cool north; sunny, warm south. 7–14 Rain to snow, then sunny, cold. 15–17 Sunny north, t-storms south; cool. 18–22 Periods of rain and snow north; sunny, warm south. 23–30 Showers, then sunny, warm.

**MAY 2011:** Temp. 57.5° (3° below avg. north, 2° above south); precip. 1.5" (1" below avg.). 1–6 Rain to snow, then sunny, cool. 7–15 Scattered t-storms, turning warm. 16–23 Sunny; cool, then warm. 24–31 T-storms, cool north; t-storms, then sunny, warm south.

**JUNE 2011:** Temp. 67° (avg.); precip. 2.5" (0.5" below avg.). 1–7 T-storms, then sunny, cool. 8–13 Scattered t-storms, warm. 14–17 T-storms; cool north, warm south. 18–21 Sunny, turning hot. 22–30 Scattered t-storms, hot.

**JULY 2011:** Temp. 74° (2° above avg.); precip. 2.5" (0.5" above avg.). 1–4 Sunny, hot. 5–16 Scattered t-storms, hot. 17–23 T-storms, then sunny, cooler. 24–31 A few t-storms, seasonable.

**AUG. 2011:** Temp. 69° (2° below avg.); precip. 2.5" (0.5" above avg.). 1–5 Scattered t-storms, cool. 6–10 Sunny, seasonable. 11–17 Rainy periods, cool. 18–22 Sunny, turning warm. 23–27 T-storms, then sunny, cool. 28–31 Sunny, warm.

**SEPT. 2011:** Temp. 63° (2° above avg.); precip. 2.5" (1" above avg.). 1–3 Sunny; warm north, cool south. 4–9 T-storms, cool. 10–15 Sunny, turning very warm. 16–25 Rainy periods, turning cooler. 26–30 Sunny, turning mild.

**OCT. 2011:** Temp. 48° (1° below avg.); precip. 0.5" (0.5" below avg.). 1–4 Sunny. 5–9 Rain to snow, then sunny, chilly. 10–12 T-storms, then sunny, cool. 13–15 Rain and snow. 16–23 Sunny, warm. 24–27 Rain and snow, then sunny, cool. 28–31 Snowstorm, cold north; sunny, warm south.

WEATHER

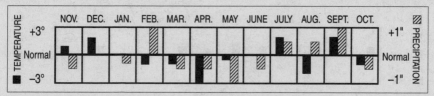

# Intermountain

**SUMMARY:** Winter temperatures will be above normal, especially in the south, with the coldest periods in late December, mid-January, and early February. Precipitation will be below normal, with near- to below-normal snowfall. The snowiest periods will occur in early and mid-December and early and late February.

April and May will be warmer and drier than normal.

Summer will be drier than normal, with near-normal temperatures, on average. The hottest periods will be in late July and mid-August.

September and October will be slightly drier than normal, with near-normal temperatures.

**NOV. 2010:** Temp. 40° (1° above avg.); precip. 1.5" (avg.). 1–6 Rainy periods north, sunny south; mild. 7–14 Rainy periods, quite mild. 15–22 Rain to snow, then sunny, cold. 23–30 Showers north, sunny south; mild.

**DEC. 2010:** Temp. 34° (3° above avg.); precip. 2" (0.5" above avg.). 1–9 Snowy periods, turning colder. 10–13 Sunny, cold. 14–17 Snow showers north, heavy snow south; cold. 18–21 Snow to rain north, sunny south. 22–28 Snowy periods, cold. 29–31 Rain, then sunny, mild.

**JAN. 2011:** Temp. 31° (1° above avg.); precip. 0.5" (1" below avg.). 1–8 Periods of rain and snow north, sunny south; mild. 9–12 Flurries north, snowy periods south; cold. 13–17 Snowy periods north, sunny south; very cold. 18–21 Sunny, turning milder. 22–29 Snowy periods, then sunny, seasonable. 30–31 Snow showers.

**FEB. 2011:** Temp. 33° (2° below avg. north, 2° above south); precip. 1" (0.5" below avg.). 1–10 Snow, then sunny, cold. 11–15 Sunny, milder. 16–21 Occasional rain and snow, seasonable. 22–25 Sunny north, snowstorm south; cold. 26–28 Snow north, sunny south; seasonable.

**MAR. 2011:** Temp. 43° (1° above avg.); precip. 0.5" (1" below avg.). 1–12 Rainy periods north, sunny south; mild. 13–17 Rain to snow, then sunny, cold. 18–26 Showers, then sunny, warm. 27–31 Sunny; cool, then warm.

**APR. 2011:** Temp. 50.5° (1.5° above avg.); precip. 0.5" (0.5" below avg.). 1–5 Showers, cool north; sunny, mild south. 6–9 Sunny, warm. 10–14 Rain and snow, chilly. 15–18 Sunny, seasonable. 19–22 Showers, then sunny, cool. 23–30 Sunny, turning very warm.

**MAY 2011:** Temp. 54.5° (1° below avg. north, 2° above south); precip. 0.5" (0.5" below avg.). 1–7 T-storms, then sunny, cool. 8–10 Showers, cool north; sunny, warm south. 11–13 Sunny, warm. 14–19 Showers, then sunny, warm. 20–31 Showers, cool north; sunny, seasonable south.

**JUNE 2011:** Temp. 67° (1° above avg.); precip. 0.2" (0.3" below avg.). 1–6 Showers, then sunny, cool. 7–11 Sunny, warm. 12–18 Showers, then sunny, cool. 19–21 Sunny, warm. 22–26 Scattered t-storms, cool. 27–30 Sunny, warm.

**JULY 2011:** Temp. 73° (avg.); precip. 0.2" (0.3" below avg.). 1–7 Isolated t-storms, seasonable. 8–16 Sunny, hot north; scattered t-storms, warm south. 17–31 Sunny north, scattered t-storms south; very warm.

**AUG. 2011:** Temp. 71° (1° below avg.); precip. 0.5" (0.5" below avg.). 1–4 Sunny, seasonable. 5–14 T-storms, then sunny, cool north; scattered t-storms, seasonable south. 15–18 Sunny, hot. 19–26 Scattered t-storms, then sunny, cool. 27–31 Sunny, hot north; scattered t-storms south.

**SEPT. 2011:** Temp. 63° (1° above avg.); precip. 1" (avg.). 1–9 Scattered showers, cool. 10–16 Sunny north, scattered t-storms south; very warm. 17–25 Scattered showers, warm. 26–30 Sunny, warm north; showers, cool south.

**OCT. 2011:** Temp. 50° (1° below avg.); precip. 0.5" (0.5" below avg.). 1–4 Scattered showers, seasonable. 5–11 Showers, then sunny, cool. 12–16 Rain and snow showers, chilly north; sunny, mild south. 17–27 Sunny, mild. 28–31 Showers, turning cooler.

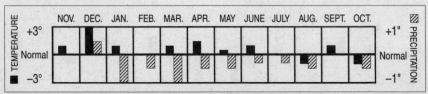

*Get your local forecast at Almanac.com/Weather.*

# Desert Southwest

**SUMMARY:** Winter temperatures will be about 1 degree above normal, on average, with the coldest periods in mid-January and mid-February. Precipitation and snowfall will be below normal, with the snowiest periods in mid-January and late February.

April and May will be slightly warmer than normal, with near-normal rainfall.

Summer will be rainier than normal, with near-normal temperatures, on average. The hottest periods will be in mid-July and early August.

September and October will be cooler and drier than normal.

**NOV. 2010:** Temp. 58° (3° above avg.); precip. 0.8" (0.5" below avg. east, 1" above west). 1–5 Sunny, seasonable. 6–10 Sunny, very warm east; showers west. 11–13 Sunny, warm east; t-storms, cool west. 19–22 Sunny, cool. 23–30 Showers, then sunny, warm east; sunny, turning warmer west.

**DEC. 2010:** Temp. 48° (1° above avg.); precip. 0.2" (0.3" below avg.). 1–4 Showers, mild. 5–6 Sunny, cool. 7–10 Rain and snow, cold. 11–14 Sunny, cool. 15–21 Showers, then sunny, cool. 22–31 Showers, then sunny, cold.

**JAN. 2011:** Temp. 48° (1° above avg.); precip. 0.5" (avg.). 1–9 Sunny; mild, then cool. 10–14 Snowy periods east, sunny west; cold. 15–22 Sunny; cold, then milder. 23–30 Rain and showers, then sunny, seasonable. 31 Rain.

**FEB. 2011:** Temp. 50° (avg.); precip. 0.2" (0.3" below avg.). 1–11 Showers and flurries, then sunny, cold. 12–18 Sunny; mild, then cold. 19–22 Showers, then sunny, cool. 23–28 Showers and flurries, then sunny, cool.

**MAR. 2011:** Temp. 58° (1° above avg.); precip. 0.2" (0.3" below avg.). 1–14 Sunny, warm. 15–20 Scattered showers, cool. 21–26 Sunny, turning very warm. 27–31 Sunny, seasonable.

**APR. 2011:** Temp. 64° (avg.); precip. 0.5" (avg.). 1–4 Sunny, warm. 5–10 Showers, then sunny, warm. 11–17 Scattered t-storms, cool. 18–23 Sunny, seasonable. 24–30 Sunny; cool east, hot west.

**MAY 2011:** Temp. 73.5° (0.5° above avg.); precip. 0.5" (avg.). 1–6 Showers, then sunny, cool. 7–18 Showers, then sunny, hot. 19–23 Showers, then sunny, seasonable. 24–31 T-storms, then sunny, warm.

**JUNE 2011:** Temp. 83° (avg.); precip. 1" (1" above avg. east, avg. west). 1–8 Sunny; cool, then hot. 9–17 Scattered t-storms, cool. 18–23 T-storms, cool east; sunny, hot west. 24–30 Sunny, seasonable.

**JULY 2011:** Temp. 88° (1° above avg.); precip. 1.5" (avg.). 1–8 Scattered t-storms east, sunny west; cool. 9–13 A few t-storms east, sunny west; seasonable. 14–25 A few t-storms, hot and humid. 26–31 Scattered t-storms, cool east; sunny, hot west.

**AUG. 2011:** Temp. 84° (1° below avg.); precip. 2" (0.5" above avg.). 1–5 Scattered t-storms east; sunny, hot west. 6–13 Scattered t-storms, cool. 14–21 Scattered t-storms, cool east; sunny, warm west. 22–29 Scattered t-storms east, sunny west; cool. 30–31 Sunny, warm.

**SEPT. 2011:** Temp. 76° (2° below avg.); precip. 1" (avg.). 1–3 Sunny; cool east, hot west. 4–8 A few t-storms, cool. 9–15 Scattered t-storms, then sunny, warm. 16–21 Scattered t-storms, very warm. 22–30 A few t-storms, cool.

**OCT. 2011:** Temp. 65° (2° below avg.); precip. 0.5" (0.5" below avg.). 1–3 Sunny, warm. 4–16 T-storms, then sunny, cool. 17–25 Sunny; cool east, warm west. 26–31 Sunny, seasonable.

W E A T H E R

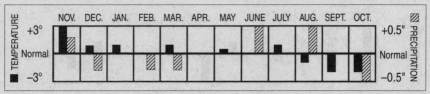

# Pacific Northwest

**SUMMARY:** Winter temperatures will be slightly above normal, on average, with slightly below-normal precipitation but above-normal snowfall in most places. The coldest periods will occur in mid-December and mid- to late February, with the snowiest periods in mid-December and late February.

April and May will be cooler and drier than normal.

Summer will be drier than normal, with below-normal temperatures, on average, in Washington and above-normal temperatures in Oregon and California. The hottest periods will occur in late July and early August.

September and October will be slightly drier than normal, with near-normal temperatures.

**NOV. 2010:** Temp. 49° (2° above avg.); precip. 5.5" (1" below avg.). 1–7 Rainy periods, mild. 8–11 Showers, mild. 12–14 Rainy, mild. 15–19 Showers, chilly. 20–22 Partly sunny, seasonable. 23–30 Rainy periods, cool.

**DEC. 2010:** Temp. 42° (avg.); precip. 10.5" (4" above avg.). 1–5 Occasional rain, cool. 6–10 Rain to snow, then sunny, cold. 11–15 Showers, mild. 16–18 Snowstorm, then sunny, cold. 19–25 Heavy rain, some wet snow, chilly. 26–31 Heavy rain, mild.

**JAN. 2011:** Temp. 42° (avg.); precip. 3" (3" below avg.). 1–7 Rainy periods, mild. 8–14 Misty, cool. 15–23 Occasional rain, mild. 24–26 Partly sunny, cool. 27–31 Rainy, mild.

**FEB. 2011:** Temp. 44.5° (0.5° above avg.); precip. 4" (1" below avg.). 1–7 Periods of rain and drizzle, seasonable. 8–11 Partly sunny, cool. 12–15 Showers, windy, mild. 16–19 Sprinkles, mild. 20–25 Periods of rain and snow, cold. 26–28 Rainy, cool.

**MAR. 2011:** Temp. 47.5° (0.5° above avg.); precip. 4" (avg.). 1–4 Heavy rain, then partly sunny, cool. 5–8 Rainy, mild. 9–10 Partly sunny, cool. 11–14 Rain and snow, chilly. 15–22 Sunny, turning warm. 23–26 Showers, seasonable. 27–31 Sunny, warm.

**APR. 2011:** Temp. 51° (1° above avg.); precip. 2" (1" below avg.). 1–7 Rainy periods, seasonable. 8–12 Sunny, pleasant. 13–19 Rainy periods, cool. 20–27 Sunny, turning warm. 28–30 Showers, mild.

**MAY 2011:** Temp. 53° (2° below avg.); precip. 1" (1" below avg.). 1–2 Sunny, warm. 3–8 Showers, cool. 9–13 Sunny, cool. 14–18 Showers, then sunny, warm. 19–23 Showers, then sunny, cool. 24–28 Rain and mist, cool. 29–31 Sunny, warm.

**JUNE 2011:** Temp. 60° (2° below avg. north, 2° above south); precip. 2" (0.5" above avg.). 1–6 Scattered showers, cool. 7–11 Sunny, warm. 12–19 Scattered showers, cool. 20–23 Rain, then sunny, cool. 24–26 Rain and mist, cool. 27–30 Sunny, seasonable.

**JULY 2011:** Temp. 64.5° (2° below avg. north, 2° above south); precip. 0.2" (0.3" below avg.). 1–9 Scattered t-storms, cool. 10–15 Sunny, cool. 16–22 Showers, then sunny, warm. 23–27 Sunny, hot. 28–31 Scattered t-storms, warm.

**AUG. 2011:** Temp. 65° (avg.); precip. 0.5" (0.5" below avg.). 1–6 Scattered t-storms, warm. 7–12 Sunny, pleasant. 13–17 Sunny, cool. 18–25 T-storms, then sunny, cool. 26–31 Sunny, seasonable.

**SEPT. 2011:** Temp. 62° (1° above avg.); precip. 2" (0.5" above avg.). 1–8 Showers, then sunny, cool. 9–14 Rain, then sunny, warm. 15–19 Rainy periods, seasonable. 20–23 Sunny, warm. 24–28 Showers, then sunny, warm. 29–30 Rain, mild.

**OCT. 2011:** Temp. 53° (1° below avg.); precip. 2" (1" below avg.). 1–3 Sunny, cool. 4–10 Rain, then sunny, chilly. 11–15 Rain, cool. 16–19 Showers, warm. 20–24 Sunny, then showers, seasonable. 25–31 Sunny, then showers, cool.

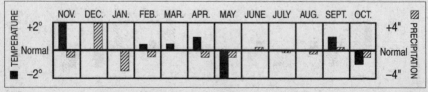

# Pacific Southwest

**SUMMARY:** Winter temperatures will be near normal, on average, with above-normal rainfall. The coldest periods will be in mid-January and early February. The stormiest periods will be in early to mid-November and December, with December being the snowiest period in the mountains.

April and May will be warmer and drier than normal.

Summer will be cooler than normal, with near-normal rainfall and the hottest periods in mid-July and mid-August.

September and October will have near-normal temperatures, on average, with rainfall below normal in the north and above normal in the south. Expect hot weather near the coast in mid- to late September and mid- to late October.

**NOV. 2010:** Temp. 58° (avg.); precip. 5.5" (4" above avg.). 1–4 Sunny. 5–11 Stormy, heavy rain and t-storms. 12–18 Sunny, then rain and t-storms, cool. 19–24 Sunny, cool. 25–30 Low clouds and fog, cool north; sunny, warm south.

**DEC. 2010:** Temp. 53° (avg.); precip. 4" (2" above avg.). 1–9 Stormy periods, especially south; cool. 10–12 Sunny, cool. 13–18 T-storms, especially north; cool. 19–20 Sunny, mild. 21–24 Stormy, heavy rain and t-storms. 25–27 Sunny, cool. 28–31 T-storms, then sunny north; sunny south.

**JAN. 2011:** Temp. 53° (avg.); precip. 2" (1" below avg.). 1–4 Sunny, cool coast; fog inland. 5–10 A.M. clouds, P.M. sun; cool. 11–19 Showers, then sunny, cool. 20–25 Stormy. 26–29 T-storms north; cool south. 30–31 Rainy.

**FEB. 2011:** Temp. 53° (2° below avg.); precip. 1" (2" below avg.). 1–2 Sunny, chilly. 3–10 Showers, then sunny, cool. 11–15 Showers north; sunny, warmer south. 16–19 Rainy periods, cool. 20–22 Sunny, cool. 23–25 Showers, then sunny, cool. 26–28 Showers north, sunny south.

**MAR. 2011:** Temp. 59° (2° above avg.); precip. 0.5" (1.5" below avg.). 1–4 Showers, then sunny, cool. 5–12 Showers north, sunny south; cool. 13–16 Sunny, warm. 17–23 Rain, then mostly cloudy coast; sunny, warm inland. 24–31 A.M. clouds, P.M. sun coast; sunny, very warm inland.

**APR. 2011:** Temp. 62° (2° above avg.); precip. 0.5" (0.5" below avg.). 1–5 Rainy periods north, sunny south. 6–10 Sunny, very warm. 11–14 Showers, then sunny, cool. 15–20 Sunny, very warm. 21–26 A.M. clouds, P.M. sun coast; sunny, very warm inland. 27–30 Showers, then sunny.

**MAY 2011:** Temp. 63° (1° below avg.); precip. 0.5" (avg.). 1–10 Showers, then sunny, seasonable. 11–20 Clouds and fog, cool coast; sunny, very warm inland. 21–28 Showers, then sunny, cool. 29–31 Showers north, sunny south.

**JUNE 2011:** Temp. 68° (avg.); precip. 0.1" (avg.). 1–4 Coastal fog and drizzle; sunny, hot inland. 5–8 Sprinkles southwest; sunny, hot elsewhere. 9–14 Sunny, seasonable. 15–22 Sprinkles southwest, sunny elsewhere; seasonable coast, turning hot inland. 23–30 A.M. clouds, P.M. sun, seasonable coast; sunny, cool inland.

**JULY 2011:** Temp. 70° (1° below avg.); precip. 0" (avg.). 1–11 A.M. clouds, P.M. sun, seasonable coast; sunny, cool inland. 12–19 Sunny; cool coast, turning hot inland. 20–27 Scattered showers, then sunny, warm. 28–31 A.M. clouds, P.M. sun coast; sunny inland.

**AUG. 2011:** Temp. 71.5° (0.5° below avg.); precip. 0.1" (avg.). 1–6 Sunny, seasonable. 7–13 Scattered t-storms, then sunny, hot. 14–21 Sunny, seasonable. 22–27 Scattered showers, then sunny, cool. 28–31 Sunny; cool coast, hot inland.

**SEPT. 2011:** Temp. 69° (1° below avg.); precip. 0.2" (avg.). 1–10 Sunny; cool, then seasonable. 11–15 Showers, then sunny. 16–19 Low clouds and fog coast, sunny inland; seasonable. 20–23 Sunny, hot north; scattered showers south. 24–30 Low clouds, drizzle coast; sunny inland.

**OCT. 2011:** Temp. 66° (1° above avg.); precip. 0.8" (0.4" below avg. north, 1" above south). 1–2 Sunny, warm. 3–5 Sunny, warm north; t-storms south. 6–10 Sunny; cool north, warm south. 11–13 Sunny, Santa Ana winds; hot coast, warm inland. 14–16 Sunny, cool. 17–19 Sunny, Santa Ana winds; hot coast, warm inland. 20–26 Sunny; cool, then hot. 27–31 T-storms, then cooler.

San Francisco

Fresno

Los Angeles

San Diego

WEATHER

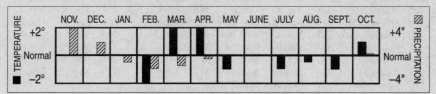

## Frosts and Growing Seasons

■ Dates given are normal averages for a light freeze; local weather and topography may cause considerable variations. The possibility of frost occurring after the spring dates and before the fall dates is 50 percent. The classification of freeze temperatures is usually based on their effect on plants. **Light freeze:** 29° to 32°F—tender plants killed. **Moderate freeze:** 25° to 28°F—widely destructive effect on most vegetation. **Severe freeze:** 24°F and colder—heavy damage to most plants. *–courtesy of National Climatic Data Center*

| State | City | Growing Season (days) | Last Spring Frost | First Fall Frost | State | City | Growing Season (days) | Last Spring Frost | First Fall Frost |
|---|---|---|---|---|---|---|---|---|---|
| AK | Juneau | 148 | May 8 | Oct. 4 | ND | Bismarck | 129 | May 14 | Sept. 21 |
| AL | Mobile | 273 | Feb. 28 | Nov. 29 | NE | Blair | 167 | Apr. 25 | Oct. 10 |
| AR | Pine Bluff | 240 | Mar. 16 | Nov. 12 | NE | North Platte | 137 | May 9 | Sept. 24 |
| AZ | Phoenix | * | * | * | NH | Concord | 124 | May 20 | Sept. 21 |
| AZ | Tucson | 324 | Jan. 19 | Dec. 18 | NJ | Newark | 217 | Apr. 3 | Nov. 7 |
| CA | Eureka | 323 | Jan. 27 | Dec. 16 | NM | Carlsbad | 215 | Mar. 31 | Nov. 2 |
| CA | Sacramento | 296 | Feb. 10 | Dec. 4 | NM | Los Alamos | 149 | May 11 | Oct. 8 |
| CA | San Francisco | * | * | * | NV | Las Vegas | 283 | Feb. 16 | Nov. 27 |
| CO | Denver | 157 | Apr. 30 | Oct. 4 | NY | Albany | 153 | May 2 | Oct. 3 |
| CT | Hartford | 166 | Apr. 26 | Oct. 9 | NY | Syracuse | 168 | Apr. 28 | Oct. 13 |
| DE | Wilmington | 202 | Apr. 10 | Oct. 30 | OH | Akron | 192 | Apr. 18 | Oct. 28 |
| FL | Miami | * | * | * | OH | Cincinnati | 192 | Apr. 13 | Oct. 23 |
| FL | Tallahassee | 239 | Mar. 22 | Nov. 17 | OK | Lawton | 223 | Mar. 29 | Nov. 7 |
| GA | Athens | 227 | Mar. 24 | Nov. 7 | OK | Tulsa | 225 | Mar. 27 | Nov. 7 |
| GA | Savannah | 268 | Mar. 1 | Nov. 25 | OR | Pendleton | 187 | Apr. 13 | Oct. 18 |
| IA | Atlantic | 148 | May 2 | Sept. 28 | OR | Portland | 236 | Mar. 23 | Nov. 15 |
| IA | Cedar Rapids | 163 | Apr. 25 | Oct. 6 | PA | Franklin | 164 | May 6 | Oct. 17 |
| ID | Boise | 147 | May 10 | Oct. 6 | PA | Williamsport | 168 | Apr. 30 | Oct. 15 |
| IL | Chicago | 187 | Apr. 20 | Oct. 24 | RI | Kingston | 147 | May 8 | Oct. 3 |
| IL | Springfield | 182 | Apr. 13 | Oct. 13 | SC | Charleston | 260 | Mar. 9 | Nov. 25 |
| IN | Indianapolis | 181 | Apr. 17 | Oct. 16 | SC | Columbia | 214 | Apr. 1 | Nov. 1 |
| IN | South Bend | 175 | Apr. 26 | Oct. 19 | SD | Rapid City | 140 | May 9 | Sept. 27 |
| KS | Topeka | 174 | Apr. 19 | Oct. 11 | TN | Memphis | 235 | Mar. 22 | Nov. 13 |
| KY | Lexington | 192 | Apr. 15 | Oct. 25 | TN | Nashville | 204 | Apr. 6 | Oct. 28 |
| LA | Monroe | 256 | Mar. 3 | Nov. 15 | TX | Amarillo | 185 | Apr. 18 | Oct. 20 |
| LA | New Orleans | 300 | Feb. 12 | Dec. 11 | TX | Denton | 243 | Mar. 18 | Nov. 16 |
| MA | Worcester | 170 | Apr. 26 | Oct. 14 | TX | San Antonio | 270 | Feb. 28 | Nov. 25 |
| MD | Baltimore | 200 | Apr. 11 | Oct. 29 | UT | Cedar City | 133 | May 21 | Oct. 1 |
| ME | Portland | 156 | May 2 | Oct. 6 | UT | Spanish Fork | 167 | May 1 | Oct. 16 |
| MI | Lansing | 145 | May 10 | Oct. 3 | VA | Norfolk | 247 | Mar. 20 | Nov. 23 |
| MI | Marquette | 154 | May 11 | Oct. 13 | VA | Richmond | 206 | Apr. 6 | Oct. 30 |
| MN | Duluth | 124 | May 21 | Sept. 23 | VT | Burlington | 147 | May 8 | Oct. 3 |
| MN | Willmar | 154 | Apr. 30 | Oct. 1 | WA | Seattle | 251 | Mar. 10 | Nov. 17 |
| MO | Jefferson City | 188 | Apr. 13 | Oct. 18 | WA | Spokane | 153 | May 2 | Oct. 3 |
| MS | Columbia | 248 | Mar. 13 | Nov. 16 | WI | Green Bay | 150 | May 6 | Oct. 4 |
| MS | Vicksburg | 240 | Mar. 20 | Nov. 16 | WI | Sparta | 133 | May 13 | Sept. 24 |
| MT | Fort Peck | 141 | May 8 | Sept. 26 | WV | Parkersburg | 183 | Apr. 21 | Oct. 22 |
| MT | Helena | 121 | May 19 | Sept. 18 | WY | Casper | 120 | May 22 | Sept. 19 |
| NC | Fayetteville | 222 | Mar. 28 | Nov. 5 | | | | | |

*Frosts do not occur every year.*

# The Best Times to Fertilize Vegetables

| Crop | Time of Application |
|------|---------------------|
| Asparagus | before growth starts in the spring |
| Beans | after blossoming and set of pods |
| Beets | at time of planting |
| Broccoli | three weeks after transplanting |
| Brussels sprouts | three weeks after transplanting |
| Cabbage | three weeks after transplanting |
| Carrots | in the fall for the following spring |
| Cauliflower | three weeks after transplanting |
| Celery | at time of transplanting |
| Corn | when plants are 8 to 10 inches tall and again when silk first appears |
| Cucumbers | one week after blossoming and again three weeks later |
| Eggplants | after first fruit-set |
| Garlic | before planting and when growth starts in the spring |
| Kale | when plants are one-third grown |
| Lettuce (head) | two to three weeks after transplanting |
| Muskmelons | one week after blossoming and again three weeks later |
| Okra | when plants are 6 to 8 inches tall and again three weeks later |
| Onions | when bulbs begin to swell and again when plants are 1 foot tall |
| Peas | after blossoming and set of pods |
| Peppers | after first fruit-set |
| Potatoes | at blossom time or time of second hilling |
| Pumpkins | just before vines start to run, when plants are about 1 foot tall |
| Radishes | before spring planting |
| Spinach | when plants are one-third grown |
| Squashes | just before vines start to run, when plants are about 1 foot tall |
| Sweet potatoes | when vines start to run |
| Tomatoes | one to two weeks before first picking and again two weeks after |
| Watermelons | just before vines start to run, when plants are about 1 foot tall |

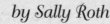

by Sally Roth

# SNAKES in the HOUSE!

## True tales of lurking serpents

**Alicia Bailey didn't bother to turn on** the light when she visited her bathroom one summer night in her Jacksonville, Florida, home a few years ago. Big mistake. Just as she was about to sit down, a water moccasin sank its fangs into her flesh.

"I freaked," she says.

Scrambling to get out, she closed the door on herself, so that only she and the snake were in the dark room. Her husband ran to the rescue, pulled her out and started back for the snake.

"My throat started closing, and I said, 'Richard, we gotta go!,'" she recounts.

While she was at the hospital for 3 days, her family was desperately trying to find the snake. They emptied the house of furniture, sliced open mattresses and sofas, and had the air-conditioning vents thoroughly examined. No viper to be seen.

It took months for Bailey's anxiety to dissipate. Then, in early spring, it happened again. She had climbed into bed and was sleeping peacefully with her dog when a pygmy rattlesnake under the bedcovers punctured her arm with fangs like little red-hot pokers. This time, she had the presence of mind to grab the snake through the blanket so that her husband, who had been snoozing in his recliner, could dispatch it.

Now, she says, "My eyes don't rest. I'm constantly scanning everything."

Bailey's experiences aside, most snake stories are a lot like fish tales— the snake gets bigger and meaner with every retelling. Some simply aren't true. The family that builds their home on top of a rattlesnake den? A tall tale that feeds on the primal fear of snakes that many of us have.

What might be true is a recent Carnegie Mellon University study that says that women are four times more fearful of snakes than men, but this depends on whom you ask.

Mimi Castaldi of Washington, D.C., recalls, "It started with a large family of mice that was living between our basement ceiling and our first floor. We had a little leak, which turned out to be fortuitous. When the plumber cut a hole in the ceiling, it gave me better access to the mice.

"Later, I noticed what I thought was a dusty piece of rope under the hole. When I went to pick it up, it moved. I screamed and ran upstairs.

"When I crawled back downstairs, I found that the snake's head was stuck in a glue trap, wrapped around a mouse that was still with us."

She tried to put both invaders out of their misery in a bucket of water, but the garter snake was having none of it. When it managed to wriggle free, "I figured he deserved to live." She and her husband, Mark, put a plate over the bucket and drove him to the woods, where he slithered away.

## Something's in the Ceiling!

**A horde of mice attracts snakes in a** hurry, and white rats are just as appealing, as Mark Dauble of Bloomington, Indiana, discovered.

As a teenager, Dauble kept white rats at home. Soon, much to his parents' dismay, a male and female escaped and, he recalls, "white rats were scurrying everywhere." He was live-trapping the

## Out, Out, SNAKES!

*When you really mean it . . .*

**1** Get rid of rodents in the house. They can quickly attract snakes.

**2** Don't let pet food sit in an outside bowl, and keep bird-feeding areas tidy to avoid attracting mice.

**3** Mow the grass closely around the house and avoid dense foundation plantings, especially near your doorstep and sidewalk. Snakes sometimes lie on a stone or concrete front step or walkway at night, because the material retains heat.

**4** Cover the openings of floor drains and any outside pipe outlets with a layer of wire mesh.

**5** Plug steel wool or expanding foam into every opening you can find along your foundation or walls. Baby snakes can fit through a ¼-inch hole, says snake specialist Steve Thompson.

*A group of snakes can be called a bed, den, knot, nest, pit, rhumba (rattlesnakes), or slither.*

rats as fast as he could, but before long, he began to hear "unnerving" noises in the suspended ceiling. "Finally, I saw the source of the noise slithering across the translucent panel of the ceiling light—the largest black king snake I've ever seen." He nabbed it and eventually released it back into the wild.

Wendell Little of New Harmony, Indiana, has no fear of the king snake that lives in his garage, keeping the mice under control. "I'd rather have him than the mice," he says. "King snakes eat the venomous snakes."

It's true. These powerful constrictors are immune to the venom of rattlesnakes and copperheads and often make a meal of them. Besides, Little adds, "We hardly ever see it."

## There's a Slither in the Cellar!

**Snakes have a knack for staying out** of sight, even when dozens of them share the house, as they do in a rental property near Chicago. More than a decade ago, the tenants found scores of western fox snakes hibernating in the cellar.

Wildlife biologist Gary Glowacki, of nearby Lake County Forest Preserve, says that 50 to 100 fox snakes may winter in the house. An exact count is tricky. The snakes "mostly" stay in the basement, he says.

In 2009, Glowacki and others constructed and installed an alternate "hibernaculum" into which the snakes were encouraged to move.

If you can't afford to construct a separate living space for a snake in your house, you can try to catch it by hand—but do not attempt to catch any snake that you can't properly identify. If this doesn't work, trap it. Snake educator Steve Thompson of Pierre, South Dakota, who has been helping people with household serpents for 35 years, recommends setting glue traps along the walls. "Lean a board against the wall to cover the trap," he suggests, so that kids and pets don't come in contact with the super-sticky surface. To release a caught snake from a glue trap, spray cooking oil on it.

In the meantime, follow Alicia Bailey's lead and be wary of every possible lurking place.  □□

**HAVE YOU EVER HAD A SNAKE IN YOUR HOUSE?**
Share your experience— and recommendations on evicting snakes—at **Almanac.com/Snake.**

**Sally Roth** shared a home for years with a 5-foot-long black rat snake that ate mice inside the house and moles outside.

# Tracker's Guide

Off for a walk in the woods? Keep an eye out for signs of these woodland creatures.

*text compiled by Sarah Perreault*

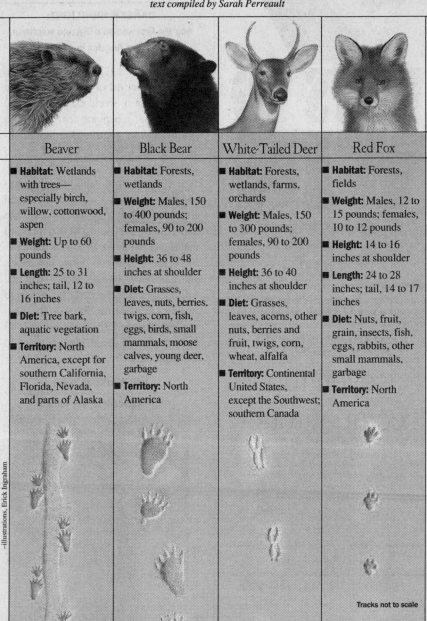

| Beaver | Black Bear | White-Tailed Deer | Red Fox |
|---|---|---|---|
| ■ **Habitat:** Wetlands with trees—especially birch, willow, cottonwood, aspen | ■ **Habitat:** Forests, wetlands | ■ **Habitat:** Forests, wetlands, farms, orchards | ■ **Habitat:** Forests, fields |
| ■ **Weight:** Up to 60 pounds | ■ **Weight:** Males, 150 to 400 pounds; females, 90 to 200 pounds | ■ **Weight:** Males, 150 to 300 pounds; females, 90 to 200 pounds | ■ **Weight:** Males, 12 to 15 pounds; females, 10 to 12 pounds |
| ■ **Length:** 25 to 31 inches; tail, 12 to 16 inches | ■ **Height:** 36 to 48 inches at shoulder | ■ **Height:** 36 to 40 inches at shoulder | ■ **Height:** 14 to 16 inches at shoulder |
| ■ **Diet:** Tree bark, aquatic vegetation | ■ **Diet:** Grasses, leaves, nuts, berries, twigs, corn, fish, eggs, birds, small mammals, moose calves, young deer, garbage | ■ **Diet:** Grasses, leaves, acorns, other nuts, berries and fruit, twigs, corn, wheat, alfalfa | ■ **Length:** 24 to 28 inches; tail, 14 to 17 inches |
| ■ **Territory:** North America, except for southern California, Florida, Nevada, and parts of Alaska | ■ **Territory:** North America | ■ **Territory:** Continental United States, except the Southwest; southern Canada | ■ **Diet:** Nuts, fruit, grain, insects, fish, eggs, rabbits, other small mammals, garbage |
| | | | ■ **Territory:** North America |

Tracks not to scale

# 7 WAYS TO WIN

Secrets behind the success of seven top competitors.

by Alice Cary

## JOAN BENOIT

marathoner

**CAREER HIGHLIGHT:**
won the first women's Olympic marathon, in Los Angeles in 1984

In Maine in 1973, 15-year-old Joan Benoit dreamed of achieving athletic greatness as a world-class skier. She trained hard, practicing for hours on a nearby slalom course. One winter afternoon, she lost her concentration and crashed into a gate, breaking her leg. Her recovery went well, but in the following winter she discovered that when she stood at the top of the ski slope, she had fear in her heart. Benoit realized that she could never be a great competitor if she were afraid. Since her injury, she had been running more—and she loved it. That sport became her means to realizing her dream. She won the Boston Marathon in 1979 and again in 1983 (setting a world record) before going to the Olympics.

**THE WINNING WAY:**

Change course, not focus.

–Tony Duffy/Getty Images

# SUSAN BUTCHER

## dog musher

**CAREER HIGHLIGHTS:**
won Alaska's multiday Iditarod race in
1986, '87, '88, and '90

**W**hile attending the first grade in Cambridge, Massachusetts, Susan Butcher wrote: "I hate the city. I love the country." She also loved animals—so much so that friends thought

−Betty Udesen/*The Seattle Times*

that she might become a veterinarian. She didn't love school (perhaps because she was dyslexic). At age 20, Butcher headed to Alaska with her two dogs. "I lived alone for 9 years, following my dream," she said. Her nearest neighbor was 40 miles away. "It was tough times for me," she said, "but I was never discontented." Her care and treatment of her sled dogs revolutionized the sport of sled dog racing. She was the first woman to dominate the sport, and in 1979 she helped to lead the first dog

team to the summit of Mt. McKinley, North America's highest peak.

Butcher, who died of leukemia at age 51 in 2006, lived her life her way. "I really feel that I had a strong sense of myself from my earliest memories," she said. "I knew very much who I was and approximately what I wanted to do."

**THE WINNING WAY:**

Know yourself.

# NADIA COMANECI

## gymnast

**CAREER HIGHLIGHTS:**
first gymnast to score a 10 in the Olympics,
first to earn seven 10s

−Central Press/Getty Images

**B**ela Karolyi, coach of the Romanian gymnasts during the 1970s, trained his athletes to stand out in the crowd. This attitude led him and Nadia Comaneci to develop two new moves: the Comaneci Dismount and the Comaneci

> "Trying to be someone else may get you through the door, but being unique will get you noticed."
>
> –Nadia Comaneci

Salto ("salto" is a gymnastics term for "somersault"). In the Salto, she cast away from the uneven bars, did a straddled front somersault, and then regrasped the same bar. She performed these moves during the 1976 Olympics and earned a score of 10, which is considered perfect. In *Letters to a Young Gymnast* (Basic Books, 2003), Comaneci wrote: "I believe that Bela's theory is true in life, too. Trying to be someone else may get you through the door, but being unique will get you noticed."

**THE WINNING WAY:**

**Be original.**

# JULIE KRONE

## jockey

**CAREER HIGHLIGHT:**
first woman to win a Triple Crown race, 1993

Although she stands only 4 feet 10 inches tall and when competing weighed 100 pounds, Julie Krone has never let anything stand in her way. At age 9, she harnessed a Great Dane to a sled and went for a ride in the snow. When she was 15, she got a job at Churchill Downs in Louisville, Kentucky. She proved wrong the trainers and horse owners who thought that women weren't strong enough to handle 1,200-pound racehorses, and she

–Susan Ragan/Painet Inc.

always aimed high, saying: "I don't want to be the best female jockey in the world. I want to be the best jockey."

In 2000, when Krone became the first woman accepted into thoroughbred racing's Hall of Fame, she said, "I want this to be a lesson to all kids everywhere. If the stable gate is closed, climb the fence."

**THE WINNING WAY:**

**Overcome any hurdles.**

# JACK NICKLAUS

## golfer

**CAREER HIGHLIGHTS:**
won 73 PGA Tour events and 10
Champions Tour events

In 1959, 19-year-old Jack Nicklaus was among the best amateur golfers in the nation and part of a small group invited to play in the Masters. As an amateur, he was allowed to practice at the revered Augusta National Golf

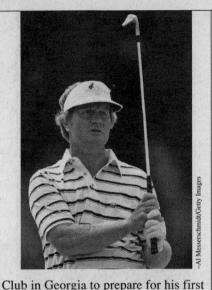

unless you become physically incapacitated to the point of not being able either to walk or to swing a golf club."

**THE WINNING WAY:**

**Finish what you start.**

# JESSE OWENS

## track and field athlete

**CAREER HIGHLIGHTS:**
set three world records and tied a fourth at the Big Ten Championships, 1935; won four gold medals at the 1936 Berlin Olympics

Club in Georgia to prepare for his first professional tournament. The club's steak dinners, which he got at a bargain rate of two dollars, were an added bonus.

It wasn't long before Nicklaus decided that he needed some experience in professional competition, so he asked permission to enter the Azalea Open in North Carolina. He was successful in qualifying and then played well in the event: After the first two rounds, he was just six strokes off the lead. The weather turned nasty, though, and Nicklaus didn't like the course, so he withdrew and headed back to Augusta for a steak. A short time later, a Professional Golfers' Association official read him the riot act, explaining that golfers can't just quit in the middle of a tournament, and that had he stayed, he could have won.

Nicklaus says that the lesson stayed with him his entire career: "When you enter a golf tournament, you stay in that golf tournament to its beautiful or bitter end,

**A**t about age 15, Jesse Owens ran his first official race, a quarter mile, and lost. His coach, Charles Riley, told him that his mistake was in trying to stare down his competitors instead of running them down. When Owens didn't understand, Riley took him to a horse

*(continued)*

racetrack. As Owens studied the horses' gaits, Riley asked him about the horses' faces. Owens said that he didn't see anything in their faces.

Soon after, Owens ran another race. At the end, when the race had been won (but not by Owens), he was still running hard, pushing himself past the finish line and his opponents. Riley congratulated him for working hard and overcoming his greatest opponent—himself.

From that day on, Owens seldom lost. He seemed to run effortlessly; like a racehorse, he seldom revealed strain or emotion in his face.

**THE WINNING WAY:**

**Run your own race.**

# NOLAN RYAN

### baseball pitcher

**CAREER HIGHLIGHTS:**

**holds the Major League career record for strikeouts (5,714) and no-hitters (seven)**

Once Nolan Ryan got to the Major Leagues, he enjoyed many successes but also endured occasional injuries and slumps. As a new member of the California Angels in 1972, Ryan decided to increase his stamina and his upper-body strength by working out in the ballpark's weight room. At the time, baseball managers and coaches discouraged such routines, believing that weight lifting would cause players to be "muscle-bound" and unable to hit or throw well. In fact, Ryan felt more

—Focus on Sports/Getty Images

limber and stronger after workouts. He installed a gym at home, began swimming, and developed a conditioning routine that he used for years. The hard work paid off. In his first 3 years with the Angels, Ryan pitched a total of more than 1,000 innings.

Ryan observed: "If it hadn't been for that weight room, I would have been out of the game many years ago. Not only has it helped me to prevent injury, but also it's kept me strong so that I could continue to hold up over the long grind."

**THE WINNING WAY:**

**Go the extra mile.**

☐☐

**Alice Cary,** a frequent Almanac contributor, goes the extra mile and overcomes any hurdle to calmly watch her kids finish their sports events.

# Got Game?

**Match each term with the correct sport. (One sport has no match.)**
**We bet that even the most knowledgeable fans will be stumped by some of these.**

| | | | |
|---|---|---|---|
| ____ | 1. **Balk** | A. | Badminton |
| ____ | 2. **Bonk** | B. | Baseball |
| ____ | 3. **Carom** | C. | Basketball |
| ____ | 4. **Catch a crab** | D. | Billiards |
| ____ | 5. **Cradling** | E. | Bowling |
| ____ | 6. **Dink** | F. | Bicycling |
| ____ | 7. **Gimme** | G. | Curling |
| ____ | 8. **Grind** | H. | Fencing |
| ____ | 9. **Hog** | I. | Football |
| ____ | 10. **Jerk** | J. | Golf |
| ____ | 11. **Kiss** | K. | Gymnastics |
| ____ | 12. **Lollipop** | L. | Ice hockey |
| ____ | 13. **Maul** | M. | Lacrosse |
| ____ | 14. **Red zone** | N. | Rowing |
| ____ | 15. **Riposte** | O. | Rugby |
| ____ | 16. **Schuss** | P. | Skateboarding |
| ____ | 17. **Slash** | Q. | Skiing |
| ____ | 18. **Sling** | R. | Snowboarding |
| ____ | 19. **Stutz** | S. | Soccer |
| ____ | 20. **Sur place** | T. | Surfing |
| ____ | 21. **Tip-off** | U. | Swimming |
| ____ | 22. **Touch out** | V. | Tennis |
| ____ | 23. **Trap** | W. | Track & field |
| ____ | 24. **Turkey** | X. | Volleyball |
| | | Y. | Weightlifting |

☞ *For definitions of these terms, go to* **Almanac.com/SportsTerms.**

**Answers:** 1. B; 2. R; 3. L; 4. N; 5. M; 6. V; 7. J; 8. P; 9. G; 10. Y; 11. D; 12. X; 13. O; 14. I; 15. H; 16. Q; 17. T; 18. A; 19. K; 20. F; 21. C; 22. U; 23. S; 24. E; not used: W.

# GET THE BEST
## OF YOUR
# BOSS

-------------------------------------------------

### and improve your chances for success.

*A little knowledge about your boss's zodiac profile can yield valuable insights into her or his work style—and make you a star!*

## ARIES • *March 21–April 20*

Aries are **self-motivated, energetic,** and **pioneering.** Spontaneous and fearless, this boss has little, if any, lag time between thoughts and actions or impulses and deeds. Clearly able to "just do it," s/he respects and admires subordinates who can pick up and run with a project. This boss invites new ideas as long as they mesh with the overall plan but also enjoys a little chivalrous push-back, as sparring is an integral part of her/his nature. Always lead with your best idea; this boss has no time for weakness

or excuses. You know where you stand with this individual: What you see is what you get.

## TAURUS • *April 21–May 20*

Taureans are **practical, grounded,** and **value-oriented.** Sensual and earthy, this boss has a strongly developed sense of touch (her/his clothing is usually made of natural fibers). S/he loves the best that money can buy but seldom pays top dollar; "bargain" could be her/his middle name. To get this boss's attention, heed the importance of the bottom line and implement cost efficiencies but never diminish the quality of the product or service. Be aware that s/he will not be pushed but can be coaxed. Remember to turn off lights and computers when you leave and to always reuse paper clips.

## GEMINI • *May 21–June 20*

Geminis are **witty, effervescent,** and **mercurial.** This boss thrives on change,

## by Celeste Longacre

–illustrations, Virginia Allyn

"dancing" from place to place, flitting among topics, or juggling many projects. Here is a boss who values diversity (s/he bores quite easily) and loves to know everything that happens in the office. S/he will appreciate your ability to brighten dull reports with innovative headings, sidebars, and illustrations. Moving the furniture around your office to achieve greater efficiency will be noticed and approved. A sense of humor is vital here to avoid being considered officious.

## CANCER • *June 21–July 22*

Cancers are **sensitive, patriotic,** and **fiercely loyal** to home and family. This boss works primarily to benefit loved ones. Leadership comes naturally, but s/he is often introspective, with obtuse reasoning. A side-stepper like her/his totem (the crab), this boss is characterized by hints and innuendo that precede direct suggestions. You will be greatly rewarded if you can respond to these early warning signals and follow up with your own concise questions for

clarity. Understand, too, that her/his tough exterior shields a soft interior. Treat her/him like family (remembering her/his relatives' names and particulars will be noticed), and benefits will follow.

## LEO • *July 23–August 22*

Leos are **bold, leadership-oriented,** and **magnanimous.** This boss likes to do things in a grand style, and success is achieved by force of personality (like cream, this boss seems to naturally rise to the top). Being strong and independent, s/he will admire the same qualities in you. Know, however, that this boss wants the spotlight; your ideas will be more readily accepted if they reflect her/his personal beliefs. For best results, weave your proposals into flattering constructs and show how they benefit the boss's brilliant plans.

## VIRGO • *August 23–September 22*

Virgos are **precise, analytical,** and **detail-oriented.** This boss is able to spot the flaw in a given situation instantly and has no tolerance for sloppy work, misplaced files, or halfhearted effort. S/he seeks perfection in all things and will value a diligent employee who dots all the i's and crosses all the t's. Punctuality is imperative; this boss will not endure anyone who is chronically late or absent from appointments. Sharp, focused business proposals and neat, crisp attire win the day—and the rewards.

**(continued)**

especially extra effort, such as late hours or work done from home—on her/his behalf is noticed and rewarded. Be warned: This boss forgets nothing; consider fully all consequences before taking any professional action. S/he is almost assured of success, so hang on to her/his coattails for a great ride!

## LIBRA • *September 23–October 22*

Libras are **relationship-oriented, charming,** and **graceful.** This boss continually weighs and balances each decision because s/he is concerned with her/his impact on others; justice is extremely important. Pleasant surroundings are important, as s/he—perhaps more than a boss with any other sign—is extremely sensitive to her/his enclosures (s/he can not abide dirty environs). Your tactfulness is appreciated, and your willingness to debate and compromise will be noticed. S/he wants a peaceful office, so play fair and practice kindness. Sincere compliments will find favor.

## SCORPIO • *October 23–November 22*

Scorpios are **passionate, intense, driven,** and **career-oriented.** This boss understands the ways of the world: S/he always has a plan, yes, and a backup. Corporate organization and the ability to strategize are important. S/he likes to present a complex package to potential clients, so thorough research—

## SAGITTARIUS •

*November 23–December 21*

Sagittarians are **independent, philosophical,** and **freedom-oriented.** This boss is dedicated to the truth and will not tolerate any deviations from it. S/he is also drawn to foreign places, so expect travel to be in her/his game plan. Being able to anticipate the many possible ramifications of business decisions, s/he will notice you for being thorough with your research and recommendations. Expect lively discussions in the boardroom, and because her/his interests include nearly everything, showing your own diverse intellect will be rewarded everywhere. Know, though,

that Truth Is King here and that any attempt to subvert or hide it will be met with immediate dismissal.

## CAPRICORN •
*December 22–January 19*

Capricorns are **worldly, determined,** and **success-oriented.** This boss has figured out that slow, sure, steady steps lead to the mountain peak (or corner office). S/he has made sacrifices to achieve her/his current success; a bit of respect and admiration is greatly appreciated. S/he is organized and methodical, so your ability to set and reach goals is noticed and rewarded. Extra effort earns points, as does fastidiousness and proper attire. A good standing in the local community is important to this boss; your help in assisting her/him in attaining and keeping this standing will be noticed.

## AQUARIUS •
*January 20–February 19*

Aquarians are **humanitarian, intuitive,** and **future-oriented.** This boss is an unconventional thinker naturally drawn to like minds. Having an inventive nature, s/he anticipates new trends and instinctively knows how to fill the public's needs and satiate desires. If you can present unique stratagems and bold, new marketing plans, s/he will shower you with attention and rewards. Your efforts to improve the future for humanity, such as your support of local civic organizations, will delight this soul.

## PISCES • *February 20–March 20*

Pisces are **sensitive, empathic,** and **creative.** Unlike bosses with other signs, this one doesn't possess a particular energy; rather, s/he is a blend of the entire zodiac. This boss has the ability to intuit others' thoughts and feelings, so be aware of your state of mind. S/he may sometimes need protection or comforting words; encouraging her/him to close the door or take a walk for a general respite is appreciated. Know that s/he is often found in leadership positions because s/he can appreciate everyone's point of view. When sharing new proposals and ideas, use a soft approach, as s/he is averse to harsh words and criticisms. Understanding is this one's gift, so expect a sympathetic ear if difficulties arise.  □□

**Celeste Longacre,** the Almanac's astrologer, has the work style of an Aries: What you see is what you get.

# Secrets of the Zodiac

## The Man of the Signs

Ancient astrologers believed that each astrological sign influenced a specific part of the body. The first sign of the zodiac—Aries—was attributed to the head, with the rest of the signs moving down the body, ending with Pisces at the feet.

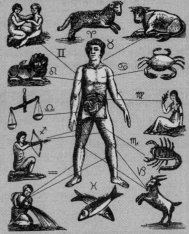

♈ Aries, head . . . . . . **ARI**   *Mar. 21–Apr. 20*
♉ Taurus, neck . . . . **TAU**   *Apr. 21–May 20*
♊ Gemini, arms . . . **GEM**   *May 21–June 20*
♋ Cancer, breast . . . **CAN**   *June 21–July 22*
♌ Leo, heart . . . . . . **LEO**   *July 23–Aug. 22*
♍ Virgo, belly . . . . **VIR**   *Aug. 23–Sept. 22*
♎ Libra, reins . . . . . **LIB**   *Sept. 23–Oct. 22*
♏ Scorpio, secrets . . **SCO**   *Oct. 23–Nov. 22*
♐ Sagittarius, thighs **SAG**   *Nov. 23–Dec. 21*
♑ Capricorn, knees . **CAP**   *Dec. 22–Jan. 19*
♒ Aquarius, legs . . **AQU**   *Jan. 20–Feb. 19*
♓ Pisces, feet . . . . . **PSC**   *Feb. 20–Mar. 20*

## Astrology vs. Astronomy

■ **Astrology** is a tool we use to plan events according to the placements of the Sun, the Moon, and the planets in the 12 signs of the zodiac. In astrology, the planetary movements do not cause events; rather, they explain the path, or "flow," that events tend to follow. **Astronomy** is the study of the actual placement of the known planets and constellations. *(The placement of the planets in the signs of the zodiac is not the same astrologically and astronomically.)* The Moon's astrological place is given on **page 230;** its astronomical place is given in the **Left-Hand Calendar Pages, 114–140.**

The dates in the **Best Days table, page 231,** are based on the astrological passage of the Moon. However, consider all indicators before making any major decisions.

## When Mercury Is Retrograde

■ Sometimes the other planets appear to be traveling backward through the zodiac; this is an illusion. We call this illusion *retrograde motion.*

Mercury's retrograde periods can cause our plans to go awry. However, this is an excellent time to reflect on the past. Intuition is high during these periods, and coincidences can be extraordinary.

When Mercury is retrograde, remain flexible, allow extra time for travel, and avoid signing contracts. Review projects and plans at these times, but wait until Mercury is direct again to make any final decisions.

In 2011, Mercury will be retrograde from March 30–April 22, August 3–25, and November 24–December 13.

*–Celeste Longacre*

## Gardening by the Moon's Sign

Use the chart on the next page to find the best dates for the following garden tasks:

■ **Plant, transplant, and graft:** Cancer, Scorpio, or Pisces. Taurus, Virgo, and Capricorn are good second choices.

■ **Build/fix fences or garden beds:** Capricorn.

■ **Control insect pests, plow, and weed:** Aries, Gemini, Leo, Sagittarius, or Aquarius.

■ **Prune:** Aries, Leo, or Sagittarius. During a waxing Moon, pruning encourages growth; during a waning Moon, it discourages growth.

■ **Clean out the garden shed:** Virgo.

**(continued)**

## Secrets of the Zodiac (continued)

### Setting Eggs by the Moon's Sign

■ Chicks take about 21 days to hatch. Those born under a waxing Moon, in the fruitful signs of Cancer, Scorpio, and Pisces, are healthier and mature faster. To ensure that chicks are born during these times, determine the best days to "set eggs" (to place eggs in an incubator or under a hen). To calculate, find the three fruitful birth signs on the chart below. Use the Left-Hand Calendar Pages, 114–140, to find the dates of the new and full Moons.

Using only the fruitful dates between the new and full Moons, count back 21 days to find the best days to set eggs.

**E X A M P L E :**

The Moon is new on June 1 and full on June 15. Between these dates, on June 3 and 4, the Moon is in the sign of Cancer. To have chicks born on June 3, count back 21 days; set eggs on May 13.

## The Moon's Astrological Place, 2010–11

|    | Nov. | Dec. | Jan. | Feb. | Mar. | Apr. | May | June | July | Aug. | Sept. | Oct. | Nov. | Dec. |
|----|------|------|------|------|------|------|-----|------|------|------|-------|------|------|------|
| 1  | VIR | LIB | SAG | CAP | AQU | PSC | ARI | GEM | CAN | VIR | LIB | SAG | CAP | PSC |
| 2  | VIR | SCO | SAG | AQU | AQU | ARI | TAU | GEM | CAN | VIR | SCO | SAG | AQU | PSC |
| 3  | LIB | SCO | CAP | AQU | PSC | ARI | TAU | CAN | LEO | LIB | SCO | CAP | AQU | PSC |
| 4  | LIB | SCO | CAP | PSC | PSC | ARI | GEM | CAN | LEO | LIB | SAG | CAP | PSC | ARI |
| 5  | SCO | SAG | AQU | PSC | PSC | TAU | GEM | LEO | VIR | SCO | SAG | AQU | PSC | ARI |
| 6  | SCO | SAG | AQU | PSC | ARI | TAU | GEM | LEO | VIR | SCO | CAP | AQU | PSC | TAU |
| 7  | SAG | CAP | AQU | ARI | ARI | GEM | CAN | LEO | LIB | SAG | CAP | AQU | ARI | TAU |
| 8  | SAG | CAP | PSC | ARI | TAU | GEM | CAN | VIR | LIB | SAG | AQU | PSC | ARI | TAU |
| 9  | CAP | AQU | PSC | TAU | TAU | GEM | LEO | VIR | SCO | SAG | AQU | PSC | TAU | GEM |
| 10 | CAP | AQU | ARI | TAU | TAU | CAN | LEO | LIB | SCO | CAP | AQU | ARI | TAU | GEM |
| 11 | CAP | AQU | ARI | TAU | GEM | CAN | VIR | LIB | SAG | CAP | PSC | ARI | TAU | CAN |
| 12 | AQU | PSC | ARI | GEM | GEM | LEO | VIR | SCO | SAG | AQU | PSC | ARI | GEM | CAN |
| 13 | AQU | PSC | TAU | GEM | CAN | LEO | LIB | SCO | CAP | AQU | ARI | TAU | GEM | CAN |
| 14 | PSC | ARI | TAU | CAN | CAN | VIR | LIB | SAG | CAP | PSC | ARI | TAU | CAN | LEO |
| 15 | PSC | ARI | GEM | CAN | CAN | VIR | SCO | SAG | CAP | PSC | ARI | GEM | CAN | LEO |
| 16 | PSC | ARI | GEM | LEO | LEO | LIB | SCO | CAP | AQU | PSC | TAU | GEM | LEO | VIR |
| 17 | ARI | TAU | GEM | LEO | LEO | LIB | SAG | CAP | AQU | ARI | TAU | GEM | LEO | VIR |
| 18 | ARI | TAU | CAN | VIR | VIR | SCO | SAG | AQU | PSC | ARI | GEM | CAN | LEO | LIB |
| 19 | TAU | GEM | CAN | VIR | VIR | SCO | SAG | AQU | PSC | TAU | GEM | CAN | VIR | LIB |
| 20 | TAU | GEM | LEO | LIB | LIB | SAG | CAP | AQU | ARI | TAU | GEM | LEO | VIR | SCO |
| 21 | TAU | CAN | LEO | LIB | LIB | SAG | CAP | PSC | ARI | TAU | CAN | LEO | LIB | SCO |
| 22 | GEM | CAN | VIR | SCO | SCO | CAP | AQU | PSC | ARI | GEM | CAN | VIR | LIB | SAG |
| 23 | GEM | LEO | VIR | SCO | SCO | CAP | AQU | ARI | TAU | GEM | LEO | VIR | SCO | SAG |
| 24 | CAN | LEO | LIB | SAG | SAG | CAP | PSC | ARI | TAU | CAN | LEO | LIB | SCO | CAP |
| 25 | CAN | VIR | LIB | SAG | SAG | AQU | PSC | ARI | GEM | CAN | VIR | LIB | SAG | CAP |
| 26 | LEO | VIR | SCO | SAG | CAP | AQU | PSC | TAU | GEM | LEO | VIR | SCO | SAG | AQU |
| 27 | LEO | VIR | SCO | CAP | CAP | PSC | ARI | TAU | GEM | LEO | LIB | SCO | CAP | AQU |
| 28 | VIR | LIB | SAG | CAP | AQU | PSC | ARI | GEM | CAN | LEO | LIB | SAG | CAP | AQU |
| 29 | VIR | LIB | SAG | — | AQU | ARI | TAU | GEM | CAN | VIR | SCO | SAG | AQU | PSC |
| 30 | LIB | SCO | CAP | — | AQU | ARI | TAU | CAN | LEO | VIR | SCO | CAP | AQU | PSC |
| 31 | — | SCO | CAP | — | PSC | — | TAU | — | LEO | LIB | — | CAP | — | ARI |

## Best Days for 2011

This chart is based on the Moon's sign and shows the best days each month for certain activities.

*—Celeste Longacre*

| | Jan | Feb | Mar | Apr | May | Jun | Jul | Aug | Sep | Oct | Nov | Dec |
|---|---|---|---|---|---|---|---|---|---|---|---|---|
| **Quit smoking** | 22, 23, 26, 27 | 18, 22, 23 | 22, 31 | 1, 22, 23 | 2, 24, 29 | 21, 26 | 18, 23 | 14, 19 | 16, 25 | 13, 22 | 19, 23 | 16, 20 |
| **Begin diet to lose weight** | 22, 23, 26, 27 | 18, 22, 23 | 22, 31 | 1, 22, 23 | 2, 24, 29 | 21, 26 | 18, 23 | 14, 19 | 16, 25 | 13, 22 | 19, 23 | 16, 20 |
| **Begin diet to gain weight** | 8, 9, 13, 14 | 4, 5, 9 | 9, 13, 14 | 5, 14 | 11, 15, 16 | 8, 12 | 5, 9 | 1, 5 | 2, 11, 29 | 8, 27 | 4, 5 | 1, 6, 29 |
| **Cut hair to encourage growth** | 13, 14 | 9, 10 | 9, 10 | 5, 6, 16, 17 | 13, 14 | 10, 11 | 7, 8 | 3, 4 | 1, 11, 28 | 8, 9 | 4, 5, 9 | 7, 8, 29, 30 |
| **Cut hair to discourage growth** | 24, 25 | 20, 21 | 20, 21 | 27, 28 | 2, 29, 30, 31 | 26, 27 | 23, 24 | 19, 20 | 16, 17 | 14, 15, 25 | 21, 22 | 14, 15 |
| **Have dental care** | 22, 23 | 18, 19 | 18, 19 | 14, 15 | 11, 12 | 8, 9 | 5, 6 | 1, 2, 29, 30 | 25, 26 | 22, 23 | 19, 20 | 16, 17 |
| **Start projects** | 5, 6 | 4, 5 | 5, 6 | 4, 5 | 4, 5 | 2, 3 | 2, 3 | 30, 31 | 28, 29 | 27, 28 | 26, 27 | 25, 26 |
| **End projects** | 2, 3 | 1, 2 | 2, 3 | 1, 2 | 1, 2 | 29, 30 | 28, 29 | 27, 28 | 25, 26 | 24, 25 | 23, 24 | 22, 23 |
| **Go camping** | 28, 29 | 24, 25 | 24, 25 | 20, 21 | 17, 18, 19 | 14, 15 | 11, 12 | 7, 8 | 4, 5 | 1, 2, 28, 29 | 25, 26 | 22, 23 |
| **Plant aboveground crops** | 8, 9, 18 | 5, 14, 15 | 13, 14 | 10, 11 | 7, 8, 16 | 3, 4, 12, 13 | 9, 10 | 5, 6 | 2, 3, 29, 30 | 8, 9, 27 | 4, 5 | 2, 3, 29, 30 |
| **Plant belowground crops** | 26, 27 | 22, 23 | 22, 23 | 1, 27, 28 | 24, 25, 26 | 21, 22 | 18, 19, 28, 29 | 14, 15, 24, 25 | 21, 22 | 18, 19 | 14, 15, 23, 24 | 11, 12, 13 |
| **Destroy pests and weeds** | 11, 12 | 7, 8 | 6, 7 | 2, 3, 4, 30 | 1, 27, 28 | 23, 24 | 21, 22 | 17, 18 | 13, 14 | 11, 12 | 7, 8 | 4, 5, 31 |
| **Graft or pollinate** | 18, 19 | 14, 15 | 13, 14 | 10, 11 | 7, 8 | 3, 4, 30 | 1, 2, 28, 29 | 24, 25 | 21, 22 | 18, 19 | 14, 15 | 11, 12, 13 |
| **Prune to encourage growth** | 11, 12 | 7, 8 | 6, 7, 16, 17 | 3, 4, 12, 13 | 9, 10 | 6, 7 | 3, 4 | 7, 8 | 4, 5 | 1, 2, 28, 29 | 7, 8 | 4, 5, 31 |
| **Prune to discourage growth** | 28, 29 | 24, 25 | 24, 25 | 20, 21 | 27, 28 | 23, 24 | 21, 22 | 17, 18 | 23, 24 | 20, 21 | 17, 18 | 14, 15 |
| **Harvest above-ground crops** | 13, 14 | 9, 10 | 9, 10 | 5, 6 | 11, 12 | 8, 9 | 5, 6 | 1, 2 | 6, 7 | 3, 4 | 9, 27, 28 | 7, 8 |
| **Harvest below-ground crops** | 3, 22, 23 | 27, 28 | 26, 27 | 22, 23 | 20, 21, 30, 31 | 17, 26, 27 | 23, 24 | 20, 21 | 16, 17 | 13, 22, 23 | 19, 20 | 16, 17 |
| **Can, pickle, or make sauerkraut** | 26, 27 | 22, 23 | 22, 23 | 1, 27, 28 | 25, 26 | 21, 22 | 28, 29 | 14, 15 | 21, 22 | 18, 19 | 14, 15 | 12, 13 |
| **Cut hay** | 11, 12 | 7, 8 | 6, 7 | 2, 3, 4, 30 | 1, 27, 28 | 23, 24 | 21, 22 | 17, 18 | 13, 14 | 11, 12 | 7, 8 | 4, 5, 31 |
| **Begin logging** | 3, 4, 30, 31 | 1, 27, 28 | 26, 27 | 22, 23 | 20, 21 | 16, 17 | 13, 14 | 10, 11 | 6, 7 | 3, 4, 31 | 1, 27, 28 | 24, 25 |
| **Set posts or pour concrete** | 3, 4, 30, 31 | 1, 27, 28 | 26, 27 | 22, 23 | 20, 21 | 16, 17 | 13, 14 | 10, 11 | 6, 7 | 3, 4, 31 | 1, 27, 28 | 24, 25 |
| **Breed animals** | 26, 27 | 22, 23 | 22, 23 | 18, 19 | 15, 16 | 12, 13 | 9, 10 | 5, 6 | 2, 3, 29, 30 | 26, 27 | 23, 24 | 20, 21 |
| **Wean animals or children** | 22, 23, 26, 27 | 18, 22, 23 | 22, 31 | 1, 22, 23 | 2, 24, 29 | 21, 26 | 18, 23 | 14, 19 | 16, 25 | 13, 22 | 19, 23 | 16, 20 |
| **Castrate animals** | 6, 7 | 2, 3 | 1, 2, 28, 29 | 25, 26 | 22, 23 | 18, 19 | 16, 17 | 12, 13 | 8, 9 | 6, 7 | 2, 3, 29, 30 | 27, 28 |
| **Slaughter livestock** | 26, 27 | 22, 23 | 22, 23 | 18, 19 | 15, 16 | 12, 13 | 9, 10 | 5, 6 | 2, 3, 29, 30 | 26, 27 | 23, 24 | 20, 21 |

# Planting by the Moon's Phase

*This age-old practice suggests that the Moon in its cycles affects plant growth.*

■ Plant flowers and vegetables that bear crops above ground during the light, or waxing, of the Moon: from the day the Moon is new to the day it is full.

■ Plant flowering bulbs and vegetables that bear crops below ground during the dark, or waning, of the Moon: from the day after it is full to the day before it is new again.

The Moon Favorable columns give the best planting days based on the Moon's phases for 2011. (See the **Left-Hand Calendar Pages, 114–140,** for the exact days of the new and full Moons.) The Planting Dates columns give the safe periods for planting in areas that receive frost. See **Frosts and Growing Seasons, page 212,** for first/last frost dates and the average length of the growing season in your area.

Get local seed-sowing dates at Almanac.com/PlantingTable.

■ Aboveground crops are marked *.
■ (E) means early;  (L) means late.
■ Map shades correspond to shades of date columns.

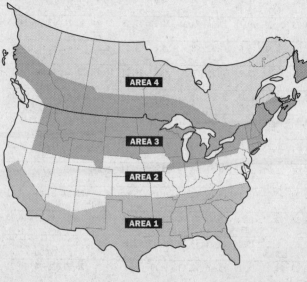

| | |
|---|---|
| * Barley | |
| * Beans | (E) |
| | (L) |
| Beets | (E) |
| | (L) |
| * Broccoli plants | (E) |
| | (L) |
| * Brussels sprouts | |
| * Cabbage plants | |
| Carrots | (E) |
| | (L) |
| * Cauliflower plants | (E) |
| | (L) |
| * Celery plants | (E) |
| | (L) |
| * Collards | (E) |
| | (L) |
| * Corn, sweet | (E) |
| | (L) |
| * Cucumbers | |
| * Eggplant plants | |
| * Endive | (E) |
| | (L) |
| * Kale | (E) |
| | (L) |
| Leek plants | |
| * Lettuce | |
| * Muskmelons | |
| * Okra | |
| Onion sets | |
| * Parsley | |
| Parsnips | |
| * Peas | (E) |
| | (L) |
| * Pepper plants | |
| Potatoes | |
| * Pumpkins | |
| Radishes | (E) |
| | (L) |
| * Spinach | (E) |
| | (L) |
| * Squashes | |
| Sweet potatoes | |
| * Swiss chard | |
| * Tomato plants | |
| Turnips | (E) |
| | (L) |
| * Watermelons | |
| * Wheat, spring | |
| * Wheat, winter | |

| | AREA 1 | | | AREA 2 | | | AREA 3 | | | AREA 4 | |
|---|---|---|---|---|---|---|---|---|---|---|---|
| Planting Dates | Moon Favorable | | Planting Dates | Moon Favorable | | Planting Dates | Moon Favorable | | Planting Dates | Moon Favorable | |
| 2/15–3/7 | 2/15–18, 3/4–7 | | 3/15–4/7 | 3/15–19, 4/3–7 | | 5/15–6/21 | 5/15–19, 6/1–15 | | 6/1–30 | 6/1–15 | |
| 3/15–4/7 | 3/15–19, 4/3–7 | | 4/15–30 | 4/15–17 | | 5/7–6/21 | 5/7–17, 6/1–15 | | 5/30–6/15 | 6/1–15 | |
| 8/7–31 | 8/7–13, 8/28–31 | | 7/1–21 | 7/1–15 | | 6/15–7/15 | 6/15, 7/1–15 | | — | — | |
| 2/7–28 | 2/19–28 | | 3/15–4/3 | 3/20–4/2 | | 5/1–15 | 5/1–2 | | 5/25–6/10 | 5/25–31 | |
| 9/1–30 | 9/13–26 | | 8/15–31 | 8/15–27 | | 7/15–8/15 | 7/16–29, 8/14–15 | | 6/15–7/8 | 6/16–30 | |
| 2/15–3/15 | 2/15–18, 3/4–15 | | 3/7–31 | 3/7–19 | | 5/15–31 | 5/15–17 | | 6/1–25 | 6/1–15 | |
| 9/7–30 | 9/7–12, 9/27–30 | | 8/1–20 | 8/1–13 | | 6/15–7/7 | 6/15, 7/1–7 | | — | — | |
| 2/11–3/20 | 2/11–18, 3/4–19 | | 3/7–4/15 | 3/7–19, 4/3–15 | | 5/15–31 | 5/15–17 | | 6/1–25 | 6/1–15 | |
| 2/11–3/20 | 2/11–18, 3/4–19 | | 3/7–4/15 | 3/7–19, 4/3–15 | | 5/15–31 | 5/15–17 | | 6/1–25 | 6/1–15 | |
| 2/15–3/7 | 2/19–3/3 | | 3/7–31 | 3/20–31 | | 5/15–31 | 5/18–31 | | 5/25–6/10 | 5/25–31 | |
| 8/1–9/7 | 8/14–27 | | 7/7–31 | 7/16–29 | | 6/15–7/21 | 6/16–30, 7/16–21 | | 6/15–7/8 | 6/16–30 | |
| 2/15–3/7 | 2/15–18, 3/4–7 | | 3/15–4/7 | 3/15–19, 4/3–7 | | 5/15–31 | 5/15–17 | | 6/1–25 | 6/1–15 | |
| 8/7–31 | 8/7–13, 8/28–31 | | 7/1–8/7 | 7/1–15, 7/30–8/7 | | 6/15–7/21 | 6/15, 7/1–15 | | — | — | |
| 2/15–28 | 2/15–18 | | 3/7–31 | 3/7–19 | | 5/15–6/30 | 5/15–17, 6/1–15 | | 6/1–30 | 6/1–15 | |
| 9/15–30 | 9/27–30 | | 8/15–9/7 | 8/28–9/7 | | 7/15–8/15 | 7/15, 7/30–8/13 | | — | — | |
| 2/11–3/20 | 2/11–18, 3/4–19 | | 3/7–4/7 | 3/7–19, 4/3–7 | | 5/15–31 | 5/15–17 | | 6/1–25 | 6/1–15 | |
| 9/7–30 | 9/7–12, 9/27–30 | | 8/15–31 | 8/28–31 | | 7/1–8/7 | 7/1–15, 7/30–8/7 | | — | — | |
| 3/15–31 | 3/15–19 | | 4/1–17 | 4/3–17 | | 5/10–6/15 | 5/10–17, 6/1–15 | | 5/30–6/20 | 6/1–15 | |
| 8/7–31 | 8/7–13, 8/28–31 | | 7/7–21 | 7/7–15 | | 6/15–30 | 6/15 | | — | — | |
| 3/7–4/15 | 3/7–19, 4/3–15 | | 4/7–5/15 | 4/7–17, 5/3–15 | | 5/7–6/20 | 5/7–17, 6/1–15 | | 5/30–6/15 | 6/1–15 | |
| 3/7–4/15 | 3/7–19, 4/3–15 | | 4/7–5/15 | 4/7–17, 5/3–15 | | 6/1–30 | 6/1–15 | | 6/15–30 | 6/15 | |
| 2/15–3/20 | 2/15–18, 3/4–19 | | 4/7–5/15 | 4/7–17, 5/3–15 | | 5/15–31 | 5/15–17 | | 6/1–25 | 6/1–15 | |
| 8/15–9/7 | 8/28–9/7 | | 7/15–8/15 | 7/15, 7/30–8/13 | | 6/7–30 | 6/7–15 | | — | — | |
| 2/11–3/20 | 2/11–18, 3/4–19 | | 3/7–4/7 | 3/7–19, 4/3–7 | | 5/15–31 | 5/15–17 | | 6/1–15 | 6/1–15 | |
| 9/7–30 | 9/7–12, 9/27–30 | | 8/15–31 | 8/28–31 | | 7/1–8/7 | 7/1–15, 7/30–8/7 | | 6/25–7/15 | 7/1–15 | |
| 2/15–4/15 | 2/19–3/3, 3/20–4/2 | | 3/7–4/7 | 3/20–4/2 | | 5/15–31 | 5/18–31 | | 6/1–25 | 6/16–25 | |
| 2/15–3/7 | 2/15–18, 3/4–7 | | 3/1–31 | 3/4–19 | | 5/15–6/30 | 5/15–17, 6/1–15 | | 6/1–30 | 6/1–15 | |
| 3/15–4/7 | 3/15–19, 4/3–7 | | 4/15–5/7 | 4/15–17, 5/3–7 | | 5/15–6/30 | 5/15–17, 6/1–15 | | 6/1–30 | 6/1–15 | |
| 4/15–6/1 | 4/15–17, 5/3–17, 6/1 | | 5/25–6/15 | 6/1–15 | | 6/15–7/10 | 6/15, 7/1–10 | | 6/25–7/7 | 7/1–7 | |
| 2/1–28 | 2/1, 2/19–28 | | 3/1–31 | 3/1–3, 3/20–31 | | 5/15–6/7 | 5/18–31 | | 6/1–25 | 6/16–25 | |
| 2/20–3/15 | 3/4–15 | | 3/1–31 | 3/4–19 | | 5/15–31 | 5/15–17 | | 6/1–15 | 6/1–15 | |
| 1/15–2/4 | 1/20–2/1 | | 3/7–31 | 3/20–31 | | 4/1–30 | 4/1–2, 4/18–30 | | 5/10–31 | 5/18–31 | |
| 1/15–2/7 | 1/15–19, 2/2–7 | | 3/7–31 | 3/7–19 | | 4/15–5/7 | 4/15–17, 5/3–7 | | 5/15–31 | 5/15–17 | |
| 9/15–30 | 9/27–30 | | 8/7–31 | 8/7–13, 8/28–31 | | 7/15–31 | 7/15, 7/30–31 | | 7/10–25 | 7/10–15 | |
| 3/1–20 | 3/4–19 | | 4/1–30 | 4/3–17 | | 5/15–6/30 | 5/15–17, 6/1–15 | | 6/1–30 | 6/1–15 | |
| 2/10–28 | 2/19–28 | | 4/1–30 | 4/1–2, 4/18–30 | | 5/1–31 | 5/1–2, 5/18–31 | | 6/1–25 | 6/16–25 | |
| 3/7–20 | 3/7–19 | | 4/23–5/15 | 5/3–15 | | 5/15–31 | 5/15–17 | | 6/1–30 | 6/1–15 | |
| 1/21–3/1 | 1/21–2/1, 2/19–3/1 | | 3/7–31 | 3/20–31 | | 4/15–30 | 4/18–30 | | 5/15–6/5 | 5/18–31 | |
| 10/1–21 | 10/12–21 | | 9/7–30 | 9/13–26 | | 8/15–31 | 8/15–27 | | 7/10–31 | 7/16–29 | |
| 2/7–3/15 | 2/7–18, 3/4–15 | | 3/15–4/20 | 3/15–19, 4/3–17 | | 5/15–31 | 5/15–17 | | 6/1–25 | 6/1–15 | |
| 10/1–21 | 10/1–11 | | 8/1–9/15 | 8/1–13, 8/28–9/12 | | 7/17–9/7 | 7/30–8/13, 8/28–9/7 | | 7/20–8/5 | 7/30–8/5 | |
| 3/15–4/15 | 3/15–19, 4/3–15 | | 4/15–30 | 4/15–17 | | 5/15–6/15 | 5/15–17, 6/1–15 | | 6/1–30 | 6/1–15 | |
| 3/23–4/6 | 3/23–4/2 | | 4/21–5/9 | 4/21–5/2 | | 5/15–6/15 | 5/18–31 | | 6/1–30 | 6/16–30 | |
| 2/7–3/15 | 2/7–18, 3/4–15 | | 3/15–4/15 | 3/15–19, 4/3–15 | | 5/1–31 | 5/3–17 | | 5/15–31 | 5/15–17 | |
| 3/7–20 | 3/7–19 | | 4/7–30 | 4/7–17 | | 5/15–31 | 5/15–17 | | 6/1–15 | 6/1–15 | |
| 1/20–2/15 | 1/20–2/1 | | 3/15–31 | 3/20–31 | | 4/7–30 | 4/18–30 | | 5/10–31 | 5/18–31 | |
| 9/1–10/15 | 9/13–26, 10/12–15 | | 8/1–20 | 8/14–20 | | 7/1–8/15 | 7/16–29, 8/14–15 | | — | — | |
| 3/15–4/7 | 3/15–19, 4/3–7 | | 4/15–5/7 | 4/15–17, 5/3–7 | | 5/15–6/30 | 5/15–17, 6/1–15 | | 6/1–30 | 6/1–15 | |
| 2/15–28 | 2/15–18 | | 3/1–20 | 3/4–19 | | 4/7–30 | 4/7–17 | | 5/15–6/10 | 5/15–17, 6/1–10 | |
| 10/15–12/7 | 10/26–11/10, 11/25–12/7 | | 9/15–10/20 | 9/27–10/11 | | 8/11–9/15 | 8/11–13, 8/28–9/12 | | 8/5–30 | 8/5–13, 8/28–30 | |

# Time Corrections

■ Astronomical data for Boston is given on **pages 90, 94–95,** and **114–140.** Use the Key Letter shown to the right of each time on those pages with this table to find the number of minutes that you must add to or subtract from Boston time to get the correct time for your city. (Because of complex calculations for different locales, times are approximate.) For more information on the use of Key Letters and this table, **see How to Use This Almanac, page 110.**

**Get times simply and specifically:** Purchase astronomical times calculated for your zip code and presented like a Left-Hand Calendar page at **MyLocalAlmanac.com.**

**TIME ZONES:** Codes represent *standard time.* Atlantic is −1, Eastern is 0, Central is 1, Mountain is 2, Pacific is 3, Alaska is 4, and Hawaii-Aleutian is 5.

| State | City | North Latitude ° | ′ | West Longitude ° | ′ | Time Zone Code | A (min.) | B (min.) | C (min.) | D (min.) | E (min.) |
|---|---|---|---|---|---|---|---|---|---|---|---|
| AK | Anchorage | 61 | 10 | 149 | 59 | 4 | −46 | +27 | +71 | +122 | +171 |
| AK | Cordova | 60 | 33 | 145 | 45 | 4 | −55 | +13 | +55 | +103 | +149 |
| AK | Fairbanks | 64 | 48 | 147 | 51 | 4 | −127 | +2 | +61 | +131 | +205 |
| AK | Juneau | 58 | 18 | 134 | 25 | 4 | −76 | −23 | +10 | +49 | +86 |
| AK | Ketchikan | 55 | 21 | 131 | 39 | 4 | −62 | −25 | 0 | +29 | +56 |
| AK | Kodiak | 57 | 47 | 152 | 24 | 4 | 0 | +49 | +82 | +120 | +154 |
| AL | Birmingham | 33 | 31 | 86 | 49 | 1 | +30 | +15 | +3 | −10 | −20 |
| AL | Decatur | 34 | 36 | 86 | 59 | 1 | +27 | +14 | +4 | −7 | −17 |
| AL | Mobile | 30 | 42 | 88 | 3 | 1 | +42 | +23 | +8 | −8 | −22 |
| AL | Montgomery | 32 | 23 | 86 | 19 | 1 | +31 | +14 | +1 | −13 | −25 |
| AR | Fort Smith | 35 | 23 | 94 | 25 | 1 | +55 | +43 | +33 | +22 | +14 |
| AR | Little Rock | 34 | 45 | 92 | 17 | 1 | +48 | +35 | +25 | +13 | +4 |
| AR | Texarkana | 33 | 26 | 94 | 3 | 1 | +59 | +44 | +32 | +18 | +8 |
| AZ | Flagstaff | 35 | 12 | 111 | 39 | 2 | +64 | +52 | +42 | +31 | +22 |
| AZ | Phoenix | 33 | 27 | 112 | 4 | 2 | +71 | +56 | +44 | +30 | +20 |
| AZ | Tucson | 32 | 13 | 110 | 58 | 2 | +70 | +53 | +40 | +24 | +12 |
| AZ | Yuma | 32 | 43 | 114 | 37 | 2 | +83 | +67 | +54 | +40 | +28 |
| CA | Bakersfield | 35 | 23 | 119 | 1 | 3 | +33 | +21 | +12 | +1 | −7 |
| CA | Barstow | 34 | 54 | 117 | 1 | 3 | +27 | +14 | +4 | −7 | −16 |
| CA | Fresno | 36 | 44 | 119 | 47 | 3 | +32 | +22 | +15 | +6 | 0 |
| CA | Los Angeles–Pasadena– Santa Monica | 34 | 3 | 118 | 14 | 3 | +34 | +20 | +9 | −3 | −13 |
| CA | Palm Springs | 33 | 49 | 116 | 32 | 3 | +28 | +13 | +1 | −12 | −22 |
| CA | Redding | 40 | 35 | 122 | 24 | 3 | +31 | +27 | +25 | +22 | +19 |
| CA | Sacramento | 38 | 35 | 121 | 30 | 3 | +34 | +27 | +21 | +15 | +10 |
| CA | San Diego | 32 | 43 | 117 | 9 | 3 | +33 | +17 | +4 | −9 | −21 |
| CA | San Francisco–Oakland– San Jose | 37 | 47 | 122 | 25 | 3 | +40 | +31 | +25 | +18 | +12 |
| CO | Craig | 40 | 31 | 107 | 33 | 2 | +32 | +28 | +25 | +22 | +20 |
| CO | Denver–Boulder | 39 | 44 | 104 | 59 | 2 | +24 | +19 | +15 | +11 | +7 |
| CO | Grand Junction | 39 | 4 | 108 | 33 | 2 | +40 | +34 | +29 | +24 | +20 |
| CO | Pueblo | 38 | 16 | 104 | 37 | 2 | +27 | +20 | +14 | +7 | +2 |
| CO | Trinidad | 37 | 10 | 104 | 31 | 2 | +30 | +21 | +13 | +5 | 0 |
| CT | Bridgeport | 41 | 11 | 73 | 11 | 0 | +12 | +10 | +8 | +6 | +4 |
| CT | Hartford–New Britain | 41 | 46 | 72 | 41 | 0 | +8 | +7 | +6 | +5 | +4 |
| CT | New Haven | 41 | 18 | 72 | 56 | 0 | +11 | +8 | +7 | +5 | +4 |
| CT | New London | 41 | 22 | 72 | 6 | 0 | +7 | +5 | +4 | +2 | +1 |
| CT | Norwalk–Stamford | 41 | 7 | 73 | 22 | 0 | +13 | +10 | +9 | +7 | +5 |
| CT | Waterbury–Meriden | 41 | 33 | 73 | 3 | 0 | +10 | +9 | +7 | +6 | +5 |
| DC | Washington | 38 | 54 | 77 | 1 | 0 | +35 | +28 | +23 | +18 | +13 |
| DE | Wilmington | 39 | 45 | 75 | 33 | 0 | +26 | +21 | +18 | +13 | +10 |

| State | City | North Latitude ° | ' | West Longitude ° | ' | Time Zone Code | A (min.) | B (min.) | C (min.) | D (min.) | E (min.) |
|---|---|---|---|---|---|---|---|---|---|---|---|
| FL | Fort Myers | 26 | 38 | 81 | 52 | 0 | +87 | +63 | +44 | +21 | +4 |
| FL | Jacksonville | 30 | 20 | 81 | 40 | 0 | +77 | +58 | +43 | +25 | +11 |
| FL | Miami | 25 | 47 | 80 | 12 | 0 | +88 | +57 | +37 | +14 | −3 |
| FL | Orlando | 28 | 32 | 81 | 22 | 0 | +80 | +59 | +42 | +22 | +6 |
| FL | Pensacola | 30 | 25 | 87 | 13 | 1 | +39 | +20 | +5 | −12 | −26 |
| FL | St. Petersburg | 27 | 46 | 82 | 39 | 0 | +87 | +65 | +47 | +26 | +10 |
| FL | Tallahassee | 30 | 27 | 84 | 17 | 0 | +87 | +68 | +53 | +35 | +22 |
| FL | Tampa | 27 | 57 | 82 | 27 | 0 | +86 | +64 | +46 | +25 | +9 |
| FL | West Palm Beach | 26 | 43 | 80 | 3 | 0 | +79 | +55 | +36 | +14 | −2 |
| GA | Atlanta | 33 | 45 | 84 | 24 | 0 | +79 | +65 | +53 | +40 | +30 |
| GA | Augusta | 33 | 28 | 81 | 58 | 0 | +70 | +55 | +44 | +30 | +19 |
| GA | Macon | 32 | 50 | 83 | 38 | 0 | +79 | +63 | +50 | +36 | +24 |
| GA | Savannah | 32 | 5 | 81 | 6 | 0 | +70 | +54 | +40 | +25 | +13 |
| HI | Hilo | 19 | 44 | 155 | 5 | 5 | +94 | +62 | +37 | +7 | −15 |
| HI | Honolulu | 21 | 18 | 157 | 52 | 5 | +102 | +72 | +48 | +19 | −1 |
| HI | Lanai City | 20 | 50 | 156 | 55 | 5 | +99 | +69 | +44 | +15 | −6 |
| HI | Lihue | 21 | 59 | 159 | 23 | 5 | +107 | +77 | +54 | +26 | +5 |
| IA | Davenport | 41 | 32 | 90 | 35 | 1 | +20 | +19 | +17 | +16 | +15 |
| IA | Des Moines | 41 | 35 | 93 | 37 | 1 | +32 | +31 | +30 | +28 | +27 |
| IA | Dubuque | 42 | 30 | 90 | 41 | 1 | +17 | +18 | +18 | +18 | +18 |
| IA | Waterloo | 42 | 30 | 92 | 20 | 1 | +24 | +24 | +24 | +25 | +25 |
| ID | Boise | 43 | 37 | 116 | 12 | 2 | +55 | +58 | +60 | +62 | +64 |
| ID | Lewiston | 46 | 25 | 117 | 1 | 3 | −12 | −3 | +2 | +10 | +17 |
| ID | Pocatello | 42 | 52 | 112 | 27 | 2 | +43 | +44 | +45 | +46 | +46 |
| IL | Cairo | 37 | 0 | 89 | 11 | 1 | +29 | +20 | +12 | +4 | −2 |
| IL | Chicago–Oak Park | 41 | 52 | 87 | 38 | 1 | +7 | +6 | +6 | +5 | +4 |
| IL | Danville | 40 | 8 | 87 | 37 | 1 | +13 | +9 | +6 | +2 | 0 |
| IL | Decatur | 39 | 51 | 88 | 57 | 1 | +19 | +15 | +11 | +7 | +4 |
| IL | Peoria | 40 | 42 | 89 | 36 | 1 | +19 | +16 | +14 | +11 | +9 |
| IL | Springfield | 39 | 48 | 89 | 39 | 1 | +22 | +18 | +14 | +10 | +6 |
| IN | Fort Wayne | 41 | 4 | 85 | 9 | 0 | +60 | +58 | +56 | +54 | +52 |
| IN | Gary | 41 | 36 | 87 | 20 | 1 | +7 | +6 | +4 | +3 | +2 |
| IN | Indianapolis | 39 | 46 | 86 | 10 | 0 | +69 | +64 | +60 | +56 | +52 |
| IN | Muncie | 40 | 12 | 85 | 23 | 0 | +64 | +60 | +57 | +53 | +50 |
| IN | South Bend | 41 | 41 | 86 | 15 | 0 | +62 | +61 | +60 | +59 | +58 |
| IN | Terre Haute | 39 | 28 | 87 | 24 | 0 | +74 | +69 | +65 | +60 | +56 |
| KS | Fort Scott | 37 | 50 | 94 | 42 | 1 | +49 | +41 | +34 | +27 | +21 |
| KS | Liberal | 37 | 3 | 100 | 55 | 1 | +76 | +66 | +59 | +51 | +44 |
| KS | Oakley | 39 | 8 | 100 | 51 | 1 | +69 | +63 | +59 | +53 | +49 |
| KS | Salina | 38 | 50 | 97 | 37 | 1 | +57 | +51 | +46 | +40 | +35 |
| KS | Topeka | 39 | 3 | 95 | 40 | 1 | +49 | +43 | +38 | +32 | +28 |
| KS | Wichita | 37 | 42 | 97 | 20 | 1 | +60 | +51 | +45 | +37 | +31 |
| KY | Lexington–Frankfort | 38 | 3 | 84 | 30 | 0 | +67 | +59 | +53 | +46 | +41 |
| KY | Louisville | 38 | 15 | 85 | 46 | 0 | +72 | +64 | +58 | +52 | +46 |
| LA | Alexandria | 31 | 18 | 92 | 27 | 1 | +58 | +40 | +26 | +9 | −3 |
| LA | Baton Rouge | 30 | 27 | 91 | 11 | 1 | +55 | +36 | +21 | +3 | −10 |
| LA | Lake Charles | 30 | 14 | 93 | 13 | 1 | +64 | +44 | +29 | +11 | −2 |
| LA | Monroe | 32 | 30 | 92 | 7 | 1 | +53 | +37 | +24 | +9 | −1 |
| LA | New Orleans | 29 | 57 | 90 | 4 | 1 | +52 | +32 | +16 | −1 | −15 |
| LA | Shreveport | 32 | 31 | 93 | 45 | 1 | +60 | +44 | +31 | +16 | +4 |
| MA | Brockton | 42 | 5 | 71 | 1 | 0 | 0 | 0 | 0 | 0 | −1 |
| MA | Fall River–New Bedford | 41 | 42 | 71 | 9 | 0 | +2 | +1 | 0 | 0 | −1 |
| MA | Lawrence–Lowell | 42 | 42 | 71 | 10 | 0 | 0 | 0 | 0 | 0 | +1 |
| MA | Pittsfield | 42 | 27 | 73 | 15 | 0 | +8 | +8 | +8 | +8 | +8 |
| MA | Springfield–Holyoke | 42 | 6 | 72 | 36 | 0 | +6 | +6 | +6 | +5 | +5 |
| MA | Worcester | 42 | 16 | 71 | 48 | 0 | +3 | +2 | +2 | +2 | +2 |

# Time Corrections

| State | City | North Latitude ° | ' | West Longitude ° | ' | Time Zone Code | A (min.) | B (min.) | C (min.) | D (min.) | E (min.) |
|---|---|---|---|---|---|---|---|---|---|---|---|
| MD | Baltimore | 39 | 17 | 76 | 37 | 0 | +32 | +26 | +22 | +17 | +13 |
| MD | Hagerstown | 39 | 39 | 77 | 43 | 0 | +35 | +30 | +26 | +22 | +18 |
| MD | Salisbury | 38 | 22 | 75 | 36 | 0 | +31 | +23 | +18 | +11 | +6 |
| ME | Augusta | 44 | 19 | 69 | 46 | 0 | −12 | −8 | −5 | −1 | 0 |
| ME | Bangor | 44 | 48 | 68 | 46 | 0 | −18 | −13 | −9 | −5 | −1 |
| ME | Eastport | 44 | 54 | 67 | 0 | 0 | −26 | −20 | −16 | −11 | −8 |
| ME | Ellsworth | 44 | 33 | 68 | 25 | 0 | −18 | −14 | −10 | −6 | −3 |
| ME | Portland | 43 | 40 | 70 | 15 | 0 | −8 | −5 | −3 | −1 | 0 |
| ME | Presque Isle | 46 | 41 | 68 | 1 | 0 | −29 | −19 | −12 | −4 | +2 |
| MI | Cheboygan | 45 | 39 | 84 | 29 | 0 | +40 | +47 | +53 | +59 | +64 |
| MI | Detroit–Dearborn | 42 | 20 | 83 | 3 | 0 | +47 | +47 | +47 | +47 | +47 |
| MI | Flint | 43 | 1 | 83 | 41 | 0 | +47 | +49 | +50 | +51 | +52 |
| MI | Ironwood | 46 | 27 | 90 | 9 | 1 | 0 | +9 | +15 | +23 | +29 |
| MI | Jackson | 42 | 15 | 84 | 24 | 0 | +53 | +53 | +53 | +52 | +52 |
| MI | Kalamazoo | 42 | 17 | 85 | 35 | 0 | +58 | +57 | +57 | +57 | +57 |
| MI | Lansing | 42 | 44 | 84 | 33 | 0 | +52 | +53 | +53 | +54 | +54 |
| MI | St. Joseph | 42 | 5 | 86 | 26 | 0 | +61 | +61 | +60 | +60 | +59 |
| MI | Traverse City | 44 | 46 | 85 | 38 | 0 | +49 | +54 | +57 | +62 | +65 |
| MN | Albert Lea | 43 | 39 | 93 | 22 | 1 | +24 | +26 | +28 | +31 | +33 |
| MN | Bemidji | 47 | 28 | 94 | 53 | 1 | +14 | +26 | +34 | +44 | +52 |
| MN | Duluth | 46 | 47 | 92 | 6 | 1 | +6 | +16 | +23 | +31 | +38 |
| MN | Minneapolis–St. Paul | 44 | 59 | 93 | 16 | 1 | +18 | +24 | +28 | +33 | +37 |
| MN | Ortonville | 45 | 19 | 96 | 27 | 1 | +30 | +36 | +40 | +46 | +51 |
| MO | Jefferson City | 38 | 34 | 92 | 10 | 1 | +36 | +29 | +24 | +18 | +13 |
| MO | Joplin | 37 | 6 | 94 | 30 | 1 | +50 | +41 | +33 | +25 | +18 |
| MO | Kansas City | 39 | 1 | 94 | 20 | 1 | +44 | +37 | +33 | +27 | +23 |
| MO | Poplar Bluff | 36 | 46 | 90 | 24 | 1 | +35 | +25 | +17 | +8 | +1 |
| MO | St. Joseph | 39 | 46 | 94 | 50 | 1 | +43 | +38 | +35 | +30 | +27 |
| MO | St. Louis | 38 | 37 | 90 | 12 | 1 | +28 | +21 | +16 | +10 | +5 |
| MO | Springfield | 37 | 13 | 93 | 18 | 1 | +45 | +36 | +29 | +20 | +14 |
| MS | Biloxi | 30 | 24 | 88 | 53 | 1 | +46 | +27 | +11 | −5 | −19 |
| MS | Jackson | 32 | 18 | 90 | 11 | 1 | +46 | +30 | +17 | +1 | −10 |
| MS | Meridian | 32 | 22 | 88 | 42 | 1 | +40 | +24 | +11 | −4 | −15 |
| MS | Tupelo | 34 | 16 | 88 | 34 | 1 | +35 | +21 | +10 | −2 | −11 |
| MT | Billings | 45 | 47 | 108 | 30 | 2 | +16 | +23 | +29 | +35 | +40 |
| MT | Butte | 46 | 1 | 112 | 32 | 2 | +31 | +39 | +45 | +52 | +57 |
| MT | Glasgow | 48 | 12 | 106 | 38 | 2 | −1 | +11 | +21 | +32 | +42 |
| MT | Great Falls | 47 | 30 | 111 | 17 | 2 | +20 | +31 | +39 | +49 | +58 |
| MT | Helena | 46 | 36 | 112 | 2 | 2 | +27 | +36 | +43 | +51 | +57 |
| MT | Miles City | 46 | 25 | 105 | 51 | 2 | +3 | +11 | +18 | +26 | +32 |
| NC | Asheville | 35 | 36 | 82 | 33 | 0 | +67 | +55 | +46 | +35 | +27 |
| NC | Charlotte | 35 | 14 | 80 | 51 | 0 | +61 | +49 | +39 | +28 | +19 |
| NC | Durham | 36 | 0 | 78 | 55 | 0 | +51 | +40 | +31 | +21 | +13 |
| NC | Greensboro | 36 | 4 | 79 | 47 | 0 | +54 | +43 | +35 | +25 | +17 |
| NC | Raleigh | 35 | 47 | 78 | 38 | 0 | +51 | +39 | +30 | +20 | +12 |
| NC | Wilmington | 34 | 14 | 77 | 55 | 0 | +52 | +38 | +27 | +15 | +5 |
| ND | Bismarck | 46 | 48 | 100 | 47 | 1 | +41 | +50 | +58 | +66 | +73 |
| ND | Fargo | 46 | 53 | 96 | 47 | 1 | +24 | +34 | +42 | +50 | +57 |
| ND | Grand Forks | 47 | 55 | 97 | 3 | 1 | +21 | +33 | +43 | +53 | +62 |
| ND | Minot | 48 | 14 | 101 | 18 | 1 | +36 | +50 | +59 | +71 | +81 |
| ND | Williston | 48 | 9 | 103 | 37 | 1 | +46 | +59 | +69 | +80 | +90 |
| NE | Grand Island | 40 | 55 | 98 | 21 | 1 | +53 | +51 | +49 | +46 | +44 |
| NE | Lincoln | 40 | 49 | 96 | 41 | 1 | +47 | +44 | +42 | +39 | +37 |
| NE | North Platte | 41 | 8 | 100 | 46 | 1 | +62 | +60 | +58 | +56 | +54 |
| NE | Omaha | 41 | 16 | 95 | 56 | 1 | +43 | +40 | +39 | +37 | +36 |
| NH | Berlin | 44 | 28 | 71 | 11 | 0 | −7 | −3 | 0 | +3 | +7 |
| NH | Keene | 42 | 56 | 72 | 17 | 0 | +2 | +3 | +4 | +5 | +6 |

*Get local rise, set, and tide times at* Almanac.com/Astronomy.

| State | City | North Latitude ° | North Latitude ' | West Longitude ° | West Longitude ' | Time Zone Code | A (min.) | B (min.) | C (min.) | D (min.) | E (min.) |
|---|---|---|---|---|---|---|---|---|---|---|---|
| NH | Manchester–Concord | 42 | 59 | 71 | 28 | 0 | 0 | 0 | +1 | +2 | +3 |
| NH | Portsmouth | 43 | 5 | 70 | 45 | 0 | −4 | −2 | −1 | 0 | 0 |
| NJ | Atlantic City | 39 | 22 | 74 | 26 | 0 | +23 | +17 | +13 | +8 | +4 |
| NJ | Camden | 39 | 57 | 75 | 7 | 0 | +24 | +19 | +16 | +12 | +9 |
| NJ | Cape May | 38 | 56 | 74 | 56 | 0 | +26 | +20 | +15 | +9 | +5 |
| NJ | Newark–East Orange | 40 | 44 | 74 | 10 | 0 | +17 | +14 | +12 | +9 | +7 |
| NJ | Paterson | 40 | 55 | 74 | 10 | 0 | +17 | +14 | +12 | +9 | +7 |
| NJ | Trenton | 40 | 13 | 74 | 46 | 0 | +21 | +17 | +14 | +11 | +8 |
| NM | Albuquerque | 35 | 5 | 106 | 39 | 2 | +45 | +32 | +22 | +11 | +2 |
| NM | Gallup | 35 | 32 | 108 | 45 | 2 | +52 | +40 | +31 | +20 | +11 |
| NM | Las Cruces | 32 | 19 | 106 | 47 | 2 | +53 | +36 | +23 | +8 | −3 |
| NM | Roswell | 33 | 24 | 104 | 32 | 2 | +41 | +26 | +14 | 0 | −10 |
| NM | Santa Fe | 35 | 41 | 105 | 56 | 2 | +40 | +28 | +19 | +9 | 0 |
| NV | Carson City–Reno | 39 | 10 | 119 | 46 | 3 | +25 | +19 | +14 | +9 | +5 |
| NV | Elko | 40 | 50 | 115 | 46 | 3 | +3 | 0 | −1 | −3 | −5 |
| NV | Las Vegas | 36 | 10 | 115 | 9 | 3 | +16 | +4 | −3 | −13 | −20 |
| NY | Albany | 42 | 39 | 73 | 45 | 0 | +9 | +10 | +10 | +11 | +11 |
| NY | Binghamton | 42 | 6 | 75 | 55 | 0 | +20 | +19 | +19 | +18 | +18 |
| NY | Buffalo | 42 | 53 | 78 | 52 | 0 | +29 | +30 | +30 | +31 | +32 |
| NY | New York | 40 | 45 | 74 | 0 | 0 | +17 | +14 | +11 | +9 | +6 |
| NY | Ogdensburg | 44 | 42 | 75 | 30 | 0 | +8 | +13 | +17 | +21 | +25 |
| NY | Syracuse | 43 | 3 | 76 | 9 | 0 | +17 | +19 | +20 | +21 | +22 |
| OH | Akron | 41 | 5 | 81 | 31 | 0 | +46 | +43 | +41 | +39 | +37 |
| OH | Canton | 40 | 48 | 81 | 23 | 0 | +46 | +43 | +41 | +38 | +36 |
| OH | Cincinnati–Hamilton | 39 | 6 | 84 | 31 | 0 | +64 | +58 | +53 | +48 | +44 |
| OH | Cleveland–Lakewood | 41 | 30 | 81 | 42 | 0 | +45 | +43 | +42 | +40 | +39 |
| OH | Columbus | 39 | 57 | 83 | 1 | 0 | +55 | +51 | +47 | +43 | +40 |
| OH | Dayton | 39 | 45 | 84 | 10 | 0 | +61 | +56 | +52 | +48 | +44 |
| OH | Toledo | 41 | 39 | 83 | 33 | 0 | +52 | +50 | +49 | +48 | +47 |
| OH | Youngstown | 41 | 6 | 80 | 39 | 0 | +42 | +40 | +38 | +36 | +34 |
| OK | Oklahoma City | 35 | 28 | 97 | 31 | 1 | +67 | +55 | +46 | +35 | +26 |
| OK | Tulsa | 36 | 9 | 95 | 60 | 1 | +59 | +48 | +40 | +30 | +22 |
| OR | Eugene | 44 | 3 | 123 | 6 | 3 | +21 | +24 | +27 | +30 | +33 |
| OR | Pendleton | 45 | 40 | 118 | 47 | 3 | −1 | +4 | +10 | +16 | +21 |
| OR | Portland | 45 | 31 | 122 | 41 | 3 | +14 | +20 | +25 | +31 | +36 |
| OR | Salem | 44 | 57 | 123 | 1 | 3 | +17 | +23 | +27 | +31 | +35 |
| PA | Allentown–Bethlehem | 40 | 36 | 75 | 28 | 0 | +23 | +20 | +17 | +14 | +12 |
| PA | Erie | 42 | 7 | 80 | 5 | 0 | +36 | +36 | +35 | +35 | +35 |
| PA | Harrisburg | 40 | 16 | 76 | 53 | 0 | +30 | +26 | +23 | +19 | +16 |
| PA | Lancaster | 40 | 2 | 76 | 18 | 0 | +28 | +24 | +20 | +17 | +13 |
| PA | Philadelphia–Chester | 39 | 57 | 75 | 9 | 0 | +24 | +19 | +16 | +12 | +9 |
| PA | Pittsburgh–McKeesport | 40 | 26 | 80 | 0 | 0 | +42 | +38 | +35 | +32 | +29 |
| PA | Reading | 40 | 20 | 75 | 56 | 0 | +26 | +22 | +19 | +16 | +13 |
| PA | Scranton–Wilkes-Barre | 41 | 25 | 75 | 40 | 0 | +21 | +19 | +18 | +16 | +15 |
| PA | York | 39 | 58 | 76 | 43 | 0 | +30 | +26 | +22 | +18 | +15 |
| RI | Providence | 41 | 50 | 71 | 25 | 0 | +3 | +2 | +1 | 0 | 0 |
| SC | Charleston | 32 | 47 | 79 | 56 | 0 | +64 | +48 | +36 | +21 | +10 |
| SC | Columbia | 34 | 0 | 81 | 2 | 0 | +65 | +51 | +40 | +27 | +17 |
| SC | Spartanburg | 34 | 56 | 81 | 57 | 0 | +66 | +53 | +43 | +32 | +23 |
| SD | Aberdeen | 45 | 28 | 98 | 29 | 1 | +37 | +44 | +49 | +54 | +59 |
| SD | Pierre | 44 | 22 | 100 | 21 | 1 | +49 | +53 | +56 | +60 | +63 |
| SD | Rapid City | 44 | 5 | 103 | 14 | 2 | +2 | +5 | +8 | +11 | +13 |
| SD | Sioux Falls | 43 | 33 | 96 | 44 | 1 | +38 | +40 | +42 | +44 | +46 |
| TN | Chattanooga | 35 | 3 | 85 | 19 | 0 | +79 | +67 | +57 | +45 | +36 |
| TN | Knoxville | 35 | 58 | 83 | 55 | 0 | +71 | +60 | +51 | +41 | +33 |
| TN | Memphis | 35 | 9 | 90 | 3 | 1 | +38 | +26 | +16 | +5 | −3 |
| TN | Nashville | 36 | 10 | 86 | 47 | 1 | +22 | +11 | +3 | −6 | −14 |

# Time Corrections

| State/Province | City | North Latitude ° | North Latitude ′ | West Longitude ° | West Longitude ′ | Time Zone Code | A (min.) | B (min.) | C (min.) | D (min.) | E (min.) |
|---|---|---|---|---|---|---|---|---|---|---|---|
| TX | Amarillo | 35 | 12 | 101 | 50 | 1 | +85 | +73 | +63 | +52 | +43 |
| TX | Austin | 30 | 16 | 97 | 45 | 1 | +82 | +62 | +47 | +29 | +15 |
| TX | Beaumont | 30 | 5 | 94 | 6 | 1 | +67 | +48 | +32 | +14 | 0 |
| TX | Brownsville | 25 | 54 | 97 | 30 | 1 | +91 | +66 | +46 | +23 | +5 |
| TX | Corpus Christi | 27 | 48 | 97 | 24 | 1 | +86 | +64 | +46 | +25 | +9 |
| TX | Dallas–Fort Worth | 32 | 47 | 96 | 48 | 1 | +71 | +55 | +43 | +28 | +17 |
| TX | El Paso | 31 | 45 | 106 | 29 | 2 | +53 | +35 | +22 | +6 | −6 |
| TX | Galveston | 29 | 18 | 94 | 48 | 1 | +72 | +52 | +35 | +16 | +1 |
| TX | Houston | 29 | 45 | 95 | 22 | 1 | +73 | +53 | +37 | +19 | +5 |
| TX | McAllen | 26 | 12 | 98 | 14 | 1 | +93 | +69 | +49 | +26 | +9 |
| TX | San Antonio | 29 | 25 | 98 | 30 | 1 | +87 | +66 | +50 | +31 | +16 |
| UT | Kanab | 37 | 3 | 112 | 32 | 2 | +62 | +53 | +46 | +37 | +30 |
| UT | Moab | 38 | 35 | 109 | 33 | 2 | +46 | +39 | +33 | +27 | +22 |
| UT | Ogden | 41 | 13 | 111 | 58 | 2 | +47 | +45 | +43 | +41 | +40 |
| UT | Salt Lake City | 40 | 45 | 111 | 53 | 2 | +48 | +45 | +43 | +40 | +38 |
| UT | Vernal | 40 | 27 | 109 | 32 | 2 | +40 | +36 | +33 | +30 | +28 |
| VA | Charlottesville | 38 | 2 | 78 | 30 | 0 | +43 | +35 | +29 | +22 | +17 |
| VA | Danville | 36 | 36 | 79 | 23 | 0 | +51 | +41 | +33 | +24 | +17 |
| VA | Norfolk | 36 | 51 | 76 | 17 | 0 | +38 | +28 | +21 | +12 | +5 |
| VA | Richmond | 37 | 32 | 77 | 26 | 0 | +41 | +32 | +25 | +17 | +11 |
| VA | Roanoke | 37 | 16 | 79 | 57 | 0 | +51 | +42 | +35 | +27 | +21 |
| VA | Winchester | 39 | 11 | 78 | 10 | 0 | +38 | +33 | +28 | +23 | +19 |
| VT | Brattleboro | 42 | 51 | 72 | 34 | 0 | +4 | +5 | +5 | +6 | +7 |
| VT | Burlington | 44 | 29 | 73 | 13 | 0 | 0 | +4 | +8 | +12 | +15 |
| VT | Rutland | 43 | 37 | 72 | 58 | 0 | +2 | +5 | +7 | +9 | +11 |
| VT | St. Johnsbury | 44 | 25 | 72 | 1 | 0 | −4 | 0 | +3 | +7 | +10 |
| WA | Bellingham | 48 | 45 | 122 | 29 | 3 | 0 | +13 | +24 | +37 | +47 |
| WA | Seattle–Tacoma–Olympia | 47 | 37 | 122 | 20 | 3 | +3 | +15 | +24 | +34 | +42 |
| WA | Spokane | 47 | 40 | 117 | 24 | 3 | −16 | −4 | +4 | +14 | +23 |
| WA | Walla Walla | 46 | 4 | 118 | 20 | 3 | −5 | +2 | +8 | +15 | +21 |
| WI | Eau Claire | 44 | 49 | 91 | 30 | 1 | +12 | +17 | +21 | +25 | +29 |
| WI | Green Bay | 44 | 31 | 88 | 0 | 1 | 0 | +3 | +7 | +11 | +14 |
| WI | La Crosse | 43 | 48 | 91 | 15 | 1 | +15 | +18 | +20 | +22 | +25 |
| WI | Madison | 43 | 4 | 89 | 23 | 1 | +10 | +11 | +12 | +14 | +15 |
| WI | Milwaukee | 43 | 2 | 87 | 54 | 1 | +4 | +6 | +7 | +8 | +9 |
| WI | Oshkosh | 44 | 1 | 88 | 33 | 1 | +3 | +6 | +9 | +12 | +15 |
| WI | Wausau | 44 | 58 | 89 | 38 | 1 | +4 | +9 | +13 | +18 | +22 |
| WV | Charleston | 38 | 21 | 81 | 38 | 0 | +55 | +48 | +42 | +35 | +30 |
| WV | Parkersburg | 39 | 16 | 81 | 34 | 0 | +52 | +46 | +42 | +36 | +32 |
| WY | Casper | 42 | 51 | 106 | 19 | 2 | +19 | +19 | +20 | +21 | +22 |
| WY | Cheyenne | 41 | 8 | 104 | 49 | 2 | +19 | +16 | +14 | +12 | +11 |
| WY | Sheridan | 44 | 48 | 106 | 58 | 2 | +14 | +19 | +23 | +27 | +31 |
| **CANADA** | | | | | | | | | | | |
| AB | Calgary | 51 | 5 | 114 | 5 | 2 | +13 | +35 | +50 | +68 | +84 |
| AB | Edmonton | 53 | 34 | 113 | 25 | 2 | −3 | +26 | +47 | +72 | +93 |
| BC | Vancouver | 49 | 13 | 123 | 6 | 3 | 0 | +15 | +26 | +40 | +52 |
| MB | Winnipeg | 49 | 53 | 97 | 10 | 1 | +12 | +30 | +43 | +58 | +71 |
| NB | Saint John | 45 | 16 | 66 | 3 | −1 | +28 | +34 | +39 | +44 | +49 |
| NS | Halifax | 44 | 38 | 63 | 35 | −1 | +21 | +26 | +29 | +33 | +37 |
| NS | Sydney | 46 | 10 | 60 | 10 | −1 | +1 | +9 | +15 | +23 | +28 |
| ON | Ottawa | 45 | 25 | 75 | 43 | 0 | +6 | +13 | +18 | +23 | +28 |
| ON | Peterborough | 44 | 18 | 78 | 19 | 0 | +21 | +25 | +28 | +32 | +35 |
| ON | Thunder Bay | 48 | 27 | 89 | 12 | 0 | +47 | +61 | +71 | +83 | +93 |
| ON | Toronto | 43 | 39 | 79 | 23 | 0 | +28 | +30 | +32 | +35 | +37 |
| QC | Montreal | 45 | 28 | 73 | 39 | 0 | −1 | +4 | +9 | +15 | +20 |
| SK | Saskatoon | 52 | 10 | 106 | 40 | 1 | +37 | +63 | +80 | +101 | +119 |

*Get local rise, set, and tide times at* Almanac.com/Astronomy.

# Tide Corrections

■ Many factors affect the times and heights of the tides: the shoreline, the time of the Moon's southing (crossing the meridian), and the Moon's phase. The High Tide column on the **Left-Hand Calendar Pages, 114–140,** lists the times of high tide at Commonwealth Pier in Boston Harbor. The heights of some of these tides, reckoned from Mean Lower Low Water, are given on the **Right-Hand Calendar Pages, 115–141.** Use the table below to calculate the approximate times and heights of high tide at the places shown. Apply the time difference to the times of high tide at Boston and the height difference to the heights at Boston. A tide calculator can be found at **Almanac.com/Tides.**

**E X A M P L E :**

The conversion of the times and heights of the tides at Boston to those at Cape Fear, North Carolina, is given below:

| | |
|---|---|
| High tide at Boston | 11:45 A.M. |
| Correction for Cape Fear | – 3 55 |
| High tide at Cape Fear | 7:50 A.M. |
| | |
| Tide height at Boston | 11.6 ft. |
| Correction for Cape Fear | – 5.0 ft. |
| Tide height at Cape Fear | 6.6 ft. |

Estimations derived from this table are *not* meant to be used for navigation. *The Old Farmer's Almanac* accepts no responsibility for errors or any consequences ensuing from the use of this table.

| Tidal Site | Difference: Time (h. m.) | Height (ft.) |
|---|---|---|
| **Canada** | | |
| Alberton, PE | *–5 45 | –7.5 |
| Charlottetown, PE | *–0 45 | –3.5 |
| Halifax, NS. | –3 23 | –4.5 |
| North Sydney, NS | –3 15 | –6.5 |
| Saint John, NB | +0 30 | +15.0 |
| St. John's, NL | –4 00 | –6.5 |
| Yarmouth, NS | –0 40 | +3.0 |
| **Maine** | | |
| Bar Harbor | –0 34 | +0.9 |
| Belfast | –0 20 | +0.4 |
| Boothbay Harbor | –0 18 | –0.8 |
| Chebeague Island | –0 16 | –0.6 |
| Eastport | –0 28 | +8.4 |
| Kennebunkport | +0 04 | –1.0 |
| Machias | –0 28 | +2.8 |
| Monhegan Island | –0 25 | –0.8 |
| Old Orchard | 0 00 | –0.8 |
| Portland | –0 12 | –0.6 |
| Rockland | –0 28 | +0.1 |
| Stonington | –0 30 | +0.1 |
| York | –0 09 | –1.0 |
| **New Hampshire** | | |
| Hampton | +0 02 | –1.3 |
| Portsmouth | +0 11 | –1.5 |
| Rye Beach | –0 09 | –0.9 |
| **Massachusetts** | | |
| Annisquam | –0 02 | –1.1 |
| Beverly Farms | 0 00 | –0.5 |
| Boston | 0 00 | 0.0 |

| Tidal Site | Difference: Time (h. m.) | Height (ft.) |
|---|---|---|
| Cape Cod Canal | | |
| East Entrance | –0 01 | –0.8 |
| West Entrance | –2 16 | –5.9 |
| Chatham Outer Coast | +0 30 | –2.8 |
| Inside | +1 54 | **0.4 |
| Cohasset | +0 02 | –0.07 |
| Cotuit Highlands | +1 15 | **0.3 |
| Dennis Port | +1 01 | **0.4 |
| Duxbury–Gurnet Point | +0 02 | –0.3 |
| Fall River | –3 03 | –5.0 |
| Gloucester | –0 03 | –0.8 |
| Hingham | +0 07 | 0.0 |
| Hull | +0 03 | –0.2 |
| Hyannis Port | +1 01 | **0.3 |
| Magnolia–Manchester | –0 02 | –0.7 |
| Marblehead | –0 02 | –0.4 |
| Marion | –3 22 | –5.4 |
| Monument Beach | –3 08 | –5.4 |
| Nahant | –0 01 | –0.5 |
| Nantasket | +0 04 | –0.1 |
| Nantucket | +0 56 | **0.3 |
| Nauset Beach | +0 30 | **0.6 |
| New Bedford | –3 24 | –5.7 |
| Newburyport | +0 19 | –1.8 |
| Oak Bluffs | +0 30 | **0.2 |
| Onset–R.R. Bridge | –2 16 | –5.9 |
| Plymouth | +0 05 | 0.0 |
| Provincetown | +0 14 | –0.4 |
| Revere Beach | –0 01 | –0.3 |
| Rockport | –0 08 | –1.0 |
| Salem | 0 00 | –0.5 |
| Scituate | –0 05 | –0.7 |

# Tide Corrections

| Tidal Site | Difference: Time (h. m.) | Height (ft.) |
|---|---|---|
| Wareham | −3 09 | −5.3 |
| Wellfleet | +0 12 | +0.5 |
| West Falmouth | −3 10 | −5.4 |
| Westport Harbor | −3 22 | −6.4 |
| Woods Hole | | |
| Little Harbor | −2 50 | **0.2 |
| Oceanographic | | |
| Institute | −3 07 | **0.2 |
| **Rhode Island** | | |
| Bristol | −3 24 | −5.3 |
| Narragansett Pier | −3 42 | −6.2 |
| Newport | −3 34 | −5.9 |
| Point Judith | −3 41 | −6.3 |
| Providence | −3 20 | −4.8 |
| Sakonnet | −3 44 | −5.6 |
| Watch Hill | −2 50 | −6.8 |
| **Connecticut** | | |
| Bridgeport | +0 01 | −2.6 |
| Madison | −0 22 | −2.3 |
| New Haven | −0 11 | −3.2 |
| New London | −1 54 | −6.7 |
| Norwalk | +0 01 | −2.2 |
| Old Lyme | | |
| Highway Bridge | −0 30 | −6.2 |
| Stamford | +0 01 | −2.2 |
| Stonington | −2 27 | −6.6 |
| **New York** | | |
| Coney Island | −3 33 | −4.9 |
| Fire Island Light | −2 43 | **0.1 |
| Long Beach | −3 11 | −5.7 |
| Montauk Harbor | −2 19 | −7.4 |
| New York City–Battery | −2 43 | −5.0 |
| Oyster Bay | +0 04 | −1.8 |
| Port Chester | −0 09 | −2.2 |
| Port Washington | −0 01 | −2.1 |
| Sag Harbor | −0 55 | −6.8 |
| Southampton | | |
| Shinnecock Inlet | −4 20 | **0.2 |
| Willets Point | 0 00 | −2.3 |
| **New Jersey** | | |
| Asbury Park | −4 04 | −5.3 |
| Atlantic City | −3 56 | −5.5 |
| Bay Head–Sea Girt | −4 04 | −5.3 |
| Beach Haven | −1 43 | **0.24 |
| Cape May | −3 28 | −5.3 |
| Ocean City | −3 06 | −5.9 |
| Sandy Hook | −3 30 | −5.0 |
| Seaside Park | −4 03 | −5.4 |
| **Pennsylvania** | | |
| Philadelphia | +2 40 | −3.5 |
| **Delaware** | | |
| Cape Henlopen | −2 48 | −5.3 |

| Tidal Site | Difference: Time (h. m.) | Height (ft.) |
|---|---|---|
| Rehoboth Beach | −3 37 | −5.7 |
| Wilmington | +1 56 | −3.8 |
| **Maryland** | | |
| Annapolis | +6 23 | −8.5 |
| Baltimore | +7 59 | −8.3 |
| Cambridge | +5 05 | −7.8 |
| Havre de Grace | +11 21 | −7.7 |
| Point No Point | +2 28 | −8.1 |
| Prince Frederick | | |
| Plum Point | +4 25 | −8.5 |
| **Virginia** | | |
| Cape Charles | −2 20 | −7.0 |
| Hampton Roads | −2 02 | −6.9 |
| Norfolk | −2 06 | −6.6 |
| Virginia Beach | −4 00 | −6.0 |
| Yorktown | −2 13 | −7.0 |
| **North Carolina** | | |
| Cape Fear | −3 55 | −5.0 |
| Cape Lookout | −4 28 | −5.7 |
| Currituck | −4 10 | −5.8 |
| Hatteras | | |
| Inlet | −4 03 | −7.4 |
| Kitty Hawk | −4 14 | −6.2 |
| Ocean | −4 26 | −6.0 |
| **South Carolina** | | |
| Charleston | −3 22 | −4.3 |
| Georgetown | −1 48 | **0.36 |
| Hilton Head | −3 22 | −2.9 |
| Myrtle Beach | −3 49 | −4.4 |
| St. Helena | | |
| Harbor Entrance | −3 15 | −3.4 |
| **Georgia** | | |
| Jekyll Island | −3 46 | −2.9 |
| St. Simon's Island | −2 50 | −2.9 |
| Savannah Beach | | |
| River Entrance | −3 14 | −5.5 |
| Tybee Light | −3 22 | −2.7 |
| **Florida** | | |
| Cape Canaveral | −3 59 | −6.0 |
| Daytona Beach | −3 28 | −5.3 |
| Fort Lauderdale | −2 50 | −7.2 |
| Fort Pierce Inlet | −3 32 | −6.9 |
| Jacksonville | | |
| Railroad Bridge | −6 55 | **0.1 |
| Miami Harbor Entrance | −3 18 | −7.0 |
| St. Augustine | −2 55 | −4.9 |

*Varies widely; accurate within only 1½ hours. Consult local tide tables for precise times and heights.

**Where the difference in the Height column is so marked, the height at Boston should be multiplied by this ratio.

# Tidal Glossary

**Apogean Tide:** A monthly tide of decreased range that occurs when the Moon is at apogee (farthest from Earth).

**Diurnal Tide:** A tide with one high water and one low water in a tidal day of approximately 24 hours.

**Mean Lower Low Water:** The arithmetic mean of the lesser of a daily pair of low waters, observed over a specific 19-year cycle called the National Tidal Datum Epoch.

**Neap Tide:** A tide of decreased range that occurs twice a month, when the Moon is in quadrature (during its first and last quarters, when the Sun and the Moon are at right angles to each other relative to Earth).

**Perigean Tide:** A monthly tide of increased range that occurs when the Moon is at perigee (closest to Earth).

**Semidiurnal Tide:** A tide with one high water and one low water every half day. East Coast tides, for example, are semidiurnal, with two highs and two lows during a tidal day of approximately 24 hours.

**Spring Tide:** A tide of increased range that occurs at times of syzygy each month. Named not for the season of spring but from the German *springen* ("to leap up"), a spring tide also brings a lower low water.

**Syzygy:** The nearly straight-line configuration that occurs twice a month, when the Sun and the Moon are in conjunction (on the same side of Earth, at the new Moon) and when they are in opposition (on opposite sides of Earth, at the full Moon). In both cases, the gravitational effects of the Sun and the Moon reinforce each other, and tidal range is increased.

**Vanishing Tide:** A mixed tide of considerable inequality in the two highs and two lows, so that the lower high (or higher low) may appear to vanish. □□

# The Old Farmer's

# General Store

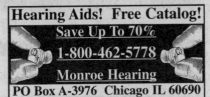

# General Store Classifieds

**For advertising information, contact Bernie Gallagher, 203-263-7171.**

## BEEKEEPING

## BEER & WINE MAKING

## BUILDING

# Classifieds

## INVENTORS/INVENTIONS/PATENTS

INVENTORS: We can help try to submit ideas to industry. Patent referral services. 800-INVENTION. www.InventHelp.com

## OLD PHONOGRAPH RECORDS

**OLD PHONOGRAPH RECORDS WANTED**
Buying blues, jazz, rock, and country!
78s, 45s, and LPs from 1920s–1960s
Paying as high as $12,000 for certain blues
78-rpm records! Will come to you!
John, "The Record Man":
**800-955-1326**

## OPEN-POLLINATED SEED

OPEN-POLLINATED CORN SEED. Silage, grain, wildlife. Available certified organic, 75-85-87-90-120-day. Green Haven, 607-566-9253. Visit online: www.openpollinated.com

## PERSONAL

GET YOUR LETTER FROM SANTA. Visit online: www.santa-mailbag.com

## PERSONALS

ASIAN BRIDES! Overseas. Romance, love, marriage! Details, photos: Box 4601-OFA, Thousand Oaks CA 91362. 805-492-8040. www.pacisl.com

## POULTRY

GOSLINGS, DUCKLINGS, GUINEAS, chicks, turkeys, bantams, game birds. Books and equipment. 717-365-3694. Hoffman Hatchery, PO Box 129P, Gratz PA 17030. www.hoffmanhatchery.com

## PUBLICATIONS/BOOKS/CATALOGS

FREE BOOKLETS: Life, Immortality, Soul, Pollution Crisis, Judgment Day, Restitution. Sample magazine. Bible Standard (OF), 1156 St. Matthews Road, Chester Springs PA 19425. Visit: www.biblestandard.com

FREE BOOKLET: Pro and Con assessment of Jehovah's Witnesses teachings. Bible Standard (OFA), 1156 St. Matthews Road, Chester Springs PA 19425. www.biblestandard.com

## SEEDS & PLANTS

LIVE HERB PLANTS for culinary, medicinal, and aromatherapy. Gourmet vegetables, plants, seeds, and teas. Call 724-735-4700. Visit us online: www.AlwaysSummerHerbs.com

GROW YOUR OWN tobacco, medicinal plants and herbs, houseplants, heirloom veggies, and more. Free catalog. E.O.N.S., Dept. FA, PO Box 4604, Hallandale FL 33008. Call 954-382-8281. Visit us online: www.eonseed.com

## SPIRITUAL ADVICE

SOPHIA GREEN: Don't tell me, I'll tell you. Help with all problems. Help reuniting lovers. You will be satisfied. 956-878-7053.

DONNA BELLA, Spiritual Reader, cleanses evil that blocks you from progressing. Healing Oils and Lucky Powders. 954-324-6160.

NEED HELP FAST! Spiritualist Leza cures all evil spells. Reunites lovers; potions; luck. Valdosta, GA. 229-630-5386 or 229-244-1306.

SISTER CHEROKEE, Gifted Indian Reader. Gives good luck, blessings, guidance, winning hits. Originally from Egypt. 3848 North Druid Hills Rd., Decatur GA 30033. 404-325-7336.

## SPIRITUAL HEALERS

OTHERS FAILED? Indian healer Rev. Ginger, Louisiana spiritualist, permanently restores stolen lovers immediately! 504-416-0958.

**MOTHER THOMPSON**
Healing Spiritualist
Born with a veil, she has the spiritual power to reunite lovers, help in health, business, marriage. One call will achieve your life goals, claim your destiny, gain personal power, and overcome blocks of negativity. **323-383-8857**

SPIRITUAL HEALER and advisor. Guaranteed help in all problems in life, such as love, marriage, business, and health. One free question. Call today: 817-613-0509.

BROTHER ROY. Spiritual root worker. Healing oils, health, luck. Success guaranteed. Call today: 912-262-6897.

**EVANGELIST DOCTOR ADAMS**
Spiritual Healer
100% guarantee. $39 to cast love spells.
Bring that man or woman back.
Results in hours, no matter the spell you need.
Write 1770 Howell Mill Rd., Atlanta GA 30318
or call **770-622-9191**

SISTER MOSES, Indian Healer. Helps in Luck, Love, Health, Farming Grounds, works with Holy Spirit. 678-677-1144.

**MOTHER DIVINE**
Guaranteed to succeed where others have failed.
Brings loved one back instantly.
Removes all bad luck and evil in your life.
Call now to see results immediately.
**812-309-0067**

## TREES & SHRUBS

**SPRUCE, FIR, PINE SEEDLINGS**
for reforestation, Christmas trees, landscaping,
windbreaks. Wholesale prices.
Free catalog. Flickingers' Nursery,
Box 245, Sagamore PA 16250
**www.flicknursery.com**
**800-368-7381**

## WANTED TO BUY

**CASH FOR 78-RPM RECORDS!**
Send $2 (refundable) for illustrated booklet
identifying collectible labels, numbers, with
actual prices I pay.
Docks, Box 780218(FA),
San Antonio TX 78278-0218

## WINE & BEER MAKING

**FREE ILLUSTRATED CATALOG**
Fast service. Since 1967.
Kraus, PO Box 7850-YB,
Independence MO 64054
**www.eckraus.com/offers/fd.asp**
**800-841-7404**

*The Old Farmer's Almanac* consistently reaches a proven,
responsive audience and is known for delivering readers who
are active buyers. The 2012 edition closes on May 2, 2011.
Ad opportunities are available in the *All-Seasons Garden
Guide*, which closes on January 7, 2011, and on our Web
site, Almanac.com. For ad rates, Web classifieds, or ad
information, please contact Bernie Gallagher by e-mail at
OFAads@aol.com, by phone at 203-263-7171, by fax at
203-263-7174, or by mail at The Old Farmer's Almanac,
PO Box 959, Woodbury CT 06798.

# Got Kids Looking for Things to Do?

*The Old Farmer's Almanac for Kids* keeps
youngsters busy for hours, with fun facts,
great stories, and easy (and educational)
projects and activities, such as how to:

❖ **Grow a sunflower house.**

❖ **Plant beet seeds.**

❖ **Make a scarecrow.**

❖ **Grow loofah that become
sponges.**

❖ **Match Moons with Moon
names.**

❖ **Grow plants under glass.**

❖ **Create paper snowflakes.**

**Look for** *The Old Farmer's Almanac for Kids,*
**Volume 3, in bookstores and at Almanac.com/Store or call 1-800-ALMANAC.**
Mention code: YKPA1KDS

# Index to Advertisers

*There's more of everything at* Almanac.com.

# ANECDOTES & Pleasantries

**A sampling from the hundreds of letters, clippings, articles, and e-mails sent to us by Almanac readers from all over the United States and Canada during the past year.**

## The Top 15 Things We Can Learn From the Movies

*Bet you can think of a half-dozen more . . .*

*–courtesy of R.S.H., Glen Ridge, New Jersey*

**15.** Beds have special, L-shape top sheets that reach up to the woman's armpit but only to the waist of the man lying beside her.

**14.** The ventilation system of any building is the perfect hiding place. No one will ever think of looking for you in there, and you can travel to any other part of the building without difficulty.

**13.** Should you wish to pass yourself off as a German officer, it will not be necessary to speak the language. A German accent will do.

**12.** A man will show no pain while taking the most ferocious beating but will wince when a woman tries to clean his wounds.

**11.** A cough is usually the sign of a terminal illness.

**10.** When confronted by an evil international terrorist, sarcasm and wisecracks are your best weapons.

**9.** One man shooting at 20 men has a better chance of killing them than 20 men firing at one man.

**8.** Taxi drivers don't require exact or even approximate payment; the first bill you pull from your pocket is always correct.

**7.** A detective can only solve a case once he has been suspended from duty.

**6.** Most people keep a scrapbook of newspaper clippings, especially if any of their family or friends have died in a strange boating accident.

**5.** All grocery shopping bags contain at least one stick of French bread.

**4.** If a large pane of glass is visible, someone will be thrown through it before long.

**3.** The Eiffel Tower can be seen from any window in Paris.

**2.** You're likely to survive any battle in any war unless you make the mistake of showing someone a picture of your sweetheart back home.

**1.** If you find yourself caught up in a misunderstanding that could be cleared up quickly with a simple explanation, for goodness' sake, keep your mouth shut.

## Four Reasons to Marry Four Times

*—courtesy of S. L., St. Louis, Missouri*

**O**n the occasion of her fourth wedding, a reporter asked an elderly Indiana woman about her spouses. She explained that her first husband had been a banker; her second, a circus performer; her third, an attorney. This latest marriage was to a funeral director. The reporter then asked why the woman had been attracted to men with such diverse interests. She replied, "I chose number one for the money, two for the show, three to get ready, and four to go."

## 10 Things People Actually Said During Job Interviews

*Honesty is good, but sometimes discretion is better.*

*—courtesy of J. B., Washington, D.C., who cites Rachel Zupek at CareerBuilder.com*

■ "What do you want me to do if I can not walk to work if it's raining? Can you pick me up?"

■ "So, how much do they pay you for doing these interviews?"

■ "What is your company's policy on Monday absences?"

■ "When you do background checks on candidates, do things like public drunkenness arrests come up?"

■ "I was fired from my last job because they were forcing me to attend anger management classes."

■ "I'm really not a big learner. I'd much rather work at a place where the job is pretty stagnant and doesn't change a lot."

■ "My parents told me that I need to get a job, so that is why I'm here."

■ "I saw the job posted on Twitter and thought, Why not?"

■ "What is two weeks' notice? I've never quit a job before—I've always been fired."

■ "If this doesn't work out, can I call you to go out sometime?"

continued

# How Would You Answer These Four Questions?

*90 percent of adults get every one wrong. But preschoolers do well!*

*—courtesy of C.W.F., Shaker Heights, Ohio*

**QUESTION 1:** *How would you put a giraffe into a refrigerator?*

**The correct answer:** Open the refrigerator, put in the giraffe, and close the door. (This question tests whether you tend to do simple things in an overly complicated way.)

**QUESTION 2:** *How would you put an elephant into a refrigerator?*

**The correct answer:** Same as above? Wrong. Open the refrigerator, take out the giraffe, put in the elephant, and close the door. (This tests your ability to think through the repercussions of your previous actions.)

**QUESTION 3:** *The Lion King is hosting an animal conference. All animals attend, except one. Which animal does not attend?*

**The correct answer:** The elephant. The elephant is in the refrigerator. You just put him in there. (This tests your memory.)

**QUESTION 4:** *There is a river you must cross, but it is known to be frequented by crocodiles, and you do not have a boat. How do you manage?*

**The correct answer:** You jump into the river and swim across. All the crocodiles are attending the animal conference. (This tests whether you learn from your mistakes.)

# It's Apparent

*—courtesy of P. B., aka "Mr. B," Laramie, Wyoming, from years of substitute teaching*

What is the difference between a bald man, a prince, an orphan, and a monkey's mother?

- A bald man has no hair apparent.

- A prince is an heir apparent.

- An orphan has nary a parent.

- A monkey's mother is a hairy parent.

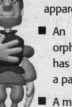

# Plain Speaking

*Why didn't we think of this?*

*—also courtesy of "Mr. B"*

- ◆ There is no such thing as exactly the same.

- ◆ Seeking security will never give you the security you seek.

- ◆ The status quo is never sustainable.

## How to Verify Your Age

*If you're really bored sometime, try this . . .*

*–courtesy of D. M., Cannon Beach, Oregon*

➡ Write down your age.

➡ Multiply by 2 and then add 5.

➡ Multiply that by 50.

➡ Subtract 365.

➡ Add the loose change in your pocket under $1.00.

➡ Add 115.

➡ The first two figures in the resulting number are your age.

➡ The last two are the change in your pocket.

# The 5-Second Rule: Myth or Fact?

*–courtesy of C.R.B., Woodland Park, Colorado, who cites the newsletter of the Colorado State University Extension*

Ever dropped a cookie on the floor, yelled "5-second rule!," then quickly picked it up and popped it into your mouth? The assumption is that 5 seconds is not a long enough time for the food to pick up harmful bacteria.

Or is it?

Jillian Clarke, a high school student doing an apprenticeship in Hans Blaschek's University of Illinois laboratory, decided to test the validity of the 5-second rule. Clarke took swab samples from floors around campus to determine bacteria counts. The floors were surprisingly clean.

Next, she inoculated rough and smooth floor tiles with *E. coli* bacteria. She placed gummy bears and fudge-stripe cookies on the inoculated tiles for 5 seconds, then examined the foods under a high-power microscope.

Her findings showed that in all cases, *E. coli* was transferred from the tile to the food, demonstrating that microorganisms can be transferred from ceramic tile to food in 5 seconds or less. Clarke found that more *E. coli* was transferred from smooth tiles than from rough tiles and that both the dry cookies and the gummy bears became contaminated from only 5 seconds of contact with the inoculated tiles.

So, the next time that some yummy morsel falls to the floor, resist the temptation to pick it up quickly and eat it. Just trash it. ▫▫

---

**SHARE YOUR ANECDOTES & PLEASANTRIES**

Send your contributions for the 2012 edition of *The Old Farmer's Almanac* by January 28, 2011, to "A & P," The Old Farmer's Almanac, P.O. Box 520, Dublin, NH 03444, or contact us at Almanac .com/Feedback (subject: A & P).

# Vinegar Can Be Used For WHAT?

CANTON (Special)- Research from the U.S. to Asia reports that VINEGAR-- *Mother Nature's Liquid Gold*-- is one of the most powerful aids for a healthier, longer life.

Each golden drop is a natural store-house of vitamins and minerals to help fight ailments and extend life. In fact:

- Studies show it helps boost the immune system to help prevent cancer, ease arthritic pain, and fight cholesterol build-up in arteries.

And that's not all!

*Want to control Your weight?*

Since ancient times a teaspoon of apple cider vinegar in water at meals has been the answer. Try it.

*Worried about age spots? Troubled by headaches? Aches and pain?*

You'll find a vinegar home remedy for your problem among the 308 researched and available for the first time in the exclusive *"The Vinegar Book,"* by natural health author Emily Thacker.

As *The Wall Street Journal* wrote in a vinegar article: "Have a Problem? Chances are Vinegar can help solve it."

This fascinating book shows you step by step how to mix *inexpensive* vinegar with kitchen staples to help:

- Lower blood pressure
- Speed up your metabolism
- Fight pesky coughs, colds
- Relieve painful leg cramps
- Soothe aching muscles
- Fade away headaches
- Gain soft, radiant skin
- Help lower cholesterol
- Boost immune system in its prevention of cancer
- Fight liver spots
- Natural arthritis reliever
- Use for eye and ear problems
- Destroy bacteria in foods
- Relieve itches, insect bites
- Skin rashes, athlete's foot
- Heart and circulatory care, and so much more

You'll learn it's easy to combine vinegar and herbs to create tenderizers, mild laxatives, tension relievers.

Enjoy bottling your own original and delicious vinegars. And tasty pickles and pickling treats that win raves!

You'll discover vinegar's amazing history through the ages *PLUS easy-to-make cleaning formulas that save you hundreds of dollars every year.*

*"The Vinegar Book"* is so amazing that you're invited to use and enjoy its wisdom on a **90 day No-Risk Trial basis. If not delighted simply tear off and return** *the cover only* **for a prompt refund.** To order right from the publisher at the introductory low price of $12.95 plus $3.98 postage & handling (total of $16.93, OH residents please add 6% sales tax) do this now:

Write "Vinegar Preview" on a piece of paper and mail it along with your check or money order payable to: James Direct Inc., Dept. V1277, 500 S. Prospect Ave., Box 980, Hartville, Ohio 44632.

You can charge to your VISA, MasterCard, Discover or American Express by mail. Be sure to include your card number, expiration date and signature.

*Want to save even more?* Do a favor for a relative or friend and order 2 books for only $20 postpaid. It's such a thoughtful gift.

*Remember: It's not available in book stores at this time. And you're protected by the publisher's 90-Day Money Back Guarantee.*

SPECIAL BONUS - Act promptly and you'll also receive Brain & Health Power Foods booklet absolutely FREE. It's yours to keep just for previewing *"The Vinegar Book."* Supplies are limited. Order today.

©2010 JDI V0121S03

*http://www.jamesdirect.com*

# A Reference Compendium

R
E
F
E
R
E
N
C
E

compiled by Mare-Anne Jarvela

# A Table Foretelling the Weather Through All the Lunations of Each Year, or Forever

■ This table is the result of many years of actual observation and shows what sort of weather will probably follow the Moon's entrance into any of its quarters. For example, the table shows that the week following January 12, 2011, will be stormy, because the Moon enters the first quarter that day at 6:31 A.M. EST. (See the **Left-Hand Calendar Pages, 114–140,** for 2011 Moon phases.)

**Editor's note: Although the data in this table is taken into consideration in the yearlong process of compiling the annual long-range weather forecasts for** *The Old Farmer's Almanac,* **we rely far more on our projections of solar activity.**

| Time of Change | Summer | Winter |
|---|---|---|
| Midnight to 2 A.M. | Fair | Hard frost, unless wind is south or west |
| 2 A.M. to 4 A.M. | Cold, with frequent showers | Snow and stormy |
| 4 A.M. to 6 A.M. | Rain | Rain |
| 6 A.M. to 8 A.M. | Wind and rain | Stormy |
| 8 A.M. to 10 A.M. | Changeable | Cold rain if wind is west; snow, if east |
| 10 A.M. to noon | Frequent showers | Cold with high winds |
| Noon to 2 P.M. | Very rainy | Snow or rain |
| 2 P.M. to 4 P.M. | Changeable | Fair and mild |
| 4 P.M. to 6 P.M. | Fair | Fair |
| 6 P.M. to 10 P.M. | Fair if wind is northwest; rain if wind is south or southwest | Fair and frosty if wind is north or northeast; rain or snow if wind is south or southwest |
| 10 P.M. to midnight | Fair | Fair and frosty |

*This table was created more than 175 years ago by Dr. Herschell for the* Boston Courier; *it first appeared in* The Old Farmer's Almanac *in 1834.*

# Safe Ice Thickness*

| Ice Thickness | Permissible Load | Ice Thickness | Permissible Load |
|---|---|---|---|
| 3 inches | Single person on foot | 12 inches | Heavy truck (8-ton gross) |
| 4 inches | Group in single file | 15 inches | 10 tons |
| 7½ inches | Passenger car (2-ton gross) | 20 inches | 25 tons |
| 8 inches | Light truck (2½-ton gross) | 30 inches | 70 tons |
| 10 inches | Medium truck (3½-ton gross) | 36 inches | 110 tons |

**\*Solid, clear, blue/black pond and lake ice**

*Slush ice has only half the strength of blue ice. The strength value of river ice is 15 percent less.*

# The UV Index for Measuring Ultraviolet Radiation Risk

The U.S. National Weather Service's daily forecasts of ultraviolet levels use these numbers for various exposure levels:

| UV Index Number | Exposure Level | Time to Burn | Actions to Take |
|---|---|---|---|
| 0, 1, 2 | Minimal | 60 minutes | Apply SPF 15 sunscreen |
| 3, 4 | Low | 45 minutes | Apply SPF 15 sunscreen; wear a hat |
| 5, 6 | Moderate | 30 minutes | Apply SPF 15 sunscreen; wear a hat |
| 7, 8, 9 | High | 15–25 minutes | Apply SPF 15 to 30 sunscreen; wear a hat and sunglasses |
| 10 or higher | Very high | 10 minutes | Apply SPF 30 sunscreen; wear a hat, sunglasses, and protective clothing |

"Time to Burn" and "Actions to Take" apply to people with fair skin that sometimes tans but usually burns. People with lighter skin need to be more cautious. People with darker skin may be able to tolerate more exposure.

R
E
F
E
R
E
N
C
E

## What Are Cooling/ Heating Degree Days?

■ Each degree of a day's average temperature above 65°F is considered one cooling degree day, an attempt to measure the need for air-conditioning. If the average of the day's high and low temperatures is 75°, that's ten cooling degree days.

Similarly, each degree of a day's average temperature below 65°F is considered one heating degree and is an attempt to measure the need for fuel consumption. For example, a day with temperatures ranging from 60°F to 40°F results in an average of 50°, or 15 degrees less than 65°. Hence, that day would be credited as 15 heating degree days.

## How to Measure Earthquakes

■ Seismologists have developed a new measurement of earthquake size, called Moment Magnitude, that is more accurate than the previously used Richter scale, which is precise only for earthquakes of a certain size and at a certain distance from a seismometer. All earthquakes can now be compared on the same scale.

| Magnitude | Effect |
|---|---|
| Less than 3 | Micro |
| 3–3.9 | Minor |
| 4–4.9 | Light |
| 5–5.9 | Moderate |
| 6–6.9 | Strong |
| 7–7.9 | Major |
| 8 or more | Great |

# Heat Index °F (°C)

| | | **RELATIVE HUMIDITY (%)** | | | | | | | |
|---|---|---|---|---|---|---|---|---|---|
| **TEMPERATURE °F (°C)** | | **40** | **45** | **50** | **55** | **60** | **65** | **70** | **75** | **80** |
| **100 (38)** | 109 (43) | 114 (46) | 118 (48) | 124 (51) | 129 (54) | 136 (58) | | | |
| **98 (37)** | 105 (41) | 109 (43) | 113 (45) | 117 (47) | 123 (51) | 128 (53) | 134 (57) | | |
| **96 (36)** | 101 (38) | 104 (40) | 108 (42) | 112 (44) | 116 (47) | 121 (49) | 126 (52) | 132 (56) | |
| **94 (34)** | 97 (36) | 100 (38) | 103 (39) | 106 (41) | 110 (43) | 114 (46) | 119 (48) | 124 (51) | 129 (54) |
| **92 (33)** | 94 (34) | 96 (36) | 99 (37) | 101 (38) | 105 (41) | 108 (42) | 112 (44) | 116 (47) | 121 (49) |
| **90 (32)** | 91 (33) | 93 (34) | 95 (35) | 97 (36) | 100 (38) | 103 (39) | 106 (41) | 109 (43) | 113 (45) |
| **88 (31)** | 88 (31) | 89 (32) | 91 (33) | 93 (34) | 95 (35) | 98 (37) | 100 (38) | 103 (39) | 106 (41) |
| **86 (30)** | 85 (29) | 87 (31) | 88 (31) | 89 (32) | 91 (33) | 93 (34) | 95 (35) | 97 (36) | 100 (38) |
| **84 (29)** | 83 (28) | 84 (29) | 85 (29) | 86 (30) | 88 (31) | 89 (32) | 90 (32) | 92 (33) | 94 (34) |
| **82 (28)** | 81 (27) | 82 (28) | 83 (28) | 84 (29) | 84 (29) | 85 (29) | 86 (30) | 88 (31) | 89 (32) |
| **80 (27)** | 80 (27) | 80 (27) | 81 (27) | 81 (27) | 82 (28) | 82 (28) | 83 (28) | 84 (29) | 84 (29) |

**EXAMPLE:** *When the temperature is 88°F (31°C) and the relative humidity is 60 percent, the heat index,*

**Clouds have many characteristics and are classified by altitude and type**

### HIGH CLOUDS
**(bases start above 20,000 feet, on average)**

**Cirrus:** Thin, featherlike, crystal clouds.

**Cirrocumulus:** Thin clouds that appear as small "cotton patches."

**Cirrostratus:** Thin white clouds that resemble veils.

### MIDDLE CLOUDS
**(bases start at between 6,500 and 20,000 feet)**

**Altocumulus:** Gray or white layer or patches of solid clouds with rounded shapes.

**Altostratus:** Grayish or bluish layer of clouds that can obscure the Sun.

### LOW CLOUDS
**(bases start below 6,500 feet)**

**Stratus:** Thin, gray, sheetlike clouds with low bases; may bring drizzle or snow.

**Stratocumulus:** Rounded cloud masses that form in a layer.

**Nimbostratus:** Dark, gray, shapeless cloud layers containing rain, snow, or ice pellets.

| | 85 | 90 | 95 | 100 |
|---|---|---|---|---|
| | 135 (57) | | | |
| | 126 (52) | 131 (55) | | |
| | 117 (47) | 122 (50) | 127 (53) | 132 (56) |
| | 110 (43) | 113 (45) | 117 (47) | 121 (49) |
| | 102 (39) | 105 (41) | 108 (42) | 112 (44) |
| | 96 (36) | 98 (37) | 100 (38) | 103 (39) |
| | 90 (32) | 91 (33) | 93 (34) | 95 (35) |
| | 85 (29) | 86 (30) | 86 (30) | 87 (31) |

*how hot it feels, is 95°F (35°C).*

## CLOUDS WITH VERTICAL DEVELOPMENT

**(form at almost any altitude and can reach to more than 39,000 feet)**

**Cumulus:** Fair-weather clouds with flat bases and dome-shape tops.

**Cumulonimbus:** Large, dark, vertical clouds with bulging tops that bring showers, thunder, and lightning.

# How to Measure Hail

■ The **Torro Hailstorm Intensity Scale** was introduced by Jonathan Webb of Oxford, England, in 1986 as a means of categorizing hailstorms. The name derives from the private and mostly British research body named the TORnado and storm Research Organisation.

### INTENSITY/DESCRIPTION OF HAIL DAMAGE

**H0** True hail of pea size causes no damage

**H1** Leaves and flower petals are punctured and torn

**H2** Leaves are stripped from trees and plants

**H3** Panes of glass are broken; auto bodies are dented

**H4** Some house windows are broken; small tree branches are broken off; birds are killed

**H5** Many windows are smashed; small animals are injured; large tree branches are broken off

**H6** Shingle roofs are breached; metal roofs are scored; wooden window frames are broken away

**H7** Roofs are shattered to expose rafters; cars are seriously damaged

**H8** Shingle and tile roofs are destroyed; small tree trunks are split; people are seriously injured

**H9** Concrete roofs are broken; large tree trunks are split and knocked down; people are at risk of fatal injuries

**H10** Brick houses are damaged; people are at risk of fatal injuries

REFERENCE

# How to Measure Wind Speed

■ The **Beaufort Wind Force Scale** is a common way of estimating wind speed. It was developed in 1805 by Admiral Sir Francis Beaufort of the British Navy to measure wind at sea. We can also use it to measure wind on land.

Admiral Beaufort arranged the numbers 0 to 12 to indicate the strength of the wind from calm, force 0, to hurricane, force 12. Here's a scale adapted to land.

*"Used Mostly at Sea but of Help to All Who Are Interested in the Weather"*

| Beaufort Force | Description | When You See or Feel This Effect | Wind Speed (mph) | (km/h) |
|---|---|---|---|---|
| 0 | Calm | Smoke goes straight up | less than 1 | less than 2 |
| 1 | Light air | Wind direction is shown by smoke drift but not by wind vane | 1–3 | 2–5 |
| 2 | Light breeze | Wind is felt on the face; leaves rustle; wind vanes move | 4–7 | 6–11 |
| 3 | Gentle breeze | Leaves and small twigs move steadily; wind extends small flags straight out | 8–12 | 12–19 |
| 4 | Moderate breeze | Wind raises dust and loose paper; small branches move | 13–18 | 20–29 |
| 5 | Fresh breeze | Small trees sway; waves form on lakes | 19–24 | 30–39 |
| 6 | Strong breeze | Large branches move; wires whistle; umbrellas are difficult to use | 25–31 | 40–50 |
| 7 | Moderate gale | Whole trees are in motion; walking against the wind is difficult | 32–38 | 51–61 |
| 8 | Fresh gale | Twigs break from trees; walking against the wind is very difficult | 39–46 | 62–74 |
| 9 | Strong gale | Buildings suffer minimal damage; roof shingles are removed | 47–54 | 75–87 |
| 10 | Whole gale | Trees are uprooted | 55–63 | 88–101 |
| 11 | Violent storm | Widespread damage | 64–72 | 102–116 |
| 12 | Hurricane | Widespread destruction | 73+ | 117+ |

## Retired Atlantic Hurricane Names

**These storms have been some of the most destructive and costly; as a result, their names have been retired from the six-year rotating list of names.**

| NAME | YEAR | NAME | YEAR | NAME | YEAR |
|---|---|---|---|---|---|
| Jeanne | 2004 | Stan | 2005 | Noel | 2007 |
| Dennis | 2005 | Wilma | 2005 | Gustav | 2008 |
| Katrina | 2005 | Dean | 2007 | Ike | 2008 |
| Rita | 2005 | Felix | 2007 | Paloma | 2008 |

| Atlantic Tropical (and Subtropical) Storm Names for 2011 | | | Eastern North-Pacific Tropical (and Subtropical) Storm Names for 2011 | | |
|---|---|---|---|---|---|
| Arlene | Jose | Tammy | Adrian | Jova | Todd |
| Bret | Katia | Vince | Beatriz | Kenneth | Veronica |
| Cindy | Lee | Whitney | Calvin | Lidia | Wiley |
| Don | Maria | | Dora | Max | Xina |
| Emily | Nate | | Eugene | Norma | York |
| Franklin | Ophelia | | Fernanda | Otis | Zelda |
| Gert | Philippe | | Greg | Pilar | |
| Harvey | Rina | | Hilary | Ramon | |
| Irene | Sean | | Irwin | Selma | |

# How to Measure Hurricane Strength

■ The **Saffir-Simpson Hurricane Scale** assigns a rating from 1 to 5 based on a hurricane's intensity. It is used to give an estimate of the potential property damage and flooding expected along the coast from a hurricane landfall. Wind speed is the determining factor in the scale, as storm surge values are highly dependent on the slope of the continental shelf in the landfall region. Wind speeds are measured using a 1-minute average.

**CATEGORY ONE.** Average wind: 74–95 mph. No real damage to building structures. Damage primarily to unanchored mobile homes, shrubbery, and trees. Also, some coastal road flooding and minor pier damage.

**CATEGORY TWO.** Average wind: 96–110 mph. Some roofing material, door, and window damage to buildings. Considerable damage to vegetation, mobile homes, and piers. Coastal and low-lying escape routes flood 2 to 4 hours before arrival of center. Small craft in unprotected anchorages break moorings.

**CATEGORY THREE.** Average wind: 111–130 mph. Some structural damage to small residences and utility buildings; minor amount of curtainwall failures. Mobile homes destroyed. Flooding near coast destroys smaller structures; larger structures damaged by floating debris.

**CATEGORY FOUR.** Average wind: 131–155 mph. More extensive curtainwall failures with some complete roof failures on small residences. Major beach erosion. Major damage to lower floors near the shore.

**CATEGORY FIVE.** Average wind: 156+ mph. Complete roof failures on many residences and industrial buildings. Some complete building failures; small buildings blown over or away. Major damage to lower floors located less than 15 feet above sea level (ASL) and within 500 yards of the shoreline.

REFERENCE

# How to Measure a Tornado

■ The original **Fujita Scale** (or F Scale) was developed by Dr. Theodore Fujita to classify tornadoes based on wind damage. All tornadoes, and other severe local windstorms, were assigned a number according to the most intense damage caused by the storm. An enhanced F scale (EF) was implemented in the United States on February 1, 2007. The new EF scale uses three-second gust estimates based on a more detailed system for assessing damage, taking into account different building materials.

| F SCALE | | EF SCALE (U.S.) |
|---|---|---|
| F0 • 40–72 mph (64–116 km/h) | light damage | EF0 • 65–85 mph (105–137 km/h) |
| F1 • 73–112 mph (117–180 km/h) | moderate damage | EF1 • 86–110 mph (138–178 km/h) |
| F2 • 113–157 mph (181–253 km/h) | considerable damage | EF2 • 111–135 mph (179–218 km/h) |
| F3 • 158–207 mph (254–332 km/h) | severe damage | EF3 • 136–165 mph (219–266 km/h) |
| F4 • 208–260 mph (333–419 km/h) | devastating damage | EF4 • 166–200 mph (267–322 km/h) |
| F5 • 261–318 mph (420–512 km/h) | incredible damage | EF5 • over 200 mph (over 322 km/h) |

# Wind/Barometer Table

| Barometer (Reduced to Sea Level) | Wind Direction | Character of Weather Indicated |
|---|---|---|
| 30.00 to 30.20, and steady | westerly | Fair, with slight changes in temperature, for one to two days. |
| 30.00 to 30.20, and rising rapidly | westerly | Fair, followed within two days by warmer and rain. |
| 30.00 to 30.20, and falling rapidly | south to east | Warmer, and rain within 24 hours. |
| 30.20 or above, and falling rapidly | south to east | Warmer, and rain within 36 hours. |
| 30.20 or above, and falling rapidly | west to north | Cold and clear, quickly followed by warmer and rain. |
| 30.20 or above, and steady | variable | No early change. |
| 30.00 or below, and falling slowly | south to east | Rain within 18 hours that will continue a day or two. |
| 30.00 or below, and falling rapidly | southeast to northeast | Rain, with high wind, followed within two days by clearing, colder. |
| 30.00 or below, and rising | south to west | Clearing and colder within 12 hours. |
| 29.80 or below, and falling rapidly | south to east | Severe storm of wind and rain imminent. In winter, snow or cold wave within 24 hours. |
| 29.80 or below, and falling rapidly | east to north | Severe northeast gales and heavy rain or snow, followed in winter by cold wave. |
| 29.80 or below, and rising rapidly | going to west | Clearing and colder. |

**Note:** *A barometer should be adjusted to show equivalent sea-level pressure for the altitude at which it is to be used. A change of 100 feet in elevation will cause a decrease of ¹/₁₀ inch in the reading.*

# Windchill Table

■ As wind speed increases, your body loses heat more rapidly, making the air feel colder than it really is. The combination of cold temperature and high wind can create a cooling effect so severe that exposed flesh can freeze.

| | | | | | | | TEMPERATURE (°F) | | | | | | | | |
|---|---|---|---|---|---|---|---|---|---|---|---|---|---|---|---|
| **Calm** | **35** | **30** | **25** | **20** | **15** | **10** | **5** | **0** | **−5** | **−10** | **−15** | **−20** | **−25** | **−30** | **−35** |
| **5** | 31 | 25 | 19 | 13 | 7 | 1 | −5 | −11 | −16 | −22 | −28 | −34 | −40 | −46 | −52 |
| **10** | 27 | 21 | 15 | 9 | 3 | −4 | −10 | −16 | −22 | −28 | −35 | −41 | −47 | −53 | −59 |
| **15** | 25 | 19 | 13 | 6 | 0 | −7 | −13 | −19 | −26 | −32 | −39 | −45 | −51 | −58 | −64 |
| **20** | 24 | 17 | 11 | 4 | −2 | −9 | −15 | −22 | −29 | −35 | −42 | −48 | −55 | −61 | −68 |
| **25** | 23 | 16 | 9 | 3 | −4 | −11 | −17 | −24 | −31 | −37 | −44 | −51 | −58 | −64 | −71 |
| **30** | 22 | 15 | 8 | 1 | −5 | −12 | −19 | −26 | −33 | −39 | −46 | −53 | −60 | −67 | −73 |
| **35** | 21 | 14 | 7 | 0 | −7 | −14 | −21 | −27 | −34 | −41 | −48 | −55 | −62 | −69 | −76 |
| **40** | 20 | 13 | 6 | −1 | −8 | −15 | −22 | −29 | −36 | −43 | −50 | −57 | −64 | −71 | −78 |
| **45** | 19 | 12 | 5 | −2 | −9 | −16 | −23 | −30 | −37 | −44 | −51 | −58 | −65 | −72 | −79 |
| **50** | 19 | 12 | 4 | −3 | −10 | −17 | −24 | −31 | −38 | −45 | −52 | −60 | −67 | −74 | −81 |
| **55** | 18 | 11 | 4 | −3 | −11 | −18 | −25 | −32 | −39 | −46 | −54 | −61 | −68 | −75 | −82 |
| **60** | 17 | 10 | 3 | −4 | −11 | −19 | −26 | −33 | −40 | −48 | −55 | −62 | −69 | −76 | −84 |

(WIND SPEED (mph))

Frostbite occurs in     30 minutes     10 minutes     5 minutes

**EXAMPLE: When the temperature is 15°F and the wind speed is 30 miles per hour, the windchill, or how cold it feels, is −5°F. For a Celsius version of this table, visit Almanac.com/Windchill.**

*−courtesy National Weather Service*

# How to Measure Volcanic Eruptions

### The Volcanic Explosivity Index (VEI)

| VEI/Description | Plume | Volume Height | Classification | Frequency |
|---|---|---|---|---|
| **0** Nonexplosive | <100 m | 1,000 m³ | Hawaiian | Daily |
| **1** Gentle | 100–1,000 m | 10,000 m³ | Hawaiian/Strombolian | Daily |
| **2** Explosive | 1–5 km | 1,000,000 m³ | Strombolian/Vulcanian | Weekly |
| **3** Severe | 3–15 km | 10,000,000 m³ | Vulcanian | Yearly |
| **4** Cataclysmic | 10–25 km | 100,000,000 m³ | Vulcanian/Plinian | 10 years |
| **5** Paroxysmal | >25 km | 1 km³ | Plinian | 100 years |
| **6** Colossal | >25 km | 10 km³ | Plinian/Ultra-Plinian | 100 years |
| **7** Supercolossal | >25 km | 100 km³ | Ultra-Plinian | 1,000 years |
| **8** Megacolossal | >25 km | 1,000 km³ | Ultra-Plinian | 10,000 years |

REFERENCE

# Weather Lore Calendar

■ For centuries, farmers and sailors—people whose livelihoods depended on the weather—relied on lore to forecast the weather. They quickly connected changes in nature with rhythms or patterns of the weather. Here is a collection of proverbs relating to months, weeks, and days.

## January

- *Fog in January brings a wet spring.*
- *[13th] St. Hilary, the coldest day of the year.*
- *[22nd] If the Sun shine on St. Vincent, there shall be much wind.*

## February

- *There is always one fine week in February.*
- *If bees get out in February, the next day will be windy and rainy.*
- *Fogs in February mean frosts in May.*
- *Winter's back breaks about the middle of February.*

## March

- *When March has April weather, April will have March weather.*
- *Thunder in March betokens a fruitful year.*
- *Dust in March brings grass and foliage.*
- *A March Sun sticks like a lock of wool.*

## April

- *If it thunders on All Fools' Day, it brings good crops of corn and hay.*
- *Moist April, clear June.*
- *Cloudy April, dewy May.*
- *Snow in April is manure.*

## May

- *Hoar frost on May 1st indicates a good harvest.*
- *A swarm of bees in May is worth a load of hay.*
- *In the middle of May comes the tail of winter.*

## June

- *A good leak in June, sets all in tune.*
- *When it is hottest in June, it will be coldest in the corresponding days of the next February.*
- *[24th] Rain on St. John's Day, and we may expect a wet harvest.*

## July

- *If the 1st of July be rainy weather, it will rain more or less for three weeks together.*
- *Ne'er trust a July sky.*
- *[3rd] Dog days bright and clear, indicate a happy year.*

## August

- *If the first week in August is unusually warm, the winter will be white and long.*
- *[24th] Thunderstorms after St. Bartholomew are mostly violent.*
- *When it rains in August, it rains honey and wine.*

## September

- *Fair on September 1st, fair for the month.*
- *Heavy September rains bring drought.*
- *If on September 19th there is a storm from the south, a mild winter may be expected.*
- *[29th] If St. Michael's brings many acorns, Christmas will cover the fields with snow.*

## October

- *Much rain in October, much wind in December.*
- *For every fog in October, a snow in the winter.*
- *Full Moon in October without frost, no frost till full Moon in November.*

## November

- *A heavy November snow will last till April.*
- *Thunder in November, a fertile year to come.*
- *Flowers in bloom late in autumn indicate a bad winter.*

## December

- *Thunder in December presages fine weather.*
- *A green Christmas, a white Easter.*
- *As the days lengthen, so the cold strengthens.*
- *If it rains much during the twelve days after Christmas, it will be a wet year.*

# Animal Signs of the Chinese Zodiac

■ The animal designations of the Chinese zodiac follow a 12-year cycle and are always used in the same sequence. The Chinese year of 354 days begins three to seven weeks into the western 365-day year, so the animal designation changes at that time, rather than on January 1. **See page 113** for the exact date of the start of the Chinese New Year.

## Rat

Ambitious and sincere, you can be generous with your money. Compatible with the dragon and the monkey. Your opposite is the horse.

| 1900 | 1936 | 1984 |
|------|------|------|
| 1912 | 1948 | 1996 |
| 1924 | 1960 | 2008 |
| 1972 |      |      |

## Ox or Buffalo

A leader, you are bright, patient, and cheerful. Compatible with the snake and the rooster. Your opposite is the sheep.

| 1901 | 1937 | 1985 |
|------|------|------|
| 1913 | 1949 | 1997 |
| 1925 | 1961 | 2009 |
| 1973 |      |      |

## Tiger

Forthright and sensitive, you possess great courage. Compatible with the horse and the dog. Your opposite is the monkey.

| 1902 | 1938 | 1986 |
|------|------|------|
| 1914 | 1950 | 1998 |
| 1926 | 1962 | 2010 |
| 1974 |      |      |

## Rabbit or Hare

Talented and affectionate, you are a seeker of tranquility. Compatible with the sheep and the pig. Your opposite is the rooster.

| 1903 | 1939 | 1987 |
|------|------|------|
| 1915 | 1951 | 1999 |
| 1927 | 1963 | 2011 |
| 1975 |      |      |

## Dragon

Robust and passionate, your life is filled with complexity. Compatible with the monkey and the rat. Your opposite is the dog.

| 1904 | 1940 | 1988 |
|------|------|------|
| 1916 | 1952 | 2000 |
| 1928 | 1964 | 2012 |
| 1976 |      |      |

## Snake

Strong-willed and intense, you display great wisdom. Compatible with the rooster and the ox. Your opposite is the pig.

| 1905 | 1941 | 1989 |
|------|------|------|
| 1917 | 1953 | 2001 |
| 1929 | 1965 | 2013 |
| 1977 |      |      |

## Horse

Physically attractive and popular, you like the company of others. Compatible with the tiger and the dog. Your opposite is the rat.

| 1906 | 1942 | 1990 |
|------|------|------|
| 1918 | 1954 | 2002 |
| 1930 | 1966 | 2014 |
| 1978 |      |      |

## Sheep or Goat

Aesthetic and stylish, you enjoy being a private person. Compatible with the pig and the rabbit. Your opposite is the ox.

| 1907 | 1943 | 1991 |
|------|------|------|
| 1919 | 1955 | 2003 |
| 1931 | 1967 | 2015 |
| 1979 |      |      |

## Monkey

Persuasive, skillful, and intelligent, you strive to excel. Compatible with the dragon and the rat. Your opposite is the tiger.

| 1908 | 1944 | 1992 |
|------|------|------|
| 1920 | 1956 | 2004 |
| 1932 | 1968 | 2016 |
| 1980 |      |      |

## Rooster or Cock

Seeking wisdom and truth, you have a pioneering spirit. Compatible with the snake and the ox. Your opposite is the rabbit.

| 1909 | 1945 | 1993 |
|------|------|------|
| 1921 | 1957 | 2005 |
| 1933 | 1969 | 2017 |
| 1981 |      |      |

## Dog

Generous and loyal, you have the ability to work well with others. Compatible with the horse and the tiger. Your opposite is the dragon.

| 1910 | 1946 | 1994 |
|------|------|------|
| 1922 | 1958 | 2006 |
| 1934 | 1970 | 2018 |
| 1982 |      |      |

## Pig or Boar

Gallant and noble, your friends will remain at your side. Compatible with the rabbit and the sheep. Your opposite is the snake.

| 1911 | 1947 | 1995 |
|------|------|------|
| 1923 | 1959 | 2007 |
| 1935 | 1971 | 2019 |
| 1983 |      |      |

R E F E R E N C E

## PHASES OF THE MOON

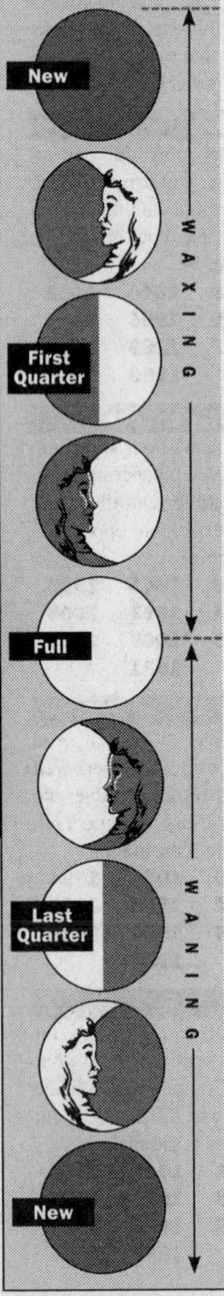

New

WAXING

First Quarter

Full

WANING

Last Quarter

New

# The Origin of Full-Moon Names

■ Historically, the Native Americans who lived in the area that is now the northern and eastern United States kept track of the seasons by giving a distinctive name to each recurring full Moon. This name was applied to the entire month in which it occurred. These names, and some variations, were used by the Algonquin tribes from New England to Lake Superior.

| Name | Month | Variations |
|---|---|---|
| Full Wolf Moon | January | Full Old Moon |
| Full Snow Moon | February | Full Hunger Moon |
| Full Worm Moon | March | Full Crow Moon<br>Full Crust Moon<br>Full Sugar Moon<br>Full Sap Moon |
| Full Pink Moon | April | Full Sprouting Grass Moon<br>Full Egg Moon<br>Full Fish Moon |
| Full Flower Moon | May | Full Corn Planting Moon<br>Full Milk Moon |
| Full Strawberry Moon | June | Full Rose Moon<br>Full Hot Moon |
| Full Buck Moon | July | Full Thunder Moon<br>Full Hay Moon |
| Full Sturgeon Moon | August | Full Red Moon<br>Full Green Corn Moon |
| Full Harvest Moon* | September | Full Corn Moon<br>Full Barley Moon |
| Full Hunter's Moon | October | Full Travel Moon<br>Full Dying Grass Moon |
| Full Beaver Moon | November | Full Frost Moon |
| Full Cold Moon | December | Full Long Nights Moon |

*The Harvest Moon is always the full Moon closest to the autumnal equinox. If the Harvest Moon occurs in October, the September full Moon is usually called the Corn Moon.

Many Moons Ago

**January's** full Moon was called the **Wolf Moon** because it appeared when wolves howled in hunger outside the villages.

**February's** full Moon was called the **Snow Moon** because it was a time of heavy snow. It was also called the **Hunger Moon** because hunting was difficult and hunger often resulted.

**March's** full Moon was called the **Worm Moon** because, as the Sun increasingly warmed the soil, earthworms became active and their castings (excrement) began to appear.

**April's** full Moon was called the **Pink Moon** because it heralded the appearance of the grass pink, or wild ground phlox—one of the first spring flowers.

**May's** full Moon was called the **Flower Moon** because blossoms were abundant everywhere at this time.

**June's** full Moon was called the **Strawberry Moon** because it appeared when the strawberry harvest took place.

**July's** full Moon was called the **Buck Moon** because it arrived when male deer started growing new antlers.

**August's** full Moon was called the **Sturgeon Moon** because that large fish, which is found in the Great Lakes and Lake Champlain, was caught easily at this time.

**September's** full Moon was called the **Corn Moon** because this was the time to harvest corn.

The **Harvest Moon** is the full Moon that occurs closest to the autumnal equinox. It can occur in either **September** or **October.** At this time, crops such as corn, pumpkins, squash, and wild rice are ready for gathering.

**October's** full Moon was called the **Hunter's Moon** because this was the time to hunt in preparation for winter.

**November's** full Moon was called the **Beaver Moon** because it was the time to set beaver traps, before the waters froze over.

**December's** full Moon was called the **Cold Moon.** It was also called the **Long Nights Moon** because nights at this time of year were the longest.

REFERENCE

# When Will the Moon Rise Today?

■ A lunar puzzle involves the timing of moonrise. If you enjoy the out-of-doors and the wonders of nature, you may wish to commit to memory the following gem:

 **The new Moon always rises at sunrise**

 **And the first quarter at noon.**

 **The full Moon always rises at sunset**

**And the last quarter at midnight.**

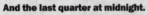

■ Moonrise occurs about 50 minutes later each day.

■ The new Moon is invisible because its illuminated side faces away from Earth, which occurs when the Moon lines up between Earth and the Sun.

■ One or two days after the date of the new Moon, you can see a thin crescent setting just after sunset in the western sky as the lunar cycle continues. (**See pages 114–140** for exact **rise and set times.**)

## The Origin of Month Names

**JANUARY.** Named for the Roman god Janus, protector of gates and doorways. Janus is depicted with two faces, one looking into the past, the other into the future.

**FEBRUARY.** From the Latin word *februa,* "to cleanse." The Roman Februalia was a month of purification and atonement.

**MARCH.** Named for the Roman god of war, Mars. This was the time of year to resume military campaigns that had been interrupted by winter.

**APRIL.** From the Latin word *aperio,* "to open (bud)," because plants begin to grow in this month.

**MAY.** Named for the Roman goddess Maia, who oversaw the growth of plants. Also from the Latin word *maiores,* "elders," who were celebrated during this month.

**JUNE.** Named for the Roman goddess Juno, patroness of marriage and the well-being of women. Also from the Latin word *juvenis,* "young people."

**JULY.** Named to honor Roman dictator Julius Caesar (100 B.C.–44 B.C.). In 46 B.C., Julius Caesar made one of his greatest contributions to history: With the help of Sosigenes, he developed the Julian calendar, the precursor to the Gregorian calendar we use today.

**AUGUST.** Named to honor the first Roman emperor (and grandnephew of Julius Caesar), Augustus Caesar (63 B.C.–A.D. 14).

**SEPTEMBER.** From the Latin word *septem,* "seven," because this had been the seventh month of the early Roman calendar.

**OCTOBER.** From the Latin word *octo,* "eight," because this had been the eighth month of the early Roman calendar.

**NOVEMBER.** From the Latin word *novem,* "nine," because this had been the ninth month of the early Roman calendar.

**DECEMBER.** From the Latin word *decem,* "ten," because this had been the tenth month of the early Roman calendar.

# The Origin of Day Names

■ The days of the week were named by ancient Romans with the Latin words for the Sun, the Moon, and the five known planets. These names have survived in European languages, but English names also reflect Anglo-Saxon and Norse influences.

| English | Latin | French | Italian | Spanish | Anglo-Saxon and Norse |
|---------|-------|--------|---------|---------|----------------------|
| **SUNDAY** | dies Solis (Sol's day) | dimanche | domenica | domingo | Sunnandaeg (Sun's day) |
| | | *from the Latin for "Lord's day"* | | | |
| **MONDAY** | dies Lunae (Luna's day) | lundi | lunedì | lunes | Monandaeg (Moon's day) |
| **TUESDAY** | dies Martis (Mars's day) | mardi | martedì | martes | Tiwesdaeg (Tiw's day) |
| **WEDNESDAY** | dies Mercurii (Mercury's day) | mercredi | mercoledì | miércoles | Wodnesdaeg (Woden's day) |
| **THURSDAY** | dies Jovis (Jupiter's day) | jeudi | giovedì | jueves | Thursdaeg (Thor's day) |
| **FRIDAY** | dies Veneris (Venus's day) | vendredi | venerdì | viernes | Frigedaeg (Frigga's day) |
| **SATURDAY** | dies Saturni (Saturn's day) | samedi | sabato | sábado | Saeterndaeg (Saturn's day) |
| | | *from the Latin for "Sabbath"* | | | |

# Best Planetary Encounters of the 21st Century

Me = Mercury    V = Venus    Mn = Moon    Ma = Mars    J = Jupiter    S = Saturn

**In all of these cases, face west between twilight and 10:00 P.M. to see the conjunction.**

| DATE | OBJECTS | DATE | OBJECTS |
|------|---------|------|---------|
| February 20, 2015 | V, Mn, Ma | June 28, 2076 | Ma, J |
| June 30–July 1, 2015 | V, J | October 31, 2076 | Mn, Ma, S |
| July 18, 2015 | V, Mn, J | February 27, 2079 | V, Ma |
| December 20, 2020 | J, S | November 7, 2080 | Ma, J, S |
| March 1, 2023 | V, J | November 15, 2080 | Ma, J, S |
| December 1–2, 2033 | Ma, J | November 17, 2080 | Mn, Ma, J, S |
| February 23, 2047 | V, Ma | December 24, 2080 | V, J |
| March 7, 2047 | V, J | March 6, 2082 | V, J |
| May 13, 2066 | V, Ma | April 28, 2085 | Mn, Ma, J |
| July 1, 2066 | V, S | June 13, 2085 | Me, V, J |
| March 14, 2071 | V, J | May 15, 2098 | V, Ma |
| June 21, 2074 | V, J | June 29, 2098 | V, J |
| June 27, 2074 | V, Mn, J | | |

REFERENCE

# How to Find the Day of the Week for Any Given Date

**To compute the day of the week for any given date as far back as the mid–18th century, proceed as follows:**

■ Add the last two digits of the year to one-quarter of the last two digits (discard any remainder), the day of the month, and the month key from the key box below. Divide the sum by 7; the remainder is the day of the week (1 is Sunday, 2 is Monday, and so on). If there is no remainder, the day is Saturday. If you're searching for a weekday prior to 1900, add 2 to the sum before dividing; prior to 1800, add 4. The formula doesn't work for days prior to 1753. From 2000 to 2099, subtract 1 from the sum before dividing.

*Example:*

**The Dayton Flood was on March 25, 1913.**

| | |
|---|---|
| Last two digits of year: ....................... | 13 |
| One-quarter of these two digits: ......... | 3 |
| Given day of month: ............................ | 25 |
| Key number for March: ....................... | 4 |
| Sum: | 45 |

**45 ÷ 7 = 6, with a remainder of 3. The flood took place on Tuesday, the third day of the week.**

| KEY | |
|---|---|
| January .............. | 1 |
|    leap year .......... | 0 |
| February............. | 4 |
|    leap year .......... | 3 |
| March ............... | 4 |
| April................ | 0 |
| May ................. | 2 |
| June ................ | 5 |
| July ................ | 0 |
| August .............. | 3 |
| September ........... | 6 |
| October ............. | 1 |
| November............ | 4 |
| December ........... | 6 |

# Easter Dates (2011–15)

■ Christian churches that follow the Gregorian calendar celebrate Easter on the first Sunday after the paschal full Moon on or just after the vernal equinox.

| YEAR | EASTER |
|---|---|
| 2011 .................... | April 24 |
| 2012 .................... | April 8 |
| 2013 ................... | March 31 |
| 2014 .................... | April 20 |
| 2015 .................... | April 5 |

■ Eastern Orthodox churches follow the Julian calendar.

| YEAR | EASTER |
|---|---|
| 2011 .................... | April 24 |
| 2012 .................... | April 15 |
| 2013 .................... | May 5 |
| 2014 .................... | April 20 |
| 2015 .................... | April 12 |

# Friggatriskaidekaphobia Trivia

Here are a few facts about Friday the 13th:

■ In the 14 possible configurations for the annual calendar (see any perpetual calendar), the occurrence of Friday the 13th is this:

**6 of 14 years have one Friday the 13th.**
**6 of 14 years have two Fridays the 13th.**
**2 of 14 years have three Fridays the 13th.**

■ There is no year without one Friday the 13th, and no year with more than three.

■ There is one Friday the 13th in 2011, in May.

■ We say "Fridays the 13th" because it is hard to say "Friday the 13ths."

## Sowing Vegetable Seeds

| | |
|---|---|
| **Sow or plant in cool weather** | Beets, broccoli, brussels sprouts, cabbage, lettuce, onions, parsley, peas, radishes, spinach, Swiss chard, turnips |
| **Sow or plant in warm weather** | Beans, carrots, corn, cucumbers, eggplant, melons, okra, peppers, squash, tomatoes |
| **Sow or plant for one crop per season** | Corn, eggplant, leeks, melons, peppers, potatoes, spinach (New Zealand), squash, tomatoes |
| **Resow for additional crops** | Beans, beets, cabbage, carrots, kohlrabi, lettuce, radishes, rutabagas, spinach, turnips |

## A Beginner's Vegetable Garden

■ A good size for a beginner's vegetable garden is 10x16 feet. It should have crops that are easy to grow. A plot this size, planted as suggested below, can feed a family of four for one summer, with a little extra for canning and freezing (or giving away).

Make 11 rows, 10 feet long, with 6 inches between them. Ideally, the rows should run north and south to take full advantage of the sunlight. Plant the following:

| ROW | | ROW | |
|---|---|---|---|
| **1** | Zucchini (4 plants) | **5** | Bush beans |
| **2** | Tomatoes (5 plants, staked) | **6** | Lettuce |
| **3** | Peppers (6 plants) | **7** | Beets |
| **4** | Cabbage | **8** | Carrots |
| | | **9** | Chard |
| | | **10** | Radishes |
| | | **11** | Marigolds (to discourage rabbits!) |

## Traditional Planting Times

■ Plant **corn** when elm leaves are the size of a squirrel's ear, when oak leaves are the size of a mouse's ear, when apple blossoms begin to fall, or when the dogwoods are in full bloom.

■ Plant **lettuce, spinach, peas,** and other cool-weather vegetables when the lilacs show their first leaves or when daffodils begin to bloom.

■ Plant **tomatoes, early corn,** and **peppers** when dogwoods are in peak bloom or when daylilies start to bloom.

■ Plant **cucumbers** and **squashes** when lilac flowers fade.

■ Plant **perennials** when maple leaves begin to unfurl.

■ Plant **morning glories** when maple trees have full-size leaves.

■ Plant **pansies, snapdragons,** and other hardy annuals after the aspen and chokecherry trees leaf out.

■ Plant **beets** and **carrots** when dandelions are blooming.

## Flowers and Herbs That Attract Butterflies

Allium . . . . . . . . . . . . . . . . . . . . *Allium*
Aster . . . . . . . . . . . . . . . . . . . . . . *Aster*
Bee balm . . . . . . . . . . . . . . *Monarda*
Butterfly bush . . . . . . . . . . . . . *Buddleia*
Catmint . . . . . . . . . . . . . . . . . . . .*Nepeta*
Clove pink . . . . . . . . . . . . . . *Dianthus*
Cornflower . . . . . . . . . . . . . *Centaurea*
Creeping thyme . . . . .*Thymus serpyllum*
Daylily . . . . . . . . . . . . . *Hemerocallis*
Dill . . . . . . . . . . . .*Anethum graveolens*
False indigo . . . . . . . . . . . . . *Baptisia*
Fleabane . . . . . . . . . . . . . . . . *Erigeron*
Floss flower . . . . . . . . . . . . . *Ageratum*
Globe thistle . . . . . . . . . . . . . *Echinops*
Goldenrod . . . . . . . . . . . . . . . *Solidago*
Helen's flower . . . . . . . . . . . *Helenium*
Hollyhock . . . . . . . . . . . . . . . . . *Alcea*
Honeysuckle . . . . . . . . . . . . *Lonicera*
Lavender . . . . . . . . . . . . . . . . *Lavendula*
Lilac . . . . . . . . . . . . . . . . . . . *Syringa*
Lupine . . . . . . . . . . . . . . . . . *Lupinus*
Lychnis . . . . . . . . . . . . . . . . . *Lychnis*

Mallow . . . . . . . . . . . . . . . . . . . *Malva*
Mealycup sage . . . . . . . *Salvia farinacea*
Milkweed . . . . . . . . . . . . . . . *Asclepias*
Mint . . . . . . . . . . . . . . . . . . . . *Mentha*
Oregano . . . . . . . . . *Origanum vulgare*
Pansy . . . . . . . . . . . . . . . . . . . . . *Viola*
Parsley . . . . . . . . . . . . . . . .*Petroselinum crispum*
Phlox . . . . . . . . . . . . . . . . . . . . *Phlox*
Privet . . . . . . . . . . . . . . . . . *Ligustrum*
Purple coneflower . *Echinacea purpurea*
Purple loosestrife . . . . . . . . . . . *Lythrum*
Rock cress . . . . . . . . . . . . . . . . .*Arabis*
Sea holly . . . . . . . . . . . . . . . . *Eryngium*
Shasta daisy . . . . . . . . . *Chrysanthemum*
Snapdragon . . . . . . . . . . . . *Antirrhinum*
Stonecrop . . . . . . . . . . . . . . . . . *Sedum*
Sweet alyssum . . . . . . . . . . . *Lobularia*
Sweet marjoram . . .*Origanum majorana*
Sweet rocket . . . . . . . . . . . . . . *Hesperis*
Tickseed . . . . . . . . . . . . . . . . *Coreopsis*
Zinnia . . . . . . . . . . . . . . . . . . . . *Zinnia*

## Flowers* That Attract Hummingbirds

Beard tongue . . . . . . . . . . . . *Penstemon*
Bee balm . . . . . . . . . . . . . . . . *Monarda*
Butterfly bush . . . . . . . . . . . . . *Buddleia*
Catmint . . . . . . . . . . . . . . . . . . *Nepeta*
Clove pink . . . . . . . . . . . . . . *Dianthus*
Columbine . . . . . . . . . . . . . *Aquilegia*
Coral bells . . . . . . . . . . . . . . *Heuchera*
Daylily . . . . . . . . . . . . . *Hemerocallis*
Desert candle . . . . . . . . . . . . . . *Yucca*
Flag iris . . . . . . . . . . . . . . . . . . . . *Iris*
Flowering tobacco . . . . . *Nicotiana alata*
Foxglove . . . . . . . . . . . . . . . . *Digitalis*
Larkspur . . . . . . . . . . . . . . .*Delphinium*
Lily . . . . . . . . . . . . . . . . . . . . . *Lilium*
Lupine . . . . . . . . . . . . . . . . . *Lupinus*
Petunia . . . . . . . . . . . . . . . . . *Petunia*
Pincushion flower . . . . . . . . . *Scabiosa*
Red-hot poker . . . . . . . . . . . *Kniphofia*
Scarlet sage . . . . . . . . *Salvia splendens*

Soapwort . . . . . . . . . . . . . . . *Saponaria*
Summer phlox . . . . . . *Phlox paniculata*
Trumpet honeysuckle . . . . . . . *Lonicera sempervirens*
Verbena . . . . . . . . . . . . . . . . . *Verbena*
Weigela . . . . . . . . . . . . . . . . . *Weigela*

**\*Note: Choose varieties in red and orange shades.**

# pH Preferences of Trees, Shrubs, Vegetables, and Flowers

■ An accurate soil test will tell you your soil pH and will specify the amount of lime or sulfur that is needed to bring it up or down to the appropriate level. A pH of 6.5 is just about right for most home gardens, since most plants thrive in the 6.0 to 7.0 (slightly acidic to neutral) range. Some plants (azaleas, blueberries) prefer more strongly acidic soil in the 4.0 to 6.0 range, while a few (asparagus, plums) do best in soil that is neutral to slightly alkaline. Acidic (sour, below 7.0) soil is counteracted by applying finely ground limestone, and alkaline (sweet, above 7.0) soil is treated with ground sulfur.

| Common Name | Optimum pH Range | Common Name | Optimum pH Range | Common Name | Optimum pH Range |
|---|---|---|---|---|---|
| **TREES AND SHRUBS** | | Walnut, black | 6.0–8.0 | Carnation | 6.0–7.0 |
| Apple | 5.0–6.5 | Willow | 6.0–8.0 | Chrysanthemum | 6.0–7.5 |
| Ash | 6.0–7.5 | | | Clematis | 5.5–7.0 |
| Azalea | 4.5–6.0 | **VEGETABLES** | | Coleus | 6.0–7.0 |
| Basswood | 6.0–7.5 | Asparagus | 6.0–8.0 | Coneflower, purple | 5.0–7.5 |
| Beautybush | 6.0–7.5 | Bean, pole | 6.0–7.5 | Cosmos | 5.0–8.0 |
| Birch | 5.0–6.5 | Beet | 6.0–7.5 | Crocus | 6.0–8.0 |
| Blackberry | 5.0–6.0 | Broccoli | 6.0–7.0 | Daffodil | 6.0–6.5 |
| Blueberry | 4.0–6.0 | Brussels sprout | 6.0–7.5 | Dahlia | 6.0–7.5 |
| Boxwood | 6.0–7.5 | Carrot | 5.5–7.0 | Daisy, Shasta | 6.0–8.0 |
| Cherry, sour | 6.0–7.0 | Cauliflower | 5.5–7.5 | Daylily | 6.0–8.0 |
| Chestnut | 5.0–6.5 | Celery | 5.8–7.0 | Delphinium | 6.0–7.5 |
| Crab apple | 6.0–7.5 | Chive | 6.0–7.0 | Foxglove | 6.0–7.5 |
| Dogwood | 5.0–7.0 | Cucumber | 5.5–7.0 | Geranium | 6.0–8.0 |
| Elder, box | 6.0–8.0 | Garlic | 5.5–8.0 | Gladiolus | 5.0–7.0 |
| Fir, balsam | 5.0–6.0 | Kale | 6.0–7.5 | Hibiscus | 6.0–8.0 |
| Fir, Douglas | 6.0–7.0 | Lettuce | 6.0–7.0 | Hollyhock | 6.0–8.0 |
| Hemlock | 5.0–6.0 | Pea, sweet | 6.0–7.5 | Hyacinth | 6.5–7.5 |
| Hydrangea, blue-flowered | 4.0–5.0 | Pepper, sweet | 5.5–7.0 | Iris, blue flag | 5.0–7.5 |
| Hydrangea, pink-flowered | 6.0–7.0 | Potato | 4.8–6.5 | Lily-of-the-valley | 4.5–6.0 |
| Juniper | 5.0–6.0 | Pumpkin | 5.5–7.5 | Lupine | 5.0–6.5 |
| Laurel, mountain | 4.5–6.0 | Radish | 6.0–7.0 | Marigold | 5.5–7.5 |
| Lemon | 6.0–7.5 | Spinach | 6.0–7.5 | Morning glory | 6.0–7.5 |
| Lilac | 6.0–7.5 | Squash, crookneck | 6.0–7.5 | Narcissus, trumpet | 5.5–6.5 |
| Maple, sugar | 6.0–7.5 | Squash, Hubbard | 5.5–7.0 | Nasturtium | 5.5–7.5 |
| Oak, white | 5.0–6.5 | Tomato | 5.5–7.5 | Pansy | 5.5–6.5 |
| Orange | 6.0–7.5 | | | Peony | 6.0–7.5 |
| Peach | 6.0–7.0 | **FLOWERS** | | Petunia | 6.0–7.5 |
| Pear | 6.0–7.5 | Alyssum | 6.0–7.5 | Phlox, summer | 6.0–8.0 |
| Pecan | 6.4–8.0 | Aster, New England | 6.0–8.0 | Poppy, oriental | 6.0–7.5 |
| Pine, red | 5.0–6.0 | Baby's breath | 6.0–7.0 | Rose, hybrid tea | 5.5–7.0 |
| Pine, white | 4.5–6.0 | Bachelor's button | 6.0–7.5 | Rose, rugosa | 6.0–7.0 |
| Plum | 6.0–8.0 | Bee balm | 6.0–7.5 | Snapdragon | 5.5–7.0 |
| Raspberry, red | 5.5–7.0 | Begonia | 5.5–7.0 | Sunflower | 6.0–7.5 |
| Rhododendron | 4.5–6.0 | Black-eyed Susan | 5.5–7.0 | Tulip | 6.0–7.0 |
| Spruce | 5.0–6.0 | Bleeding heart | 6.0–7.5 | Zinnia | 5.5–7.0 |
| | | Canna | 6.0–8.0 | | |

R
E
F
E
R
E
N
C
E

## How to Grow Vegetables

| VEGETABLE | START SEEDS INDOORS (weeks before last spring frost) | START SEEDS OUTDOORS (weeks before or after last spring frost) | MINIMUM SOIL TEMPERATURE TO TO GERMINATE (°F) | COLD HARDINESS |
|---|---|---|---|---|
| Beans | | Anytime after | 48–50 | Tender |
| Beets | | 4 before to 4 after | 39–41 | Half-hardy |
| Broccoli | 6–8 | 4 before | 55–75 | Hardy |
| Brussels sprouts | 6–8 | | 55–75 | Hardy |
| Cabbage | 6–8 | Anytime after | 38–40 | Hardy |
| Carrots | | 4–6 before | 39–41 | Half-hardy |
| Cauliflower | 6–8 | 4 before | 65–75 | Half-hardy |
| Celery | 6–8 | | 60–70 | Tender |
| Corn | | 2 after | 46–50 | Tender |
| Cucumbers | 3–4 | 1–2 after | 65–70 | Very tender |
| Lettuce | 4–6 | 2–3 after | 40–75 | Half-hardy |
| Melons | 3–4 | 2 after | 55–60 | Very tender |
| Onion sets | | 4 before | 34–36 | Hardy |
| Parsnips | | 2–4 before | 55–70 | Hardy |
| Peas | | 4–6 before | 34–36 | Hardy |
| Peppers | 8–10 | | 70–80 | Very tender |
| Potato tubers | | 2–4 before | 55–70 | Half-hardy |
| Pumpkins | 3–4 | 1 after | 55–60 | Tender |
| Radishes | | 4–6 before | 39–41 | Hardy |
| Spinach | | 4–6 before | 55–65 | Hardy |
| Squash, summer | 3–4 | 1 after | 55–60 | Very tender |
| Squash, winter | 3–4 | 1 after | 55–60 | Tender |
| Tomatoes | 6–8 | | 50–55 | Tender |

REFERENCE

| WHEN TO FERTILIZE | WHEN TO WATER |
|---|---|
| After heavy bloom and set of pods | Regularly, from start of pod to set |
| At time of planting | Only during drought conditions |
| Three weeks after transplanting | Only during drought conditions |
| Three weeks after transplanting | At transplanting |
| Three weeks after transplanting | Two to three weeks before harvest |
| Preferably in the fall for the following spring | Only during drought conditions |
| Three weeks after transplanting | Once, three weeks before harvest |
| At time of transplanting | Once a week |
| When eight to ten inches tall, and again when first silk appears | When tassels appear and cobs start to swell |
| One week after bloom, and again three weeks later | Frequently, especially when fruits form |
| Two to three weeks after transplanting | Once a week |
| One week after bloom, and again three weeks later | Once a week |
| When bulbs begin to swell, and again when plants are one foot tall | Only during drought conditions |
| One year before planting | Only during drought conditions |
| After heavy bloom and set of pods | Regularly, from start of pod to set |
| After first fruit-set | Once a week |
| At bloom time or time of second hilling | Regularly, when tubers start to form |
| Just before vines start to run, when plants are about one foot tall | Only during drought conditions |
| Before spring planting | Once a week |
| When plants are one-third grown | Once a week |
| Just before vines start to run, when plants are about one foot tall | Only during drought conditions |
| Just before vines start to run, when plants are about one foot tall | Only during drought conditions |
| Two weeks before, and after first picking | Twice a week |

## Lawn-Growing Tips

■ Test your soil: The pH balance should be 7.0 or more; 6.2 to 6.7 puts your lawn at risk for fungal diseases. If the pH is too low, correct it with liming, best done in the fall.

■ The best time to apply fertilizer is just before it rains.

■ If you put lime and fertilizer on your lawn, spread half of it as you walk north to south, the other half as you walk east to west to cut down on missed areas.

■ Any feeding of lawns in the fall should be done with a low-nitrogen, slow-acting fertilizer.

■ In areas of your lawn where tree roots compete with the grass, apply some extra fertilizer to benefit both.

■ Moss and sorrel in lawns usually means poor soil, poor aeration or drainage, or excessive acidity.

■ Control weeds by promoting healthy lawn growth with natural fertilizers in spring and early fall.

■ Raise the level of your lawn-mower blades during the hot summer days. Taller grass resists drought better than short.

■ You can reduce mowing time by redesigning your lawn, reducing sharp corners and adding sweeping curves.

■ During a drought, let the grass grow longer between mowings, and reduce fertilizer.

■ Water your lawn early in the morning or in the evening.

## Herbs to Plant in Lawns

**Choose plants that suit your soil and your climate. All these can withstand mowing and considerable foot traffic.**

Ajuga or bugleweed (*Ajuga reptans*)
Corsican mint (*Mentha requienii*)
Dwarf cinquefoil (*Potentilla tabernaemontani*)
English pennyroyal (*Mentha pulegium*)
Green Irish moss (*Sagina subulata*)
Pearly everlasting (*Anaphalis margaritacea*)
Roman chamomile (*Chamaemelum nobile*)
Rupturewort (*Herniaria glabra*)
Speedwell (*Veronica officinalis*)
Stonecrop (*Sedum ternatum*)
Sweet violets (*Viola odorata* or
  *V. tricolor*)
Thyme (*Thymus serpyllum*)
White clover (*Trifolium
  repens*)
Wild strawberries
  (*Fragaria virginiana*)
Wintergreen or
  partridgeberry
  (*Mitchella repens*)

### A Gardener's Worst Phobias

| Name of Fear | Object Feared |
|---|---|
| Alliumphobia | Garlic |
| Anthophobia | Flowers |
| Apiphobia | Bees |
| Arachnophobia | Spiders |
| Batonophobia | Plants |
| Bufonophobia | Toads |
| Dendrophobia | Trees |
| Entomophobia | Insects |
| Lachanophobia | Vegetables |
| Melissophobia | Bees |
| Mottephobia | Moths |
| Myrmecophobia | Ants |
| Ornithophobia | Birds |
| Ranidaphobia | Frogs |
| Rupophobia | Dirt |
| Scoleciphobia | Worms |
| Spheksophobia | Wasps |

# Cooperative Extension Services

■ Contact your local state cooperative extension Web site to get help with tricky insect problems, best varieties to plant in your area, or general maintenance of your garden.

**Alabama**
www.aces.edu

**Alaska**
www.uaf.edu/coop-ext

**Arizona**
extension.arizona.edu

**Arkansas**
www.uaex.edu

**California**
www.ucanr.org

**Colorado**
www.ext.colostate.edu

**Connecticut**
www.extension.uconn.edu

**Delaware**
ag.udel.edu/extension

**Florida**
www.solutionsforyourlife
.ufl.edu

**Georgia**
www.caes.uga.edu/exten-
sion

**Hawaii**
www.ctahr.hawaii.edu/ext

**Idaho**
www.extension.uidaho.edu

**Illinois**
web.extension.illinois.edu/
state/index.html

**Indiana**
www.ces.purdue.edu

**Iowa**
www.extension.iastate.edu

**Kansas**
www.ksre.ksu.edu

**Kentucky**
www.ca.uky.edu/ces

**Louisiana**
www.lsuagcenter.com

**Maine**
extension.umaine.edu

**Maryland**
extension.umd.edu

**Massachusetts**
www.umassextension.org

**Michigan**
www.msue.msu.edu

**Minnesota**
www.extension.umn.edu

**Mississippi**
www.msucares.com

**Missouri**
www.extension.missouri.
edu

**Montana**
www.extn.msu.montana.edu

**Nebraska**
www.extension.unl.edu

**Nevada**
www.unce.unr.edu

**New Hampshire**
www.extension.unh.edu

**New Jersey**
www.njaes.rutgers.edu

**New Mexico**
extension.nmsu.edu

**New York**
www.cce.cornell.edu

**North Carolina**
www.ces.ncsu.edu

**North Dakota**
www.ext.nodak.edu

**Ohio**
extension.osu.edu

**Oklahoma**
www.oces.okstate.edu

**Oregon**
extension.oregonstate.edu

**Pennsylvania**
extension.psu.edu

**Rhode Island**
cels.uri.edu/ce

**South Carolina**
www.clemson.edu/
extension

**South Dakota**
sdces.sdstate.edu

**Tennessee**
utextension.tennessee.edu

**Texas**
texasextension.tamu.edu

**Utah**
www.extension.usu.edu

**Vermont**
www.uvm.edu/extension

**Virginia**
www.ext.vt.edu

**Washington**
ext.wsu.edu

**West Virginia**
www.wvu.edu/~exten

**Wisconsin**
www.uwex.edu/ces

**Wyoming**
ces.uwyo.edu

# How to Grow Herbs

| HERB | PROPAGATION METHOD | START SEEDS INDOORS (weeks before last spring frost) | START SEEDS OUTDOORS (weeks before or after last spring frost) | MINIMUM SOIL TEMPERATURE TO GERMINATE (°F) | HEIGHT (inches) |
|---|---|---|---|---|---|
| Basil | Seeds, transplants | 6–8 | Anytime after | 70 | 12–24 |
| Borage | Seeds, division, cuttings | Not recommended | Anytime after | 70 | 12–36 |
| Chervil | Seeds | Not recommended | 3–4 before | 55 | 12–24 |
| Chives | Seeds, division | 8–10 | 3–4 before | 60–70 | 12–18 |
| Cilantro/ coriander | Seeds | Not recommended | Anytime after | 60 | 12–36 |
| Dill | Seeds | Not recommended | 4–5 before | 60–70 | 36–48 |
| Fennel | Seeds | 4–6 | Anytime after | 60–70 | 48–80 |
| Lavender, English | Seeds, cuttings | 8–12 | 1–2 before | 70–75 | 18–36 |
| Lavender, French | Transplants | Not recommended | Not recommended | — | 18–36 |
| Lemon balm | Seeds, division, cuttings | 6–10 | 2–3 before | 70 | 12–24 |
| Lovage | Seeds, division | 6–8 | 2–3 before | 70 | 36–72 |
| Oregano | Seeds, division, cuttings | 6–10 | Anytime after | 70 | 12–24 |
| Parsley | Seeds | 10–12 | 3–4 before | 70 | 18–24 |
| Rosemary | Seeds, division, cuttings | 8–10 | Anytime after | 70 | 48–72 |
| Sage | Seeds, division, cuttings | 6–10 | 1–2 before | 60–70 | 12–48 |
| Sorrel | Seeds, division | 6–10 | 2–3 after | 60–70 | 20–48 |
| Spearmint | Division, cuttings | Not recommended | Not recommended | — | 12–24 |
| Summer savory | Seeds | 4–6 | Anytime after | 60–70 | 4–15 |
| Sweet cicely | Seeds, division | 6–8 | 2–3 after | 60–70 | 36–72 |
| Tarragon, French | Cuttings, transplants | Not recommended | Not recommended | — | 24–36 |
| Thyme, common | Seeds, division, cuttings | 6–10 | 2–3 before | 70 | 2–12 |

| SPREAD (inches) | BLOOMING SEASON | USES | SOIL | LIGHT* | GROWTH TYPE |
|---|---|---|---|---|---|
| 12 | Midsummer | Culinary | Rich, moist | ○ | Annual |
| 12 | Early to midsummer | Culinary | Rich, well-drained, dry | ○ | Annual, biennial |
| 8 | Early to midsummer | Culinary | Rich, moist | ◑ | Annual, biennial |
| 18 | Early summer | Culinary | Rich, moist | ○ | Perennial |
| 4 | Midsummer | Culinary | Light | ○◑ | Annual |
| 12 | Early summer | Culinary | Rich | ○ | Annual |
| 18 | Mid- to late summer | Culinary | Rich | ○ | Annual |
| 24 | Early to late summer | Ornamental, medicinal | Moderately fertile, well-drained | ○ | Perennial |
| 24 | Early to late summer | Ornamental, medicinal | Moderately fertile, well-drained | ○ | Tender perennial |
| 18 | Midsummer to early fall | Culinary, ornamental | Rich, well-drained | ○◑ | Perennial |
| 36 | Early to late summer | Culinary | Fertile, sandy | ○◑ | Perennial |
| 18 | Mid- to late summer | Culinary | Poor | ○ | Tender perennial |
| 6–8 | Mid- to late summer | Culinary | Medium-rich | ◑ | Biennial |
| 48 | Early summer | Culinary | Not too acid | ○ | Tender perennial |
| 30 | Early to late summer | Culinary, ornamental | Well-drained | ○ | Perennial |
| 12–14 | Late spring to early summer | Culinary, medicinal | Rich, organic | ○ | Perennial |
| 18 | Early to midsummer | Culinary, medicinal, ornamental | Rich, moist | ◑ | Perennial |
| 6 | Early summer | Culinary | Medium rich | ○ | Annual |
| 36 | Late spring | Culinary | Moderately fertile, well-drained | ○◑ | Perennial |
| 12 | Late summer | Culinary, medicinal | Well-drained | ○◑ | Perennial |
| 7–12 | Early to midsummer | Culinary | Fertile, well-drained | ○◑ | Perennial |

* ○ full sun   ◑ partial shade

# How to Grow Bulbs

## SPRING-PLANTED BULBS

| COMMON NAME | LATIN NAME | HARDINESS ZONE | SOIL | SUN/ SHADE* | SPACING (Inches) |
|---|---|---|---|---|---|
| Allium | Allium | 3–10 | Well-drained/moist | ○ | 12 |
| Begonia, tuberous | Begonia | 10–11 | Well-drained/moist | ◑● | 12–15 |
| Blazing star/ gayfeather | Liatris | 7–10 | Well-drained | ○ | 6 |
| Caladium | Caladium | 10–11 | Well-drained/moist | ◑● | 8–12 |
| Calla lily | Zantedeschia | 8–10 | Well-drained/moist | ○◑ | 8–24 |
| Canna | Canna | 8–11 | Well-drained/moist | ○ | 12–24 |
| Cyclamen | Cyclamen | 7–9 | Well-drained/moist | ◑ | 4 |
| Dahlia | Dahlia | 9–11 | Well-drained/fertile | ○ | 12–36 |
| Daylily | Hemerocallis | 3–10 | Adaptable to most soils | ○◑ | 12–24 |
| Freesia | Freesia | 9–11 | Well-drained/moist/sandy | ○◑ | 2–4 |
| Garden gloxinia | Incarvillea | 4–8 | Well-drained/moist | ○ | 12 |
| Gladiolus | Gladiolus | 4–11 | Well-drained/fertile | ○◑ | 4–9 |
| Iris | Iris | 3–10 | Well-drained/sandy | ○ | 3–6 |
| Lily, Asiatic/Oriental | Lilium | 3–8 | Well-drained | ○◑ | 8–12 |
| Peacock flower | Tigridia | 8–10 | Well-drained | ○ | 5–6 |
| Shamrock/sorrel | Oxalis | 5–9 | Well-drained | ○◑ | 4–6 |
| Windflower | Anemone | 3–9 | Well-drained/moist | ○◑ | 3–6 |

## FALL-PLANTED BULBS

| COMMON NAME | LATIN NAME | HARDINESS ZONE | SOIL | SUN/ SHADE* | SPACING (Inches) |
|---|---|---|---|---|---|
| Bluebell | Hyacinthoides | 4–9 | Well-drained/fertile | ○◑ | 4 |
| Christmas rose/ hellebore | Helleborus | 4–8 | Neutral–alkaline | ○◑ | 18 |
| Crocus | Crocus | 3–8 | Well-drained/moist/fertile | ○◑ | 4 |
| Daffodil | Narcissus | 3–10 | Well-drained/moist/fertile | ○◑ | 6 |
| Fritillary | Fritillaria | 3–9 | Well-drained/sandy | ○◑ | 3 |
| Glory of the snow | Chionodoxa | 3–9 | Well-drained/moist | ○◑ | 3 |
| Grape hyacinth | Muscari | 4–10 | Well-drained/moist/fertile | ○◑ | 3–4 |
| Iris, bearded | Iris | 3–9 | Well-drained | ○◑ | 4 |
| Iris, Siberian | Iris | 4–9 | Well-drained | ○◑ | 4 |
| Ornamental onion | Allium | 3–10 | Well-drained/moist/fertile | ○ | 12 |
| Snowdrop | Galanthus | 3–9 | Well-drained/moist/fertile | ○◑ | 3 |
| Snowflake | Leucojum | 5–9 | Well-drained/moist/sandy | ○◑ | 4 |
| Spring starflower | Ipheion uniflorum | 6–9 | Well-drained loam | ○◑ | 3–6 |
| Star of Bethlehem | Ornithogalum | 5–10 | Well-drained/moist | ○◑ | 2–5 |
| Striped squill | Puschkinia scilloides | 3–9 | Well-drained | ○◑ | 6 |
| Tulip | Tulipa | 4–8 | Well-drained/fertile | ○◑ | 3–6 |
| Winter aconite | Eranthis | 4–9 | Well-drained/moist/fertile | ○◑ | 3 |

REFERENCE

| DEPTH (Inches) | BLOOMING SEASON | HEIGHT (Inches) | NOTES |
|---|---|---|---|
| 3–4 | Spring to summer | 6–60 | Usually pest-free; a great cut flower |
| 1–2 | Summer to fall | 8–18 | North of Zone 10, lift in fall |
| 4 | Summer to fall | 8–20 | An excellent flower for drying; north of Zone 7, plant in spring, lift in fall |
| 2 | Summer | 8–24 | North of Zone 10, plant in spring, lift in fall |
| 1–4 | Summer | 24–36 | Fragrant; north of Zone 8, plant in spring, lift in fall |
| Level | Summer | 18–60 | North of Zone 8, plant in spring, lift in fall |
| 1–2 | Spring to fall | 3–12 | Naturalizes well in warm areas; north of Zone 7, lift in fall |
| 4–6 | Late summer | 12–60 | North of Zone 9, lift in fall |
| 2 | Summer | 12–36 | Mulch in winter in Zones 3 to 6 |
| 2 | Summer | 12–24 | Fragrant; can be grown outdoors in warm climates |
| 3–4 | Summer | 6–20 | Does well in woodland settings |
| 3–6 | Early summer to early fall | 12–80 | North of Zone 10, lift in fall |
| 4 | Spring to late summer | 3–72 | Divide and replant rhizomes every two to five years |
| 4–6 | Early summer | 36 | Fragrant; self-sows; requires excellent drainage |
| 4 | Summer | 18–24 | North of Zone 8, lift in fall |
| 2 | Summer | 2–12 | Plant in confined area to control |
| 2 | Early summer | 3–18 | North of Zone 6, lift in fall |
| 3–4 | Spring | 8–20 | Excellent for borders, rock gardens and naturalizing |
| 1–2 | Spring | 12 | Hardy, but requires shelter from strong, cold winds |
| 3 | Early spring | 5 | Naturalizes well in grass |
| 6 | Early spring | 14–24 | Plant under shrubs or in a border |
| 3 | Midspring | 6–30 | Different species can be planted in rock gardens, woodland gardens, or borders |
| 3 | Spring | 4–10 | Self-sows easily; plant in rock gardens, raised beds, or under shrubs |
| 2–3 | Late winter to spring | 6–12 | Use as a border plant or in wildflower and rock gardens; self-sows easily |
| 4 | Early spring to early summer | 3–48 | Naturalizes well; good cut flower |
| 4 | Early spring to midsummer | 18–48 | An excellent cut flower |
| 3–4 | Late spring to early summer | 6–60 | Usually pest-free; a great cut flower |
| 3 | Spring | 6–12 | Best when clustered and planted in an area that will not dry out in summer |
| 4 | Spring | 6–18 | Naturalizes well |
| 3 | Spring | 4–6 | Fragrant; naturalizes easily |
| 4 | Spring to summer | 6–24 | North of Zone 5, plant in spring, lift in fall |
| 3 | Spring | 4–6 | Naturalizes easily; makes an attractive edging |
| 4–6 | Early to late spring | 8–30 | Excellent for borders, rock gardens, and naturalizing |
| 2–3 | Late winter to spring | 2–4 | Self-sows and naturalizes easily |

R
E
F
E
R
E
N
C
E

# Plastics

■ In your quest to go green, use this guide to use and sort plastic. The number, usually found with a triangle symbol on a container, indicates the type of resin used to produce the plastic. Call **1-800-CLEANUP** for recycling information in your state.

**PETE**

**Number 1** • *PETE or PET (polyethylene terephthalate)*

**IS USED IN** . . . . . . . . . microwavable food trays; salad dressing, soft drink, water, and beer bottles

**STATUS** . . . . . . . . . . . hard to clean; absorbs bacteria and flavors; avoid reusing

**IS RECYCLED TO MAKE** . . carpet, furniture, new containers, Polar fleece

**HDPE**

**Number 2** • *HDPE (high-density polyethylene)*

**IS USED IN** . . . . . . . . . household cleaner and shampoo bottles, milk jugs, yogurt tubs

**STATUS** . . . . . . . . . . . transmits no known chemicals into food

**IS RECYCLED TO MAKE** . . detergent bottles, fencing, floor tiles, pens

**V**

**Number 3** • *V or PVC (vinyl)*

**IS USED IN** . . . . . . . . . cooking oil bottles, clear food packaging, mouthwash bottles

**STATUS** . . . . . . . . . . . is believed to contain phalates that interfere with hormonal development; avoid

**IS RECYCLED TO MAKE** . . cables, mudflaps, paneling, roadway gutters

**LDPE**

**Number 4** • *LDPE (low-density polyethylene)*

**IS USED IN** . . . . . . . . . bread and shopping bags, carpet, clothing, furniture

**STATUS** . . . . . . . . . . . transmits no known chemicals into food

**IS RECYCLED TO MAKE** . . envelopes, floor tiles, lumber, trash-can liners

**PP**

**Number 5** • *PP (polypropylene)*

**IS USED IN** . . . . . . . . . ketchup bottles, medicine and syrup bottles, drinking straws

**STATUS** . . . . . . . . . . . transmits no known chemicals into food

**IS RECYCLED TO MAKE** . . battery cables, brooms, ice scrapers, rakes

**PS**

**Number 6** • *PS (polystyrene)*

**IS USED IN** . . . . . . . . . disposable cups and plates, egg cartons, take-out containers

**STATUS** . . . . . . . . . . . is believed to leach styrene, a possible human carcinogen, into food; avoid

**IS RECYCLED TO MAKE** . . foam packaging, insulation, light switchplates, rulers

**OTHER**

**Number 7** • *Other (miscellaneous)*

**IS USED IN** . . . . . . . . . 3- and 5-gallon water jugs, nylon, some food containers

**STATUS** . . . . . . . . . . . contains bisphenol A, which has been linked to heart disease and obesity; avoid

**IS RECYCLED TO MAKE** . . custom-made products

# Tile and Vinyl Flooring

■ Make a scale drawing of your room with all measurements clearly marked, and take it with you when you shop for tile flooring. Ask the salespeople to help you calculate your needs if you have rooms that feature bay windows, unusual jogs or turns, or if you plan to use special floor patterns or tiles with designs.

## Ceramic Tile

■ Ceramic tiles for floors and walls come in a range of sizes, from 1x1-inch mosaics up to 12x12-inch (or larger) squares. The most popular size is the 4¼-inch-square tile, but there is a trend toward larger tiles (8x8s, 10x10s, 12x12s). Installing these larger tiles can be a challenge because the underlayment must be absolutely even and level.

■ Small, one-inch mosaic tiles are usually joined together in 12x12-inch or 12x24-inch sheets to make them easier to install. You can have a custom pattern made, or you can mix different-color tiles to create your own mosaic borders, patterns, and pictures.

## Sheet Vinyl

■ Sheet vinyl typically comes in 6- and 12-foot widths. If your floor requires two or more pieces, your estimate must include enough overlap to allow you to match the pattern.

## Vinyl Tile

■ Vinyl tiles generally come in 9- and 12-inch squares. To find the number of 12-inch tiles you need, just multiply the length of the room by the width in feet (rounding fractions up to the next foot) to get the number of tiles you need. Add 5 percent extra for cutting and waste. Measure any obstructions on the floor that you will be tiling around (such

as appliances and cabinets), and subtract that square footage from the total. To calculate the number of 9-inch tiles, divide the room's length (in inches) by 9, then divide the room's width by 9. Multiply those two numbers together to get the number of tiles you need, and then add 5 percent extra for cutting and waste.

# Wallpaper

■ Before choosing your wallpaper, keep in mind that wallpaper with little or no pattern to match at the seams and the ceiling will be the easiest to apply, thus resulting in the least amount of wasted wallpaper. If you choose a patterned wallpaper, a small repeating pattern will result in less waste than a large repeating pattern. And a pattern that is aligned horizontally (matching on each column of paper) will waste less than one that drops or alternates its pattern (matching on every other column).

**To determine the amount of wall space you're covering:**

■ Measure the length of each wall, add these figures together, and multiply by the height of the walls to get the area (square footage) of the room's walls.

■ Calculate the square footage of each door, window, and other opening in the room. Add these figures together and subtract the total from the area of the room's walls.

■ Take that figure and multiply by 1.15, to account for a waste rate of about 15 percent in your wallpaper project. You'll end up with a target amount to purchase when you shop.

■ Wallpaper is sold in single, double, and triple rolls. Coverage can vary, so be sure to refer to the roll's label for the proper square footage. (The average coverage for a double roll, for example, is 56 square feet.) After choosing a paper, divide the coverage figure (from the label) into the total square footage of the walls of the room you're papering. Round the answer up to the nearest whole number. This is the number of rolls you need to buy.

■ Save leftover wallpaper rolls, carefully wrapped to keep clean.

### HOW MUCH DO YOU NEED?

## Interior Paint

■ Estimate your room size and paint needs before you go to the store. Running out of a custom color halfway through the job could mean disaster. For the sake of the following exercise, assume that you have a 10x15-foot room with an 8-foot ceiling. The room has two doors and two windows.

### For Walls

■ Measure the total distance (perimeter) around the room:
 **(10 ft. + 15 ft.) x 2 = 50 ft.**

■ Multiply the perimeter by the ceiling height to get the total wall area:
 **50 ft. x 8 ft. = 400 sq. ft.**

■ Doors are usually 21 square feet (there are two in this exercise):
 **21 sq. ft. x 2 = 42 sq. ft.**

■ Windows average 15 square feet (there are two in this exercise):
 **15 sq. ft. x 2 = 30 sq. ft.**

■ Take the total wall area and subtract the area for the doors and windows to get the wall surface to be painted:

 **400 sq. ft. (wall area)**
 **– 42 sq. ft. (doors)**
 **– 30 sq. ft. (windows)**
 **328 sq. ft.**

■ As a rule of thumb, one gallon of quality paint will usually cover 400 square feet. One quart will cover 100 square feet. Because you need to cover 328 square feet in this example, one gallon will be adequate to give one coat of paint to the walls. (Coverage will be affected by the porosity and texture of the surface. In addition, bright colors may require a minimum of two coats.)

### For Ceilings

■ Using the rule of thumb for coverage above, you can calculate the quantity of paint needed for the ceiling by multiplying the width by the length:
 **10 ft. x 15 ft. = 150 sq. ft.**
This ceiling will require approximately two quarts of paint. (A flat finish is recommended to minimize surface imperfections.)

### For Doors, Windows, and Trim

■ The area for the doors and windows has been calculated above. (The windowpane area that does not get painted should allow for enough paint for any trim around doors and windows.) Determine the baseboard trim by taking the perimeter of the room, less 3 feet per door (3 ft. x 2 = 6 ft.), and multiplying this by the average trim width of your baseboard, which in this example is 6 inches (or 0.5 feet).

 **50 ft. (perimeter) – 6 ft. = 44 ft.**
 **44 ft. x 0.5 ft. = 22 sq. ft.**

■ Add the area for doors, windows, and baseboard trim.

 **42 sq. ft. (doors)**
 **+30 sq. ft. (windows)**
 **+22 sq. ft. (baseboard trim)**
 **94 sq. ft.**

One quart will be sufficient to cover the doors, windows, and trim in this example.

*–courtesy M.A.B. Paints*